OPEN
Hands:
Reconciliation,
justice
and peace work
around the world

OPEN
Hands:
Reconciliation,
justice
and peace work
around the world

Edited by **Barbara Butler**
Foreword by **Archbishop Desmond Tutu**

Kevin
Mayhew

First published in 1998 by
KEVIN MAYHEW LTD
Rattlesden
Bury St Edmunds
Suffolk IP30 0SZ

0 1 2 3 4 5 6 7 8 9

ISBN 1 84003 202 2
Catalogue No 1500209

Cover illustration: *The child and the seed* by Jyoti Sahi
Cover design by Jaquetta Sergeant
Printed and bound in Finland by
WSOY – Book Printing Division

Contents

The Contributors

Desmond Tutu Anglican Archbishop and Chairperson of the Truth and Reconciliation Commission in South Africa

Barbara Butler Executive Secretary, Christians Aware

Paul Oestreicher Recent Director of International Ministry, Coventry Cathedral

Adam Curle Quaker writer and peace worker

Keith Clements General Secretary of the Conference of European Churches

Roger Williamson Theologian and peace researcher

Elizabeth Salter Member of the Religious Society of Friends, recently with special responsibility for the World Council of Churches' Programme to Overcome Violence

Kathryn Spink Writer

Kenneth Greet Former Chair of the World Methodist Council

Cyril Okorocha Recent Director for Mission and Evangelism of the Anglican Communion

John McConnell Quaker writer and teacher who has lived and worked in Buddhist countries in South and South-East Asia

B. J. Prashantam Director of the Christian Counselling Centre, Vellore, India

Livingstone Ngwewu Lecturer and chaplain, University of the Transkei, South Africa

Clive Larkin Former lieutenant-colonel who had lived in Mozambique; monitor in the Mozambique elections

Kenneth Ross Senior lecturer in Theology and Religious Studies, University of Malawi

Michael Ipgrave Anglican priest in Leicester who has lived and ministered in Japan

Adrian Hastings Theologian and writer

Derick Wilson Former Director of the Corrymeela Centre in Ballycastle; senior lecturer in Community Relations in the University of Ulster

Akuila D. Yabaki World Church Secretary (Asia and Pacific), the Methodist Church

Marigold Best Recent Programme Co-ordinator for Latin America at Quaker Peace and Service

Pamela Hussey Officer in the Latin America Section of the Catholic Institute for International Relations; member of the Society of the Holy Child Jesus

Marcella Althaus-Reid Argentine feminist theologian; lecturer in Christian Ethics and Practical Theology at the University of Edinburgh

Aldo M. Etchegoyen Methodist bishop in Argentina; former Moderator of the Advisory Group of Human Rights, World Council of Churches

Remember, as you read, and as you live:
Nothing is ever simple. Nothing.
The more it looks black and white,
the deeper you should dig
to find the grey.
Grey sounds dull.
But it is the colour of the mind.

Lynne Reid Banks

Acknowledgements

I would like to thank all the contributors to this book for sharing their concerns, hopes and fears for the future peace of the world and for the work they do or have done to bring this about.

Thank you to Donald and Jane Arden for their encouragement in the creation of this book.

Thank you to Jeanne Coker for her help with the computer work.

Thank you to Ann Collins for proof-reading the book.

Thank you to Margery Hyde for her translation of the chapter 'Struggling for Human Rights in Latin America'.

Barbara Butler

The publishers wish to express their gratitude to the following for permission to use copyright material in this book:

Macmillan Publishers, 25 Eccleston Place, London SW1F 9NF, for *Gitanjali* by Rabindranath Tagore.

Anthea Dove for *The Light of the World*.

Lynne Reid Banks for *Remember, as you read*.

Scripture quotations are from the New Revised Standard Version of the Bible, copyright 1989 by the Division of Christian Education of the National Council of the Churches of Christ in the USA. Used by permission. All rights reserved.

Foreword

I have a favourite book of cartoons entitled 'My God' by the late Observer Cartoonist. They are charming line drawings. One of these shows God somewhat disconsolate saying, 'Oh dear, I think I've lost my copy of the divine plan.' Looking at the state of the world one is often tempted to say, 'I wonder whether God had a plan at all.' What with floods in one part and droughts in another, couldn't God have arranged it better with enough water for everyone everywhere? Be that as it may, for our purposes it is enough to point to the horrendous state of so many countries with regard to peace, justice and human rights. There have been and continue to be some quite devastating civil wars and the world is pockmarked with conflicts, with depressing lines of ragged humanity making their weary and desperate way to yet another refugee camp. Look at Bosnia, Afghanistan, Sri Lanka, Burma, the Sudan, Somalia, Nigeria, Sierra Leone. We have not yet recovered from the genocide in Kampuchea and Rwanda and the latter country is still unstable, as is her neighbour, Burundi. In fact the entire Great Lakes region of Central Africa is highly volatile. And we have had what might be regarded as the hardy annual of the Middle East where peace talks have stalled. But as I write on Easter Monday, it is not all gloom and disaster, for we are celebrating the Northern Ireland Peace Accord signed just before Good Friday and the dove of peace seems not to be too ruffled. There have been unification talks in Japan between North and South Korea. In all the countries we have referred to there has been, or there is, turmoil and conflict. This is because certain people have felt hard done by because their human rights have been violated or the conflict has happened because people have felt that their identity, their culture, their language, their religion – things they hold dear – were threatened or trampled underfoot and their continued existence as a distinct people was in jeopardy. What it means is that there would one day arise the need for erstwhile adversaries to sit down and deal with their past in a way that would help to heal the wounds inflicted on those who were at one another's throats for whatever reasons.

The fact of the matter is that forgiveness, reconciliation, reparation, etc. are no longer regarded as confined exclusively to the spiritual or religious realm and as being somewhat nebulous and perhaps vaguely interesting but really of no earthly use in dealing with the tough issues of practical politics. No, these are now being acknowledged however grudgingly as the stuff of realpolitik, of helping to ensure that new societies coming out of a past characterised by conflict, hatred and gross violations of human rights, that societies emerging from such a painful past can have a chance to survive and can be consolidated.

Forgiveness has to do with practical politics. Without forgiveness there is no future, there can be no real future. Forgiveness deals with the past in such a way that the future becomes possible.

I went to Kigali in Rwanda soon after the genocide that wracked that beautiful country. At a rally in the stadium I preached and said that if justice (retributive justice that is) was their last word, then they had had it. Their history could be said to be a rivalry – a bloody rivalry about who would be topdog between the Hutu and Tutsi. The Hutu topdogs wanted to uphold their position of dominance whilst the Tutsi underdog strove to become the topdog and when they did succeed they visited the erstwhile topdog with ghastly retribution and reprisal. The new underdog, now Hutu, would strive to topple the new topdog and when they succeeded they did so with a ruthlessness that we had seen with revulsion and horror in the last genocide – and so they would go on. And a tribunal would not really solve the problem, because as is the case now, the Hutu accused would claim they were being found guilty really only because they were Hutu and this would be added to their store of resentment against the Tutsi and they would bide their time until there would be a day of reckoning for the Tutsis. The only way out of this spiral was to go beyond justice (certainly retributive justice) through forgiveness. This was not to allow for impunity because amnesty and forgiveness would come only after the perpetrator had acknowledged their wrong publicly, had accepted responsibility and accountability and perhaps be ready to pay reparation to the victims even symbolically in an effort to redress the moral balance. This is restorative justice which is concerned not so much with punishment as with healing, with restoring the state of affairs to what it would have been had the atrocity not been perpetrated. That is what we are trying to do in South Africa – to seek to rehabilitate the humanity of both victim and perpetrator.

We have often been overwhelmed by the depth of depravity exposed in the disclosures in amnesty applications, but that is just one side of the story. The other side has been that quite frequently we have been exhilarated and humbled by the magnanimity, the nobility of spirit of those who though they have suffered so horrendously are yet willing to forgive that they are not consumed by bitterness or a lust for revenge. Our President is the spectacular and most famous embodiment of this. But he is not alone. A white woman, a victim of a hand grenade attack on a golf clubhouse, was so badly injured that when she got out of hospital she had her children looking after her, bathing, clothing and feeding her. She still can't go through the security checkpoint at an airport because all sorts of alarms go off since she is full of shrapnel. She said of this traumatic experience that it had enriched her life. Incredible! She said she wanted to meet the perpetrator in a spirit of forgiveness. That was remarkable enough. But then she went on to say, 'I want to forgive him and I hope he forgives me.' Now, that is quite something. Another moving example was at the TRC hearing on the Bisho massacre that

11

happened after the ANC sought to challenge the decree of Brigadier Gqozo who was Head of State of the former Bantustan homeland, Ciskei, in which he banned demonstrations in Bisho the capital of the then Ciskei. The hall in which the hearing was held was packed with people, some of whom had been injured during the massacre when the Ciskeian Defence Force (CDF) opened fire on unarmed civilians, others were relatives of those who had been killed in that incident. The former head of the CDF testified and riled the audience with his unrepentant tone. The next witnesses were four former officers of the CDF, one of whom was white and was their spokesperson. He said that they had given the orders to the troops to open fire on the fateful day, and then he turned to the audience and said, 'Please forgive us. Please receive my colleagues back into the community.' That highly incensed audience broke out into rapturous applause. Afterwards I said that we should be still because we were in the presence of something holy. Actually we should really take off our shoes, because we were standing on holy ground.

I don't know why it is happening here. Perhaps it is because we have prayed for a much longer time than any other troubled spot and much more intensely, so if miracles were going to happen anywhere, they had to take place in South Africa. But we are not peculiar.

May God bless all who read this anthology and may they be encouraged to hope that their nightmares too will end as ours has ended.

Desmond Tutu
April 1998

Leave this chanting and singing and
telling of beads! Whom dost thou worship in
this lonely dark corner of the temple with doors all shut?
Open thine eyes and see
thy God is not before thee!

He is there where the tiller is tilling
the hard ground
and where the pathmaker is breaking stones.
He is with them in sun and in shower,
and his garment is covered with dust.
Put off thy holy mantle and even like him
come down on the dusty soil!

Deliverance? Where is this deliverance
to be found?
Our master himself has joyfully taken upon him
the bonds of creation;
he is bound with us forever.

Come out of thy meditations and leave aside
thy flowers and incense!
What harm is there if thy clothes become tattered
and stained?
Meet him and stand by him in toil
and in the sweat of thy brow.

Rabindranath Tagore. From *Gitanjali* (Macmillan, India)

Introduction

Barbara Butler

The front cover of this book is from an oil painting by the Indian artist Jyoti Sahi. It is a painting showing openness and bridge building. The open hands of the mother are making contact with God. They are both appealing to God and giving something to God. The mother is linking earth and heaven. She is seated on the earth and yet she is almost taking off with the dove she is releasing into the mountains and the heavens beyond. The child is more earthbound, a growing seed himself; feeding the earthbound birds with the new life given to him by his mother so that they gradually rise, gaining life and light and hope as they do so.

The painting is a painting of hope and possibility but it is also an angry painting. Many people I have shown it to have said that they found it 'frightening'. The mother's hands are strong, but are they threatening as well as appealing? Is the child threatened by the birds he has chosen to feed? Perhaps it is because the painting is one of anger, as well as hope, that it is a dignified painting. The invocation of the mother and the generous vulnerability of the child do not arise from powerlessness or fragility but rather from work, energy and courage. The barely discernible spirit within both mother and child are linked to the Spirit beyond all things, and strangely there is a natural equality between them.

Jesus mixed with people naturally, in their homes and in the countryside. He came to earth as an ordinary child and throughout his life and ministry he continued to link earth and heaven, God and the ordinary, and people to God and to each other. In Ephesians we read that Christ's purpose was . . . 'to create in himself one new person out of two, thus making peace.' People of faith are called to be links in today's world, between God and everyday life and people, between different areas of life and between people who are separated from each other. There is nothing that can be outside the concern and responsibility of people of faith, outside the sphere of prayer and action and towards reconciliation. If reconciliation is to be at all possible this commitment must be irrespective of whether there will be a successful outcome and whether the people, area or issue are judged 'good' or 'bad,' which very often depends upon who is making the judgement.

The many conflicts and divisions in the Middle East for instance will never be resolved so long as the people, and the wider world, put the various groups into 'good' or 'bad' camps and act accordingly. The twentieth century has been one of suffering and trouble for the Jewish people and also for the Palestinians, Christian and Muslim alike, and this suffering continues as the century moves towards its close and people persist in persecuting, killing and maiming each other. It is not helpful to take sides and to see either the Jewish or the Palestinian cause as just. It is essential to empathise with the Jewish people and their attempts to build Israel because they have been so cruelly treated over the centuries, the last and most terrible straw being the holocaust. Heart-rending stories have been told by the few survivors of the holocaust. I met a woman whose story took several hours to tell, because she wept as she spoke, and this was fifty years after the unrepeatable events took place. Rabbi Hugo Gryn's memory of being deported to Auschwitz was of being exhausted, totally demoralised and frightened. Modern Israelis not only have their recent history to contend with, but are also very aware of their precarious position as a small minority group in the Middle East and of the necessity therefore to build up their defences. It is essential, however, also to empathise with the Palestinian people, who have had their land and villages taken over, their houses and their nationhood destroyed, so that, in the second half of the twentieth century, many have become refugees. A Quaker, Jean Zaru, has spoken of the war of 1948. 'I can remember very clearly the fears, hiding in a basement, and the Palestinian refugees from the coastal plains of Palestine. My father and older brother, hearing of their plight, took a truck with water and bread and rescued many of the children and women who were running away from the dangers of war but could not go on walking because of the heat, thirst, hunger and pain. About fifty of these refugees shared our house for a period of six weeks. Another hundred camped under our pine trees. Our meeting house sheltered many families. I have lived most of my life next to a refugee camp.' It is necessary to realise that there are problems and signs of hope in all communities. I return to the Middle East in the chapter on reconciliation and the world faiths. What is needed there, in the words of Elias Chakour, the Melkite priest who wrote *Blood Brothers* and *We Belong to the Land*, is '. . . a bridge-builder between us', and he continues, 'If you are the friend of the Palestinians and the enemy of my Jewish neighbour, I do not need your friendship at all.'

The challenge of faith is then to relate to the total reality of any community, anywhere in the world, beautiful and ugly, good and bad, as the Christians from the Holy Land were seeking to do. The challenge is never easy in a world where war, crime and violence, racism and fanaticism are so obvious and where religion may be part of the problem rather than part of the solution. Elizabeth Salter, in her chapter on 'Overcoming Violence', touches on wars of religion down the ages. It is sad at the end of the twentieth century to reflect that Rwanda has suffered such cruel division and death in spite of having a high percentage of Christian people. Struggling to explain this situation, some people, including Cyril Okorocha in his chapter from Africa, have suggested that the traditional focus on personal faith in the Rwandan churches has not been balanced by awareness of others or by any stimulation to social responsibility.

This book has been written by people of faith most of whom have struggled with the realities of life, sometimes near to the edge of disaster. The *modus operandi* are not offered as easy or even difficult ways towards reconciliation and justice; and they do not all end in 'success'. The value of the book is rather in the sharing of the experiences and in the commitment of the people of faith to being links, to going on, sometimes in the face of failure and suffering. Most of the time there are no special insights or results but simply hard work and perseverance. What is inspiring is that people have faith enough to go on struggling as if the world can be changed but without any evidence that it will ever be any different from the way it has always been.

A Buddhist story of struggle and faith tells of a bandit who, having killed someone, fled, arriving at the mountain range which would lead him into another country. He joined the straggling line of travellers towards the shoulder of the mountain and onto a narrow path which gradually disappeared. He saw a young man in front of the queue edging forward until he slipped and began to fall. He pulled him back to safety and learnt that this dangerous crossing was the only way into the other country where there might be less poverty and suffering. The bandit bought a rope, secured it and helped people across the ravine, until one day he was ill, and two people slipped into the ravine and died. He decided to dig a tunnel, and bought a pick. As he dug, deeper and deeper into the mountain, the villagers supported him with food and water. As he dug on and on, the son of the man he had killed caught up with him, but realising that it would take another ten years to dig the tunnel, he went away, returning ten years later. The village was now known as the 'village of the digging saint'. The avenger climbed up the mountain to see the 'saint', the man who had killed his father. The tunnel was almost complete and gradually the young man joined the older one to help him finish his task. He resolved to fight and kill him as soon as the tunnel was complete. The two men worked together in silence and one day the pick broke through into fresh air. They ripped the hole until it was wide enough for them to see out. As they looked down, the tunnel ended in the face of a cliff higher, steeper, wider and more deadly than the one they had cut through. The bandit said, 'I was so sure of the direction. But that's it. I've finished.' The younger man, having forgotten his plan to fight and kill the bandit, tried to persuade him to continue, but he walked away, calling over his shoulder, 'No more. It's all yours. You must make of it what you can.'

Jesus was an example, a challenger and a link person in his world, especially in relation to the Jews and the Gentiles who did not understand each other and who lived completely separate lives. The story of Jesus asking the Samaritan woman at the well for water is one of the many stories of Jesus being a link person, and thus working towards understanding, justice and bringing the qualities of the kingdom of God a little nearer. The woman at the well was seen as unclean by the Jewish people. Jesus should not, according to tradition and culture, have spoken to her, let alone have asked her for a drink of the water which was seen as polluted by her handling it. But he did speak, and focused his full attention upon her, treating her as a real person and as an equal when he asked her to help him. Jyoti Sahi has painted several pictures of Jesus and the woman at the well. One of them shows Jesus as an Eastern holy man, towering over the woman. But the woman is painted in blue and is part of the water spurting out of the well. She is the one giving Jesus new life as she serves him with the water. In Indian culture she is the one bringing the things of God to him, because in India blue is the colour of the gods.

Jesus' gift to the Samaritan woman was the gift of giving. He empowered her to accept him, a representative of her oppressors. How different this inspirational story is from much of the reality of the late twentieth century world, a world where atrocities happen every day. I met three women

19

from Shrebrenitsa who had all lost members of their families – sons, husbands and fathers – in the terrible massacre which took place when they thought they were in a safe place. There have been so many massacres in Algeria that the country may never recover. I read of a son who killed his father and of a man who killed his sister. The cruelty of life is perhaps epitomised by a five year old Indian Dalit girl, who had taken water from a well reserved for the high caste people and was beaten until she went blind. And yet in the same country the people of faith keep open hands and hearts, working for justice and never giving up hope that one day it may be a reality.

Jesus brought people together, making one person out of two, he opened eyes and hearts to God and to the world and he opened hands to work for all people, especially the suffering. In the words of Brother Roger of the Taizé community in France, 'In the heart of God, the church is as large as all the world.' Indigenous people the world over suffer in the modern world, as their lands are taken over and they are pushed to the edge in every sense. In the far north of Argentina for instance, in the Chaco area, the peaceful Wichi Indians endure harassment, malnutrition and violence as a result of the invasion of their lands. Their claims to their land, which they have lived on for hundreds of years, are normally ignored by the Argentinian government and settlers continue to arrive. The Anglican church began to work with the Wichi people in 1964, arranging meetings and finally receiving permission to measure out areas of land along the banks of the river which could be ceded to the Wichi. Bishop Patrick Harris remembers spending a lot of time cutting through the forests to demarcate the areas which could belong to the Wichi. These were put onto maps and sent to the provincial government. The hard work resulted in the passing of a decree giving the rights in the chosen areas to the Wichi. However, the work goes on as the church continues to press for the deeds to the land to be passed to the people. In 1995 there was conflict when an international bridge was planned over the river, with a road going through the lands of the Wichi who have built gardens. The people challenged the building of the road and were able to refer to the decree of 1964, which was discovered, bringing the road building to a halt. However, the struggle continues as the government continues to build the bridge and the church continues to work for the rights of the Indian people. A moving account has been written of one synod meeting when support for the Indian cause was sought, when, 'An old Indian standing at the front held out a very large plastic bag and people were invited to come forward with their gifts. Since the majority of the delegates live precariously from day to day I could not see how the sack would be filled. However, forward they came, some with money, others with their craft products, beautiful carvings and weavings. The sack was more than filled.' Our book shows people of faith from every continent who hack through the forests in their search for reconciliation, justice and peace, sometimes in the face of apparently impossible situations.

In Australia, Christians have used their religion for many years as a tool to crush the cultural identity of the indigenous peoples, and it is only in recent years that they have offered solidarity and strengthening support. The British took possession of Australia in the eighteenth century as if it was unoccupied land, because most of them were totally ignorant of the Aboriginal culture based on family, clan and tribe and on the understanding of the land as mother. In *My Mother the Land*, by Revd Dr Djiniyini Gondarra, we read, 'The land is my mother. Like a human mother, the land gives us protection, enjoyment, and provides of our needs – economic, social, religious. We have a human relationship with the land.' Each clan belonged to an area of land which was the source of their physical and spiritual life for there was no separation between the two. The whole way of life of the people was related to the land and there were rich ceremonies to

21

maintain its fertility. The people cared for the land and were brutally driven away from it. Many people were massacred, many caught diseases and many despaired and turned to alcohol. Until quite recently attempts were made to assimilate the surviving Aborigine people into the white culture by taking children of mixed race marriages away to be brought up as white children in foster homes. It is surprising that there seems to be no record of any church condemning this practice, which left parents and children traumatised. Many Christians did provide homes for the children who had been taken away from their parents and obviously did so lovingly and with the best interests of the children, as they understood them, at heart. It is not surprising that attempts by Christians in Australia, mainly in recent years, to be reconciled to the Aborigine people have not been easy. Some of the churches have, over the last eighty years or so, worked to strengthen Aborigine people and culture and to support their demands for the recognition of their right to the land. In 1982 the Uniting Aboriginal and Islander Christian Congress was formed and has led the way in developing solidarity with the Aborigine and Islander people in their struggles for justice. The Congress acts in the firm faith that Jesus Christ has always stood with the Aborigine people in their resistance to oppression and in their affirmation of their own identity. In January 1988, when Australia celebrated the arrival of the British fleet, the Congress organised a nation-wide march for freedom, justice and hope. Approximately thirty thousand people rallied in Sydney. A covenant has also been agreed between the Congress and the Uniting Church of Australia and the Australian Parliament has established a Council for Aboriginal Reconciliation. When the World Council of Churches Assembly took place in Canberra in 1990 it provided a platform for the Aboriginal people to tell their story and to invite solidarity from all over the world. Every participant to the assembly passed through the purifying smoke of the aboriginal fire on the way into the worship tent for the opening worship, where there was an Aborigine dance of welcome. Bishop Arthur Malcolm, Anglican Aborigine Bishop of North Queensland, also gave a welcome. 'Walk carefully as you come here for God is here before you. Walk softly as you come here for the Spirit may speak in the silence of the ancient place.' But it remains true that Aboriginal and Torres Strait Islander peoples are still the poorest, the unhealthiest, least employed, worst housed and most imprisoned Australians. There is a long way to go in bringing justice, but understanding is being developed; understanding of history and culture, of disadvantage and the need for dignity and control.

When the World Council of Churches held its conference on mission in Salvador in Brazil, at the end of 1996, over six hundred people gathered from sixty countries. Members of the conference listened to each other's ways and wisdoms; they heard the cries of pain from the indigenous people; they learnt about doing theology with street children and from those living in multi-faith societies. For many participants the most moving part of the conference was the early morning service of worship at the dockside where, for centuries, the slaves from Africa were unloaded, separated from their loved ones and sold. People from all over the world wept together and repented together by the 'Stone of Weeping', truly becoming one person instead of many, however fleetingly. People from Europe and people from Africa repented for the part their ancestors had played in this utterly cruel trade. People from every continent committed themselves to work against oppression and for justice and peace.

This book has concentrated on the Christian vision and work for reconciliation, justice and peace but it is vital to recognise that the world faiths all have their visions of a just world and their challenges towards understanding and reconciliation, and work for justice and peace. We include a chapter on Buddhist insights into peacemaking, which brings out the need for detached, neutral compassion in situations of conflict. The way of the Buddha is close to the ways of

23

modern mediators who aim to listen to people on all sides without interruption and then to enable those in conflict to make decisions.

The world faiths all have their link people who set a good example of going on, and on.

Perhaps the best twentieth century example of a link person came from the Hindu Religion. Mahatma Gandhi was someone who practised being a link person throughout his life. He asked people to discover the 'truth' or goodness of those they opposed and thus to develop their own awareness of the humanity of the 'enemy' and of the links between them.

One of the challenges of being a link person is to see the world in new ways, through new eyes. Many people tend to see life and every issue from their own places and cultures. The challenge to people of faith is to look through new eyes and in new directions, towards an understanding of what may seem new ways and wisdoms, new visions and plans.

On one occasion when I travelled to Kenya I stayed in a family where the mother, who was also a primary school teacher, seemed to be doing everything about the house and on the small farm. She fed and milked the cows and goats, she kept hens and ducks, she grew thriving crops; arrowroot, maize, coffee, sugar cane, tea and many fruits. She always gathered and cooked the food, and also cared for her four children and the elderly relative who lived with her family. I felt that the poor woman did not share the pleasures of life which her husband enjoyed, but was rather exhausted by everything she faced. I suggested that next time a group came to England the husband should stay at home whilst she had the opportunity to travel. She thought, for a moment, and then said, 'I will come one day, perhaps when the children are older, but now, when he goes we just simply carry on, but if I were to go away he could not manage.' I had looked at her through Western cultural spectacles. I had mistaken her strength for weakness and had dug a totally unnecessary pit between us.

The gap between myself and the Kenyan woman was easily

bridged, once I had stopped to listen to her. We were both serious and committed to developing our relationship which is the necessary first step towards understanding and trust. There are gaps between people in some circumstances and places which prove much harder, sometimes almost impossible, to bridge.

As Adam Curle has pointed out, the mark of tyrants is that they do not listen or change. They deepen their power by demonising the 'enemy'. Their work is the direct opposite of Gandhi's work. Perhaps there is the temptation towards tyranny in every person at some time, the temptation to believing that one's own culture or country is superior, towards the undermining of the 'other'. This temptation is especially well illustrated in the chapter on relationships between Japan and Britain, markedly after World War Two.

In many of the places where people are divided their religious affiliation seems rather to add fuel to the flames of hatred and division than to enable understanding. This may be because sometimes religion may encourage people to withdraw into their own communities rather than to look outwards, thus making it impossible for them to understand anyone in another community let alone trust them. Fear may so easily become the dominating emotion, leading to total isolation broken only by violence and more violence. In the words of Albert Camus, 'The moment despair is alone, sure of itself, pitiless in its consequences, it has a merciless power.' Religion is strong in many of the bleak situations in the world; religious people may be pitiless to other religious people and sometimes to members of their own communities. Christians in Rwanda and in Northern Ireland, Buddhists, Hindus, Muslims and Christians in Sri Lanka live with violence.

Every time the fragile work for peace breaks down in Northern Ireland it is because people have felt that their culture and identity were being threatened by the 'others' or even by the efforts towards peace which would bring advantage to the others as well as to themselves. When Billy Wright, a convicted murderer, was assassinated in the Maze Prison in January 1998 his death led to reprisal killings and to the stirring up of old and deep hatreds in all the communities. The danger of open conflict breaking out could only be immediately averted by the Secretary of State for Northern Ireland, Mo Mowlam, herself demonstrating that all the people are respected by going into the prison, to meet people on all sides and to listen to them.

Sri Lanka has been devastated by a long civil war which has divided Tamil people, mostly Hindu, from the Sinhala people, mostly Buddhist. The early struggle of the Tamil people for equal recognition, including civil rights for those who came from India to work in the tea plantations, has developed into a struggle for the devolution of power to the Tamil areas in the north and east of the country. As the struggles have been resisted by the Sinhala Buddhist majority, many of the young men have been killed so that there are many widows and children. Unemployment is high and the refugee problem is great with over one million people internally displaced by the fighting. The fiftieth anniversary of the independence of the country, early in 1998, was marked by the bombing of the outer area of the most famous Buddhist temple, the Temple of the Tooth in Kandy. A place of peaceful pilgrimage has been turned into a place of war damage and suffering. The fighting and the gross human rights abuses continue daily, and all in a country where most ordinary people are people of faith who want peace and instead see their children enlist and go to the front line, only returning to them as corpses. Many people of faith in Sri Lanka are working for peace, including the World Solidarity Forum for Justice and Peace which is aiming for a massive peace movement to challenge the present climate of violence. An encouraging story is of the couple who have mortgaged their home to build an inter-cultural research centre so that classes can be offered in inter-cultural and inter-racial understanding. The project has begun, ten miles outside Colombo, in a garage with twenty five students. The Centre for Society and Religion in Colombo is made up of people of the Buddhist, Hindu, Muslim and Christian faiths and offers opportunities for people of different persuasions to meet each other, even if they meet to argue and shout before they listen.

In any circumstances the discipline of listening and sharing is not an easy one to develop. It may often involve a hard struggle for people from opposed groups to meet at all. It may include the setting up of opportunities for people to share by shouting at each other; but shouting is much better than shooting and may lead to some understanding. The community of 'Neve Shalom/Wahat al-Salaam' was formed in 1972 and is situated on a hill overlooking the Vale of Ayalon in an area with a history of struggle and war from the days of Joshua. The community name means 'oasis of peace' and it sets up programmes for meeting and working together for every stage of life for Jews and Palestinians. The encounters are often traumatic and often people shout at each other, because it is hard for a Palestinian to meet a Jew who will one day go into the Israeli army, and it is hard for a Jew to meet a Palestinian who supports an independent Palestine. The hope of the meetings is that they will break down some of the ignorance and fear and may be the beginning of change for some people as they begin to understand that there is more than one truth. The work of 'Neve Shalom/ Wahat al-Salaam' is in the fine tradition of the Hebrew prophets who spoke of God bringing light and justice to the earth. Ezekiel told the people of Israel that truth-telling was the condition for peace making.

When practised, listening and sharing may, with time, lead not only to understanding but to respect for the other person or people even though differences and even disagreements may remain. Respect must lead to work for change and justice of course, otherwise there is the danger of what the Argentinians have called 'Ostrich Theology'. Open hands are only useful if they are strong and if they belong to people who do not seek reconciliation and forgiveness out of weakness but out of strength and a commitment to justice. The Mahatma Gandhi told the story of the cat and the mouse. He said that there was no point in facing a cat by being like a mouse, by accepting weakness and passivity and going on to be taunted and tortured, and finally killed. The only result of such weakness is to strengthen the 'other', whether it is a cat, person, group or nation. Gandhi taught that the only way to face a cat was for supposed 'mice' to struggle, however painful it might be, towards a transformed frame of mind, towards responsibility and the strength and cleverness of the cat; bringing with it the respect of the 'others'. Only then is work for change, by level-headed challenge, by denouncing unjust situations and by working for justice, a realistic option.

The history of the struggle of the South African people against apartheid is an excellent example of the psychological transformation of a people, encouraged by the shining lights of Desmond Tutu and Nelson Mandela and by many other less well known people who have defied all attempts to denigrate and belittle them, and who have set an example of dignified defiance, leading to the ending of apartheid. The chapter on South Africa tells the story well. A novel set in South Africa described one person who refused to be crushed by his own obscurity, disfigurement and poverty. He represents many such people, all over the world. J. M. Coetzee, in *The Life and Times of Michael K*, introduced a person who lived in war-torn and apartheid-ridden South Africa and struggled bravely to become a real person and to find his own creative life. His struggle began when he laboured to make a cart to push his aged and sick mother back to the farm where she was a girl. He refused to compromise, so that when a 'newcomer' to the farm began to tell him what to do, he left. He also wept when he thought of the seeds he had lovingly planted and cared for, and left behind.

He chose isolation and frequently faced hunger and possible death in his search towards himself and his life and dignity. His moments of ecstasy were touchingly simple, one being when he tasted the first pumpkin he had grown himself and 'chewed with tears of joy in his eyes'. This is a novel about the possibility of human freedom, creativity and responsibility which may be released in every person but are only too easily stifled in many.

There is no better example of a contemporary person in a weak position who struggled to become strong than Rigoberta Menchu, who won the 1992 Nobel Peace Prize in recognition of her human rights work amongst her people, the Mayan Indians of Guatemala. Rigoberta, in her autobiography, written in Spanish and translated into English, writes, 'My story is the story of all poor Guatemalans.' She writes of her parents setting up home on the mountainside near Chajul in the North of El Quiche, where they cleared the land and nurtured it for eight or nine years before even maize and beans would grow. She tells of her early childhood with five older brothers and sisters, a childhood divided between home in the mountains and the coastal region where there was work in the coffee, cotton and sugar cane harvesting on the big plantations. She writes, 'I had a great friend. Her name was Maria. One day she died when they were spraying the cotton. From then on I was very depressed about life.' Rigoberta went to work in a plantation house when she was thirteen, and writes that she felt lower than the animals in the house. She returned home to further suffering when the government threw her family and others off the land, even smashing the cooking pots, because the landowners wanted to grow cash crops. Her father, who tried to secure union help, was imprisoned and later released, beaten up and threatened, so that he could never walk freely and had to leave the community. Rigoberta herself went away also and began to travel around, to learn Spanish and to speak to a variety of people, including the plantation workers at the coast. She tells how gradually, 'We realised that the root of the problem was that the country's riches were all in the hands of the few.' In 1979 her young brother was killed after being beaten by the army. Then her father was killed, along with many others, when he tried to occupy the Spanish embassy in order to let people know what was happening. Her mother, who had helped people in the mountain community, was kidnapped and died. Rigoberta then committed herself to remain single and to work hard for the community, teaching people Spanish and reading and writing, and also self-defence and the organising of a strike for better pay on the plantations. Her work meant that she was a wanted person, and had to hide by working as a maid in a convent and then by leaving for Mexico. She has since returned home to Guatemala, has continued her work for her community, and has also travelled widely, giving talks on behalf of her people. She received a message from Emilio Castro when she won the Nobel Peace Prize which read, 'Through you, the heroic and long struggle of the indigenous people for dignity and integrity is uplifted and honoured.'

Wilfred Brown was a dedicated professional singer who died in 1971. In 1968 he wrote:

On behalf of everyone present I have to render articulate things that are stirring in my heart, but which without me would have no point of focus. Without the aspirations of the listener I am as powerless to kindle a flame as a burning glass on a summer's day.

'Yet were it not for the mediator the poem would remain so much print, the melody a crazy string of dots – mere ink. The dormant cyphers can be brought to life only by the exercise of a sacramental gift. God has generously given the gift to people like me . . . It is therefore my duty to stand in all weathers at the crossroads of human experience, assimilating all that I may observe, so that the quintessence of any given emotion may irradiate my voice as I sing of it, and my listeners thrill to this as being the articulation of something within themselves'.

Our book includes inspiring examples of individuals and groups who, like Rigoberta Menchu, are strong in working for reconciliation, justice and peace in harrowing situations and also brave in public and often dangerous mediation work. They are the hope of all who suffer.

The Light of the World

What if electricity
failed over the whole world?
Imagine the stars dimmed
and the smooth shining disc of the moon
eclipsed for ever.
Suppose the sun,
that flushes the sky with glory,
never rose again,
the little leaves on the silver birch
lost their November gold,
and every candle flame
flickered for the last time
and died . . .
Even then,
we would not live in darkness,
because, in the moment of Incarnation,
a great light shone,
a child was born,
and God became human.

Anthea Dove.

Reconciliation: a Search for Its Meaning

Paul Oestreicher

The victims of oppression whose watchword has, for the past generation, been liberation, ask whether their anguish can be smoothed away by the balm of reconciliation. They are wary of this word that has now moved to centre stage. Once confined to the world of theology, it has now entered the language of political science. It is a sign of the times that Coventry University has established, in its School of Law, a Centre for the Study of Forgiveness and Reconciliation, its patron Mary Robinson, the former President of Ireland. No longer is this the exclusive business of the cathedral across the road.

That the churches of Europe chose reconciliation as the theme of their 1997 Assembly in Graz, reflects an almost universal longing to find ways of transcending violent conflict, not at the expense of justice, but as an ethically – and politically – better way of achieving it.

Is there a contemporary model? The world points with wonder at South Africa. But like the Jews, the victims of apartheid ask what it means to forgive. Nelson Mandela reminds us that many who typified the abuse of power are being granted amnesties. He goes on to say, 'Intellectually and politically, one understands why this is necessary. But deep in your heart, and when you are alone with your memories, this is no easy matter.'

This is a remarkable reversal of the common assumption that forgiveness is a personal virtue while in the realm of public life justice must prevail. Here now is a man whom the world honours as a moral and political giant declaring that mercy, however hard it may be to show in one's heart, is a demand of political wisdom, is enlightened realpolitik.

There are, as yet, few protagonists on the world stage with comparable insights. Forgiveness, in the South African context – amnesty is its political expression – is not to be confused with the erasing of memory. On the contrary, both the oppressors and their victims are being encouraged to face their common history. And, from the start, there is the honest recognition that a liberation movement also has its criminals who need to be forgiven. 'Forgive and forget' is not a South African slogan. 'Remember and forgive' is. And the admission that 'all have sinned' is no longer only a spiritual insight. At the end of a bitter conflict there are no innocent parties. All need forgiveness if the wounds of history are to be healed.

These insights challenge Christians anew to explore the meaning and application of reconciliation as a demand of Christian discipleship; and then to turn again to its social and political consequences. This is the time to rescue the Sermon on the Mount from its religious ghetto.

The teaching of the radical rabbi Jesus of Nazareth is the right point of departure. The Hebrew doctrine of an eye for an eye was not an evil, primitive principle. It put clear limits on retaliation. If your enemy hurts you, you are not entitled to take revenge on his wife and children. (A war ending with Hiroshima recognised no such restraints.) But Jesus went much further. 'Love your enemies, do good to those who persecute you. Do not repay evil with evil.' St Paul concludes, 'If your enemy is hungry, feed him . . . and so put your enemy to shame. Do not let evil defeat you, but defeat evil with goodness.' So much for exhortation. When it was put to the ultimate test, Jesus found the strength to pray for his executioners: 'Father forgive them.' Stephen, the first martyr, found the strength to do the same.

For ten years I have been privileged to share responsibility for Coventry Cathedral's ministry of reconciliation, which was born on the 14th November 1940 when the city and its cathedral were destroyed by Hitler's Luftwaffe. At Christmas that year, Provost Howard, standing in the ruins of his cathedral at a BBC microphone, preached to the British Empire: 'Hard as we may find it, we must seek to put away all thoughts of revenge. In the days when this strife is over we will try to build a kinder, more Christlike sort of world.' Of course his words fell on deaf ears in the seats of power. One by one the cities of Germany were, in the cold clinical language of war, taken out.

Provost Howard meant what he had said. And the city caught on to this spirit. In 1947, with Coventry still in ruins, a partner city was sought and found in Germany, Kiel, also in ruins. It was the first civic gesture of friendship from Britain, where many people had been taught by the propaganda of war that the only good German was a dead German.

The fruits of that first act of forgiveness have been many. Around it a mythology has grown to which people respond from many corners of the earth. As Coventry Cathedral's International Director I am, as it were, a keeper of that inheritance. Yet I find myself using the word reconciliation less and less.

Reconciliation, to the comfortable and rich who badly need to be disturbed, gives the all too easy assurance of a quiet life. To the oppressed, uprooted, homeless and disturbed it seems to signify that nothing much will change. We seem to be back with 'the rich man in his castle, the poor man at his gate . . .'

The grave injustices in our land and in our world cry out for redress. Between me and a child banished to the streets, between me and the countless mothers whose children die of hunger, a great gulf is fixed. We are not reconciled.

So what kind of language can I speak and be understood? In my experience, the language of Jesus makes sense. Where reconciliation is both a need and a task, I now put that word into cold storage and start to talk about loving enemies. That provokes a strong reaction.

Most people, Christians included, hold this demand to be at best idealistic, at worst irresponsible or – given human nature – simply impossible. The dialogue starts to take off when I hasten to add that, in this context, loving does not mean liking. It is to wish someone (or a whole nation) well, someone (or a whole group of people) whom we may intensely – and with good reason – dislike. It is, at the deepest level, to refuse to despise anyone, and to admit of no exception.

Given this frame of mind, it is of course even possible for enemies to like each other. Yet not imperative. Kidnapped and kidnapper can and often do discover each other's humanity. Collective enmity (Serb and Croat/Palestinian and Israeli) does not readily lend itself to such personal (Mandela/ de Klerk?) chemistry. Feelings are one thing. Loving enemies is not the same thing. More often than not, it will go against the grain.

The essence of reconciliation, of this loving process, is bound up with the complex relationship between forgiveness and repentance. They, in a mixture which cannot be accurately defined, are the practical ingredients. There is a major debate about which is the more important, the *sine qua non*, the precondition for all that follows. At this point it is tempting to dogmatise. I will try to avoid it.

Both biblical insight and experience have convinced me that normally the unconditional offer of forgiveness is the first step to the overcoming of enmity. The offer remains valid, whether accepted or not. The victim makes the first move. The prisoner has often retained the humanity her jailer has lost. Sheila Cassidy found it possible in a Chilean jail to pray for those who had stripped her, as they plied her with electrodes: the Jesus option.

That makes psychological sense when the victim has the insight to see in the enemy a person like himself, like herself. It is a lesson my father taught me. His mother died in the Holocaust. He escaped from Germany with my mother and with me. 'How lucky I am to have been born a Jew,' he often said, in a reversal of roles. 'There is dignity in being a victim of persecution, there is shame in persecuting others. Being born a Jew, my role was clear. I could not even be tempted to side with the devil.' In other words, he knew in his heart of hearts that he too, in different circumstances, might have been the persecutor. We all have demonic as well as divine potential. The survivor of Auschwitz can all too easily become the torturer of Palestinians. The world is plagued by the rekindling of historic conflicts. Collective memory without the collective will to forgive and to ask for forgiveness is a virulent poison. Northern Ireland and the former Yugoslavia are classic examples. So is the bitterness between Tutsi and Hutu. Invariably, both sides believe themselves more sinned against than sinning. As in bitter personal conflict, the offer of forgiveness from an assumed position of moral superiority will not suffice. Healing is unlikely to happen until both sides recognise the beam in their own eye. And so we face the complex and subtle relationship between forgiveness and repentance.

It may seem obvious that in 1939 Hitler launched a criminally aggressive war. Yet he had successfully persuaded most Germans that they were simply righting the injustices of the Treaty of Versailles. It is a rare example of corporate maturity – of learning from history – that after World War II the great majority of Germans accepted their guilt, and this despite the fact that the victors occupied and divided their land and ethnically cleansed Germany's eastern provinces of their population, some eight million people. Two million Germans died in the process.

Germany's neighbours in East and West have good reasons to hate Germans. Germans have reasons enough to return that hatred. It has not happened. The reasons are complex but by far the most important is the recognition that friendship is possible and imperative because in the conflicts of the past century all have failed. There are no hero nations. There is little fertile soil left for national chauvinism.

Britain's problem with the rest of Europe – though not one of overt enmity – is that in Britain there is no corporate recognition of failure. Few Europeans could understand the corporate euphoria over Britain's (or should it be England's?) Falkland victory. Serbs and Croats, perhaps Greeks and Turks, the European exceptions, can understand our jingoism more readily.

A threatened marriage is on the road to recovery if partners are able to ask for and to offer forgiveness. Corporate relationships are not fundamentally different. Had the Irish hierarchy enabled the Pope, on his visit to Ireland, to ask for as well as to offer forgiveness to the Protestant Community, he would have been a more credible peacemaker. If the many followers of Ian Paisley could only see that they are mirror images of the IRA, peace would begin to be possible. If the British could only acknowledge their historic guilt towards Ireland, they might begin to cease being an integral part of the Irish problem. (Nicholas Frayling, the Rector of Liverpool, has convincingly argued that in his book *Pardon and Peace*.)

If that is an important part of the truth, then reconciliation is in large measure about the politics of penitence. And that is in short supply. Yet I return also to the previous insight, exemplified in South Africa, that the politics of forgiveness is equally if not even more important. The vicious circle of retaliation – often described with justification as justice – can sometimes only be broken by a conscious will not to insist on justice. That can be a decision of far-reaching political maturity. It is akin, within a nation or between nations, to the right of the British crown prosecution service not to prosecute an individual when it is not in the public interest.

That is never an easy course of action. To dispense with justice instead of dispensing it can be deeply hurtful to the victims of injustice. The torturers and their masters remain unpunished in many parts of Latin America and in Eastern Europe after their fall from power. And not because they have shown remorse. That is profoundly painful – and yet probably wise. At this point we are faced with the deep tension between justice and peace. No discussion of the meaning of reconciliation can escape that tension. Rightly, the psalmist dreams of the day when justice and peace will embrace. In the world as it is, they are locked in conflict. An uncompromising pursuit of justice is a recipe for conflict. It is the rationale for almost every war and every violent revolution. The end is seldom the desired end.

It is equally true that there are conditions of injustice that make a mockery of peace, 'peace, where there is no peace'. When children die of hunger, that is a declaration of war by the rich on the poor.

It is in the midst of this inescapable tension, this recognition that relative injustice is the price of peace and a constantly threatened peace the price of justice, that I return to the ethics of the Sermon on the Mount: unless, personally (and that is where it must start) and corporately, we learn and learn soon to treat our enemies with reverence, because that is how we want them to treat us, we are doomed. The interplay of injustice and violence, given our technology, will destroy us.

How much time the human race has to unlearn the destructive elements of its whole cultural history, I do not know. Will our killer instinct or our survival instinct be the stronger? Can our children and their children learn that the teaching of Jesus – with other sources of truth and wisdom – is a realistic recipe for life; that to love our enemies, however costly, is the highest form of self-love?

To say that is also to allow the psychologists to teach us that we are, each of us, in large measure our own worst enemy. To love ourselves is often the hardest thing of all, and so we project our self-hatred on to others. Social psychology teaches us that the same is true of tribes, races and nations.

We need to be saved from ourselves and reconciled with ourselves, personally and corporately. A faith that grasps the

39

reality of God's indiscriminate love for us all, a faith that reassures us that all of us are divine as well as demonic and that in Christ the demonic is already doomed, such a faith puts that healing of the world that we call reconciliation within our grasp.

There are no grounds for easy optimism, indeed for any kind of optimism. Hope is something different. It is rooted in the experience that love is what it is. And we are, when we walk in the light, capable of receiving and sharing it.

After a devastating British air raid on the German town of Pforzheim, seven airmen bailed out of their burning bomber. After five of them were captured, a Nazi officer had them driven through an enraged crowd, cornered in a church yard, and murdered on his orders by Hitler Youth teenagers.

More then forty years later, at a Communion service, the local church dedicated a plaque to the murdered airmen. The widow of one of them was invited, and came to Germany from Lancashire. An elderly man, weeping bitterly as he received communion, begged to be forgiven: 'I was one of the lads that killed them.' And then he walked away. Told of this, the widow had only one wish: 'Can't we find him, so that I can put my arms round him?'

For reconciliation, read love.

Reconciliation: Problems and Alternatives

Adam Curle

Prophesy and reconciliation

I am a member of the Society of Friends, a Quaker. The Quakers, as many people know, have been deeply concerned with peace ever since their foundation in the mid-seventeenth century; even in those early days ardent Quakers moved around Europe trying to persuade those in power to abandon war as an instrument of policy. Their approach was a religious one, essentially prophetic: war was wrong, an offence against the law of God.

More recently, however, the practice based on this belief has been supplemented by another approach: the reconciliatory. This entails attempting to get individuals – or nations – to see each other's point of view, to break down barriers of hatred, to turn enemies into friends. Wolf Mendl giving the Swarthmore Lecture to the annual gathering of British Quakers, chose to discuss this dual approach, He called his talk 'Prophets and Reconcilers'.

Social psychiatry

My own practical work as a reconciler began in 1947 some years before joining the Society of Friends. I was on the staff of the Tavistock Institute of Human Relations and many of us were very interested in what some called 'social psychiatry'. This meant using our understanding of both society and psychology to bring together people separated by misunderstanding or prejudice. We tried to apply this approach to communities, to workers and employers, and to other groups whose cohesion, effectiveness and happiness were damaged by any type of social and/or psychological division.

This carried no doctrinally 'prophetic' message, but it did express an ideal. I think that my colleagues, mostly declared atheists, felt a kind of missionary zeal in promoting the work. I have learned through this that the underlying motives of good women and men, whatever they believe, are remarkably alike.

Looking back forty years, I am surprised to recognise that the basic principles of mediation or reconciliation, as 'social psychiatry' is now called, appear to be much the same; conflict of interest among human groups is to be tackled in essentially similar ways. But the large scale armed conflicts with which I became involved later were infinitely more terrible, because of the atmosphere of violence, with its cruel turbulence and unreason, which I will discuss later.

Reconciliation

After I became a Quaker, I became involved in reconciliation on behalf of the Society. This took me to wars in Africa and Asia, and on my own behalf into the conflict in Northern Ireland. These assignments were all fairly long-lasting. My shortest involvement was two years and my longest five and a half years. This did not mean that I was 'in the field' continuously. For much of the time I was holding university appointments and was not free to be in the war zone. However, my employers were very lenient and I was almost always able to go if it seemed there was anything useful I could do.

Essentially, my associates and I tried to weaken the barriers which prevented top decision-makers on both sides of the conflict from meeting with the intention of having serious discussions about ending hostilities. (I put it like this, because at times a leader, the head of a government or of a guerrilla movement, would agree to meet his/her opposite number, not in the interests of peace, but in the belief that she/he would get some domestic or international political advantage out of seeming to pursue it.)

But before going any further I shall try to deal with an objection which is often raised. Surely, I am asked, you will compromise your principles by dealing with some of the people you must have to meet. Here such undesirables as Idi Amin or Hitler are mentioned. Well, firstly, we do not talk with people unless there is reason to suppose that they really want to make an acceptable peace, rather than to impose their tyranny. We may indeed dislike the policies of a particular leader, but such personal feelings are unimportant compared with the possibility that our efforts may help to bring an end to the miserable horrors of war afflicting thousands. And in any case, the striving for and eventual achievement of peace may well lead to a change in those policies.

Reconciliation in practice

Once it is agreed that we should consider being involved, as would-be reconcilers, in a particular conflict, we carry out what might be termed a feasibility study. What is actually happening? Is the situation one in which we can usefully intervene? Do we have any local friends? Are there any language and other difficulties? Do we have sufficient resources of qualified individuals and of cash? Above all, would we be welcomed? When all these enquiries have been satisfactory completed, we have seldom found it very hard to make contact with key decision makers (as well as a number of other people who can supply useful insights, information and friendly advice).

At this point the real difficulties begin. I shall try to define what seem to me to be the greatest problems. Chief of these is the atmosphere of violence I just mentioned. War develops a terrible momentum. As it lunges on and on, as do most contemporary wars, more bestial acts are committed by both sides. Hatred, anger and fear become the dominant emotions. Opposition, from the very start, is treasonable.

In fact the minds of non-combatant leaders become more infected by the atmosphere of violence than do those of the fighters. If decent and humane, they are overwhelmed by shame and guilt at the slaughter and destruction for which they are responsible. Very often they get rid of these intolerable emotions by projecting them outwards onto the enemy leadership, particularly such people as the head of the guerrilla group or the president of the other country if the struggle is international.

This leads to the sort of conversation I have heard a number of times. Here the mediator is addressing President A, leader of a country at war with a country led by President X:

> 'If you are interested in initiating a peace process, why do you not arrange for some of your people to meet with the representatives of President X?'
>
> 'In principle I would be glad to do so. I am very eager to bring this terrible war to an end, but you don't know X. He is a monster, a war criminal, who only wants to destroy us. Why else would he bomb our villages, killing countless women and children? And his soldiers are bloodthirsty murderers. He doesn't want peace and if he agreed to any meeting, it would simply be a trick to make me lower my guard. He is completely untrustworthy.'

And if we would then go to see President X he would use almost comparable words, and express angry amazement at what had been said about himself by President A.

This phenomenon is called the mirror image. It is the task of a mediator who wishes to achieve some degree of reconciliation between Presidents A and X to change the perceptions of the two men or women about each other. In the ambience of war it is quite incredibly difficult.

And there are many other slightly less intractable factors, such as the relative powerlessness of leaders to take what might be an independent line, the great complexity of the situation, and the need to keep in favour with aid donors.

Sometimes we have suggested a small step on the peace path, such as a short localised cease fire; this might, if all went well, demonstrate the sincerity (a much used word in this context) of the other side. But the response is usually cautious: it might be a good idea, but how do you prevent the enemy taking advantage of it to bring up more troops, improve their positions, etc.? Occasionally such an idea has been accepted, but in fact ruined by restrictive provisos. I was told things would be too risky otherwise – we can't take any chances, can't risk the losing of more lives. I answered that a greater risk is being taken by not seriously trying a measure that could shorten the war and thus save many more lives. We have then discussed ways in which the integrity of a cease fire could be monitored.

Building relationships

Above all, we concentrate on building relationships with these emotionally beleaguered leaders. They are often in fact very lonely, unsure of the loyalty of their generals and advisers. They may fear assassination – I knew one who hardly ever dared leave the barracks where he was guarded by a company of his own tribesmen. They may sometimes find it easier to confide in a person who is completely free of any local partisanship, and who is not a diplomat whose relationship with his or her own masters is of primary importance. But even here there is a psychological stumbling block: the leader cannot help realising that the reconciler has a comparable relationship with the implacable enemy whom he is fighting – how then can he be quite certain of the reconciler's friendship? There is no easy answer. All I can say is that it is crucial to maintain impeccably fair impartiality, and consistent and obvious goodwill.

This befriending is essential to building a relationship in which the mediator not only gains trust, but in the process earns the right to speak freely.

Quakers often talk about 'speaking truth to power', but this does – or should – not mean marching into the president's office, banging on the desk and denouncing his policies. This would neatly decapitate any hopes of reconciliation that the Quaker or anyone else concerned, might harbour.

However, if the mediator has been wise and truly friendly, she/he should be in a position to act as a prophet, as well as a reconciler. This adds an important moral dimension to work which is otherwise more or less purely secular diplomacy. We, who are not professional diplomats and who therefore lack many of the advantages of logistical support and communication facilities, lose much of our *raison d'être* if we cannot speak from the heart of our faith. We become just low-level ambassadors. I admit to having sometimes feared that I had acted like a rather inadequate diplomat, using the conventional strategic, political and economic arguments, and above all values, but never hinting that some acts are morally flawed.

If Quakers or any other group grounded in some ideology are to become involved in peace making, it must be obvious that they think their particular approach has something important to add. In saying this, I am not deriding or undervaluing the skills of diplomacy and negotiation – indeed we do our best to acquire them – but if we feel that our spiritual beliefs are relevant then we should find ways of expressing them. (It must, however, be said, that 'preaching' peace must be done tactfully. The reconciling mediator is, after all, talking to people who are fighting a war, often reluctantly, usually believing their cause is just.)

The uses of mediation
How effective are the procedures we have been considering? I have to acknowledge that I am aware of no instance where they have contributed in a major and obvious way to the cessation of hostilities. This usually occurs through the military defeat of one side or the intervention, forceful if not necessarily violent, of a third party. Often, however, there are many interwoven strands in the process of peace making.

Just as it is impossible to identify the part played by a single strand of a rope towing a ship into port, so it is usually impossible to determine the part of reconciliatory mediation in ending the bloodshed.

The Nigerian civil war, which it was feared would end in wholesale massacre of the defeated Biafrans, ended in an amazing spirit of reconciliatory euphoria. The victorious Federal soldiers gave money and food to their former enemies and treated their wounds. Quakers were told that, although their constant emphasis on the uselessness of war and the primacy of reconciliation, had had, for political reasons, no impact on the strategy of the war, its spirit had filtered down from the leadership to the fighting soldiers.

In another of the African conflicts, one that ended by negotiation, more than one head of state thanked them for their continuing efforts over a period of several years. One of these said that the Quakers' constant reminder that there were other ways than violence of settling quarrels, had kept his mind on the target of peace.

On the other hand, it is possible that the involvement of ardent would-be peace makers could be used by one or other party in a conflict in such a way as to worsen or prolong it. By encouraging the Quakers (or whoever was concerned) to think that they were interested in the peace process, they could win concessions or time to their own advantage. This of course could only occur when the peace makers have some influence, which in fact they always do, even though very small; otherwise they would not be allowed to carry out such sensitive work.

Limitations of reconciliation
However, the issues just discussed are very uncommon in the post-Cold War world. There are now virtually no international conflicts. Nor are there many sufficiently structured conflicts, ones comprising two definable groups with recognised leaderships, between which mediation may be carried out.

Many leaders in the confused, anarchic struggles laying waste Liberia, Afghanistan or Bosnia have had local warlords driven by autistic ambition, greed, or vanity; people with whom it is impossible to deal because they never keep a promise or follow any code of behaviour beyond self-interest. For such, the idea of reconciliation is an absurdity. They do not fight for any ideological objective, social, political, or economic, only for dominance. This is at times attempted through killing or displacing whole populations that stand in their way. Thus in Bosnia or Rwanda old men, women, and children are to be exterminated as ruthlessly as the soldiers of the other side.

In these harsh, morally arid climates, the would-be reconcilers have a hard part to play.

Where the elements of normal government survive, they will continue to behave as in the past. That is to say, to build relationships of trust and confidence with leaders on both sides. Such relationships also enable them to express their belief in the worthless evil of war and in the values – and possibilities – of peace.

However, at best the role of the contemporary peace maker is likely to be a mixture of the old and the new approaches. There will probably be much less to-ing and fro-ing between leaders, and more working with those of the people who are trying to maintain the semblance of a decent society.

A new role
This may sound over optimistic in a world committed by belief in the power of violence. We have, however, much recent evidence of the power of the people over those controlling the power of the gun. The peaceful revolutions of Czechoslovakia, East Germany and other East European countries were made by unarmed peoples. They were just as comprehensive as any other example of political metanoia. In addition, although much blood was shed over many years

in South Africa, the Middle East and Northern Ireland, the peace processes (though still vulnerable in the latter two) could never have taken place unless, during the same periods, countless individuals and groups had not come together to educate each other, to explore new ways, and to effect an enormous changing of hearts.

In 1992 I was invited to go to former Yugoslavia, then in the process of bloodily breaking up. It was expected that I should play my old part of mediator. It soon became obvious, however, that this was quite impossible in existing circumstances; the honourably fruitless efforts of such as David Owen and Cyrus Vance showed that this role, at least in this place, had become extinct. What I did find, however, was that there were individuals joining together as groups to strive for a new approach to peace. One of these is described in my book, *Another Way: Positive Approach To Violence* (Jon Carpenter, Oxford, 1995). These comprised women and men (mostly the former) who were sickened by an atmosphere virulently poisoned by hatred, fear and militarism; by the plight of the countless victims of war, and by the erosion of respect for human life and dignity and other values that constitute the foundation of a just and peaceful society.

The work of these groups in several of the countries that now make up former Yugoslavia has been immensely impressive. Their work for refugees and displaced persons, for the traumatised; in education and social provision, has transformed many communities. But perhaps the most significant transformation has been the widened consciousness of both the group members and those with whom they are in contact. Not only are the values of the past being preserved, but strengthened and given new, dynamic form.

What, then, is the role of an outsider like myself? I am demoted from the rank of 'expert foreign advisor' to a combination of odd job man, head-hunter for individuals with needed skills such as counselling children traumatised by violence, liaison work with useful organisations and funding sources in other countries, and perhaps most of all friend, supporter and giver of encouragement. I do not ever tell them what they ought to do, because I don't know – they are the ones who understand their own communities – but I am sometimes a sounding board for their own ideas. On rare occasions I may be asked to fulfil my old role and make contact with the 'enemy', but that is more or less incidental.

But former Yugoslavia is only one of many areas of a world which is widely afflicted by cruel and anarchic violence. My own experience leads me to believe that the best way for the rest of the world to help the afflicted people of these places is not to flood them with aid agencies, with advisers, with high level missions of mediators; it is not, as at last in desperation was done in Bosnia, to bully the protagonists into a precarious cessation of hostilities. It is to unobtrusively help the people to help themselves, to apply their own genius to their own problems. This entails tactfully seeking out the few (or maybe many!) people in every community who have the courage combined with both good heart and good sense to set about solving them. They will need encouragement; they will need resources of various sorts (but not very much to start with). But these should not come with governmental or UN strings attached. They might originate from these sources, but should be delivered, without instructions, by NGOs.

The more this leaven of developmental changes spreads, as in my experience it has done in several spots, the more fully will the laws of love and reason be restored.

I shall then die happy.

Building Bridges: Reconciliation as Gospel and Calling

Keith Clements

As someone who works in 'international affairs' I am all too well aware that the term sounds rather grandiose, and far removed from everyday life at home. In fact I think the real challenge we face as churches in the British Isles is to realise that our international concerns begin right here at home, on the street where we live. Remember what Martin Luther King once said: 'Before you finish eating your breakfast this morning, you have depended on half the world.' Life is a whole. Thinking internationally means not just thinking of what's going on round the other side of the world in the Pacific or in Peru, but thinking also of the international implications of what we are doing in our own kitchens. And to engage with the 'really big' issues of the day doesn't mean that they are not for so-called ordinary people at local level. Sometimes, it's precisely such people who show us just what these issues are all about.

That is certainly true of the theme of reconciliation, of building bridges. I begin with a story. Harold and Amy were a couple, nearing retiring age, in the Baptist chapel in a Cheshire village where I began my ministry, nearly 30 years ago. At first sight, they were exactly the sort of people to strike dread into the heart of a young pastor straight from college. They looked so fierce. Harold had a face like crumpled steel. He was a painter at the big ICI chemical works at the bottom of the hill. He usually had a cigarette dangling out of his mouth, and so was usually the last to take his seat in chapel for the start of the service – and for the same reason the first out as well. Amy was no less formidable in appearance, and with a voice to match. When a choir was formed for special occasions in the chapel year, Amy would always volunteer to join, and the choirmaster, with superlative diplomatic skill, would place her on the back row at the far end of the tenors where, as he put it, 'Your voice will blend in nicely with the others'. I don't think I ever saw a book in their home. But they themselves had a story, were a story which I've pondered more and more as time has gone in my ministry and career. I heard it from a number of people, and one day I heard it from Harold himself.

They'd had two sons. The older one was killed in the Second World War. He was in the Fleet Air Arm, and was lost in an attack on the huge German battleship, the *Tirpitz*. Harold told me that when the dreadful telegram came, he was so beside himself with grief and rage, he vowed that the first German he ever met, he would break his neck. Well, the war went its course, and in May 1945 came VE-Day. A week or so later in that Cheshire village came another event which, in a Baptist chapel in the north of England, was of at least equal importance: the Sunday School Anniversary. On that Sunday afternoon, Harold was standing outside the chapel door, no doubt finishing his fag, as the children in their best Sunday clothes trooped in ready to recite their poems and sing their hymns, followed by anxious parents and doting grandparents and aunts and uncles . . . when among them two young men appeared in drab grey uniforms. In somewhat thick accents they asked, 'Was ist hier today? Can we go in?' Harold replied, 'Children, lots of singing – come on in!' It took a few seconds for Harold to realise he'd broken his vow. He'd met his first Germans, and instead of breaking their necks he'd invited them into his chapel. They were of course inmates from the local prisoner-of-war camp, now allowed out at intervals.

But this was only the beginning. One night the following week, the Germans turned up again for the Young People's Fellowship – and beat all comers at table tennis. And it was only a week or two later that the gossip went round the village: 'Have you heard? Harold and Amy have had some of the German prisoners home to tea.' The first people in the whole village to welcome German lads, homeless and parentless, into their home, at the table where their own beloved son had sat, were Harold and Amy. I can still remember the look on Harold's face as he told me that story, shaking his head with a kind of wonder, a puzzlement that such things could happen. But nor did it end there. One of those Germans, called Sigmund, kept in touch with Harold and Amy after he returned to Germany. He was a keen member of his own church at Dortmund in the Ruhr. The friendship not only continued but extended. Harold and Amy visited them, the friendship was taken up by Sigmund's eventual children and the Ridings' grandchildren. It extended to our two congregations as well. When, just before I left Cheshire in 1971, we opened a new church building, we received a greeting from the pastor of the church in Dortmund. It was a card, and on it was printed those words of the Apostle Paul in his Second Letter to the Corinthians, when he crowns his great exposition on reconciliation by saying: 'So, if anyone is in Christ, there is a new creation: everything old has passed away; see, everything has become new!' (2 Cor. 5:17).

I've pondered that story increasingly over the years. For one thing, it's a salutary lesson to me, which I don't think I really appreciated at the time. I've long been deeply interested in international issues and the role of the churches in them, on the big scale. For a number of years as a teacher and writer I've dealt with the ecumenical history of Britain and Germany this century, at war and seeking reconciliation. Whenever I pass through Paddington Station I'm aware that I'm walking on ecumenically holy ground. I recall that one day in 1939 two young men, a Dutchman and a German, were to be seen walking up and down that long platform 1 for about an hour, deep in conversation. The Dutchman was

W. A. Visser't Hooft, secretary of the then nascent World Council of Churches. The German was Dietrich Bonhoeffer. They both happened to be in London at the same time, and Paddington Station was the only place where they could conveniently meet for that hour on their journeyings. They were discussing how, in the war that was inevitable and imminent, the Confessing Church inside Germany and the ecumenical fellowship outside could keep in contact across the lines of conflict, and how the brave resistors in Nazi Germany could be helped. It is one of the great stories of our ecumenical heritage how that fellowship was maintained, secretly but unbroken, during the war years. The WCC office in Geneva acted as a clandestine communications office for both sides. In 1942 Bonhoeffer was able to meet with his great English friend Bishop George Bell in neutral Sweden. And when, in April 1945, Bonhoeffer was finally taken away to Flossenbürg for execution his last message to an English fellow-prisoner was a greeting to George Bell, which stands as one of the great ecumenical testimonies of the century: 'Tell him that with him I believe in the principle of our universal Christian brotherhood which rises above all national interests, and that our victory is certain.'

There is that story of the good, the great, and the famous. It includes the story of the declaration made by the German Protestant leaders at Stuttgart after the war ended, in the autumn of 1945, confessing the guilt of their nation and their own failures, and promising a new beginning – an action which greatly contributed to rebuilding bridges between Germany and the allied countries. But I return to Harold and Amy, and Sigmund. What Bonhoeffer and Bell believed in, what Stuttgart called for, they were already doing in their own way, in their own village, in their own kitchen. And there are many other such stories that could be told. There was the very young German prisoner of war whose camp in Scotland was befriended by the local mining community, and who one day, cold and miserable and lonely, turned to the New

Testament he'd recently been given by one of those local people. He read the account of Jesus' crucifixion, and was transfixed by the cry from the cross, 'My God, my God, why have you forsaken me?' It was the turning point of his life. His name was, is, Jürgen Moltmann. And many of us who claim to know something about theology in the past thirty years know how significant that discovery has been not just for him, but for us all, as we ponder the mystery and wonder of a crucified, triune God. These apparently little stories are where the big issues of peace and reconciliation are incarnated. And so I hope that we can combine the wide vision with the focus on how these great themes can impact and be lived out in everyday life and in our local communities.

The Graz 1997 gathering underlined for me the importance of this kind of story. Christians of all traditions, Protestant, Catholic, Orthodox, Evangelical, met for Bible study, worship, celebration and exploration of what kind of Europe we want, and what kind of Christian witness for that Europe we need. The Graz theme was 'Reconciliation: Gift of God and Source of New Life'. 'Gift of God': as I contemplate that title, I see in my mind's eye Harold's face when he'd finished telling me his story, shaking his head in wonderment, in surprise that such a thing could have happened. It truly was a gift, a miracle of God's grace in their lives. 'Source of New Life': it really was life out of death for Harold and Amy, new friendship out of loss and bitterness – and moreover new life for the whole congregation, for the village, for their families to the next generation, right down to that message from the pastor in Dortmund when we opened our new building. We could spend our whole time further unpacking that story as an exposition and illustration of our theme. But we must move on to our present day and the millennium that is coming.

Reconciliation as a gift of God is where as Christians we start from. We do not start with reconciliation as a task or goal we have to achieve. I can practically hear the groans whenever a booklet is sent out with a title like 'Building Bridges' or 'Reconciliation': 'O God, not another thing we have to do, dreamt up in ecumenical headquarters somewhere, yet another impossible programme to add to our already creaking agendas, yet another dose of guilt on the way because of our inbuilt tendency to failure.' We're bound to feel like that if we start from thinking that we're being asked to put the whole world right on our own initiative and by our own resources. But we start with what God has done, is doing and will do. We start by listening again to the gospel as for example declared by the apostle Paul: 'All this is from God, who reconciled us to himself through Christ, and has given us the ministry of reconciliation; that is, in Christ God was reconciling the world to himself, not counting their trespasses against them, and entrusting the message of reconciliation to us' (2 Cor. 5:18*ff*). Our first calling is to hear again, as if for the first time, this gospel of God's initiative, God's grace, and be bowled over by the simple wonder of it. Perhaps every Christian gathering for every task ought to begin by singing the hymn 'To God be the glory, great things he has done! So loved he the world that he gave us his Son' with its refrain, 'Praise the Lord!'

God is the reconciling God. God's nature is to reconcile because God's own very being is the community of perfect love we know as holy trinity, tri-unity, the three-in-oneness of Father, Son and Holy Spirit in their boundless, ceaseless mutual love, love which overflows in creating us and this universe, and drawing all God has made into sharing that triune life of love. God as love reaches out to save and unite with himself everyone and everything in their brokenness and sickness. It is love at its deepest because it seeks precisely those at enmity with God. It is the love of the cross, where God spends all, spends himself, in reconciliation, in winning back the rebellious world from its enmity into friendship and new childhood with himself. In Jesus God lives out the life of righteous love under the conditions of our weakness and alienation. On the cross he himself becomes one of the godforsaken, so that no one and nothing need be godforsaken ever again. The apostle Paul, again, speaks of this mystery at its deepest: 'For our sake, [God] made him to be sin who knew no sin, in order that in him we might become the righteousness of God' (2 Cor. 5:21). This is the ultimacy of love, that bridge-building from God's side to ours, that we might cross to God.

If we're not continually stunned and amazed and exhilarated by this reconciliation, we've no business to be in the reconciliation business. It's on the basis of God the reconciler and his reconciling work that people are entrusted in turn with a ministry of reconciliation. Indeed, as far as I'm concerned I simply cannot survive in the reconciliation business unless this is the starting point for my faith. This came home to me recently, when I was in a meeting with about a dozen people, dealing with Rwanda and Burundi: the terrible conflicts that have, still are, taking place there, and the situation of the churches in them. In July 1995 I was in those countries myself. Things seemed bad enough already in the aftermath of the genocide in Rwanda, and the continuing bloodshed in Burundi, where every night despite a curfew in the capital of Bujumbura, the silence was broken by rifle fire and grenades. But this meeting was virtually a catalogue of despair: the desperate situation still of refugees in Zaire, the mounting toll of death in Burundi. People who had just visited these countries said, 'The kind of moderate space in political life that you saw last year has gone; in both countries church leaders seem ever more helpless, ever more compromised in their relationship to politicians.' The whole region of central Africa seems to be unravelling into a fearful situation of unstoppable conflict and unthinkable human consequences and scale of need. How can we talk of reconciliation here? How can we talk of bridge-building when even the flood-banks of the river seem to be dissolving? Only a faith that believes that God is there, the God of cross and resurrection, the God who can deal with chaos, only such a faith can go on talking about reconciliation: talk about it not as a last desperate resort but as the first resort in the hope for a new beginning, a new creation.

The reconciliation announced in the gospel is for everyone and for everything, and it cost God everything too. 'In [Christ] all the fullness of God was pleased to dwell, and through him God was pleased to reconcile to himself all things, whether on earth or in heaven, by making peace through the blood of his cross' (Col. 1:19*ff*). That's why it is entirely right to include everything human and earthly within its scope: from race to relations between women and men; from relations with people of other faiths to questions of power and wealth and poverty; from armed conflict to alienation within families; from homelessness to the preservation of our environment.

But it's just here, I recognise again, that we will start to get worried. Our calling to be reconcilers, bridge-builders, is founded on and sustained by God's reconciling grace. On that basis, we can dare to allow ourselves to be caught up into his reconciling love as his partners. We can afford to have our ministry widened out into the whole human community, the whole earth and the universe. We can risk, also, knowing how costly it can be. There is a cup to drink, a baptism to undergo, which the reconciling Lord wishes us to share with him according to the measure of our faith. I believe this means we are freed from having to think of reconciliation as a crushing and impossible task to carry out, an impossible programme to fulfil. It means rather that we are caught up into a relationship with the gracious God and we shall find thereby our particular points of responsibility, the particular pieces of service he calls us to, depending who we are, where we are. It means looking upon our world as a world in which the reconciling God is already active, and where particular possibilities will be opened to us as by faith. We wait upon the God we know in Christ, whose word we hear in our worship and at whose table we gather in fellow-ship with him and with each other.

I was helped to see this when a few years ago I visited Lebanon just as the terrible civil war there had almost ended and a very shaky peace was stumbling into place, but Terry Waite and the other western hostages were still underground we knew not where. It had been a conflict costing many thousands of lives and, tragically, it had been fought along lines of religious identity: Christians, Druze, Muslims. It had been a terribly testing time for the Christian Churches of Lebanon, who had to ask themselves: how do we break out of this tribalistic attachment of religion to groups and factions? Even before the fighting had completely stopped, they were asking what their particular ministry should be. There were of course a thousand and one tasks that they could have undertaken together, all of them useful ways of helping people and victims of the conflict. But the Council of Churches there asked the question in a more defined way. They asked: 'What sort of service, in our country, at this particular time, will most clearly manifest the kingdom of the God of reconciling love?' A lot might be done in the devas-tated city of Beirut itself, and was being done, and was well known. That was part of the trouble. But who were the people who were not at present being helped? Answer: the people of the villages up the remote end of the Bekaa Valley, out of the way and forgotten. And who among them are most in need of help and care? Answer: mentally and physi-cally handicapped children, for whom nothing is being done. And how can they be helped in a way which is most true to the God of reconciling love? Answer: by ensuring that the schools and day-centres set up for them are for Christian, Muslim and Druze children equally, are staffed by people of all those faiths, and that the schools are managed by members of all the communities equally. That, in a situation where previously society had been riven by conflict on confessional lines, was the particular ministry undertaken.

We in Britain of course find ourselves in a very different situation. But the approach, the kind of questions we ask, can be very similar. We are not called to be and do everything. We are called to a vision of the length and depth and breadth and height of the love of God in Christ, embracing everything; and within that panorama, called to identify just what specific point we are to fill in by who we are, where we are, and what we are given to use, in our responsibility before God.

It's at this point that I'd like to pick up on some of the responses to the Council of Churches for Britain and Ireland Lent Course *Building Bridges*, from a group of churches in England. A number of local groups felt that a lot of the main issues in *Building Bridges* were not relevant to their situation: race, unemployment, violent conflict and so forth. Clearly, we don't all live with these problems – especially urban ones – right on our own doorstep. But is it then fair to say that the whole theme of *Building Bridges* is not relevant to us? Or, put another way, to ask 'How is this relevant to us here?' may be the wrong question. If as God's people we are called to a vision of his love reconciling all things, ought we not rather to be asking, 'How are we relevant to it? What is our particular contribution to make, where we are and as we are?' Three points in particular are worth making.

First, even supposing your community was a perfect example of peace and harmony, both in church and village, in the midst of a leafy Essex paradise, you would not thereby be absolved from sharing in some way in God's mission of reconciliation in the world. You might find, for instance, that you had been placed there to be a special centre of prayer for those who are in the front-line; or to be means of support for them in other ways.

Second, as at least one of the response forms also pointed out, one of our greatest dangers is complacency. Can we ever assume that even in the apparently most friendly communities and congregations there are no bridges to be built? In one church I know in the west of England, someone once remarked that their church was just like a happy family, to which came a reply, 'No one in this congregation has ever invited us into their home.'

Third, there are certain crucial issues in the public sphere which concern us as citizens wherever we live. We all live in a parliamentary constituency, with a representative in Westminster to whom it is our Christian duty to convey our concerns on matters of justice and peace. The CCBI had a programme, 'Countering the Arms Trade: Churches Count the Cost', in which local churches, acting ecumenically, were encouraged to discuss arms transfers, in depth and in a critically informed way, with their MPs. The take-up for this was enormous. Groups in all kinds of areas, from the inner city to villages, throughout the United Kingdom, were activated. Issues like this which vitally concern the world of conflict today, are no respecters of location for active concern.

The vision as a whole is too much for us to manage. We are not required to – that's God's concern. We are invited to co-operate at specific points. Much is being said these days about our responsibility to creation. If John Wesley could say that the world was his parish, as today's Christians we're being challenged in an even bigger way to see the whole planet, and its eco-system, as our parish. But what can we do to save the planet? Martin Palmer is a passionate advocate of ecological ethics and of the need for Christianity to take environmental issues much more seriously. He castigates theologians for largely ignoring these issues. He suggests, however, that much of the best action is just happening where local Christians respond in the ways that they can: 'In churchyard schemes, where those precious plots of land, often in built-up areas, are no longer being mown flat or gardened into a suburban blandness but are allowed to run a little riot, thus providing habitats, feeding grounds and resources for a much wider range of flora and fauna. Over a thousand churchyards now set aside some parts to be nature reserves. Other churches have developed tree surgeries, or have established recycling projects.' (*Expository Times* January 1995 Vol. 106 No. 4 p. 104)

He goes on to describe churches auditing their buildings, their use of resources both collectively and as individual members, and the astonishing difference this can make cumulatively. Is all this, in the words of one of the respondents to *Building Bridges*, just 'sub-Greenpeace' in its approach? At least, I'm sure it's deeply consistent with our calling not to add to the suffering of a whole creation groaning in travail and longing for its liberation. We may presume to despise the doing of small, simple things, when we've actually done them, but not before. Let's not be so worried about wanting to do what we think will be specially, extraordinarily or uniquely 'Christian', until we're sure we've done what is humanly right. Yes, Jesus tells us to go the second mile – but that presupposes we've got as far as the first mile. It's the quality and direction of our actions that count, not their seeming magnitude: a quality and direction that are in line with a universe being reconciled by the God of grace.

Our ministry of reconciliation comes not by ticking off items on an endless programme of things to be done, but out of our thankful relationship to the living God who meets us in our particular time and place, and in that context we discover our particular calling. That means that the ministry of reconciliation will not always look the same in all times and all places. In fact, in some contexts 'reconciliation' is itself a difficult word to use. When reconciliation was first mooted as the main theme for the 1997 Ecumenical Assembly in Graz, it was questioned by some representatives of the churches in Central and Eastern Europe. It was felt by them to be a word that came too easily to the lips of westerners in the immediate post-Cold War period. With the downfall of Communism in eastern Europe we were all euphoric about 'Europe our common home' as Michail Gorbachev called it. But it did not at first seem like that to many in the former communist countries after 1989. Germany was re-united –

but was it reconciled? Many in the former East Germany felt that what was happening was not reconciliation but a takeover and a stripping down, economically as well as politically, of the east by the west – and to some extent even of the east German churches by the western churches.

'Reconciliation' was an even more controversial word in South Africa ten years ago, as the long campaign against apartheid reached its height and the repression by the state became ever heavier, with more and more states of emergency, more and more bannings of opposition groups, more and more detentions and arrests. In September 1985, on my first visit to South Africa, I was present at the launch of the now famous *Kairos Document* in Johannesburg, a statement by Christian activists and theologians calling for radical opposition to the state and its evil works. It was striking how the *Kairos Document* weighed into the frequent use of the term 'reconciliation' by Christians who simply wanted an end to the troubles, who called for both sides simply to talk and listen to each other and sort out their differences. I quote now in full:

> The fallacy here is that 'Reconciliation' has been made into an absolute principle that must be applied to all cases of conflict or dissension. But not all cases of conflict are the same. We can imagine a private quarrel between two people or two groups whose differences are based upon misunderstandings. In such cases it would be appropriate to talk and negotiate to sort out the misunderstandings and to reconcile the two sides. But there are other conflicts in which one side is right and the other wrong. There are conflicts where one side is a fully armed and violent oppressor while the other side is defenceless and oppressed. There are conflicts that can only be described as the struggle between justice and injustice, good and evil, God and the devil. To speak of reconciling these two is not only a mistaken application of the Christian idea of reconciliation, it is a total betrayal of all that Christian

faith has ever meant . . . We are supposed to do away with
evil, injustice, oppression and sin – not to come to terms
with it . . .

There is nothing that we want more than true reconciliation and genuine peace – the peace that God wants and
not the peace the world wants (John 14:27). The peace
that God wants is based upon truth, repentance, justice
and love. (*Kairos Document*, p. 12)

In other words, reconciliation in this situation could not be
used as a short cut. There could be no reconciliation between
a minority wielding power unjustly and the majority suffering
grievously under it – until that unjust power imbalance had
been removed. How it has come to be removed, of course, is
one of the wonders of our time. It involved, at the end, both
the willingness of President de Klerk to lead a relinquishing
of power by the minority, and a readiness of the Mandela-led
ANC to compromise on a number of their aspirations. But
the basic claim of the *Kairos Document* remains sound: reconciliation is not an alternative to justice, but must include it.
Incidentally – in fact not incidentally but very significantly
and relevantly – Christian doctrines of atonement and reconciliation through Christ have always had to wrestle with
precisely this question, of how God's love and God's justice
are united in the cross: of how, in the words of the great
Congregationalist theologian P. T. Forsyth in the early years
of this century, 'Justice is the true and only mercy.'

The point here is that reconciliation and argument are not
incompatible. Indeed, debate and disagreement may be crucial
stages in the process of reconciliation, precisely because they
expose the depth of hurt and pain that must be healed if
reconciliation is to be real and not a sham. 'The unassumed
is the unhealed' said the fourth century church father
Gregory of Nazianzus, meaning that our redemption by
Christ depends on his total and complete humanity. We
might also say, 'The unacknowledged is the unreconciled':

rifts and chasms must be realistically measured if they are to be effectively bridged. It's a message which many South Africans, both black and white, are only now really discovering. When I attended a theological conference in Cape Town it drew together theologians and church leaders and lay people both from South Africa and many parts of the world. In one sense, being a conference on a special theme it was a gathering of the like-minded. But there was one specially moving experience. While gathering material on a tape recorder for some BBC radio programmes I was making, I interviewed a young black Lutheran pastor from the northern province. He spoke of the need for confession of guilt in the new South Africa, if the past was not to haunt society in a destructive way, and of how hard it is really to talk of guilt and forgiveness with many white people. He cited the instance of how, that very morning, he'd been in conversation with another participant in the conference, a white man of his own age, from an Afrikaner background in the Dutch Reformed Church. They had had a pleasant and useful talk but when it came to exchanging experiences, things got rather difficult. The black pastor had described the grim experiences of his own family and people, cleared off their land, dumped in the so-called homeland of Bophutatswana, hungry and homeless and landless. He had asked his white colleague if he'd known about such things happening at the time. The Afrikaner had said his parents had never told him of such things. Frustration mounted in the black pastor: 'Why don't you press your parents – how could they not have known?' I went off and next day, found the young white Afrikaner in question, and got him to relate his view of their encounter. I had half expected to find a rather complacent if not arrogant individual only just emerging from a blinkered conservative existence. In fact I found someone who'd been journeying far beyond his restricted upbringing, who'd rejected much of the racist structures of the society and church in which he'd been nurtured and was working in multi-racial youth work. But, he admitted, he still had a long way to go. 'We just do not know each other's stories,' he said. When I asked him how he felt after that conversation, he said it was a deeply humbling and exhilarating experience. And quite beautifully, he said, 'It was humbling, because there was no reason why a person like that, coming out of such an experience, should give me a chance now to try to make things better. But he did.' They left the conference good friends and with plans to meet up in each other's homes soon.

Reconciliation, bridge-building, is costly and can take time. Remember, we are talking not just about crossing bridges but building them. And it's the actual building of bridges that is time-consuming and risky. Before there's any secure structure it means standing right in the swirling, muddy waters of suspicion, prejudice and fear, trying to sink piles beneath the surface, perhaps being insulted by people on both banks who say we're wasting our time and maybe even letting the side down. Some of the most courageous stories of this kind of work come to us from Northern Ireland.

There's an old legend about how bridges were invented. When God created the earth, it was a gentle plain, so that humankind could wander about freely and mix together. But the devil came down and was angry at this, and clawed up the surface of the earth into deep ravines and valleys, so that people became divided from each other and could no longer move about. When the angels saw this, they came down and bent their wings over the clefts and ravines so that people could cross over. And from these inclined angels' wings, human beings caught the idea of building bridges.

A beautiful story. It is in fact a Muslim story, told by Ivo Andrich in his wonderful book The Bridge Over the Drina, the saga of the little town in Bosnia close to the border with Serbia, and its life over the centuries. Just a little question: if before telling it I had said you were going to hear a Muslim story, how would that have affected your hearing of it? I'm not suggesting you would necessarily have been prejudiced against it – you might in fact have felt you ought to listen with extra studious impartiality to it for that reason! But building bridges with people of other faiths is one of the most sensitive, and controversial, issues for us as Christians today. For many people, it is an issue of daily life on the multi-cultural streets. Hans Küng has famously said, 'No survival without a world ethic. No world peace without peace between the religions. No peace between the religions without dialogue between the religions.' Look at the Middle East, and Jerusalem in particular. Go to the Temple Mount in Jerusalem at evening, and as the light fades hear simultaneously the prayers of the Jews at the Wailing Wall, the call of the muezzin from the Al Aqsah Mosque, and the sound of the bells from the nearby churches, and you sense the truth of Küng's remark.

Dialogue means just that: speaking and listening with one another in order to know one another more truly. On that basis, without compromising the integrity of our distinctive beliefs, we may be able to identify those values we hold in common which are crucial to human wellbeing, to justice and to peace. I must confess I'm a relative novice in this area myself, but I recognise that international affairs are increasingly inter-faith affairs: look at the Balkans and Bosnia in particular, where Muslims above all are not worrying so much about whether as Christians we'll have dialogue with them as whether we'll simply act justly towards them, and indeed simply live.

Our faith has a markedly two-fold nature. For us, Jesus is the way, the truth and the life. By faith we are related exclusively to him, and are called to the costly way of the cross in his footsteps. There can be no other gods than the God we know in him. He is our supreme loyalty. But the Jesus whom we are called to follow so exclusively is the one who was born for all, lived for all, died for all. He made himself one with all humanity in its need. We follow him, yes, but we are led by him into sharing his solidarity with all humankind in its sin and need before God. That makes it very difficult for Christian faith to accept any circumscribing of our loyalties, any divisions of the human family as ultimate. Christ is our peace, the demolisher of dividing walls of partition for the sake of a single new humanity (Ephesians 1:14). It worries me that some of our politicians say their favourite hymn is 'I vow to thee, my country, all earthly things above'. It worries me still more that it has survived so long in some of our supposedly Christian hymn books. Jesus can never be made the badge for a group loyalty over against others, not even a religious loyalty.

It is in this light that we see the real significance of our ecumenical pilgrimage. Ecumenism means a commitment to discovering Christ in one another as churches, and to allowing those new discoveries of Christ to challenge, enrich us and reshape us. Ecumenism is having a hard time at the moment. That Archbishop Derek Worlock's legacy on Merseyside should have been attacked so virulently is a sign of a time when nothing can be taken for granted. In September 1990 in Liverpool, at the inauguration of CCBI, we all processed from the Anglican to the Roman Catholic Cathedral along the significantly named Hope Street. There were cat-calls from some extreme Protestant Orangemen standing on the pavement with their banners accusing ecumenism of every known vice. We smiled then at such marginal eccentricities, but just a few years later anti-ecumenical attitudes once again became very respectable. They have to be seen in the wider context of our dangerous world. They are in part, I believe, part of a phenomenon in our society and throughout the world of a resort to group loyalties as a means of security and assurance in a world seemingly on the way to chaos. Such loyalties, whether ethnic or religious or both, often appeal to mythologised versions of a better past. We see it in the new tribalism in eastern and central Europe no less than in Rwanda and Burundi. We see its logical end-products in the horrors of ethnic cleansing and genocide. People have a fear of living with otherness and diversity. Either they resort blindly to the group they imagine they belong to, or as in many parts of western societies they go for an individualism where everyone is the same as them because the only person one knows, trusts and cares for is – oneself. Either way, the response is: up with the drawbridges. That is not what Harold and Amy did. It is not what Jesus did. Here is the real significance of ecumenical fellowship: to be a sign that the only true security, the only ultimate remedy against fear, is not the wall or fortress we try to build round ourselves, but the bridge of God's reconciling love which reaches out to us and all his creation, undeserved, unexpected and unconditional, and for ever, to God's praise and glory.

Reconciliation and Realism

Roger Williamson[1]

Introduction

Conditions for hundreds of millions of people are so drasti-
cally dehumanising that no reconciliation is possible without
fundamental political and social change. I really understood
the reason why liberation theologians speak of 'liberation'
for the first time when I went to Brazil and saw the slum
conditions of the favelas almost next door to the luxury
hotels of the visiting tourists and the rich downtown areas.
There can be no reconciliation between such appalling living
conditions and such excessive wealth; there has to be
fundamental social change.

Fanon describes this in his classic analysis of colonialism,
The Wretched of the Earth. Brazilian liberation theologians
applied such thinking to Brazil and used the term 'internal
colonialism' for what the rich élite (foreign and national)
were doing to the poor. In Fanon's text, the split is between
the settlers and the natives; the colonial city is a 'world cut in
two' which 'is inhabited by two different species . . . where
the agents of government speak the language of pure force'.[2]

The international division of wealth is alarming. According
to the 1993 United Nations Development Programme report,
the richest twenty per cent of the world's people now receive
more than one hundred and fifty times the income of the
poorest twenty per cent. Eduardo Galeano, well known for his
historical documentation of Latin America, commented as follows at the height of the military dictatorships in Latin America:

> We were not born on the moon, we don't live in seventh
> heaven. We have the good fortune and the misfortune to

belong to a tortured region of the world, Latin America, and to live in a historic period that is relentlessly oppressive. The contradictions of class society are sharper here than in the rich countries. Massive misery is the price paid by the poor countries so that six per cent of the world's population (meaning the USA) may consume with impunity half the wealth generated by the entire world. The abyss, the distance between the wellbeing of some and the misery of others, is greater in Latin America; and the methods necessary to maintain this distance are more savage.[3]

I remember a paper, talk or book on the Northern Ireland conflict some time ago: *Northern Ireland: A Question to Every Answer.* It is in this spirit that I want to write this chapter. It can be summarised by three statements which stand in deep tension, if not necessarily contradiction, to one another:

- Conflict is a deeply-ingrained element of human society.
- Reconciliation is essential for societies to function.
- Some conflicts run so deep that reconciliation is an almost superhuman task.

I want to discuss the issue primarily through four international examples.[4]

Military dictatorships in Latin America

I want to begin with the military dictatorships of Latin America of the 1960s to 1980s. The most accessible way in is the film *Death and the Maiden* by the Chilean writer Ariel Dorfman.[5] It is a powerful film and I recommend you to go and see it – when you are in a reflective mood and ready to be disturbed.

The story is well constructed to bring out the many different layers of the issue. The husband and wife who are the central characters live on the coast of the Latin American ex-dictatorship miles away from the capital city. It is winter with driving rain. The scenery is bleak and windswept. The wife is at home in the warm. The husband comes home late, soaking wet. The car had a puncture and someone who lived nearby gave him a lift. The recriminations begin. He is late for supper. She is irritated. But, he argues, it is hardly his fault he had a puncture – and in any case, why was the spare tyre flat? Why had she not had it fixed? As the story unfolds, we discover that the husband is a lawyer and has just been appointed to head the commission of the new democratic president to investigate the crimes of the former military dictatorship. The wife is pleased, until she discovers that the mandate of the new commission only extends to the cases of dead victims – not of those still alive. It emerges that she was tortured and raped while in prison herself.

The plot skilfully unfolds. The husband presents many pragmatic arguments why it is better for some of the cases to be resolved rather than none – that in fact the mandate might be renegotiable at a later stage. The character of the lawyer is presented so that one wonders whether this weak character is capable of standing up to the military. One is not inclined to believe that he would be, or that he will insist that the government change the mandate of the commission. In short, one wonders whether he is tough enough to uncover and present the truth.

Later the neighbour who helped her husband turns up with a spare wheel. It transpires that the 'doctor' with whom her husband has struck up a friendship is in fact the very man who was in charge of her torture.

The wife eventually decides to take things into her own hands.

She leaves in the car, and later returns, unsuspected, knocks out her former torturer and ties him to a chair. The mixture of violence, intimidation, humiliation and inquisition effectively turns the tables on her persecutor. The woman's husband is appalled – a guest of his is being assaulted by his own wife, in his own house. His sense of fair play is assaulted – even though the film makes clear that there is very little chance that her persecutor will be brought to justice in any other way.

The presentation operates on many levels. One is that of gender politics. Her husband, it transpires, had been having an affair while she was in prison being tortured. The two male characters thus present a weak spineless man who has an affair while his partner is in prison and a man who uses his position of power as an opportunity for violent sexual gratification and humiliation of his female prisoners.

Another level at which the film operates is the 'rough justice' of the wife's determination to take justice into her own hands, as opposed to the slow, correct, incomplete, inadequate promise of justice through 'proper channels', and how one endangers the other. What would the public think of the lawyer once it emerges that his own wife has murdered the torturer, without a trial? On the other hand, the manifest injustice of the wife's case finding no resolution is also presented.

The final scene in the play is when the couple take the torturer to the edge of a cliff and she threatens to throw him over. In the end, the couple walk away and leave him. You are left wondering whether he will 'do the decent thing' and throw himself over the cliff, and whether the woman's hurt and anger has now found some kind of cathartic resolution. For those suffering such extreme human rights abuses at the hands of those who wish to obliterate them, total rejection of the worldview of the oppressor can be a necessary survival strategy. This is expressed in one of Dorfman's poems entitled *Last Will and Testament*:

> When they tell you
> I'm not a prisoner
> don't believe them.
> They'll have to admit it
> some day.
> When they tell you
> they released me
> don't believe them.
> They'll have to admit

it's a lie
some day.
When they tell you
I betrayed the party
don't believe them.
They'll have to admit
I was loyal
some day.
When they tell you
I'm in France
don't believe them.
Don't believe them when they show you
my false I.D.
Don't believe them when they show you
the photo of my body,
don't believe them.
Don't believe them when they tell you
the moon is the moon,
if they tell you the moon is the moon,
that this is my voice on tape,
that this is my signature on a confession,
if they say a tree is a tree
don't believe them
don't believe
anything they tell you
anything they swear to
anything they show you,
don't believe them.
And finally
when
that day
comes
when they ask you
to identify the body
and a voice says
we killed him

the poor bastard died
he's dead,
when they tell you
that I am
completely absolutely definitely
dead
don't believe them,
don't believe them,
don't believe them.[6]

Is this view, the total rejection of the worldview and any statements by the oppressor, susceptible to reconciliation? On the face of it, it seems totally opposed to the possibility of reconciliation. Such an approach is superficial. Reconciliation requires a meeting as people, not a situation where the torturer has both the power and the will to determine the physical or psychological obliteration of the victim. Max Horkheimer, one of the Frankfurt School, once defined the goal of his critical theory as: 'The longing that the murderer should not triumph over his innocent victim.[7] This seems to me to be the basis for any reconciliation and, indeed, something approaching a foundation for human rights. But we know that this is simultaneously essential in terms of our desire for justice, and unachievable within human history as we know it.

The 'power of the powerless' in such situations of extreme disparity of power is quite simply the rejection (direct or indirect) of a situation in which the powerful seek and can achieve your obliteration.[8] This can involve active or passive resistance. An example of passive resistance is given in the writings of Bertolt Brecht. Following military conquest, the oppressor moves into a peasant's house and begins to treat him as a slave or servant. As oppressors often do, he also wants to be liked, so he can feel good whilst still being an oppressor. He asks the peasant in whose house he is living, 'Do you accept the position of being my servant?' The peasant makes no reply. But he cleans the occupier's shoes, brings his meals and behaves as a servant. When the war finishes, the peasant looks the occupier in the face and says, 'No.' The only chance for many people in such situations is to make the defence of one's integrity invisible, by remaining uncorrupted by the worldview of the oppressor. Open resistance in many situations is suicidal. But an open declaration of acceptance of the situation means that one has given up one's identity and integrity.

Imposed 'reconciliation' in a situation of such inequality is not reconciliation at all, it is a further nail in the coffin of the dignity of the oppressed. If one knows something of the history of the Latin American dictatorships, the film *Death and the Maiden* is even more powerful and shocking, since the kind of events portrayed are by no means exaggerated. Tens of thousands of people were disappeared, were murdered and tortured in countries like Chile and Argentina. Rape was routine for female prisoners.[9] In Central America, the entire region was dislocated by vicious wars by the military dictatorships against their own populations (Landau: 2.1; Brown: 2.3). Hundreds of priests, nuns and catechists – and many, many more lay believers – were murdered for their attempts to stand up for the poor.[10] The response of the churches varied considerably from country to country, with courageous examples of human rights work initiated by the Cardinals in Santiago, Chile (the Vicaria de la Solidaridad established by Cardinal Raul Silva Henriquez) and Sao Paulo, Brazil – the work supported by Cardinal Arns (Wechsler: 2.3). In Argentina, the Protestant churches led the work, whereas, with some notable exceptions, the Catholic hierarchy was complicit in the human rights violations (Mignone: 2.3).

How can reconciliation be achieved in situations like this? Can one hope for full justice? Won't the military who were so powerful move heaven and earth to stop their people being punished? But is it justice if the ordinary soldiers who carried the policies are punished, but not the architects of the policies, like Pinochet?

There are other even more disturbing questions. How can the people who have been through such traumatic circumstances be helped to recover? Should the relatives of the disappeared continue to insist on a full account being given of what has happened to their relatives when it is clear to most people that they are all dead?

If a new democratic regime insists on establishing the truth, will the military try to organise to obstruct this or even take over the country again to prevent the truth being told and the perpetrators of such crimes being put on trial for human rights violations, crimes against humanity, rape and murder?

Even though Argentina returned to democracy in 1983, the military have still not accepted full responsibility and those who committed the atrocities have not been punished. Recently, there have been some significant developments. A former naval captain has confessed what people involved in human rights work have known for a long time, namely that one method of dealing with the bodies of the 'disappeared' was to dump them into the River Plate from naval helicopters after they had been tortured to death in the Naval Academy.[11]

The issue of how it affects the families now – for example, those who were young children of the disappeared who are now themselves adults – must also be considered. In Argentina, army chief General Balza has accepted 'institutional responsibility' for human rights abuses during the military government. A recent article in *New Internationalist* contrasts different approaches to this by a brother and sister. The brother, Martin, says that the confessions are pointless and that the campaign of the Mothers of the Plaza de Mayo are a meaningless rehearsal of positions held for many years: 'They go on as if their sons and daughters were walking around in Paris or some place, waiting for the government to fetch them. But they are all dead. All thirty-three thousand. And nothing can be done.' For him it is a matter of drawing a line under the catastrophe and getting on with a new life, by working to set up an alternative school. His sister Adriana who only discovered the truth a year ago has joined a Protestant human rights group and feels that even this small concession of 'institutional' responsibility is helpful: 'At least it justifies our cause to those who thought we were mad. Most of all the *Madres* [Mothers]. They have been sorely abused. I've been active for a year, but they suffered for nineteen years in the face of indifference and injustice. That would have driven me mad. Then, one day, the oppressors admit to everyone: "In fact, the *Madres* were right." And you think, "finally!"'[12]

As a footnote to this, we should also remember that we were prepared to do business and even sell weapons to these murderers, long after it was known what was going on. In the case of Argentina, until they invaded the Falkland Islands, the government line was regret at the excesses of the military, but more or less business as usual.

South Africa

Some of the same questions arise with regard to South Africa. The scars run very deep but the impression which I have at the moment is that the transition to a non-racial democracy has been remarkably successful, but that much more needs to be done in the economic field.

The damage done by a theologised 'promised land' ideology of the Afrikaners, which solidified into the white system of apartheid after 1948, has done untold damage since 1652.[13]

What does reconciliation mean in the South African context? For many years, the term 'reconciliation' was viewed with suspicion by those who wanted a fundamental change in the system. Reconciliation was often presented – especially in church circles – in individual terms which would leave a fundamentally unjust social structure in place.

It is easy to see how the gospel can be used in this way. With the theological statement that everyone has sinned, the distinctions between the primary sin and the secondary sin can easily be obscured (cf. the writings of Frank Chikane).

This can be seen particularly clearly in the light of the analysis of violence in the *Kairos Document* written by a group of theologians and widely discussed in the mid-1980s at a time of very severe repression.[14] Introducing the subject of reconciliation, the *Kairos Document* says the following:

There can be no doubt that our Christian faith commits us to work for true reconciliation and genuine peace. But as so many people, including Christians, have pointed out, there can be no genuine peace without justice. Any form of peace or reconciliation that allows the sin of injustice and oppression to continue is a false peace and counterfeit reconciliation. This kind of 'reconciliation' has nothing to do with the Christian faith.[15]

The *Kairos Document* was highly critical of the way in which the churches often claimed to be against violence or condemn violence in all its forms in a way which obscured the fact that the primary violence was that of apartheid, of the dispossession of the black people of South Africa, and of the imprisonment, torture, terrorisation and outlawing of those who presented any effective organised opposition (cf. Bibliography: 3.2). In such circumstances, to be 'against violence' in a generalised sense means to deprive people of any effective categories for criticising an unjust social order. It also makes an unjustified equivalence between those who murder, dispossess and oppress a people and those who resist. At the same time, the oppressed are quite clear that armed resistance is a dangerous risk.[16] Steve Biko, in one clear passage in his writings, indicated why the black consciousness movement was necessary and why it was important for the black student (and wider social) movement of Black Consciousness to separate itself from white liberal institutions and forms of protests, in the interests of a genuine later reconciliation. White liberals, he says, see black people get kicked to the ground, and then want to tell them how to respond to the kick. It was important for black people to determine their own response.

What I have tried to show is that in South Africa political power has always rested with white society. Not only have the whites been guilty of being on the offensive but, by some skilful manoeuvres, they have managed to control the responses of the blacks to the provocation. Not only have they kicked the black but they have told him how to react to the kick. For a long time the black has been listening with patience to the advice he has been receiving on how best to respond to the kick. With painful slowness he is now beginning to show signs that it is his right and duty to respond to the kick in the way that he sees fit.[17]

The organisations developed to 'respond to the kick' included a new wave of black trade unions, various social movements like the United Democratic Front and some sectors of the church – much of the black church and some of the white church as well.

Two particularly contentious areas for those outside South Africa were the issues of the Programme to Combat Racism and of economic sanctions. What methods can and should be used to oppose injustice?[18] How can change be achieved with the least possible use of violence and with violence as a last resort? Even many nonviolent methods were also very costly – for example, only a few of the privileged white community were prepared to risk up to six years in prison as conscientious objectors, although many more just left the country in order to avoid having to attack neighbouring countries or kill black people in the townships (CIIR 1989:3.2). The symbolic importance of the rejection of the South African military was an important dimension of the End Conscription Campaign.

How, in being scrupulous about the methods of change, can change nonetheless be assured? From outside and looking back, we can now see that economic sanctions were slow but had a cumulative effect (Commonwealth:3.1). They not only had a real impact on the economy but also communicated disapproval. The sport boycott which deprived white South

Africa of the pleasure of beating the world at rugby and cricket was a particularly effective measure of isolation. There can also be little doubt that even though it was a long and massively costly process of resistance, the fact that it was mainly fought with non-violent methods has made the prospect of reconciliation much more probable. The churches (de Gruchy:3.2), particularly black church members in South Africa with inspiring figures such as Frank Chikane, Desmond Tutu (du Boulay:3.2), some white church leaders such as Beyers Naudé (ICJ; Randall:3.2), the women's movement Black Sash, successive waves of trade unionists and student groups have all played their part. So has the international ecumenical solidarity to the much-criticised Programme to Combat Racism of the World Council of Churches (Webb:3.1). Finally, however, I would also assert that the insistence for decades by the African National Congress that only a non-racial, democratic South Africa was acceptable, including the element of armed struggle within their tactics (accepted after 50 years of exclusive non-violence), was the decisive element which broke apartheid and created the basis on which reconciliation can now occur (Walshe:3.1; Simons & Simons:3.2).

Beyers Naude recently outlined his understanding of what is required for genuine reconciliation. Some of the elements are as follows:

The truth – in connection with political injustice, crime and oppression – should be brought to light. We urgently need to know the truth about those political actions involving murder and crimes in which the security services of the last government played a part. Secondly, those who were responsible should acknowledge this privately or in public. We do not demand Nuremberg-like trials because this would lead to the impression that we wish to take revenge on this whole group of oppressors. Some people in my country have asked the churches and the government to bury this painful and unhappy past. What they say is this: 'Let's not play God.

Those who are most guilty will never admit it. It will take years before one can come to any conclusions.' On the other hand, questions are being raised by the families of the fathers, sons or daughters who have been murdered. They all want to know who killed their loved ones. It reminds me of a priest in Uruguay who spoke of a mother whose child had simply disappeared. She said: 'Father, I'm willing to forgive but I don't know whom or what for.' I'd like to stress that, as a white South African, I have a special reason for wanting to know the truth about the secret actions of the security forces during the last years. Through its National Security Council, the last government, in which both President F. W. de Klerk and [Government] Minister Pik Botha both served, secretly approved and allowed many political crimes of which millions of whites know nothing. If these aren't brought to light, thousands of them will simply say: 'We don't believe those things have happened; it's simply not true.' But I also believe that other crimes need to be investigated: those committed by the ANC [African National Congress], Inkatha, the PAC [Pan-Africanist Congress] and the Kwazulu police. Matters of guilt and reconciliation ought to be addressed. The churches in South Africa have a moral obligation to do just that. The government has already done so by appointing a committee of Truth and Reconciliation. On the basis of their report, a bill will be presented in parliament soon. The notions of truth and reconciliation are basically biblical notions and not political. The government seems to be struggling with these as well, and has asked the churches for advice. I believe the findings of this committee could be relevant to other countries and churches dealing with human rights issues.[19]

Eastern Europe

A third area is the situation or situations in Eastern Europe. It is hard to get any kind of perspective on Eastern Europe because our own ideological landscape is so ideologically coloured and because the West were the 'winners' of the

Cold War (or maybe one should say 'the less obvious losers').

It is also important to notice that Eastern Europe is not one big homogenous whole. The imposition of communism suppressed many of the conflicts which have since re-emerged. The Oxford Research Group, an independent academic organisation, had already identified over 60 actual or potential conflicts by 1992.[20] A German study by a Berlin professor published last year identified nearly one hundred and fifty language and/or ethnic groups in Europe.[21] The dangers of this situation have become clear, at the very latest since the end of the Cold War. Rather than ushering in an era of free-market harmony and good-natured democracy, it is as though the dead hand of the Marxist system was lifted and the old antagonisms of history re-emerged with a vengeance. In 1990, rather than prophesying an era of sweetness and light and universal happiness in a new world order, Eric Hobsbawm commented: 'What we have now are utopias without universal hope, sectional utopias, at a time when a world increasingly globally organised, and whose problems require global treatment, actually calls for a new universalism.' The movements and groups he saw coming to the fore planned their activities in accordance with '. . . worse visions and more dangerous dreams, such as religious fundamentalism, nationalist zealotry, or more generally, that racially tinged xenophobia which looks like becoming the major mass ideology of the *fin de siècle*.'[22]

One is reminded of the gospel story of the demon being cast out of a house and seven demons returning. Slavenka Drakulic gives an important insight into this process. Her father was one of Tito's partisans who fought against fascism and genuinely hoped for and believed in a fairer society. Her father would not talk about the war, and Slavenka Drakulic and her generation grew up under a Marxist orthodoxy which instructed them to repeat slogans about 'brotherhood and unity' and to celebrate the existence of Yugoslavia (which, given what has happened since, does not seem such a bad idea, even if the unity was imposed). Drakulic comments:

'But slogans about brotherhood and unity sounded a little too abstract. Little did I know about the hate, rivalry and bloodshed that divided people in the Balkans throughout history. Little did I know about history at all. How could I know, when, according to our textbooks, history began in 1941 anyway'.

The problem was that we – all the people, not just the Pioneers – were told to shout slogans and clap our hands but never to question what those words meant. And when I did, it was too late. Brothers started to kill one another, and unity fell apart, as if Yugoslavia were only part of a communist fairy tale. Perhaps it was. Nationalism as we are witnessing it now in the former USSR, former Yugoslavia and Czechoslovakia is a legacy of that fairy tale. And it is so for at least three reasons: the communist state never allowed development of a civil society; it oppressed ethnic, national and religious beliefs, permitting only class identification; and in the end, communist leaders manipulated these beliefs, playing one nationality against another to keep themselves in power for as long as they could. Even if the price was war.[23]

In 1997 the churches of Europe held a second European Ecumenical Assembly.[24] The first was in Basel in 1989. The theme of the Second Assembly was Reconciliation. What does reconciliation mean in the European context? (Hume: 1) A French friend and colleague Professor René Coste speaks of the challenge *'vers une Europe solidaire'* – as with much in life, it loses something in translation and is ambiguous – 'towards a Europe characterised by solidarity' would be one attempt at translation. This immediately raises the questions – who is in and who is out? Is Europe in solidarity with the rest of the world or is European solidarity something for Europeans? Which Europe do we mean? When we in Britain talk about Europe, we usually mean 'them', not 'us'. We usually mean Western Europe, not Europe from the Atlantic to the Urals.

In 1989, the wall came down, but since 1989 we have

discovered that, or proved that (or ignored the fact that) exclusion does not need a Berlin Wall. Instead of an East-West divide in Europe, we have more a centre-periphery divide.

I often say that dissidents like Vaclav Havel began to speak again of 'Central Europe' and the term increasingly was taken up on the Western side. Increasingly, to Western politicians and business leaders, 'Central Europe' has come to mean those parts of Europe which we can integrate, the bits of Eastern Europe where it makes sense to invest.

What would a reconciled Europe look like? Reconciliation has happened in Europe before. But even the remarkable elements of reconciliation achieved have remained a partial process. For generations, French and Germans regarded each other as the irreconcilable, traditional enemy. War followed war, generation after generation, 1870, 1914, 1939. Now war between Germany and France is unthinkable. The common market began as a common market for certain heavy industrial goods like iron, coal and steel, but it was always informed by a vision of a Europe in which war would be prevented from breaking out.

We can look back on the events of 1989 with some distance now. What could have been done in 1989 and 1990 to help to ensure that Europe was reconciled after the end of the Cold War, rather than what has occurred? In fact what has occurred is that Western Europe has continued on an uncertain path of economic integration, and much of Eastern Europe has descended into economic disintegration. The Warsaw Pact disappeared, but NATO was retained. Certain plans are made to integrate some of the Central European countries in due course, on Western conditions. This, above all, has the dangerous effect of continuing to leave the Russians on the outside. This is not reconciliation or a model for a safe and stable future. Obviously, the blame is not all on one side. The Russians military attacks on Chechenya (condemned by the Russian Orthodox Patriarch Alexeii II), the Yeltsin government's failure (or refusal) to define Russian security interests, the indications of hankering after retention (or reassertion) of a sphere of influence and great power (if not superpower) status indicate an instability on the Russian side which is problematic – if understandable. Unless the Russian economy functions, there cannot be stability in Eastern Europe. Even if this is understood, has the West done enough to help – and, indeed, has the help been of the right kind, or were Western plans of shock therapy for the economy not an additional factor increasing the instability in Russia?

What then of Bosnia? (Glenny, Pax Christi, Sharp, Silber & Little, Vulliamy:4) What indeed. Clearly a full analysis of how things reached the current situation is important in one respect, but irrelevant in another. It is important to know who we are dealing with, how they see the world and why the Western failures of policy emerged – including deterrence which has consistently failed to deter and promises which have failed to materialise. In another sense it is irrelevant to look back and say, for example, that the Germans made a mistake by pushing for the recognition of Croatia in the early stages, or whatever analysis one comes up with. The point is: What happens now that there is a peace agreement? There are real issues to be addressed in terms of stabilising the peace; the Bosnians' right of self-defence must be assured without starting an arms race; refugees have the right of return or compensation; civil societies must be (re)built, and so on. This is not the place in which a detailed agenda for reconstruction and reconciliation can be provided.

It is hardly surprising that the Polish poet and Nobel Literature Prize winner Czeslaw Milosz (Milosz:4) criticises the well-fed West as follows: 'It is revealed now that their Europe since the beginning has been a deception, for its faith and its foundation is a nothingness.'[25]

The Israeli-Palestinian conflict
My final example is perhaps the most perplexing and painful one.

Bishop Rowan Williams has addressed it in these terms:
One of the greatest historical tragedies of this century has
been the fate of the Palestinian Arabs. Europe's attempt to
atone for a nightmare of incalculable violence against the
Jewish people has produced a new race of victims in the
Palestinians, and so set up a further chain of terrorist counter-
violence as a result of the violence (a violence which is often
made to seem intrinsic to the existence of the State of Israel,
especially by the inflexibility of its military and political
establishment in recent years) offered to the indigenous Arab
populations. It is a distressingly sharp illustration of the deadly
circularity of oppression; and we should make no mistake
about its origins in European Christian anti-semitism.[26]

Who you are determines how you tell the story. Where do
you begin? With God's promise to Abraham? What is good
news to one set of people is bad news to another set. Your
promised land is the land where my people have dwelt. It is a
land which has been promised too much or too often – to
Abraham, to both sides by the British, to the Jews as their
home, to the Muslims as Islamic land.

The 'Final Solution', the planned destruction of the whole
of the Jewish people by the Nazis is, in my view, the worst
crime of a genocidal century. But this does not mean that we
can close our eyes to the situation of the Palestinians, a
people who as the 'victims of the victims' have been
deprived of their homeland. For far too long, the two sides
have operated a politics of mutual negation, meaning that
the claims of one side would automatically mean the failure
of the claims of the other side.

At the latest from 1988, this substantially shifted, given the
readiness of the Palestinians to accept a 'two-state solution',
with them agreeing to have the substantially smaller part of
what they regard as their home country.

This process is by no means guaranteed success. It was
broadcast and heralded as 'Gaza and Jericho first' and, if it
remains only Gaza and Jericho it will fail. There are strong

forces from both the right wing in Israel and the Islamic movement Hamas on the Palestinian side who are determined to break the Peace Process. Like riding a bicycle, one cannot stop a process of this kind and balance – it either moves forward or crashes.

The concept of the Two State Solution is, I believe, one of the most promising potential models of reconciliation in recent times. Hanan Ashrawi, who was spokeswoman for the Palestinians in the early stages of the process has said the key to such a settlement is the readiness to give up one's parents' dreams for the sake of one's children's future.

The secular political task of reconciliation in the Israeli-Palestinian confrontation is also an eminently religious duty. I would argue that the churches and Jewish and Muslim leaders have a duty to try to ensure that it succeeds, rather than allowing religiously- or politically-founded maximalist claims to derail the process, either through an insistence that all of the Holy Land belongs to Israel and a continued programme of settlements, or through Christian Zionist biblical interpretations taking an uncritically anti-Palestinian position, or through an Islamic insistence that what was once Islamic land must again be, in its entirety. The secular alternative of a two-state solution also has its roots in international law, particularly if the pre-1967 War boundaries are taken as the basis (cf. UN Security Council Resolution 242) and an acceptable solution is found for Jerusalem which respects its holiness to all three main monotheistic religions and not just one of them.

Canon Naim Ateek, a leading Palestinian liberation theologian, known for his book *Justice and Only Justice* (Ateek 1989: 5.3), recently spoke in London on the theological basis for a two-state solution. His theological argument is also with those who use the Jewish scriptures (the Christian Old Testament) as a legitimation for Jewish claims for the whole of the land. He lays particular emphasis on the post-exilic, more inclusive, sharing sections of scripture rather than the earlier pre-exilic texts which present the conquest approach to the inhabitants.

Conclusion: The reign of God, the wretched of the earth, salvation and reconciliation

At the outset of this paper, I quoted the uncompromising dichotomy presented by Fanon which suggested that in the colonial setting any kind of reconciliation was illusory. We have examined four different political settings in which some kind of movement towards reconciliation has occurred or is occurring. This is not to suggest that reconciliation is easy – the processes outlined have involved great suffering, costly resistance and are by no means complete.

The vision of the reign of God (what is usually called the 'kingdom of God') transcends any political vision of the good society and acts as a critique of it. It is the reign of God for which we pray in the Lord's prayer, that God's will shall be done 'on earth as it is in heaven'. But we must beware the tendency to set the kingdom so high above what 'justice in the world' can achieve that it becomes a disconnected dream, so far away that it is unattainable and reduced to wishful thinking for the 'beyond'.

What is the content of the gospel in a divided world? There is no hope for reconciliation between the rich and poor without redistribution of wealth and power. Is the gospel about compromise or salvation? Is it about an individual's relationship with God or right relationships? Is it about here or the hereafter? Albert Nolan, the South African Dominican theologian begins his book *God in South Africa* with precisely these questions before developing a powerful plea for a gospel which required the dismantling of apartheid and a plea for reconciliation between black and white not within the existing disparities of wealth and power between the races, but as a reconciliation emerging in a non-racial, democratic South Africa.[27] This book was particularly important because it was written before it was safe, comfortable or fashionable to speak so clearly – particularly for a white theologian. Nolan argues as follows:

In practice, the content that is given to the word 'salvation' by different people depends upon their circumstances and their perceptions. It depends upon what they experience as their need for salvation and what they perceive to be wrong or sinful in their situation. Thus some will feel only the need for forgiveness to deal with their feelings of guilt, others will feel the need for justice to put right what is wrong in society, others will think that all we need is reconciliation to overcome the conflict, and still others will want liberation from oppression. Each of these projects will then become the content of the word 'salvation'. Clearly everything depends upon one's perception of what is really needed. Without a correct and comprehensive understanding of the dynamics of sin and evil in our situation, salvation will be given a limited or false content.[28]

Taking his analysis further, Nolan looks particularly at the truncation of the gospel which occurred among white South Africans, as a particular application of the European spiritualisation and individualisation of the understanding of salvation.

The most serious heresy of European Christianity, especially in the last few centuries, has been the reduction of the gospel to little more than the salvation of souls.[29]

How did this operate?

What seems to have happened is that the only need for salvation that was experienced by European Christians who benefited from capitalism and colonialism was the need to have their feelings of guilt removed. They felt no need, and could not imagine how anyone could feel any need, to be saved from oppression, from an excess of suffering, from the powers of evil, from the system. All such matters were conveniently excluded from the arena of religion and salvation by the device of calling them material and worldly problems.[30]

The net effect of this was as follows:

> It was the 'spiritualisation' and privatisation of religion
> that enabled the system of exploitation and colonialism to
> be justified, enabled it to expand through the world and to
> cause the most barbaric excess of suffering in the history
> of humankind. This kind of religion is, without doubt, the
> opium of the people.[31]

The net result, then, I would suggest, is that the social necessity of finding approximations to justice, approximations which, when they in turn become unbearably unjust need to be broken up, and the ultimate vision of the Reign of God pull in the same direction, but are not, in the last analysis the same thing. The vision of God's rule and of right relationships is always greater than the justice which can be attained within history. But we cannot be content to emphasise this gap to such an extent that the human task of creating just societies is devalued as 'only' political or secular.

For example, in the cases which I have taken, the social necessity of drawing a line under the crimes of the military at some point in Latin America is not complete justice – some kind of compromise has to be found between the demand for justice for the victims and a viable social arrangement which does not mean an endless confrontation with the military in the former dictatorships. How should one balance the demand for justice and the need for a pragmatic solution?

The ending of the Cold War was a considerable step forward, but new injustices and wars have emerged, so it cannot be said that the work of justice is completed – reconciliation in Europe is still a task which needs to be worked at.

In the South African context, the remarkable breaking down of apartheid, after the sacrificial struggle of many black and some white people, provides the non-racial basis from which a politics of reconciliation can begin to work on the economic injustice and deprivation which still prevails.

The basis for reconciliation between Israelis and Palestinians is there for the taking – I would argue primarily because of the readiness of the Palestinians to sacrifice, to forgo their claim to most of what they see as their land. But less than a two-state solution, less than a solution to the issue of Jerusalem which sees it as a holy city and symbol for both communities, and less than an economically viable Palestine, will not be sustainable.

The role of the Christian churches and indeed other religions in the politics of reconciliation is complex and often discouraging. Religion is used to harden conflicts, not provide the surplus of human values which enables blocked situations to be unblocked. The exceptions like Desmond Tutu, who was a reconciler even when he was most implacably opposed to apartheid provides an alternative dynamic to that outlined by theorists such as Fanon who saw no opportunity for reconciliation. Genuine movement towards reconciliation provides the window of opportunity which means that the rich and powerful can see an alternative between permanent oppression by them or being displaced and 'driven into the sea' (literally or metaphorically) by the others. One theme worth exploring further is the approach to conflict which Jesus had, namely making it clear what his position was, but in a way which did not threaten the opponent with destruction.

These are deep, dangerous and perplexing themes, but further praxis, and reflection on them is essential for the task of overcoming the appalling and largely unnecessary suffering in our world. The central insight of the Gospel is that within God's good creation, things could be different.

Overcoming Violence

Elizabeth Salter

Violence – an emotive word. A word which summons up so
much suffering, fear, insecurity and sorrow. A word which,
too often, characterises societies across the world struggling
with apparently insurmountable problems, at every level.
Domestic violence, where women and children are victimised
and abused; community violence, when marginalised and
neglected groups take revenge on those they mark out as their
persecutors; violence at the international level, as nations
inflict upon each other appalling suffering in the name of
narrow nationalism, ethnic purity or the pursuit of power.

Violence often takes on appearances, a more respectable
gloss: the defence of democracy by perfectly legitimate means,
with its attendant need for increasing quantities of sophisti-
cated, deadly armaments; the pursuit of economic policies
which improve the lot of many and make many others poorer
than ever; the rape of natural resources in the name of
progress; and the desire to maintain personal safety with lethal
weapons whose widespread availability increases the danger
for all of society, especially those who are most vulnerable.

Christians have struggled with the problem of violence
since the birth of the church, but for many centuries only a
minority have explored and practised the nonviolent option.
We know that in the early church Christians were deeply
committed to the Gospel message of peace, with all its
radical implications. Then, there was no doubt in the minds
of the Church Fathers that war was incompatible with
Christian belief; there is no evidence whatever of Christians
in military service in the first decades of the life of the
church. The code of conduct drawn up by Augustine ruled

that war must be just in its intent and waged only to restore peace, and the 'just war' criteria came to be those used as a guide by the majority of Christians. Tiny groups, such as the Waldensians in Italy, espoused the nonviolent way, but in Britain, it was only in the seventeenth century, when George Fox founded the Religious Society of Friends, that all the assurance of the early Church Fathers was regained. In 1650, as George Fox declined a captaincy in Cromwell's army, he made a solemn and now famous testimony to the officers: 'I told them I knew from whence all wars arose . . . and that I lived in the virtue of that life and power that took away the occasion of all wars.'

Over the following centuries, the nonviolent option has often been subject to rigorous testing, as Christian pacifists and conscientious objectors have struggled with the consequences of their moral stance at times of national crisis. There have been severe penalties, especially in countries with totalitarian regimes, for citizens refusing military service; it is only recently that Switzerland, normally considered a model of democracy and a respecter of human rights, began to reconsider the mandatory penalty of imprisonment for citizens refusing military service.

Some history
The history of problem-solving between Christians who differ in their interpretations of the Gospel and the call to be faithful servants is hardly edifying. The bitter battles between Catholics and Protestants, Anglicans and Catholics, Orthodox and Catholics, and the methods used by each side to uphold their own particular view of the truth, are records which stain the history books with blood, torture and horrendous suffering. 'See how these Christians love one another' is a description that can certainly not be applied to the Wars of Religion, or the excesses of the Reformation and Counter-Reformation.

Nor have Christians a blameless record in their dealings

with those of a different faith. The Crusades, the colonisation of Central and South America by the Spanish and Portuguese conquistadors, and the total lack of cultural sensitivity of many well-meaning but misguided missionaries, are a fearful indictment of the arrogance of Christians throughout the ages. Time and again they have often allowed themselves to be used and manipulated – advancing a political or ethnic cause, with the consequent watering down of the Gospel message of peace and goodwill to humankind in all its richness and diversity.

In recent times there have been more thoughtful attempts by the Christian churches to tackle the questions posed by violence at many levels. Jesus' call to his followers to be peacemakers is a powerful one, not an optional extra: many Christians, known or unsung, have responded to it in many differing circumstances: Martin Luther King's tremendous example of a man ardent for justice for his fellow black Americans, yet passionately determined to seek it by nonviolent means; the patient, long-term commitment of the Corrymeela Community in Northern Ireland to bring protagonists together and provide space for debate and discussion, with no predetermined agenda; the hearings held by churches in Los Angeles after race riots threatened community relations, to help rival gangs to meet, air their grievances and decide together on a common strategy; the joint endeavour by the World Council of Churches and the Lutheran World Federation, to provide for the shattered societies of Rwanda, not merely relief and rehabilitation, but the tools for long-term reconciliation as well – all responses to injustice and the violence carried out against human dignity which threatens life itself.

For many years there have been debates at the denominational level, and statements condemning war and violence of every kind. Ecumenical bodies too, have made various attempts to go further, and to explore innovative measures for the peaceful resolution of conflicts. The Sixth Assembly of the World Council of Churches in Vancouver in 1983 saw the setting up of the Council's new programme designed to explore the links between justice, peace and the integrity of creation (JPIC). A programme unit under that title was formed to tackle problems of racism, of international affairs, of economic justice, and issues affecting young people and women. At the World Convocation on JPIC, in Seoul, 1990, participants affirmed that 'we are called to seek every possible means of establishing justice, achieving peace and solving conflicts by active nonviolence'.

Practical peacemaking in Korea and the Caucasus

Serious efforts had also been made by the WCC to build bridges between peoples torn apart by war or mutual suspicion. A process begun in 1994, in Tosanzo, Japan, resulted in an historic meeting between Christians from North and South Korea, two countries divided for over forty years by an impenetrable wall – both physical and political – yet in reality a single nation for many centuries. That meeting led to others, and to ecumenical visits to the tiny Christian communities in North Korea, with the full assent of her government. Opening a tiny chink in the armour of suspicion and mistrust which had typified North-South Korean relationships for so long was an initiative which possibly only the churches could make. It allowed links to be forged, small steps to be made, prospects opened up and the walls of mutual hatred broken down.

Another WCC initiative was in response to the violent situation in the Caucasus, where, soon after the break-up of the Soviet Union and the new-found independence of her former territories, Armenia and Azerbaijan were locked in a bloody war over the tiny enclave of Nagorno-Karabagh, claimed by both states as their own. The conflict brought immense suffering to the people of Nagorno-Karabagh and the destruction of their homes and livelihoods, and to huge movements of population, with close on a million refugees on either side. As in former Yugoslavia, peoples who had lived in relative peace side by side found themselves polarised and forced into taking sides in a dangerous conflict which threatened to engulf other areas of the Caucasus.

At the height of the conflict the WCC, after long and painstaking negotiations, brought together in a private meeting the Catholicos (or Patriarch) of the Armenian Apostolic Church (the national church, and one of the founding churches of the WCC) and the Sheik-ul-Islam, the leader of the majority Muslim community in Azerbaijan and of the whole Caucasus region. The two religious leaders, after many hours of protracted discussion, signed a joint statement, affirming that the conflict was not a religious one, denouncing war as a means of settling disputes and calling on the warring parties to settle their differences by peaceful negotiation; calling, too, for an exchange of all prisoners of war and for the setting up of an international humanitarian fund for the relief of the victims of the war on both sides.

Since that meeting in 1993, the war over Nagorno-Karabagh has ended, and the slow, painful process of rebuilding trust and returning people to their homes will take many years to accomplish, but the contribution of the major religious bodies in the region was an important one. They were attempting what was most appropriate for them: bringing healing and reconciliation in a situation of terrible suffering and violence.

Programme to overcome violence

But it was only in 1994, at the Central Committee of the WCC held in Johannesburg, that, responding to a moving call from South African Methodist Bishop Stanley Mogoba, imprisoned for his firm opposition to apartheid, delegates voted unanimously for the setting up of a new programme – the Programme to Overcome Violence. The WCC, as the examples show, had since its inception been concerned to strengthen its member churches in witnessing to justice and peace. Now the time had come, as a Background Document to the Johannesburg Central Committee urged, to confront and overcome the 'spirit, logic and practice of war, and to develop new theological approaches, consonant with the teachings of Christ, which start not with war and move to peace, but with the need for justice'. 'This may indeed be a time when the churches, together, should face the challenge to give up any theological or moral justification of the use of military power, whether in war or as a part of security systems based on the notion of military deterrence, and to become a *koinonia* dedicated to the pursuit of a just peace.'

Some of the preparative groundwork for the programme was already well under way. A major consultation at the reconciliation centre of Corrymeela, in Northern Ireland, brought together church-related peace groups from around the world, including many enthusiastic young people, in June 1994. Later that summer a workshop on active non-violence, 'Living with our Differences: Nonviolent Responses to Conflict' was held in Switzerland. The questions which formed the basis of the workshop give a clear indication of its intent:

• How, as communities of faith, can we equip ourselves and others to resist this culture of violence and move towards a culture of peace?
• What inner spiritual resources can we draw upon?
• Where lies the source of our determination to seek solutions to thorny problems through active nonviolent means?

They proved to be exciting and stimulating events for participants. The experience of peace practitioners from mainstream churches throughout the world was both moving and a rich source of learning: Christians from tiny minorities in Sri Lanka and Pakistan; Christians deeply involved in the nonviolent struggle against apartheid in South Africa; Christians energised by the changes in Central and Eastern Europe, confronting new violence and the rise of nationalism, racism and ethnic strife; Christians from many parts of Africa, from New Caledonia, from the Philippines, from Central and South America . . . all with stories to tell of the paths they were following to help achieve a peaceful resolution of conflicts, close at home, in their own communities.

These major events, followed by much discussion and debate within the WCC's governing bodies, provided the framework for assumptions and principles to guide the fledgling programme. 'The WCC hopes to engage with churches, Christian groups and others committed to this work,' said a key document of the Board of the WCC's Commission of the Churches on International Affairs, meeting in June 1994, 'in a journey of transformation toward cultures of peace with justice in homes, churches, communities, nations and the world.'

It continued: 'Although no consensus exists among churches about Christian approaches to violence and nonviolence, a deep yearning to build lasting peace, grounded in justice, finds a new, more urgent expression in many churches today. Such urgency arises from the concrete experiences where churches face situations and structures of violence in arenas stretching from the local to the global. At stake may be the very survival of life in human community, sustained within creation.'

Commitment from the churches?

Now began the painstaking task of securing the commitment of the churches to the Programme to Overcome Violence in all its implications – at the local and community level, as well as at the national and international level. For some, its relevance was all too painfully clear. Conflict, a normal aspect of life in human community, all too often leads to injustice, violence and war; but the faithful witness of many Christians in conflicts which have caused intolerable suffering in their countries and regions provides us with outstanding examples of creative ways of moving forward – nonviolently.

For others, domestic and community violence, and the

desperate problems besetting the homeless, the destitute, the jobless – in the USA, in Mozambique, in Romania, for example – occupies their time and uses their skills and energies.

The first assignment was to provide materials for the churches, helping to encourage and empower them in the task of overcoming violence at the level of their own experience. A booklet, *Programme to Overcome Violence – An Introduction*, as well as an introductory leaflet and a directory of church-related peace groups throughout the world, were sent out to WCC member churches. It was essential for ordinary church members to start where they were and address the issues which were the most problematic and intractable for them. In the United Kingdom, the Churches Peace Forum, which brings together peace groups within the member churches of the Council of Churches for Britain and Ireland (CCBI) prepared its own materials, including a pack for groups and congregations, with a more specifically British and Irish focus.

A deeper concern

Behind the practical work of helping the churches to highlight issues of violence and how to deal with them lies a deeper concern. As Christians, we wring our hands over horrendous events and rush to offer succour to the victims, whether they be in Belfast or Dunblane, Bosnia or Chechnya. Where we often fail is in linking our personal lifestyles and priorities with national and international policies. It was moving to hear President Nelson Mandela of South Africa, on his visit to Britain in July 1994, thanking those who had been persistent in supporting the struggle against apartheid. What he did not say – in public at least – was that a general refusal, nationally, to have any dealings with a regime which caused so much suffering to so many for so long would have brought the apartheid government to its knees far sooner. If Christians everywhere had been more active in rejecting apartheid, and in taking personal and

political action to bring pressure to bear on their governments, it is quite probable that Nelson Mandela would have
walked free, and democratic elections would have been held,
many years before.

Nearer home, we deplore violence in the streets – mug-
gings, robberies and repeated lack of respect for human life
and property. But what kind of society have we been encouraged to create? The cult of individual enterprise, of cut-
throat competition, of the denial of the existence of 'society'
(in Margaret Thatcher's infamous phrase) has a darker side.
Whilst many succeed, and reap the benefits of their material
success, others live in insecurity and fear – badly housed,
badly fed, badly educated, with increasingly diminishing
medical services and jobs on short contract or no jobs at all.
Recent statistics show that Britain has the widest gap between
the haves and the have-nots of all the countries of Europe.

Inequalities produce anger and envy, ripe breeding
grounds for violence of every kind. Stripping many members
of our society of their human dignity is in itself a form of
violence: the homeless young people lying on our city streets,
the gradual erosion of social services for the old and the vulnerable, and even the systematic bullying which is a feature
of life in many of our schools, especially in the inner cities.

Violence against minority ethnic groups is still with us, in
spite of legislation for racial equality. Far too often, we act as
if the white, Anglo-Saxon Protestant were the only truly worthy
inhabitant of these islands. Where do Christian communities,
locally and nationally, stand on issues of social and racial
dignity? Can we see the link between our attitudes in our
homes and communities and the priorities of our local and
national government and of the international community? Do
we do anything about it? What effective steps can we take,
both as individuals and in the company of fellow Christians,
to overcome these evils, and to propose alternatives which
are both effective and creative?

103

Training for active nonviolence

To start with, we need interior preparation, learning to understand our own motivations and reactions and deepening and strengthening them, both individually and in our immediate community. Then we need to acquire the attitudes and methods of nonviolence – learning, training, preparing to control reactions, overcoming fear and discovering non-violent responses. The next step is to elaborate a strategy: defining the injustice we wish to overcome, discovering the pillars which support it, finding allies and building solidarity, and then, finally, building the alternative.

All this takes an immense amount of time, and far too often, nonviolent responses to conflict are rejected by those in authority because the results are not always obvious and are slow in coming. But they forget the long-term effects of violent responses to conflict, whether it be the resentment nursed by a battered wife or an abused child, the shattering of the confidence and self-esteem of the young person whose chances of employment are virtually nil, the long journey towards reconciliation and reconstruction of, say, the people of former Yugoslavia, or of Angola, or Rwanda.

An invitation and a challenge

The Programme to Overcome Violence is an invitation, but also a challenge, for every single Christian, calling on each and every one to be 'challenging and transforming the global culture of violence in the direction of a culture of just peace', as the call from the Johannesburg Central Committee put it. Deep commitment to the vision of a nonviolent world and the establishment of Christ's 'peaceable kingdom' is a long-term one. Peace is seldom static, but a process; conflict will always be a feature of our personal, community, national and international landscape, but as Ahab, King of Israel, told his enemy many centuries ago: 'The one who puts on his armour is not the one who can boast, but the one who takes it off'.

Can lions really lie down with lambs? Can swords truly be beaten into ploughshares? 'Blessed are the peacemakers' is not merely a statement, but a requirement from a loving God who, in the words of the Psalmist, 'means peace for his people, for his friends, if only they renounce their folly'. The challenge of the vision of the peaceable kingdom is for Christians with conviction, passion and imagination to turn that vision into a reality.

Pointers on the Way

The unity in the life and spirituality of Mother Teresa, Jean Vanier, Brother Roger and Little Sister Magdeleine

Kathryn Spink

I'd like to start with a story. It is an Indian story about four friends who stumbled upon an elephant in the dark. Unable to see the animal, they each explored its contours with their hands. The first discovered the four legs. 'Here,' he cried, 'are the columns of a great temple.' The second felt the animal's powerful flanks. 'We have surely come upon a massive fortress,' he exclaimed, while the third tugged upon the tail which he declared to be a bell rope. The fourth discovered the trunk. 'Here,' he assured his companions, 'is a huge serpent with some mystical significance.' Each had discovered and in some way experienced the reality of touching the elephant. Each interpreted the experience in his own way. No one explanation was complete in itself.

I should perhaps also say that I don't intend to keep drawing direct comparisons between my four subjects but I do invite readers to consider particularly how each one experiences the presence of God in humanity in general but especially in the poor, how belief in that presence and 'touching' it transforms their action, and how each one relates prayer/contemplation to their everyday life.

In my career as a writer, which now spans rather longer than I care to acknowledge, it has been my privilege to come into contact with quite a range of religious orders and communities, of different faiths and denominations, in many different corners of the world. As the one researching, it is usually I who ask the questions, but sometimes the table is turned and one of the questions most frequently posed of me is, in essence: 'How is it that you, an outsider, can understand our vocation or our particular commitment so well?'

I wish that I could attribute this capacity to my own extraordinary wisdom or intuition, but if I am honest it is simply that what strikes me as I travel from one group to the next is how much they have in common. It is my experience that, despite the diversity of expression, there is a 'oneness' or 'unity' which can and often does exist, both within and between different groups or communities. What is more, it exists both at the level of experience and at the level of motivating spirit. So it is that the discovery of one is not so very different from the discovery of the next. It is frequently only the very smallest of steps from the understanding of one to the understanding of another.

It would undoubtedly be possible to make out a case highlighting that which divides these same individuals or those who work or live with them, but since what I also frequently encounter in them is a sense of isolation, of struggling to live out a calling against enormous odds, and of being what Mother Teresa often referred to as 'a tiny drop in the ocean of need', I am grateful for this opportunity to concentrate on those elements which support the suggestion that, beyond what may appear diverse and separate, lies much that unifies. Since too, I understand that a particular focus of Christians Aware is on justice, peace and reconciliation I would like to suggest that those elements are also pointers to the potential for what my subjects would diversely refer to as 'peace', 'communion', 'reconciliation', 'unity'.

I have chosen here to concentrate on the lives and spirituality of Mother Teresa, Jean Vanier, Brother Roger and Little Sister Magdeleine, all of whom are Christians and all of whom know or knew each other and hold or held each other in regard. It is perhaps only to be expected then that they should have much in common. But, not insignificantly, I believe, all of the individuals I have mentioned have found a response and recognition from people who do not necessarily share their particular belief systems. Amongst those who are drawn to them and to what they stand for are people of a wide variety of creeds and world views.

Mother Teresa

I begin with Mother Teresa, the Albanian woman born and brought up in Skopje, Yugoslavia. In 1928, at the age of eighteen, Agnes Bojaxhiu as she was then, applied to join the Loreto Sisters in order to 'go out and give the life of Christ to the people'. For twenty-five years she taught history and geography in Loreto schools in Calcutta in a very unextraordinary way, until in September 1946, she experienced on a train travelling to a retreat in Darjeeling what she herself referred to as 'a call within a call'. It was an experience about which she said little: 'The call of God to be a Missionary of Charity,' she once confided, 'is the hidden treasure for me, for which I have sold all to purchase it. You remember in the gospel what the man did when he found the hidden treasure – he hid it.' The message, in whatever form it was communicated was, nevertheless, both singular and unambiguous: 'I was,' she said, 'to leave the convent and help the poor while living among them. It was an order. To fail it would have been to break the faith.'

In obedience to this order, in 1948 she stepped out into some of the world's most disease-ridden slums to live as one with the poorest of the poor and to found a new Congregation committed to their service. According to Mother Teresa's spiritual director of many years, during the retreat at Darjeeling that followed the experience on the train, Mother Teresa wrote down on small slips of paper the essentials of all that was to follow: 'The congregation she was to start would work for the poorest of the poor in the slums in a spirit of poverty and cheerfulness. There would be no institutions, hospitals or big dispensaries. There would be a special vow of charity for the poor.' The congregation first formally elected on 7th October 1950 would in fact take, in addition to the traditional vows of poverty, chastity and obedience, a fourth vow of 'wholehearted free service to the poorest of the poor'.

Today, even after her death, Mother Teresa's mission is a universal one. The work which began in the slums of Calcutta with the creation of small schools where Mother Teresa scratched the alphabet in the dust, was to lead also to the opening of children's homes, homes for the dying, mobile and static leprosy clinics. In time it spread wherever her particular geography of compassion identified a need. In 1970 she visited England. She was taken on a tour of the night spots of London by the Simon Community. She saw the strip clubs of Soho, she was shown the people sleeping under the tarpaulins which draped the scaffolding of St Martin in the Fields and she found the tramps curled up on the gratings where warm air rises from the kitchens of the London hotels. Among the methylated spirit drinkers and the drug pushers a young man, well-fed and well-dressed, took an overdose of barbiturates before her very eyes.

It is difficult to trace any particular evolution in the actual spirituality of Mother Teresa after the founding of the Missionaries of Charity, precisely because it was all there in essence in the notes she jotted down during the retreat at Darjeeling. It is evident, however, that in the course of her increasing contact with the materially rich West she was brought to a new understanding of the word 'poverty' which had always been so central to her commitment. The mental, emotional and spiritual poverty of the affluent West was, Mother Teresa pronounced, so much more complex than the physical poverty of the so-called 'Third World'. In response to the breakdown of family life she witnessed in the West, she called increasingly for people to make their homes 'another Nazareth'. And she set about meeting the 'hunger and the thirst' of those who sometimes did not even recognise their own poverty, by making them more fully aware not only of the need but also of the spiritual riches of the materially poor. According to one who was close to her during the early years, there was a time when she might have been more critical of the uncaring rich. Increasingly, however, the message was that the rich must be rich 'for a purpose'. She wanted, she said, the rich to save the poor and the poor to save the rich. Her appeal to those who in a material sense at least, have plenty, to give not from their abundance, and not from the comfort of their armchairs but until it hurts, has reached most of the sitting rooms of the Western world.

And so Mother Teresa who is remembered by her contemporaries at Loreto for her inability to light the candles in chapel, for her goodness and her conscientiousness but really for little more than benign ordinariness, became a household name. Christians have described her as a saint. Some more accustomed to the Hindu mode of thinking have chosen to see in her the 'reincarnation of Jesus', Muslims have acclaimed her as an 'evolved spirit', and people of all religious beliefs have been prepared to recognise her as a 'holy person'. In the words of India's President Giri, Mother Teresa is 'among those emancipated souls who have transcended all barriers of race, religion, creed and nation'.

What is it then that attracts such universal recognition from such diverse quarters? There are those who attribute her appeal to the idea that in a world of crumbling family relationships she conformed to a universal, archetypal ideal of motherhood. This may well be part of the explanation. There is also the fact that in an age where the media has such a powerful ability to make or break 'stars', despite all her protestations that she would rather wash a leper than face a press conference, she was a natural media personality. It was a technically far from perfect interview with Malcolm Muggeridge on BBC television in 1968 which was first strongly instrumental in making her work known, and thereafter she displayed a talent for engaging people's hearts with catch-phrases that made perfect headlines and the kind of 'photo-opportunities' of which politicians dream.

Mother Teresa undoubtedly learnt at times to use public attention to her own or rather to God's ends – for she was, she insisted, only the little pencil in the hand of God. But she was not one who deliberately set out to court the allegiance of people of different world views. Together with Brother Roger, she spoke out for the cause of Christian unity because she believed that 'Christians stand as a light to the world'. And in this context she frequently quoted the comment of Mahatma Gandhi that if all Christians were Christlike there would be no more Hindus left in India. Possibly Mother Teresa's most significant concrete contribution to the movement to break down barriers between people of different Christian denominations and indeed of different faiths was the creation of an association of lay helpers whom she termed 'co-workers' as a tribute to Gandhi, who called his own helpers 'co-workers' because they worked with him 'for the brotherhood of man under the fatherhood of God'. This Association, formally established in 1969, was open to people of good will everywhere and it bound together in action and in prayer helpers from all over the world under a non-denominational constitution.

When specifically speaking on different religious beliefs, Mother Teresa expressed tolerance: 'Every human being comes from God,' she maintained, 'and we all know what is the love of God for us. My religion is everything to me but for every individual, according to the grace God has given that soul. God has his own ways and means to work in the hearts of men and we do not know how close they are to him but by their actions we will always know whether they are at his disposal or not. Whether you are Hindu or Muslim or Christian, how you live your life is the proof that you are fully his or not.'

At the same time she remained quite uncompromising in the orthodoxy of her Roman Catholic belief, firmly rooted as it was in the faith of her devout Albanian family, particularly that of her mother whose influence appears to have been both durable and profound. Mother Teresa had no difficulty in accepting certain decisions of the Second Vatican Council, the council Pope John XXIII had given the task of renewing the life of the Church. She welcomed, for example, the approved New Mass and the use of the living language instead of Latin. That the church wanted renewal, she recognised; but she was not always comfortable with the form that renewal took. She did not approve of individual innovations or what she saw as lack of discipline. She could not accept, for instance, priests who did not wear vestments at Mass, the movement of tabernacles containing the Blessed Sacrament into obscure corners, the neglect of attention to the Virgin Mary or the rosary. Nor would she condone diminished respect for the Pope, for the teaching of the Catholic Church on marriage or sexual morality, or the failure of nuns or priests to wear religious dress.

One newly-ordained priest, sent to give instruction to the Missionaries of Charity experienced precisely how uncompromising she could be in relation to such matters. The priest was somewhat disdainful of the traditional beliefs held by the Sisters. Among other things, he claimed there was no need for them to genuflect before the Blessed Sacrament outside the Mass because the presence of Christ was limited to its duration. After he had finished speaking Mother Teresa led him to the door, thanked him for coming and informed him that he need not come again. She then spent an hour with the Sisters refuting all that he had said.

Hand in hand with her religious tolerance went a certain rigidity – both temperamental and theological. She was also quite capable of being, though possibly unconsciously, insensitive to the perspectives of non-Catholics. Outside the chapel in the Mother House in Calcutta when I was last there was one very small but concrete illustration of this fact. There on the wall of a place to which people of quite a range of different denominations come to pray was a notice, stating baldly: 'Non-Catholics must not receive the Sacraments'. I do not know whether Mother Teresa wrote it but certainly she walked past it every day, evidently oblivious to the hurt that it might cause some.

Her fidelity to the traditional authority and teachings of the Roman Catholic Church in general and her strongly expressed views on the ordination of women, birth control, divorce and abortion in particular at times provoked controversy and criticism. Sometimes what Mother Teresa actually said was perceived as quite unpalatable and not just because it was counter-cultural or in some respects more in keeping with the pre-Vatican II Catholic Church. Nor was it rejected only by the atheistic, the progressive or the feminist. For in fact the accumulative effect of the imagery, the liturgy and the general vocabulary of the Missionaries of Charity is not always to convey an atmosphere of openness to people of other Christian traditions.

Yet she was the recipient of more honorary degrees and prizes than possibly any other world figure and they were awarded to her by Christians of different denominations, by Hindus, Muslims, and by people who would not lay claim to any particular faith. When, in 1979, she received what might be considered the ultimate accolade, the Nobel prize for peace, she did so, as she received all such awards, on behalf of the poor of the world. She also said that the prize meant recognition that the works of love were also works of peace.

People responded to her 'works of love', to 'the way in which she lived her life' which she said is indicative of whether or not you 'belong to God'. Mother Teresa was not an intellectual. She was not given to clever debate. The first thing she did when people came to her, seeking to understand, was not to endeavour to explain verbally but to put them to work. She sent them out actually to touch the 'reality of the elephant', for experience had taught her that it is at the level of this action that real understanding is often born. Faith, she knew, is at its most universally articulate in action and it is at the level of action that the barriers formed by the intellect begin to topple. When Mother Teresa first opened her home for the dying in Calcutta, she encountered strong opposition from the Brahmins in the nearby Kali temple. The place to which she was taking the dying picked up from the streets had once been the pilgrims' rest home for this significant Hindu shrine. The Sisters were perceived to be encroaching on Hindu territory with the co-operation of a Muslim health officer who had afforded her the use of the building. Stones were thrown by protesting Hindus and there were those who suspected her of persuading the poor to relinquish their religion for a plate of rice. The leader of one group of young people entered Nirmal Hryday resolved to turn her out. Having witnessed, however, the care with which the suffering, emaciated bodies of the poor were tended, he returned to his fellow protesters outside with the directive that he would evict the Sisters but only on one condition: namely that they persuade their mothers and sisters to undertake the same service. Gradually Mother Teresa's concern, which she defined as 'the practical expression of God's love', commanded recognition.

The issue of the extent to which the Missionaries of Charity proselytise remains a cloudy one. To many Bengalis Mother Teresa became known as the 'preacher of love who did not preach' but the allegations of 'rice Christianity' have never been entirely dispelled. There are still those who feel that she believed that Hinduism and Islam were wrong and Catholicism right, and who question the validity of her ministering to the poor of Calcutta and the world not for their own sake but for the sake of her Catholic God. Her assertion, 'We never make those who receive become converted to Christianity,' was invariably qualified, 'However, together with our work, we bear witness of the love of God's presence'. Offset against the claim that 'If Catholics, Protestants, Buddhists or agnostics become for this better men, simply better, we will be satisfied', there is always the avowed objective of the Society of the Missionaries of Charity which is 'to satiate the thirst of Christ for love and souls'.

The more cynically inclined have wondered whether her failure to proselytise more overtly was not in fact determined by the diplomatic tightrope she walked with the Indian government. Too open an attempt at conversion would undoubtedly have jeopardised the concessions made to her, for example, in connection with customs regulations and other aspects of India's labyrinthine bureaucracy. One Indian government official once said to her, 'Tell the truth, you would like me to become a Christian, you are praying for that?' and she answered him: 'When you possess something really good, you wish your friends to share it with you. I think that Christ is the best thing in the world and I would like all to know him and love him as I do. But faith in Christ is a gift of God, who gives it to whom he likes.'

Perhaps more worthwhile than the debate about whether or not Mother Teresa set out to convert is the question of what exactly she meant by conversion. Conversion, in Mother Teresa's understanding of the word, was not bringing the atheist to believe in God or the changing of a person's belief system from one to another but 'the changing of the heart through love'. And if we apply this definition of the word, then there is no doubt that a conversion occurs in many who touch the reality of the poor, be it in the homes for the dying or in their own homes.

To work amongst the poor in countries such as India or Africa is frequently to discover that there the ecumenical impulse is pragmatic. It is often born and/or reinforced by the rejection of wasteful rivalries and the duplication of effort in the missionary work of different churches. Mother Teresa was exposed more than most to this kind of practical need and to the tendency to see differences of Christian denomination as relatively insignificant when faced with (a) the magnitude of the need and (b) the more substantial differences between, for example, Christianity and Hinduism. In the case of the Missionaries of Charity's work, however, be it in the homes for the dying, for abandoned children, for the unwanted elderly or for AIDS sufferers, the unity that is discovered extends beyond Christians of different traditions. Among the first people to come to Mother Teresa's aid were not only European women of different Christian denominations but Hindus also, and the Hindus who gathered at the bedsides of the untouchables came from different castes. The formation of the association of co-workers to co-ordinate their activity was thus in the first instance substantially pragmatic and was of necessity not confined to any particular faith or denomination. What moved it beyond the level of simply 'working together' was, however, Mother Teresa's ever increasing insistence on the need to put love and prayer into the action.

For Mother Teresa action began and ended with love: 'Today God loves the world so much that he gives you and he gives me to be his love and compassion . . .'

'Our purpose,' she said, 'is to take God's love to the poor.' At the same time, in our need for love we are all poor: 'Some call him Ishwar, some call him Allah, some simply God, but we all have to acknowledge that it is he who made us for greater things, to love and to be loved.'

Sometimes Mother Teresa was accused of failing to tackle the root causes of need. Indeed, there are some who maintain that by salving the consciences of those who might otherwise be compelled to bring about change on a wider scale, by removing some of the sources of public embarrassment, be they the dying on the pavements of Calcutta or the homeless alcoholics occupying cardboard city, she was not in fact serving the best interests of the poor but helping to preserve the status quo.

For Mother Teresa, however, what came first was not the problem to be solved but the person affected. Charged with the reproach that she should not be giving the poor fish but fishing rods with which to catch their own food, she sighed the deepest of sighs, 'Ah, my God, you should see these people. They have not even the strength to lift a fishing rod, let alone use it to fish. Giving them fish, I help them to recover the strength for the fishing of tomorrow.'

To know the problem of poverty intellectually, she maintained, was not really to comprehend it: 'It is not by reading, taking a walk in the slums, admiring and regretting the misery that we get to understand it and to discover what it has of bad and good. We have to dive into it, to live it, share it.'

Mother Teresa did not set out to transform political systems or eradicate the causes of poverty on a universal scale. She did not fail to recognise the need for such changes but she always maintained that such a calling was for others. Her vocation was to begin with the individual. 'Ek, ek, ek' – 'one by one by one' – was one of her favourite sayings, and she called on those who worked with her, not to do great things but only small things with great love. It is not the magnitude of the action which counts but the love put into it, for love, she intimated, transforms small things and makes them great.

'My revolution comes from God and is made by love,' she maintained. What she called upon the people who would follow her to do was to touch with their compassion the lepers with their maggot-ridden wounds, to love the drug addict with his running nose and needle-pricked limbs, to make time for the lonely or difficult members within their own families. And the motivation for this extraordinary love she found in the words of St Matthew's gospel: 'Just as you did it to one of the least of these who are members of my family, you did it to me.'

Mother Teresa saw Christ in everyone – the suffering Christ in the distressing disguise of the poor, Christ, hungry, thirsty, alone or rejected. To fail to understand this motivating principle is to make a nonsense of much of what she did. The inability to accept the spiritual dimension of her work –

the non-judgemental and simultaneously unsentimental love of the Christ present in every human being – necessarily renders questionable, for example, her association with right wing exploiters such as Baby Doc Duvalier of Haiti.

Someone was once rash enough to remark to Mother Teresa that they would not touch a leper for a thousand pounds. 'Neither would I,' came the instant retort, 'but I would willingly do so for the love of God.' Similarly she was convinced that it was not really possible to bring peace to the dying, tend the open wounds of the leper and nurture the tiny spark of life in babies whom others had abandoned, in other words really to love in the way that she did and her Missionaries of Charity continue to do, without prayer, without 'the pure heart which can see God'.

'It is not possible to engage in the direct apostolate,' she said, 'without being a soul at prayer.' We must be aware of oneness with Christ, as he was aware of oneness with his Father. Our activity is truly apostolic only in so far as we permit him to work in us and through us, with his power, with his desire, with his love.'

'The family that prays together stays together' was one of Mother Teresa's favourite axioms and she applied it also to the extended family of people who worked with her. So it is that those who touched the reality of poverty with her also found and find themselves praying together regardless of the belief system in which they have been born and/or bred. And sometimes in prayer there is an experience of the sense of separateness being dispelled, as the theological differences which separate religious bodies are transcended.

I have a Presbyterian friend from Scotland. She accompanied me once to Mass at one of the Missionaries of Charity houses in Rome. Had it not been for the likelihood of Mother Teresa's presence at the service, I doubt that she would even have entered the chapel, adorned as it was with colourful pictures of the Sacred Heart of Jesus and statues of the Virgin Mary. As the mass proceeded, complete with what my friend had been brought up to regard as 'bells and smells', I could sense her hackles rising but she remained for the duration of the service and for the adoration of the Sacrament that followed. Afterwards she told me how there had come a point where she had closed her eyes and ceased to focus on the unfamiliar Italian words which she could not in any case understand. She had found herself aware only of an overwhelming atmosphere of precisely the power and light and love which the ritual of her own religious training regularly verbally affirmed.

'Love to pray,' urged Mother Teresa, 'for prayer enlarges the heart until it is capable of containing God's gift of himself.'

And, she maintained, much depends on this unison of hearts. For the more united we are to God, the greater will be our love and readiness to serve the poor wholeheartedly. Hers was an understanding of the heart, not the heart as seat of the emotions but the heart as the place of direct knowledge, of clear perception 'beyond' emotion and thought. (The heart as referred to by Saul of Tarsus when he wrote to his disciples: 'I pray that the eyes of your heart may be opened that you may *know*'). Mother Teresa was not, and her Missionaries of Charity are not, social workers but contemplatives in the world. To look contemplatively is not to analyse. It is to behold not with the senses but with the eyes of the heart. It is to nurture an awareness that takes us beyond sensual perception.

So it is that the professed motivation of the society is not to remove x number of homeless people from the streets by the year 2,000, but to quench the thirst of Christ on the cross for love of souls. Such a task is not achieved through human power or through ever increasing numbers but through a sense of personal poverty which allows the free action of the Holy Spirit, through becoming the 'channel' of the prayer of St Francis which Mother Teresa used regularly.

The vision which Mother Teresa still holds out to us is that of Christ crying out for love in the broken bodies of the poor and of Christ simultaneously offering himself in the Eucharist to sustain in order that that cry might not go unheard and without response. God is expressing his love, he is actively at work in the world, through the open-hearted prayer of those instruments who place themselves at his disposal.

'Prayer to be fruitful must come from the heart and must be able to touch the heart of God.' And prayer, she insisted, is fruitful. Its fruits are 'joy, action and love'.

'Love does not live on words,' asserted Mother Teresa, 'nor can it be explained by words – especially that love which serves him, which comes from him and which finds him and touches him. We must reach the heart and to reach the heart as we must do – love is proved in deeds.'

There is oneness then at the level of 'unity of hearts' and at the level of the action which is simultaneously born of it and engenders and sustains it. Where this unity appears at times to break down is at the level of verbal expression.

Like all the great mystics, Mother Teresa knew the value of silence: 'God,' she said, 'is the friend of silence.'

'All our words will be useless, unless they come from within – words which do not give the light of Christ increase the darkness.'

Words can give the light of Christ but, like action, in order to do so they must be the fruit of prayer, of oneness with Christ, and: 'Perfect prayer does not consist in many words, but in the fervour of the desire which raised the heart of Jesus.'

'If we really want to pray we must first learn to listen, for in the silence of the heart God speaks.'

'In silence,' she said, 'we will find new energy and true unity. The energy of God will be ours to do all things well. The unity of our thoughts with his thoughts, the unity of our prayers with his prayers, the unity of our actions with his actions, of our life with his life.'

Jean Vanier
Mother Teresa did not use the word 'communion' but as we move on to look at the spirituality of l'Arche, readers might

like to consider the relationship between Mother Teresa's 'silent unity' with the God present in the Eucharist and the God present in the poor, a unity which is experienced in prayer and in 'touch', with Jean Vanier's understanding of 'communion'.

Perhaps nowhere has the value of silent presence been brought home to me more potently than during the periods I have spent in various l'Arche communities for people with a mental disability. (The emphasis in l'Arche is very much on people rather than on the mental disability). Of necessity people whose verbal communication and rational capabilities are limited call us to a different form of relationship from those we might normally have and with which we are usually comfortable

L'Arche, its founder Jean Vanier has pointed out, is distinct from many other communities, in being founded not on the word but in a very particular way on the body precisely because mentally disabled people tend to be people for whom the body with its pains, its pleasures and its capacity for expression and relationship features prominently.

'God reveals himself to people first of all by the word,' Jean Vanier claims, but he is referring to the 'word which is very close to the spirit, filled with light and touches in our intelligence and in our hearts'. (What Mother Teresa described as 'words that give the light of Christ') . . . And then there is the revelation of God through the body which seems to be the opposite to the creativity, the power, the beauty and the wisdom of the word: the littleness of the body, the fragility of the body, the ugliness, the dirt, the smell as it dies.' 'With our people here,' he says, 'there are little words and a lot of body.'

The l'Arche communities began in 1964 when, with the help of his family and friends, Jean Vanier, son of a Governor General of Canada, bought one of the unassuming houses in the village of Trosly-Breuil just north of Paris. He then invited three mentally disabled people to leave the institution where they had been living and to make their home with him. Like Mother Teresa on the train to Darjeeeling, Jean Vanier had experienced a call to the poor, which he claims he could scarcely define but which he knew to be 'irreversible'. 'In the name of Jesus,' he says of his initiation of a new life with his mentally disabled companions, 'our lives were henceforth to be bound to one another; the possibility of returning them to the dreadful living conditions of an asylum was quite out of the question.'

In his case the 'poor' took the particular form of mentally disabled people and Jean Vanier describes his life amongst them as 'sharing in a life of communion with them'. Furthermore, as in the case of Mother Teresa, who spoke readily of the 'riches of our people' who are 'free, happy and without the aggression of those who aspire to many things', and whose qualities of the heart she held up as an example to members of more materialistic societies, so in Jean Vanier's experience, what began as an act of compassion toward the suffering people he had witnessed as scarcely existing in an asylum, was to lead to the very concrete discovery of the 'riches' of people with a mental disability and the potential they have for opening the hearts of those prepared to be fully present to them.

For Jean Vanier and those who subsequently came to join him, the desire simply to live together, not as educators or carers and disabled people, but as sharers in a new form of family life, a life of 'openness to all that Jesus would show him thereafter', a life of 'communion', was to highlight by contrast the great gulf that is more often fixed between the strong and the weak, the powerful and the vulnerable, the able and the disabled.

There are, Jean Vanier was subsequently to point out, the poor, the oppressed – those who feel themselves useless and devoid of power, yet who cry out for recognition and appreciation – and there are the rich, the powerful and the effective, whose tendency is to crush others apparently less capable than themselves. The rich have work, possessions, status, but often lack that most essential quality: the capacity to love, to live relationships of communion without fear, without hiding behind the many trappings of success, power and defence. Between these two worlds there exist terrible tensions and barriers. The rich regard the poor and weak as problems and seek to resolve these problems according to their own vision, refusing to enter into a dialogue of trust with those who are oppressed and in distress. They will not listen to them. Sometimes they even want to prevent their very existence. To them it is inconceivable that the despised and the pitied might hold in the depths of their hearts the solutions to the very problems they allegedly represent. In each one of us there is a strong resistance to change and that, Jean Vanier asserts, is why the rich cannot enter into dialogue with the poor: for such a dialogue inevitably calls upon the rich to change. The cry of the person in need inconveniences those who are comfortable and satisfied with themselves and their lot. The anguish of people with a disability reveals our own anguish, their shadows our shadows, and so we turn away.

Jean Vanier did not turn away. In 1950, at the age of twenty-one, he had left the navy, as he puts it 'to follow Jesus'. He had also studied philosophy and taken his doctorate in the morals of Aristotle. None of this education in 'efficacy and competence', however, really equipped him for a life with mentally disabled people. L'Arche began in 'poverty' in every sense of the word: the small house he bought was simple in the extreme, the lack of money was a continuing reality, there was the poverty of the people with disabilities – the intolerable suffering of those who have known since childhood that they are a disappointment to their parents. There was also, Jean Vanier insists, his own poverty. Very early on in the development of l'Arche it became apparent to him that to love someone did not mean primarily to do things for that person but to reveal to them their value and beauty, to help them to rediscover their self confidence. This was by no means easy for one who knew about action, about organisation, about teaching and about generosity, but who had to learn how really to listen and to take time to understand and allow his companions to reveal the needs, the beauty and the meaning of their lives. Jean Vanier was, by his own account, to discover not only the tension between the 'poor' person and the 'rich' person outside but the same tensions within himself.

Yet the small community in Trosly-Breuil increased in number, not only of disabled people but also of 'assistants' who were also prepared not to turn away but who sought instead to share their lives. There are now about a hundred l'Arche communities scattered across the continents.

The communities which grew quite rapidly out of the small house in Trosly-Breuil and the desire to create real homes, not institutions, where disabled people and assistants could experience together all the joy and the difficulties of a community life inspired by the Beatitudes and based on reciprocity, vary considerably in their outer expression. With time the original community grew to encompass some four hundred people and more than twenty houses scattered throughout Trosly-Breuil and its neighbouring villages. It was subsequently divided into four. More recent communities may be composed of no more than six people. As in France, l'Arche in India, North America, Britain, the Ivory Coast, Honduras, Burkino Faso, Australia and elsewhere seeks to integrate with and so to express itself in terms of the local culture. Some communities are set in the heart of capital cities; others in rural areas. Some have their own workshops; in others the disabled people go out to work elsewhere. Some welcome children; some have not felt called or are not equipped to do so.

Many of the people who come to live in l'Arche are young people, students for example, who feel called to give a year or more of their lives to the community. Not all choose to make a life-long commitment. L'Arche is not a religious order. It is made up of lay people and recognised by the State as an organisation undertaking social work. In France and in some other rich countries the communities receive financial support from the State and are controlled by it. One of the challenges that l'Arche confronts, therefore, is that of being a recognised institution governed by labour laws etc. and at the same time a Christian community inspired by gospel values. In order to maintain those values, Jean Vanier claims, a priest or pastor is needed to 'reveal Jesus in the sacrament and in the word' and to serve as a constant spiritual reminder to the community. Priests in l'Arche, however, are not given positions of temporal authority, they are not at the head but at the heart of the community, 'hidden and humble like Jesus' – reminders of the mystery of the gospel.

L'Arche in Trosly Breuil has an oratory and two chapels, one of which is a converted barn. Chapels in communities elsewhere may be even simpler and more improvised: a tiny room with rush matting on the floor, a candle, an icon, a tabernacle where the blessed sacrament is reserved, an unoccupied bedroom or the corner of an attic. Some do not set aside a specific place in which to pray. In countries where the local people are not Christian, the communities are not necessarily Christian. Where people are Christian they may be of different denominations. There are also those in l'Arche who would not lay claim to any particular religious belief for religious belief is not an obligatory part of the life. Each community defines its own religious identity. Some are Roman Catholic, others are Protestant, others are inter-denominational, yet others are interfaith.

Whatever their religious background, however, those who remain in l'Arche share in a common experience. It is an experience which begins with a response to the cry of the poor, brings with it increased understanding of poverty, a sense of personal poverty on the part of those who set out to 'help' the poor and ultimately the recognition that the cry is not only the expression of the need of the world but also of its hope. Whatever their religious background, they are touching the same reality: that of the weak and the vulnerable who are yet possessed of extraordinary gifts of the heart and of what Jean Vanier frequently refers to as a 'prophetic quality'.

'The Word became flesh' – like Mother Teresa, Jean Vanier sees Jesus in the poor but again, recognising the presence of Jesus in the poor theoretically and talking about it is one thing; actually to be confronted by the poor person salivating, sometimes violent, uninhibited, intuitive, disconcertingly discerning and craving real attention is quite another. Real understanding comes with the process of *living with*. 'Conversion', if we take Mother Teresa's definition of the word as 'the changing of the heart through love', comes about through this process of 'living with' i.e. actually touching and allowing ourselves to be touched by the poor person who craves real relationship with us.

This real relationship is equatable to what Jean Vanier frequently refers to as 'communion'. 'It is communion with another' he maintains, for which every human being thirsts. What then does communion mean for him? The Second Vatican Council, he has said, made him aware of the mystery of communion with God, the source of communion between all the children of God, but he had yet to understand the full implication of the word. It was only in the actual process of living with people with disabilities that he was brought to greater understanding, to the realisation that:

'Generally speaking communion is a sense of unity deeper than working together. It is more on the level of being, and somewhere it breaks down the barriers of loneliness and gives people a sense of freedom. It has a very deep respect of difference. It is very close to the things of God. It is frequently deepened in silence and is linked much more to the body.'

'Communion is a state of being present one to another, a place in which I also discover the presence of God.

Communion is a state of grace, the fruit of shared love. It is born of a reciprocal opening to one another, a mutual and simultaneous giving devoid of expectations, based on humility and born of trust . . .'

Communion for Jean Vanier is frequently linked to gentle moments lived with the profoundly disabled, to bath time with Eric, for example, who is almost completely blind and deaf:

'It was an occasion when a deep communion could be established: when we would touch his body with gentleness, respect and love. In hot water Eric relaxes; he likes it. Water refreshes and cleanses, he has a feeling of being enveloped in a gentle warmth. Through water and the touch of the body there was a deep communion that was created between Eric and myself. It was good to be together. And because Eric was relaxed, it made me feel more relaxed. He has complete trust in the person who gives him a bath. He is completely abandoned. He no longer defends himself. He feels secure because he senses he is respected and loved. The way he welcomed me, the way he trusted me, called forth trust in me. Yes, Eric called me forth to greater gentleness and respect for his body and his being. He called forth in me all that is best. His weakness, his littleness, his yearning to be loved touched my heart and awakened in me unsuspected forces of love and tenderness. I gave him life; he also gave me life. These moments of communion are the revelation that God has created deep bonds between us'.

For me one of the most memorable experiences of l'Arche was that of watching two young men eating a meal together. They were both in their early twenties, both dark-haired and bearded, but one was bright-eyed and in this world's terms good-looking. The other, with wasted limbs and a body that did not hide his suffering, was a physically distorted reflection of the first. Severely disabled, he could not so much as swallow without a guiding hand to close his mouth and tilt his head backwards. Throughout that long and difficult meal what passed between those two was very much more than the small spoonfuls of food so gently delivered and so silently but appreciatively received. For me it brought a new and potent actuality to the word 'communion'.

Those who stay in l'Arche, Jean Vanier believes, are responding to the cry for communion which, 'whether perceived as such or not, is very close to the things of God'. Most people in the communities, be they atheist or agnostic, Hindu or Christian, can sooner or later identify with those quiet moments in which deep bonds are created. So it is that l'Arche is lived on many levels: on a level which is very tangible and physical and on a level so inexpressible that even to attempt to put the experience into words is, as one assistant put it, 'in some way to set fire to it'.

Not all relationships with mentally disabled people are as obviously characterised by gentleness as those with Eric. Some mentally disabled people are enclosed in a world of depression and revolt, and are full of violence. Jean has cited the example of Pierre with whom he shared a home for a year and whose screams of anguish and violence awakened in him the realisation that he was capable of actually physically assaulting him. Both the call to communion and the awakening to violence confront us with the truth of our being, which is simultaneously beautiful and chaotic. We are all of us, Jean Vanier maintains, tired of competition and war. But we also all have in us shadows, violence and turmoil, which we fear but which we must discover and accept if we are to live in accordance with the truth of our being and use our energies to love.

Communion with both Eric and Pierre's awakening of our murky depths, also call us to prayer: communion with Eric brings us to a realisation of the deep meaning of communion with Jesus: 'Dwell in my love'. It brings us to the realisation that 'prayer does not consist simply of uttering words or of asking God to do things or even of simply praising him, but of living in his presence'. Similarly, when we 'touch' our own shadows, our own inner turmoil, our 'incapacity to love', prayer becomes 'a cry to the Holy Spirit to descend upon our chaos and gives it meaning and life: "Come Lord Jesus"'. In discovering their wounded humanity, Jean Vanier maintains, assistants also discover the desire for Jesus to bring about the healing of hearts.

I have said that not everyone in l'Arche would lay claim to any particular religious belief, but it is also true that most assistants who stay for any length of time acknowledge the call to some form of prayer. Before a humanly speaking deformed face can be seen as extraordinarily beautiful there are often many barriers to be surmounted, there is a great deal of 'living with' to be done. The rich person in each one of us will find every possible excuse not to go to the wedding feast. The poor person cries out for love and understanding, but to respond seriously to that cry means in some way dying to ourselves: to our comforts, wealth, leisure, reputation, success, and possibly even our family and friends. It means becoming poor ourselves, not externally but internally. It means feeling ourselves poor in the presence of the poor and so being 'reduced', in the deepest meaning of the word, to prayer. As Mother Teresa expressed it: 'Self knowledge puts us on our knees.'

Precisely because of the very quality of relationship called for, life in l'Arche entails, like the Missionary of Charity commitment to loving Christ in the distressing disguise of the dying of Calcutta or the vagrants of New York, the capacity to see with the eyes of the heart – the ability to look contemplatively.

'Jesus calls his followers to love, to love one another as he loves them,' says Jean Vanier; 'not just to love others as one loves oneself. He proposes something new: to love one another with the very love of God; to see them with the eyes of the Lord. And we can only see and love them like Jesus if we have an experience in faith of Jesus loving us with a liberating love. It is only then that we can open ourselves up and become vulnerable and grow to greater openness to others and give our lives'.

Ever since the Word became flesh and dwelt among us, Jean Vanier reasons, there has been no opposition between the spiritual and the human. Jesus came to reveal to us the beauty and importance of our humanity. And l'Arche is profoundly human. Its aim is to give back to the person with the disability, the humanity that has been stolen from him or her through rejection; to enable disabled people and assistants alike to find a place in the human community, to exercise their gifts, to live a relationship with others in which they are more fully themselves.

At the same time, at the very heart of l'Arche lies the mystery of the presence of Jesus at the heart of humanity, in the poor and the weak. Among the biblical references that are regarded as 'foundation texts' for l'Arche are the words of St Luke and St Mark: 'Whoever welcomes one such child in my name welcomes me' (Luke 9:48; Mark 9:37), and the same words of St Matthew's Gospel as are so fundamental to the spirituality of Mother Teresa: 'Just as you did it to one of the least of these who are members of my family, you did it to me' (Matthew 25:40).

These mysterious words of Jesus, Jean Vanier says, mean that the welcoming of the poor person is sacramental, if we live that encounter with faith in Jesus.

Despite the diversity of religious expression, central also to life in l'Arche is the Eucharist. 'It is very clear to me,' Jean Vanier states, 'that the Eucharist is at the very heart of every community that is body-centred, and maybe every community should be body-centred.' And he relates this to another of those 'gentle moments':

> 'About two and a half years ago we welcomed a guy who was very disturbed. He couldn't stay still. We were using a lot of words with him, but then we discovered that he had athlete's foot and the doctor told us to wash his

feet three times a day. There was a transformation. His language became more coherent when we were washing his feet. There is something about the touch of the body, holding the body, respecting the body. That is the initial communication. We forget that, and yet that is at the heart of everything. Somewhere that brings us very close to the whole relationship between the Word and the Eucharist.'

'Then,' he adds, 'as you touch the Eucharistic body you touch the division of the churches, the pain, but then maybe you're touching the whole mystery of the broken body of Jesus.'

Jesus in the broken bodies of the poor, Jesus broken as bread in the Eucharist, and a mysterious relationship between the two – we move into the realm of that which defies the rational and the verbal. Yet this relationship is sensible, to those who would perceive it, in the way in which the stillness about the chapels and the oratory at Trosly is so clearly not separated from the reality of brokenness that is so much part of our world. During the daily Mass which is celebrated there, there is somehow a profound message in the relationship between the broken bread upon the altar and the broken but life-giving presence of the disabled people who may shuffle their feet, comb their hair or yawn uninhibitedly, but whom no one could judge to be irreverent.

Furthermore, precisely because we have moved into the realms that defy the rational and the verbal, perhaps we have also left behind us the level at which people are divided. It is part of the experience of l'Arche that the broken bodies and wounded hearts and minds of disabled people have drawn together and made whole many who might otherwise have remained divided. People with a mental disability have a way of leading us to the discovery that deeper even than our religious faith or the lack of it, lies our common humanity.

When l'Arche began in Muslim and Hindu parts of the world, Jean Vanier was brought very swiftly to the realisation that the tears and sufferings of a mother faced with a severely disabled child were the same whatever her religion.

And the unspoken call to awakened hearts knows no rationally based divisions.

Before the Gulf war, l'Arche had opened a community in the Muslim quarter of Bethany in Cisjordania. There they welcomed Ghadir, a young Muslim girl who was profoundly mentally disabled. She had, in the words of Jean Vanier 'an astonishing beauty and gentleness'. ' She touched and awakened the hearts of all those around her, and in her weakness and her trust she created communion between Muslims and Christians.'

Mentally disabled people do not respond to the thinking, the ideology, the articulacy, the beliefs or status of the person before them, but to his or her heart. So it is that their open hearts have a way of cutting straight through the preoccupations of others around them. They do not, for example, understand the divisions that exist between the would-be followers of Christ. Instead they simply call to a growth in love in a manner which is as universal as the vulnerability of human hearts.

L'Arche does not welcome mentally disabled people because they belong to any particular religion but because they are suffering from rejection. This has led it quite spontaneously down a road of ecumenism and inter-faith sharing. Each l'Arche community, Jean Vanier states, is ecumenical, in the sense that it is open to the welcome of people of other religious beliefs, respecting their particular journey in faith. At the same time, because l'Arche does not want to set itself apart from the rest of society, all persons, according to their desires and their potential, need to be rooted in their own church or religious tradition. So it is that l'Arche communities incorporating people of different Christian traditions in England and elsewhere have had to confront the sometimes painful necessity of sharing a life in community which has at its heart the Eucharist, but in the course of which they cannot actually receive the same sacraments. Faced with this reality, Jean Vanier nevertheless holds out a vision of unity which is open to all :

'The broken Body of the Church is the source of so many tears. Maybe today Christians are not fully one in their beliefs, their organisation and their structures. But they can be one in their love and in their yearning to follow Jesus, not always knowing the path ahead, which will be revealed little by little by the Spirit. They can be one as together they walk down the ladder with Jesus, meeting Jesus in the poorest and weakest.'

We cannot always, therefore, share in the same Eucharistic table, taking communion together, but we can all love each other, drink from the same cup of suffering and live in a communion of hearts.

L'Arche cannot work for the unity of Christians through theological meetings, but it can live this communion of hearts.

'It is true,' says Jean Vanier, 'that Christians of different traditions cannot drink today from the same chalice of the blood of Christ but we can all drink together from the same chalice of suffering: the sufferings of division, of brokenness in our world. Together we can pour the sweet oil of compassion on the wounds of humanity. Unity will come only around the treasure of the body of Jesus, his broken, rising body hidden in the Eucharist, but also through the treasure of the broken body of Jesus in the poor.'

Is not this, he asks, the most direct path to unity?

Brother Roger

Christian unity – of the four people we are looking at, Brother Roger of Taizé must surely be the one most specifically concerned with that issue. The son of a Swiss Protestant pastor, in 1940, Roger Schutz crossed the border into war-ravaged France to attempt to live out a vision of reconciliation in the tiny village of Taizé. At a time when Europe was torn asunder, Roger had asked himself why such conflict should exist between people in general, and particularly between Christians. He found himself called to establish a community in which reconciliation and peace would be made concrete day by day. Central to Brother Roger's vision of the community life he and the others who he hoped in time would join him would lead was the Christian directive to prepare the way of the Lord, and the desire to live out the words of St John's Gospel: 'Be one . . . that the world may believe' (17:21).

Roger's father had wanted him to study theology and go into the ministry. He himself had seriously considered a career as a writer. Instead he tells us how a point came when 'I found myself as if impelled to do everything I could to build a community life in which reconciliation would be realised day by day. To begin with I must start a life of prayer alone. I would find a house where there would be prayer in the morning, at midday and in the evening and I would take in those who were fleeing, those in hiding.' Once again we find the experience of knowing what he must do, a knowing which is non-rational and flies in the face of 'our little minds'.

The fruits of the step in the dark which Roger somehow knew he must take were to exceed all rational expectations. His father, himself a man of profound faith, feared that his son would end his days alone. In 1940, at the age of twenty-four Brother Roger himself dimly envisaged only a community of perhaps twelve or thirteen men. That community is now made up of some ninety brothers from more than twenty-five countries and from Protestant, Catholic and Orthodox churches. Tens of thousands of young people flock to what was once a deserted cluster of farm buildings on the undulating hills of Burgundy. Thousands more attend the meetings which take place annually in different European cities. Manifestly, people of a wide variety of Christian traditions and of other faiths also have responded to Brother Roger's vision of 'reconciliation'.

Brother Roger has, he acknowledges, always been attracted to a mystical vision of the church, that place of communion between God and humanity, the mystical body of God made human because he so loved the world and in order that all might know the truth of the resurrected Christ. The church, he insists, is the presence of the resurrected Christ in the lives of humanity. This presence creates a communion that is both visible and hidden at one and the same time. Such a vision is not easily expressed. Christ as the church is, he recognises, sometimes a little distant, a mystery, a veiled reality often perceived only in its reflection. Only from time to time, through people, events, encounters, through a word or an experience, the veil is lifted.

What Brother Roger and his Brothers set out to live, he describes as a 'parable of communion' – a parable because it is, in the Sunday school definition of the word, 'an earthly story with a heavenly meaning', i.e. its aim is to point to a reality greater than and beyond itself. For Brother Roger Christ is 'communion'. His quest for Christian unity must be seen in the context of this vision. It is an attempt to bring together the separated members of the body of Christ, the quest for the visible unity of the body of Christ.

When Brother Roger began life at Taizé the ecumenical movement had scarcely begun. The first handful of Brothers, who were Protestants, encountered grave difficulties in relation merely to the use of the local Catholic village church, despite the fact that in the wake of the French Revolution it had fallen into total disuse. Permission was granted for the Brothers to use it for their prayer only on condition that they did not allow Catholics to share in their worship. Yet the calling of the embryo community at Taizé was through their life together to communicate 'the little bit of Gospel they had grasped', to communicate 'something of Christ'.

It was through the intervention of the Cardinal Archbishop of Lyon, in whose diocese in the early 1950s the ecumenical movement was taking some of its first tentative steps, that Brother Roger made his initial contact with the Vatican. There is still wonder in his voice today when he speaks of how as a young Protestant Brother he came to meet, first Pope Pius XII and then Pope John XXIII, the man who may be said to have had more impact than any other on the developing community. 'We shall never have totally clear vision on this earth,' Brother Roger says of him, 'but that man lifted the veil a little for us.' John XXIII confirmed Taizé in its vocation. 'The church', he told Brother Roger, who was seeking to see where, if anywhere, Taizé's place might be in relation to the universal church 'is ever widening concentric circles.'

The ultimate goal of the Second Vatican Council to which Brother Roger found himself invited as an observer, that of the unity of all Christians, was one which he embraced wholeheartedly. Pope John XXIII's words at its opening: 'Let us not seek to know who was right and who was wrong. Let us be reconciled' were an 'intuition' which he would carry with him for the remainder of his life. The Council also gave him the confidence to articulate the 'intuition' to which his own reading of the gospels had brought him, namely that the spirit of the resurrected Christ was present in all created beings.

I am reminded of a recent conversation with Brother Roger, when he said, 'If the gospel alone had told me that the Holy Spirit, the resurrected Christ, was linked to every human being, that everyone had in them this image, this reflection of his presence, I doubt that I would have dared to express such a view publicly or commit it to paper. But there was the Council and there were words that had been carefully reflected upon, meditated upon, and written down, words that I have lived by since, because they could be transmitted to others, namely: "Every human being is inhabited by the Spirit of the Resurrected Christ"'.

So it is that Brother Roger's vision of reconciliation extends far beyond the unity of Christians. His mystical vision of the church, of the body of Christ, encompasses not only those who live explicitly by his example but all people and all nations. At dusk in Bangladesh a Sufi once came to him. 'All people have the same master,' the Sufi announced.

'As yet it is still an unrevealed secret but later they will realise.' His words have remained with the founder of Taizé. 'In the heart of God,' Brother Roger says, 'the church is as large as all the world.'

As it transpired, the apparent promise of the Second Vatican Council in relation to the ecumenical movement was to fall short of fulfilment. To quote Brother Roger again:

'In the sixties, on the announcement of the Council and at its opening, we were as if transported to another place in which everything seemed possible. In very large numbers we were going to live, having one same thought, one same faith, one same hope, one same understanding in this communion that is the church, Christ in his communion. And certainly a change has come about. But already by the second session of the Council the idea suggested itself to me that in our various denominations we were merely oiling the wheels to run on parallel tracks. Over the years wonderful friendships have been born, much greater understanding between people belonging to different religious traditions has come about, ecumenical groups have undertaken valuable research. Nevertheless, these same good people, on parting company from each other, have a tendency to revert to the ways that have been theirs ever since the days of historic separations.'

Yet the imperative to be reconciled remains. Brother Roger frequently cites the words of St Matthew's Gospel: 'So when you are offering your gift at the altar, if you remember that your brother or sister has something against you, leave your gift there before the altar and go; first be reconciled to your brother or sister, and then come and offer your gift.' (Matthew 5:23-24).

Furthermore, listening to young people in particular has intimated to him that some have difficulty in understanding a call to be part of a church of oppositions and separation. He is reluctant to say so too emphatically but there is a fear in him that unless the separated members of the body of Christ can be reconciled, then Christ in the form of his church may find himself once more abandoned.

Yet he remains convinced that the path forward is not closed. Brother Roger puts his trust (and trust is a key word at Taizé) in the mystery of the transfiguration, the process by which God penetrates those places within us that are hardened, incredulous, even disquieting, with the life of his Spirit and so transforms them. He traverses them to give them his face – he 'transfigures'.

Brother Roger also puts his trust in the conviction that 'living charity' is greater even than hope and faith. In love, in living charity, he maintains, there is always a response; the way can never be closed. 'There are currently blockages which exist between groups, between schools of theological thought, but let us not be too overwhelmed by them. Rather let us seek new ways.'

The trust that a way will open never leaves us, he says. 'I tell myself: "So we haven't been able to find that reconciliation of all religious persuasions in the one unique communion that is the Church. Well perhaps it is simply a case of seeking within ourselves to be ferments of communion."'

Brother Roger refers us to 'a little way which can only be a personal step, an inner way, a way of reconciliation within oneself', 'a hidden way, rooted in the secret of the Gospel, a way of forgiveness'.

Without humiliating anyone, without becoming a symbol of denial for anyone, it is possible to embrace within oneself the attention to the word of God so profoundly lived in the Reformed churches, and the treasures of the spirituality of the Orthodox churches with all the charisms of communion of the Catholic Church, daily putting one's trust in the Mystery of Faith.

Texts have their value for him, as does the intellect and indeed theology, but ultimately, Brother Roger feels, reconciliation is a question of love because 'It is by loving that we discover the mystery of God in his communion, we understand eternal life, the resurrection – solely through love'.

It is by loving that we transcend the rational and find communion: 'If only people could see that God gives us a mystical vision of communion in the church, the body of Christ and it is by this route that we shall understand and not by confrontations over what the visible church is today.' We come back then to a mystical vision of the Church and to a way which lies beyond the rational and beyond words.

More overtly than Mother Teresa and Jean Vanier, Brother Roger speaks in the language of 'intuition', 'dreams' and 'signs', of 'feeling' and 'sensing' rather than of 'thinking'. 'Intuition' is an underlying principle of the history of Taizé. It is primarily by 'intuition', Brother Roger has said, that we penetrate the mystery of faith. Asked what intuition means to him, he says: 'the ability to understand events, situations, another person, by means other than reason, a slightly mysterious ability in us which enables us to understand, grasp, even to see beyond.' Intuition, perhaps I might add, is that faculty of 'knowing what we know without knowing how we know it or, sometimes, how to express it'.

Each of the individuals mentioned has his or her own distinctive vocabulary, the result of their own personality and social, cultural, educational conditioning, and this vocabulary quite naturally has a tendency to be assumed by those who live and work with them. Mother Teresa for whom English is a second language had virtually only one positive adjective, i.e. 'beautiful'. Jean Vanier who holds a doctorate in philosophy, whose English is strongly coloured by his French Canadian background and whose French is similarly coloured by the strong English influences in his life, speaks in a very distinctive way of blockages and passages, and in images such as 'the wolf at the door of the wound' which are meaningful to those familiar with the sources from which they are drawn but are less readily comprehensible to the uninitiated. Brother Roger, who dictated poems to one of his seven sisters before he was old enough actually to commit them to paper himself, and who repeatedly emphasises the importance of the fact that he and his brothers are 'poets', draws his imagery from the natural world with which he has a spontaneous affinity (a world of deserts, springs, lights, shadows, etc.), and he speaks in the manner of one who is constantly dissatisfied with his capacity to make what he 'knows' understood to others through words.

His mode of expression is often poetic, possibly because poetry is the language which points most effectively beyond itself. And it is perhaps interesting to note that for all their differences of vocabulary Mother Teresa found and Jean Vanier often assumed a certain poetic quality when endeavouring to give expression to what they both 'knew/know', to the reality perceived with the eyes of the heart, e.g. Mother Teresa: 'Joy is a net of love by which we can catch souls.' (This is quite unlike her ordinary speech). Jean Vanier has written entire books in the form of blank verse, structured, to use his own words, 'as if in diminishing circles which spiral down, trying to pick up threads and delving ever deeper'.

In Brother Roger's case, he is also very obviously acutely conscious of the potential of words to divide and to hurt.

The Eucharist occupies a very central position in the life of the community at Taizé – 'Because,' Brother Roger believes, 'the gospel makes us attentive to this mysterious presence of Christ specially offered in the Eucharist'. He frequently cites the 'intuition' of the Orthodox Patriarch Athenagoras, who on the occasion of one of their meetings raised his hands as if lifting the chalice in a gesture which Brother Roger would never forget. Twice the Patriarch then repeated: 'The cup and the breaking of bread – there is no other solution, remember that'. Yet other than by such indirect references, the Taizé community *says* little about the Eucharist.

In 1962, in response to the unexpected influx of large numbers of young people who came to the hillside of Taizé to pray, the community was obliged to erect a building large enough to provide shelter for the worship. It has since had to be extended at various junctures and now incorporates both an Anglican and an Orthodox Chapel. A paper displayed at the entrance to this vast Church of Reconciliation explains in six languages the arrangement for the receipt of communion at Taizé:

'Catholic Mass is celebrated each day in different places. The Blessed Sacrament is reserved next to the icon of the Virgin Mary. It is from there that the Catholic Communion is distributed every morning.

For those from the churches of the Reformation, the Lord's Supper is celebrated every day. Every morning, they can receive the Lord's Supper at the entrance to the Anglican Chapel, to the right of the icon of the Resurrection.

Orthodox Mass is celebrated periodically.

For those who do not receive communion there is blessed bread which everyone can receive.'

The provision of blessed bread for those who, for a variety of reasons, do not feel it right to receive the Sacraments, based on Orthodox practice and also, in a manner which Brother Roger considers significant, on ancient custom in certain local Burgundian Catholic parishes, is an indication of the degree to which Taizé is concerned that no one should feel themselves excluded from the faith.

The centrality of the Eucharist at Taizé is related to the vision of Christ as a communion of love. The concern is always that the love of Christ should be rendered accessible to all. If, therefore, the community chooses to speak little about the subject, it is in order not to create unnecessary barriers. In the experience of the Brothers, sometimes words provoke emotive debate and division in a manner in which silence does not. Even the use of the word 'Eucharist' as opposed to words with stronger denominational overtones is an attempt to avoid separation. The fact remains, however, that it is a subject which does give rise to questions, both amongst the young people who come to Taizé and amongst visiting clergy. The question is not infrequently raised as to why the community chooses, other than on Sundays, to distribute the reserved sacrament during the morning prayer rather than to celebrate the mass or communion. The response to this query is that this practice is drawn from an ancient tradition in the church whereby the Eucharist was celebrated once a week and administered to the heads of households who afterwards took away the consecrated sacrament and distributed it to their families. Beyond this reference to long-standing tradition, Taizé endeavours to avoid debate.

People still sometimes ask when receiving the sacraments whether they are Catholic or Protestant. The answer given is that they are the love of Christ. It is then up to the individual whether or not he/she welcomes and receives that love. As Brother Roger repeatedly reminds young people (and the not so young) on a spiritual search, in the words of the first epistle of John: 'In this is love, not that we loved God but that he loved us and sent his Son to be the atoning sacrifice for our sins' (1 John 4:10).

So it is that one Russian Orthodox priest I recently met at Taizé could respond by saying, 'Taizé in my eyes symbolises what Christian love should be. The love born of the gospels. Each person arrives and leaves here with his or her own faith. Ecumenism does not consist of the confusion of rites. We each celebrate the Eucharist after our own fashion. But we communicate together in the feeling of love, friendship and mutual support.' So it is also that Hindus and Muslims have been drawn to Taizé albeit not as yet in very large numbers.

The emphasis at Taizé is generally placed strongly on listening rather than on talking and certainly not on preaching. It is one of Brother Roger's characteristics that when he speaks, he speaks as if he is listening. Still real communication, it is felt, is often best achieved through what Brother Roger calls, 'a kind of osmosis', through lived example. When Brother Roger does endeavour to communicate verbally the 'little bit of the Gospel he has grasped' to young people seeking to understand, it is often in the form of a letter, distributed throughout the world, and offered as a source of reflection and contemplation rather than as instruction. When the Taizé Brothers suggested to one prominent theologian that they would like to increase the number of such letters, he advised them instead to write as little as possible, because he said: 'For all their differences, those who come here for the communal prayer, do not argue. Quite the opposite. They are pleased to discover each other but if you once get involved in explanations, you will trigger defence mechanisms.'

Thus what the community lives is allowed to a very large extent to speak for itself, and what the brothers live revolves around and draws its energy and spiritual sustenance from the thrice daily common prayer.

The distinctive Taizé songs which form a significant part of this worship and which have become familiar in so many different parts of the world do not require much explanation. They are made up of simple sentences sung in various languages to easily accessible music, and repeated over and over again. In the great tradition of the prayer of repetition, it is intended that the essential reality expressed in these tirelessly repeated refrains and invocations, should give time to 'feel and taste inwardly' the meaning beyond the words, that they should be easily grasped by the mind, gradually absorbed into the entire person and lead spontaneously to prayer.

At the heart of the thrice-daily prayer there is always a protracted silence because, in the words of Brother Roger: 'In that silence we discover that we don't need words in order to speak to God, because there is a language of love which transcends words, which is more a state of self abandonment, an inner acceptance of no longer knowing what to say, of no longer seeking to speak but allowing God to speak to us. Silent prayer allows us to go on making discoveries from one moment to the next.'

The ways to pray are many and varied, Brother Roger acknowledges, but I once asked him what prayer was for him. In the course of his answer he drew my attention to some words of Saint Augustine which he keeps pinned to the wall of his room: 'When the soul is open before God, we are silent and our heart speaks, not to the ears of men but to those of God.' 'In prayer,' Brother Roger told me, 'a communion is given which belongs to the realms of the invisible but through which our heart is touched.' Brother Roger has been profoundly touched by St Peter's reference to Jesus Christ in his first epistle: 'Although you have not seen him, you love him; and even though you do not see him now, you believe in him and rejoice with an indescribable and glorious joy' (1 Peter 1:8), and he believes resolutely in the importance of remaining open to the invisible.

Prayer, 'contemplation', is an essential part of this process of remaining open to the invisible. At the same time the mystical vision must be a lived reality. Love, communion, must be expressed. It must be rendered concrete and visible. It must not remain something intangible but be lived. Hence the search for simple symbolic expression which he sensed from the beginning was more meaningful than words, hence Taizé, hence the need for living charity.

As a small child, Brother Roger was deeply influenced by the example of his maternal grandmother. During the First World War, she lived in the North of France very close to where the fighting was conducted. Despite the fact that two small bombs actually fell on her home, she remained there with a daughter-in-law and grandchild, turning her home into a place of refuge for old people, pregnant women and children fleeing from the battle zone. When, as the invading armies drew nearer, she was finally induced to leave, she travelled with her refugees in a cattle truck to Paris and from there on to the Dordogne, where, faithful to her Protestant origins though she was, she used to attend Mass and even receive communion in the Catholic church. To the adult

Brother Roger, this grandmother became the embodiment of the quest for reconciliation, of being 'within herself the ferment of communion'. 'She did not seek to justify her action nor talk about it,' he has said, 'but I understood that by going to the Catholic church she was effecting an immediate inner reconciliation. She was also the embodiment of compassion, of "living charity"'.

There is a difference in emphasis here between Brother Roger and Mother Teresa and Jean Vanier. Brother Roger's primary calling was not so much to the 'poor' as to living the parable of communion. Living in communion with the poor, however, has always been of vital importance to him. 'I do not think that you can understand Taizé,' he has said, 'without appreciating our intense inner desire to be close to the poorest of the poor, to live with them in gospel simplicity.'

The village in which Brother Roger chose to begin his parable of communion was what he describes as a 'desert'. The vineyards which had once provided the livelihood for its inhabitants had been blighted by disease. Many of the men folk had had to travel elsewhere to find work and the people who remained subscribed more readily to Voltaire's philosophy than to Christian belief. The determining factor in his choice of this location was the request of a poor woman who provided the young stranger with a much needed meal. 'Stay here,' she urged him. 'We are so alone. There is no one left in the village and the winters are so long and cold.' Like Jean Vanier, like Mother Teresa, like his own father, Brother Roger insists upon the importance of listening to the voice of the poor, the weak and the frail, through whom the will of God is made known.

In relation to the actual life of the community, Brother Roger prefers the use of the word 'simplicity' to the more traditional commitment to 'poverty', because, he says, 'poverty' can sometimes be used in a 'romantic' way that has little to do with the Brothers' call to provide for those whom God entrusts to them and for themselves, through their own labours. Poverty is relative to so many different factors. Poverty might convey the idea of a life with others in which everything is given up to the simple beauty of God's creation; but poverty can also mean the destitution and wretchedness that he would not wish on anyone. Thus it was 'simplicity' of life that he recognised in the very beginning was essential, because, 'Comfort invariably distances us from the depths of the "invisible", from a creation in God'.

The desire to be close to the poorest of the poor, to live with them in gospel simplicity led, in the first instance, to the taking in of Jewish refugees. After the war the community welcomed the German prisoners of war held in nearby camps. They were to be succeeded by a multitude of others with needs of different kinds, including in more recent years children caught up in the conflict in Bosnia.

The same desire has led to the Brothers going out to share the lives of the poor elsewhere. In 1951 two brothers went to live and work in a poor mining area, thirty miles north of Taizé. At the beginning of the 1970s the community opened its first provisional 'fraternity' of a few brothers sharing the lives of poverty-stricken people elsewhere in the world. In time the community turned its attention to Latin America and several brothers began life in Recife, Brazil. Later, others went into New York's Hell's Kitchen, to Kenya and Korea. This year there are small groups of Brothers living in Bangladesh, in Alagoinhas, in Seoul, Calcutta and Dacca.

In the vision of Brother Roger, to live simply, in a mud hut, has a special way of underlining what he calls the state of contemplative expectation. Like Mother Teresa, Brother Roger sees in the 'simplicity' of the community's life (she would have used the word poverty) a means of remaining open to the action of the Holy Spirit (she actually called it the 'joyful insecurity of Divine Providence'). Living in close proximity to the 'poor' in both the northern and the southern hemispheres and listening to their needs has made him aware of the suffering that is part of the universal human condition. Together with Mother Teresa, he has often referred to the existence of not only the visible homes for the dying in countries such as India but also the 'invisible homes for the dying' of Western society, of those who are deeply wounded by broken relationships, psychological neglect and spiritual doubt. Listening in the Church of Reconciliation as he does towards the end of the evening prayer to young people from Eastern and Western Europe has made him acutely aware of the less visible but no less real suffering of those who pass through Taizé in numbers which have at time threatened to overwhelm the community but which the brothers recognise are calling them to live their life of communion in 'a certain transparency'. And so Brother Roger remains for the most part in a Europe with needs which he believes are no less profound than those of other continents, emphasising the necessity for the church, the visible body of Christ, to be a place of compassion in the true sense of the word, i.e. that of 'suffering with'.

Pope John Paul II on the occasion of his visit to Taizé in October 1986 referred to the community as a source or well. The image of a place at which to draw spiritual nourishment and then move on was one which struck a special chord of recognition in the community. For many years the Brothers have been encouraging young people to go out into the world from Taizé and assume active responsibility in their own countries, their own communities, their own parishes, to become what the community calls, 'the leaven of trust in the human family'.

Taizé does not wish to immobilise any more than it wishes itself to be immobilised. Prayer/contemplation should not immobilise. At the time of the Transfiguration, Brother Roger tells us: 'the apostles contemplate the transfigured Christ and they want to remain in this dazzling light, because they know they are experiencing a powerful moment in their lives. But they have to come back down from the mountain. And that is true for all believers: we have to come down to be a reflection of God, to be bearers of peace and reconciliation amongst the divisions that exist in the Christian family and the ruptures that prevail in the human family, so that through the light of Christ in us, even those who do not believe may be drawn, without their even knowing how, towards the hope of God.'

The state of contemplation is not one which is confined to set timetables of prayer. The prayer in the Church of Reconciliation is open-ended in the sense that it has no fixed conclusion. Young people often remain there to pray, long after the Brothers have left the building to pursue their activities elsewhere. Here then is the visible expression of the invisible continuity of prayer which spills over into the whole of the rest of life, and into the action which at Taizé is often referred to as 'struggle'. 'Prayer, if we listen to what is happening in our heart of hearts has a way of leading us to the discovery that we were made to be "inhabited by Another", and if we are made for that purpose so too must others be'. Verbally at least, Brother Roger arrives at the recognition of the presence of Christ in our neighbour from a slightly different 'angle' but the end result is the same – a growth in love, in living charity.

To the young people who come to him, eager to change the world through active intervention, Brother Roger insists that it is not a question of choosing between struggle and contemplation. Contemplation and struggle are dependants one of another. They are, he says, 'sisters'. 'Sometimes,' he states, 'contemplation is perceived as the opposite of action, as leading to passivity and a flight from responsibility. But the facts suggest otherwise: Christians who are actively intervening on behalf of others draw their energy from the well of contemplation. The Brothers remain vigilant in prayer without that meaning their distancing themselves in any way from reality. Our life is given to God through both contemplation and struggle and sometimes that struggle is more like a battle in a civilisation which is penetrated by death – the announcement of the death of God, where people are in tombs even if they are not actually seen to be. We have made a commitment to the poor but that does not in any way contradict our commitment to live in a state of contemplative expectation. . .'

Little sister Magdeleine

The relationship between the call to the contemplative life and the call to be 'in the midst of humanity' is central also to the vocation of the Little Sisters of Jesus, the Congregation founded by Little Sister Magdeleine in September 1939. Little Sister Magdeleine is relatively unknown to the English speaking world. She led an essentially hidden life. Yet when she died in 1989, she left a legacy of fourteen hundred Sisters from sixty-four nations and a multitude of friends of all creeds, nationalities and classes.

Born in France in 1898, Madeleine Hutin yearned from an early age to befriend the people of the Sahara, the Muslim people who had profoundly influenced her father while he was a doctor with the French army in North Africa. A devout Catholic from childhood, well before her first communion, she experienced a call to the religious life. The response to that call, however, was to be delayed for twenty years; four of them as a consequence of the war which decimated her family, ten more because of tubercular pleurisy. During those twenty years of waiting, the one source of illumination was, she claimed, her reading of René Bazin's biography of Charles de Foucauld, the explorer and priest who spent many years sharing the life of the suffering people of the Sahara and who, shortly before the books' publication, had become the unresisting victim of rebels in Tamanrasset, Southern Algeria.

In the life and death of Charles de Foucauld, Madeleine Hutin found the ideal of which she had been dreaming: 'The gospel lived, total poverty, a life in the very midst of a people who were otherwise forgotten . . . and above all love in all its fullness: Jesus-caritas, Jesus-love.

Finally, what Little Sister Magdeleine referred to as 'the hour of God' came, in a manner which was to reinforce in her the conviction she shared with Charles de Foucauld that Jesus was 'Master of the impossible'. She had for some years been teaching at a Sacred Heart school in Nantes. The damp climate of Nantes did not, however, suit her and in March 1935 she began to experience pains which became so intense that she was obliged to give up all her activities. The final verdict of her doctor was that she would find herself crippled by acute arthritis unless she leave immediately for a place where it never rained. Both Madeleine Hutin and her spiritual director of the time, took this as a confirmation of her vocation to go to the Sahara. In October 1936, with very little notion of what lay ahead, together with her first companion and her elderly widowed mother, Madeleine Hutin set sail for Algiers and the 'land of Islam'. God, she maintained, 'had taken her by the hand' and she merely 'followed blindly'.

Here again is one for whom spirituality is not a question of thinking, reasoning and logic but of transcending rational thought. Little Sister Magdeleine was manifestly not one who came to know God through clear images and careful argument. She was essentially a very practical down-to earth woman, the kind of woman who could turn herself into builder, carpenter or plasterer as occasion demanded, and who was concerned with the mundane details of everyday living to a point which those around her sometimes found difficult to tolerate. Little Sister Magdeleine had a deep-rooted distrust of what she termed 'extraordinary ways'. Yet her life and the history of her Congregation were to be shaped by non-rational convictions, by inner lights and intuitions which she herself seems not fully to have understood and which left her constantly questioning and turning to the church and its representatives for confirmation.

Her letters and journals are full of references to feelings, intuitions, sudden realisations, the 'knowledge' that she must do something even though in human terms that action might be folly (human folly may be divine wisdom). And on the basis of her 'blind following', the extraordinary was to be accomplished despite, or perhaps precisely through, her fallibility and her weakness (although, mysteriously, ill health was not really to prove a serious problem for her again until her very old age).

It was in Sidi Boujnan, a small village nestling on a sand-dune overlooking the vastness of the desert, that she began the first of what she called 'fraternities'. The Arabs had referred to Charles de Foucauld's modest dwelling as a 'fraternity' and Little Sister Magdeleine wished to continue the associated ideas of 'brotherly' love for all human beings, of gentleness towards even the most arrogant or unjust, of kindness to all those in need. Sidi Boujnan was to be the first of many such fraternities. Initially 'those in need' took the form of the nomads suffering dreadfully from the absence of food in wartime Algeria. In time they would assume a multi-tude of other forms, be it that of the pygmies of Papua New Guinea, the prostitutes of Marseilles, or the factory workers of Leeds.

After the example of Charles de Foucauld, Little Sister Magdeleine urged her Sisters, 'You should choose to live among the poorest and most forgotten, where no one else would go': among nomads or other ignored or disregarded minorities. 'Look at the map of the world and see if you can find a handful of people scattered over a large territory and difficult to reach for those with a different form of aposto-late. You must really choose to go there, otherwise no one else may ever come to tell them that Jesus loves them, that he suffered and died for them – the lost sheep.'

The love of the Heart of Jesus was so great that it took in the whole world, Little Sister Magdeleine maintained. To return this love her Little Sisters must be ready to go to the ends of the earth. They were to do so 'crying the Gospel' – not, however, by their words but by their very life. Her Sisters were to be a 'smile upon the world', reflecting the love of God without proselytising, and recognising that it would very often be the poor who would evangelise them, who would reveal Jesus to them, rather than the other way round.

Little Sister Magdeleine was not one who made a spectacle of her spirituality or even spoke very much about her prayer life. In fact towards the end of her life she was seen to enter the chapel so infrequently that one young novice actually questioned whether the foundress ever prayed. It is only since her death that more has become known about the hidden inspiration of her life.

For a variety of reasons – her own fear of having been the subject of illusion, her mistrust of the powers of an over-active imagination, her reluctance to encourage others to pursue the 'extraordinary ways' which she found profoundly suspect – Little Sister Magdeleine said nothing of this inspiration other than to Father Voillaume, her spiritual director of many years and founder of the Little Brothers, and to one Little Sister. She certainly never used the claim to a privileged mystical experience to lend significance, grandeur or weight either to herself or to what she sought to express.

In 1937, however, during her own noviciate and before the actual foundation of her new congregation, she underwent a series of experiences which two years later, she confided to Father Voillaume in his capacity of representative of the Church, and thus of Christ. She had, she told him in a letter, gone to bed one night feeling frightened and upset:

> 'And suddenly I found myself in an inner courtyard which, by a strange coincidence, resembled the one in the noviciate. I can still see it as though it all happened only yesterday. Two or three holy persons, whom I did not know, were walking before me . . . and at the end of the courtyard on the right was the Blessed Virgin, holding the infant Jesus in her arms – an infant Jesus such as I could never have imagined in my life, for it surpassed all human

vision. I cannot even describe it because I cannot find any other words for it than 'light', 'gentleness' and, above all, 'love'. And the Blessed Virgin was preparing to give him to someone. What anguish! I was absolutely sure she would not give him to me, because my heart and soul were not pure enough to receive such a favour; and I stood back, crying more than ever because of my unworthiness. I didn't dare look – and yet, drawn to do so despite myself, I was more and more stupefied to see the first, then the second, then the third person pass in front of the Virgin Mary without noticing anything. They were in such a state of pious recollection, but I would have liked to shout at them to look. So I found myself all alone in front of this vision and . . . it was to me that the Blessed Virgin gave the little child Jesus she was holding. After that I no longer thought about my sins, but only of this joy which I cannot express in human words either. And in the great upsurging of my love I embraced and clasped the infant Jesus so closely to my heart that he became incorporated into me (and again this is something I don't know how to explain).'

Ten years later, she underwent a number of further experiences which this time took the form of participation in the Passion of Christ. Then she wrote to Fr. Voillaume of the crucifixion which she had relived 'with my eyes, in my whole being and with him, as if it were with my eyes but even more real than with my eyes, as if I were hearing it with my ears, but even more real than that'.

Whatever the objective reality of these experiences, whatever the criticisms to which they might render her prone at the level of human sensibility (criticisms which she was quite prepared to accept), they were undoubtedly the fruits of an extraordinary love for God. Equally undoubtedly they had a profound effect upon the spirituality of the congregation.

The experience of the 'incorporation' of the Christ child into her, centred her spiritual life on a particular aspect of the life of Jesus and pointed the way to the special focus of the congregation she founded. 'Always remain,' she directed her sisters, 'Little Sisters of no account, and when you are tempted to forget that, look at the crib of Bethlehem and the tiny child Jesus who was the true founder of the Little Sisters of Jesus.'

Throughout her life Little Sister Magdeleine maintained the importance of constant reference to the infant Jesus in the manger because there was to be found the truth of the whole life of Christ, the God made man in all his vulnerability and surrender. 'Perhaps you did not really stop to look at the crib, or maybe you just looked at it rather disdainfully, as an adult who thinks that the crib is for children and that it has no meaning other than at Christmas time,' she wrote to her sisters. 'You looked longer at the cross. There you found something bigger and more satisfying for your adult years.' And yet: 'This crib is something so beautiful and great because it contains the whole Christ, God and man together. And in the extension of this cradle there is the workshop of Nazareth, the passion and cross, and all the glory of the resurrection and of heaven itself.'

When Little Sister Magdeleine committed to paper the spiritual basis for her congregation, she attributed much of it to the inspiration of Charles de Foucauld. There is, however, a section in what is known as the 'Green Bulletin', in which she sets down 'the ideal' of the congregation, to which she lays more personal claim. This section contains her reflections on spiritual childhood, the state of having the eyes and the heart of a child, a spiritual obligation for all those who would enter the kingdom of heaven. 'Look at the crib and do not be put off by the childish ways in which it is sometimes pictured . . . Instead may you see in the crib only your God who is calling you to follow him and to become as a little child in total self surrender . . .' 'Childlike in heart,' she assures them, 'you will receive the little infant Jesus of the manger from the Virgin Mary his Mother.'

Little Sister Magdeleine's personal 'legacy' also includes the call to bear witness to Jesus by living in the midst of mankind as leaven in the dough and her ideal of bringing the contemplative vocation into the midst of the everyday life of humanity.

What Little Sister Magdeleine felt called to live was radical in its failure to maintain the traditional separation between religious life and the world. In order to bear witness to the love of a God who had so loved the world that he assumed the form of a vulnerable baby born in Bethlehem, her Sisters were to live in the midst of humanity as the leaven in the dough (an ideal which has also found a special resonance in the Taizé community and its fraternities). And, like the leaven which must lose itself in the dough to make it rise, the Little Sisters of Jesus were to become one with, or one of those they sought to serve.

They were to have only one model: Jesus, and like Jesus during his life on earth they were to make themselves 'all things to all people'. An Arab in the midst of Arabs, a nomad amongst nomads, a worker amongst working people, but, above all, they were to be human amongst their fellow human beings. They were in fact to be human before religious, for God, 'by making himself one of us, although he was divine, exalted our human nature by taking on our humanity'. As Little Sisters of Jesus, they must always subordinate the exterior rules of their religious life to living the Gospel. They were to put charity/love above all rules, because love was the greatest commandment of Jesus.

They were also to know how to keep 'interior silence' and to practise 'interior prayer' in the midst of all that went on around them. They must, despite the outer appearances of leading an 'apostolic' life, be truly contemplative. The contemplative life, Little Sister Magdeleine maintained, would be 'all the more luminous and fruitful', precisely because they had chosen to be plunged into the activity of everyday life.

As the tiny fraternities spread across the continents, 'everyday life' for the Little Sisters could mean travelling on the backs of lorries, living in a caravan or a mud hut, hitch-hiking, or working their passage on ships by helping to chop the vegetables for more privileged passengers. The Little Sisters became gypsies amongst the gypsies, prisoners amongst the imprisoned, circus-travellers with the circus-travellers. They lived amongst the victims of conflict and war and they became one of them.

In such circumstances, without the contemplative dimension, Little Sister Magdeleine stated as emphatically as Mother Teresa, her Sisters would not be able to live up to all that was asked of them. Mother Teresa too, urged her Sisters to be 'contemplatives in the midst of the world'. The Missionaries of Charity, however, although formally established some ten years after the Little Sisters of Jesus, are more traditional in the separation of their community life from the life of those they seek to serve. They have carefully structured times of community prayer. Their meals are taken separately from those they serve. At the end of a rigorous working day they withdraw to their convents. For the Little Sisters of Jesus, the requirement to place charity above all else and to make of their homes 'houses of Nazareth', places of joy, peace and welcome at all times, means that, as for the assistants in l'Arche who may find a mentally disabled person sitting on the end of their bed in the middle of the night, there is little or no physical withdrawal. The Little Sisters have a flexible daily rhythm of prayer but even during the time set aside for adoration of the Blessed Sacrament and the Eucharist upon which their lives are centred, they are to be available to those who seek their friendship.

In 1947 Father Voillaume ventured to say to Little Sister Magdeleine, of a vow ceremony attended by numerous guests, that as the sisters' ideal was contemplative the occasion should perhaps have been a more contemplative one. With what he himself later described as the 'reasoning of a churchman of the day' he added that a life of contact with people should not really be called 'contemplative' and that she should not juggle with words. 'Words which are the expression of an idea do not always have the same nuance of meaning,' Little Sister Magdeleine responded, 'no human language being rich enough to convey that idea, but they are enormously important . . . to change the word is to betray the idea.' 'The contemplative life,' she reminded him, 'you yourself have said it, is a life of friendship with the Person of Jesus, it is a much deeper inner life, in contact with God. Why should this friendship, this contact, not be able to co-exist with a call to souls, even a call to crowds?'

'Some people are surprised,' she wrote elsewhere, 'that the contemplative life can be lived to the full in crowded cities or on the highways as well as in a monastery, but think of Jesus, the greatest contemplative of all, think of the hidden life at Bethlehem and at Nazareth, of his public life on the roads. Jesus retired into the desert for only forty days, far from the crowds, while he lived thirty-three years among his people, simply as one of them.'

The 'contemplative vocation' was, she insisted, not an exceptional vocation, so elevated that most people could never come near it. In an attempt to define the 'essence of prayer' and the 'meaning of contemplation' she resorted, as she often did, to the spiritual writings of Charles de Foucauld:

'When we love someone, we want to speak to him endlessly. Prayer is nothing else; a familiar conversation with our Beloved. We gaze at him, we tell him we love him, we rejoice to be at his feet.'

'Praising God means to lose ourselves at his feet in words of admiration and love. It means to tell him in all the ways we know that he is infinitely perfect, infinitely worthy of love.'

In her own words she said simply that prayer was a life.

For her, contemplation was a state of intimacy between God and the soul, by no means confined to structured worship or dependent on rigid adherence to the external trappings of the religious life. This was not to dismiss the importance of such structures but it was to recognise that a contemplative vocation was as dependent on the free action of the Holy Spirit and the openness of a childlike heart turned constantly towards God, be it in the midst of the desert or on a factory production line.

She was not critical of other religious congregations who did not always subscribe to the same attitudes, attributing their differences to the fact that they had 'other aspects of the gospel to personify'. Yet Little Sister Magdeleine had to struggle for understanding and acceptance particularly from the church she loved and to which she sought always to be obedient. She struggled also for acceptance of the poverty of lifestyle she felt appropriate for her congregation. She wanted her Little Sisters to be able, without shocking any-one or being reproached for their lack of 'religious dignity', to live, be lodged and travel as the least of their brothers and sisters, 'like Jesus who lost none of his divine dignity by assuming the humanity of a poor craftsman'. She wanted them to be poor as Jesus had been, earning their living with their hands, without the dowries or income from capital which constituted the more usual source of security for religious congregations. She was repeatedly called upon to plead for this right. She struggled, too, for understanding of the absence of what the Church more usually recognised as religious ministry or 'works'. And she struggled for permission to have the Blessed Sacrament reserved in tents and caravans and mud huts in order that her tiny fraternities might themselves become tabernacles radiating the presence of Jesus (Mother Teresa also sees her foundations through-out the world as so many tabernacles), and she struggled at times for understanding simply as a human being . . .

There were certain aspects of her life which might have been better understood had she spoken of what lay at their source. Throughout her life Little Sister Magdeleine searched for an artist capable of reproducing, in the form of a statue of 'Our Lady of the Whole World', the double gesture of

Mary offering her child and of the infant Jesus holding out his arms, as though he himself were trying to escape from her hands in order to give himself to the world – the image of her 'vision/dream'. 'No one understands this gesture – forever deeply engraved as it is in my mind's eye, in my heart; I can't change it, Mary herself showed it to me,' she wrote in a notebook in 1944. It was an image full of movement and awkward to balance and Little Sister Magdeleine was never quite satisfied with numerous successive attempts by different artists to capture it. The precision of her requirements, which appeared to verge on the obsessive, would have been more readily comprehensible to some had they known of the powerful experience which lay at the roots of her exigencies, if they had realised fully that the details of the statue were important only in so far as they conveyed a profound spiritual message, the spirit which she believed to have been entrusted to her by God to pass on to her new Congregation.

This spirit was somehow not something which could be transmitted through words and was directed at the heart. 'People can't manage to understand that it is through the eyes that this devotion will enter into the heart', Little Sister Magdeleine wrote to Father Voillaume of her frustration.

Little Sister Magdeleine was acutely conscious of the pitfalls of words. In a manner which she privately protested was completely contrary to her nature, she was given to talking too much in public, and she suffered as a consequence. At the same time one senses in her as strongly as in Brother Roger the endeavour to express the ineffable through the concrete. 'Don't define, live.' Father Voillaume once wrote. This was in relation to the new understanding of the contemplative life and directed at his Little Brothers, but it seems also to have been an underlying principle of Little Sister Magdeleine's life. A deep inner life with God found its most articulate expression in something more concrete than words.

It was one of her heartfelt desires to have a fraternity of Little Sisters actually living in a tent amongst the nomadic peoples of the Sahara, tending their flocks with them and travelling with them to find fresh grazing. The realisation of this ideal after some years of struggle was a real triumph for her and when, years later, a new generation of sisters, found the foundress's deep attachment to it less readily comprehensible, their lack of understanding was a source of sadness.

Little Sister Magdeleine never actually said so, but through a multitude of intimations, once one has realised that much of what she actually sought to do with the fraternity has a symbolic language to it, it becomes clear that in a sense a nomadic life in a tent encapsulated all her intuitions and dreams. It was a life of extreme simplicity lived amongst some of the most forsaken people, in a relationship of reciprocity, in which if anything the Little Sisters were to find themselves even more vulnerable than the most marginalised who came and went between the tents with their news, their problems, and all the warmth of spontaneous relationships. It was a life devoid of barriers with only the thin, woven strips of camel and goat hair to separate the fraternity and the sacramental body of Jesus from their Muslim 'friends' and from the great contemplative silence of desert and sky. It was a life of total dependence on and surrender to the will of God amongst people for whom the expression 'inch'allah', 'God willing' was not only a *leitmotif* of conversation but also the guiding principle of their lives. It was a life from which the spiritual message must be inferred.

In her writings one can sense the presence of a constant though not explicitly defined relationship with God. And there are those who say the same about her physical presence. Interestingly enough, many who lived in close proximity to her for years had difficulty, when asked, in remembering the actual colour of her eyes. Instead they spoke of something else which shone through her gaze. In the early days of the congregation, she trudged the roads of war-time France with a small film depicting life with her nomad friends in Algeria and talked of her ideals, in the hope of raising funds for the first tiny fraternity. And young women came to join her, responding to the presence in her of what people variously described as 'a wind of the desert', 'the Holy Spirit', the 'love that shone from her', something which they sensed acting through her and on the strength of which they were prepared to offer their lives in 'immolation for the redemption of the people of Islam' and, if necessary, to die of starvation in the process.

It was not only Christians who responded to this sense that here was someone who was in deep inner contact with God. Her first companion at Sidi Boujnan felt in time that her calling was elsewhere. Her mother was unable to cope with the climate and living conditions, as were others who came to join her in a first rush of enthusiasm. For a while she found herself alone with the Arabs she had come to serve but upon whose friendship she became dependent. Like Charles de Foucauld before her, she was profoundly impressed by their faith and their worship. 'We love each other dearly,' she once wrote, 'my eyes tell them so.' In those early friendships, the human basis for much of what was to follow can be found. 'The Sister will go to heaven like us even if she doesn't say the *chahada*, because she loves us so. She gives us corn, barley, work, she is a companion to us, she has become an Arab.' Little Sister Magdeleine took this remark made by a nomad workman very much to heart. Her Arab friends responded to the fact that she struggled to provide food for them when they were starving, nursed them when they were sick, and defended their interests with the French colonial authorities. They also responded to her vulnerability and to something much more profound. Living and working along-side each other to build the first fraternity, in defiance of the climactic rigours of the desert, the Christian woman who spoke little Arabic and the Muslim desert people developed a friendship based on mutual respect and a love which had little need of words.

In 1992, many years after Little Sister Magdeleine had

paid her last visit to her friends at Sidi Boujnan, I had the opportunity to visit some of them. I remember one meeting in particular with a man who, as a boy, had helped Little Sister Magdeleine in her struggle to construct the fraternity. After listening to Tahar recounting the history of his relationship with her as if it had happened only yesterday, I found myself stating the obvious: 'It seems that she is still very present to you.' 'When a friendship is of God,' he replied, 'it lasts.' Had the fact that she was a foreign woman of a different religion never given rise to difficulties between them? 'She had her faith,' he replied, 'and we had ours. That was how it was.' God, he gave me to understand, was not interested in religious labels but in the manner in which we conduct ourselves. She had kept her holy day on Sunday and she had respected the fact that they kept theirs on Friday. There had been no attempt to 'convert' them. The respect that Little Sister Magdeleine insisted on affording every being with whose humanity Christ had identified himself so profoundly would not permit such an endeavour. Muslim or Christian, tramp or cardinal, every person was for her a brother or sister beloved of God. There was no tension between the avowed desire to offer oneself in immolation for the redemption of Islam and a profound respect for others. The two were both products of the same 'impulse of love'. So it was that she and her Muslim friends lived together in a unity which both 'parties', though very different, recognised was 'of God'.

It was specifically to these Muslim people that she had initially wanted the congregation to be consecrated. In 1946 at Sainte Baume, however, she experienced a 'sudden certainty' that the Fraternity was to spread throughout the world and become 'universal'. This time she knew that this certainty could only come from God, because it ran counter to her personal wishes. Here again was one of those intuitions, or what she on one occasion referred to as 'insights of the heart', which she could not or did not endeavour to explain but which she sought rather to turn into concrete reality. So it was that, 'knowing' that the congregation was to be 'universal', blindly following the 'Master of the impossible', having already travelled to more than forty countries and founded nearly a hundred fraternities, in 1953-4 she set off on a journey, literally round the world, seeking out always the lost sheep and leaving small numbers of sisters to live with them as one of them.

Significantly, what Little Sister Magdeleine stressed in her writings to Father Voillaume about what he describes as her 'supernatural experiences' was the transformation they wrought in her. The experience of the Passion in particular had, she felt, brought about 'a growth in love'. 'We never love enough and we can always love a little more,' she insisted. Manifestations of a lack of love became intolerable to her. Little Sister Magdeleine was no diplomat but she was acutely conscious of the potential of words to create barriers, abhorring the word 'foreigner' or the manner in which black was habitually imbued with negative associations. Words that might give offence, humour that was insensitive to the possible feelings of others, condescension, a lack of respect for anyone, rich or poor, weak or strong, became a deep source of personal sorrow, and she would clamp down on them firmly if she encountered them amongst her Little Sisters. She warned them against the risks of sentimentality but at the same time she directed them increasingly towards the goal of a universal love which could not accept divisions or barriers between people of different classes, milieux, nationalities or creeds. The yearning to see the relationship of reciprocity she had first experienced amongst the Muslim friends at Sidi Boujnan extended to all humanity became a persistent driving principle. 'Unity', she said, 'haunted' her. And, just as for her prayer was 'a life', so her 'dream' of unity must be lived. Hence the desire for fraternities in the Jewish quarter of Jerusalem and simultaneously in the Arab section, amongst both communities where people were at war. What was more, the idea was not simply to be a bridge or point of union between hostile peoples, e.g. the Tapirape Indians and the Caiapos, but to remain Tapirapes and as Tapirapes to love the Caiapos, their long-standing enemy.

Her ideal of unity had its Biblical roots in St John's Gospel: 'The glory that you have given me I have given them, so that they may be one, as we are one' (17:22). It was this ideal which determined that nowhere could be accepted as inaccessible to the love of God – not even the Iron Curtain countries. By the 1950's she simply knew that she must go next to communist countries. Accordingly, in September 1957, she set off in a specially converted van to travel behind the Iron Curtain, having waved goodbye to her Sisters, as she thought, for ever.

In fact, because of visa problems, this departure did not prove as definitive as intended. From then on until shortly before her death Little Sister Magdeleine was to spend a substantial part of each year in the various iron curtain countries with the intention of being simply a prayerful presence on the route. Under various guises Little Sisters were able to live in communist countries and to build up a network of friendships, particularly with fellow Christians but by no means exclusively so, for in the vision of Little Sister Magdeleine unity could not be a case of being for some and against others; rather it was a case of being for some whilst remaining open to others. In the course of her many visits to the Soviet Union strong links were built up with the Russian Orthodox Church but equally she wanted to remain open to the communists she met along the way. After all, communism was not all bad. It had rehabilitated the working class.

In the context of this same ideal of unity, Little Sister Magdeleine could not fail to be attracted to the idea of the breakdown of divisions between Christians in general. Little Sister Magdeleine was no more compromising in her own Roman Catholic orthodoxy than Mother Teresa. Like her, she was a loyal daughter of the Roman Catholic Church and the Pope, one for whom obedience was paramount. Yet she had really pre-empted the Second Vatican Council in many respects including its openness to non-Catholic Christians, and she welcomed it with wide open arms, calling it a 'Council of Unity'.

She was drawn to Taizé. After her first visit in July 1948 to the embryo community made up at the time of a handful of Protestant brothers, she commented simply: 'Their thinking is a little surprising – to restore the Catholic religion by their example in the village.' The relationship with these Brothers was to prove an ongoing one, as was her friendship with members of the Salvation Army and with people of a multitude of other religious beliefs.

It was in fact one of Little Sister Magdeleine's 'dreams' to have Little Sisters of other Christian denominations fully participating in the Fraternity – united in their love for God and their respect for others. Some Little Sisters who were Christian but non-Catholic actually 'joined' the Fraternity on an experimental basis. Difficulties arose not least because non-Catholics could not make their vows to the Catholic Church. For Little Sister Magdeleine such difficulties were not insurmountable, however. Characteristically she believed they could be worked out in the actual practice, in the living.

Equally characteristically, she did not believe the solution to be conversion. For her the union of diversity was too valuable, and it is an indication of her real tolerance and respect for each person's spiritual journey and for the workings of the Holy Spirit, that she said of those non-Catholics who sought to live the vocation of a Little Sister: 'Whatever happens they mustn't become Catholic!' In 1981 she was desperately disappointed that the new Constitutions of the Fraternity were not to include an article relating to non-Catholic Little Sisters. Such questions, it was then ordained, could only be resolved by official commissions dealing with relations between the Christian Churches. Nevertheless, in 1986, the first Little Sister from the Swiss Reformed Church made her final commitment to the Fraternity. An arrangement had been reached whereby the vows were made not 'into the hands' of the General Responsible but in her presence. For Little Sister Magdeleine this was a momentous occasion for which she dragged herself off her sick bed, having only the night before received the Sacrament of the Sick.

But for her ecumenism remained secondary to the goal of universality/unity. 'The love of the Heart of Jesus is so great that it took in the whole world'. For her, irretrievably bound up with considerations of different faiths, rites or denominations were the interests, problems, lives and evolution of nations and peoples of which they were frequently an expression.

It was for this reason, for instance, that Little Sister Magdeleine was deeply attracted to the Churches of the Eastern Rite. The discovery that in the East there were Catholics whose Christian worship expressed itself in the language and culture of the Islamic people to whom she wanted to draw closer in language and in prayer was irresistible. Again her 'intuition' for the fraternities in the Orient, namely that they should form part of the indigenous Church of the Eastern Rite, rather than remaining part of the Latin Church, was a radical one.

In Beirut, rather than living within the diocese of the Melkite (Greek Catholic) Patriarch Maximos IV whilst remaining dependent on their Superiors in Rome, as others had done before them, the Little Sisters would actually become part of the Melkite Church and therefore not only adopt the rite of that church and thus, as Little Sister Magdeleine put it, 'be penetrated by its spirituality' but also come under its authority. (Dependence on the Congregation for the Oriental Churches of the Eastern Rite in Rome was also for this reason very important to her.)

Furthermore, as fraternities were founded in various parts of the Orient, she found herself 'haunted by the thought' that there should be at least one fraternity in each of the churches of other Eastern countries. By 1954 in the Orient the Little Sisters had become very much part of the Melkite, Coptic and Armenian communions and shortly afterwards become part of the churches of the Chaldean, Syrian, Maronite and Syro-Malankaran Rite.

And all this was brought about more by an intuitive understanding of prevailing sensitivities than by intellectual awareness. For although she had what Father Voillaume referred to as 'an infallible theological sense', she was not a theologian in the sense of enjoying theological discussion or having devoted much time to its formal study.

Little Sister Magdeleine valued theology and insisted on her Sisters studying it, but 'unity' was not something which she sought at the level of theological debate. As one priest and friend of hers put it: 'More than a way of thinking, she had a heart so pure in its love for Jesus, that her very life, her being, was if one can say such a thing 'ecumenical'. He had, he said, been struck by the fact that long before she actually physically toured the world, its full dimensions had been encompassed by her heart.

For me the echoes of Brother Roger's 'way of reconciliation within oneself ' are quite distinct: 'In the heart of God, the church is as large as all the world . . .'

When at times in Rome Little Sister Magdeleine heard theological quarrels between various religious groups, or criticisms of particular religious orders, it made her all the more convinced of the importance of 'going beyond all that'. 'The beauty of God,' she said, 'is so much more beautiful!'

Mother Teresa, Jean Vanier, Brother Roger, Little Sister Magdeleine are all people who have entered into the mystery of the gospel message. They are all people who have responded to the God of the New Testament, the God of love and of Presence – Emmanuel – God with us. They are people of the way of the heart, the way traditionally symbolised by the cross, in which the vertical line signifies the union of the earthly with the heavenly whilst the horizontal reaches out towards and draws into this union all humanity.

Finally, I would like to offer two thoughts:

The first is that there is, of course, a value in diversity of expression and a value in verbal expression. I once sat in on a group discussion held at one of Taizé's European meetings. The young people involved were invited to discuss some of the points raised by the letter Brother Roger writes annually. Gradually it became apparent from the debate that went on haltingly in several languages that a number of people there had discovered through the letter a very simple Gospel message which they had somehow not recognised in the Bible, despite regular reading of it. I should add that I happen to know the hours of reflection and contemplation that go into the preparation of Brother Roger's letters which are often also written from a place of poverty and suffering. So it is that the words become Mother Teresa's 'words that give the light of Christ'.

The second and final thought comes actually from Dom Bede Griffiths, the Benedictine monk who, in South India, founded an ashram, a centre of prayer and meditation open to all who seek the universal and eternal truth at the heart of all religions. His life as a sannyasi brought him, he said, to the realisation that: 'As we come to the inner depth of our own tradition, we find ourselves drawing near to the depths of other traditions, and it is in that interior depth that the final meeting has to take place.'

The Methodist Peace Prize

Kenneth G. Greet

The Methodist Church came into being as the result of the eighteenth century revival of religion and the remarkable work of John Wesley and his brother Charles, the famous hymn-writer. John Wesley was both evangelist and social reformer. He founded a number of schools and placed great emphasis on the value of education. He wrote a book called 'Primitive Physic', a compendium of homely remedies for a variety of ailments. He showed an insatiable curiosity about scientific matters and produced valuable summaries of the developments taking place in his day. He expressed his views about great social evils like slavery, writing trenchant pamphlets which circulated widely. About war he said, 'Now, what an argument is this! What a method of proof! What an amazing way of deciding controversies! What must mankind be before such a thing as war could ever be known or thought of upon earth?'

This welding together of evangelism and social concern has always been a characteristic mark of the people called Methodists. For five years I was chairman of the World Methodist Council, a body which now represents some sixty million Methodists in more than 100 countries. The agendas of that Council reflect the multi-faceted involvement of Methodist churches across the world for justice, peace and the integrity of creation. At every meeting for many years the Council has received reports from the Methodist Church of Southern Africa. I myself went in 1986 on a tour of the Republic with the express purpose of supporting those who were involved in the struggle against apartheid. It was an experience I shall never forget and I came away with many memories of magnificent people, black and white, who were seeking to bring that hateful system to an end and to build a new South Africa. I have been thrilled by the recent developments under the presidency of Nelson Mandela.

I want to write here of one particular action taken by the World Methodist Council in the interests of peace. In 1976, the year I became its chairman, the Council met in Dublin. At that time the 'peace women' were very active and staged a march. Some three thousand Methodists attending our world gathering decided to join them. In the wake of this moving experience it was suggested that we should establish a World Methodist Peace Award to be presented annually to some person who had shown special devotion to the cause of peace. The criteria for the Award are courage, creativity and consistency. The annual decision about who should receive the Award is made by the officers of the WMC. It is no easy task. Obviously our knowledge of the world is limited and we rely on representatives of the Methodist churches in many countries to advise us of the names of those who might be considered. There is the need to ensure that the Award goes to various parts of the world. One teasing question that we have had to face is this: how much importance should we attach to the public profile of the recipient? There is the temptation to go for well-known people in order to enhance the publicity value of the award while neglecting some little-known folk whose service for peace has been outstanding.

Another real difficulty arises from the fact that Christians vary in their views about peace and how they should respond to the commission of Christ to be peacemakers. Some, like the present writer, are pacifists and believe that the church should renounce war as a means of settling disputes and expound the concept of non-violence as the way of life to which our Lord calls his people. Others believe that the pursuit of peace sometimes involves the resort to arms. Among those who have received the Peace Award are individuals who represent both these positions. For example, to mention two well-known men, Lord Soper has consistently preached pacifism over the long years of his distinguished ministry; President Carter on the other hand was inevitably involved as Commander-in-Chief of the armed forces of the USA in sanctioning military action. But all of those who have been honoured have given outstanding service of various kinds to the cause of peace, working within their own understandings of how they can best contribute to the ending of war.

The Award consists of a medallion and a cheque which recipients use to further their work. It has several purposes. Obviously it is a way of recognising individuals who have made a significant contribution to the work for peace and to encourage others who labour with similar devotion. It is also a means of witnessing to the church's commitment to peace-making. Beyond that the publicity attending the award ceremony is a means of telling worthwhile stories. In a world where so often the news is bad there is value in emphasising some of the positive things that are being achieved by often unsung heroes. In what follows I want to tell a little of the story of the Peace Award so far and of those who have received it, lingering a little on my own involvement with a few of them. The list contains some famous names that have echoed round the world and others known only within the locality or the country where their work has been done. Not all of them are Methodists. Taken together these names reflect the inspiring fact that there are people on every continent who believe that peace is possible and are not unwilling to attempt the impossible in pursuit of it.

Sadie Patterson of Belfast

The first Award was appropriately made to Miss Sadie Patterson and I travelled to Belfast on a bitter winter's day with Dr Joe Hale, the Council's General Secretary, to make the presentation. This remarkable lady had spent the whole of her life in an attempt to bring peace and reconciliation to Ireland. She was trusted by all sides in the saga of violence, hatred and revenge which has gone on for so long. She was often exposed to danger. Although some take the cynical view that peace in Ireland is a lost cause, when eventually sanity comes to that deeply divided island the work of Sadie Patterson and others like her will be recognised as foundation stones in a building constructed only after infinite patience and persistence.

On the very day when I presented the Award to Sadie Patterson her grand-nephew, Robin Smyrl aged 25, was gunned down by the IRA on a deserted country road as he drove to work. Her immediate reaction was to say that she would continue the struggle to save her country in spite of the overwhelming sadness which she felt.

President Anwar Sadat of Egypt

The following year we decided to ask the President of Egypt if he would accept the Award in recognition of his courage in making his historic visit to Israel to address the Knesset – an action which opened up the possibility of new relationships between two traditional enemies. Within twenty-four hours of our contacting the Egyptian Embassy in London we received a warm acceptance from President Sadat.

I flew to Cairo and, to my astonishment, found a sleek limousine accompanied by police outriders waiting on the tarmac to whisk me off to a hotel on the banks of the Nile. Two armed guards were posted at the entrance to my suite of rooms and they accompanied me wherever I went. Anwar Sadat's initiative had not been universally popular and it was evidently felt that I was at some risk. I am bound to say that the screech of sirens from the outriders as we sped through the city did nothing to add to my sense of security. Even when I visited the great Pyramid and penetrated to the dark burial chamber at its heart, the ever-present police followed me like a shadow.

On the day of the presentation I was taken to the old royal palace. I sat on a golden chair as also did Joe Hale who had flown in from America. A most distinguished group of people had gathered for the occasion. This included the whole of the Egyptian cabinet and representatives of all the major religious organisations. In his acceptance speech the President said how moved he was to know that he, a leading Muslim, was being recognised by the Methodist Church. The ceremony was reported in all the papers and was headline news on the television channels.

Before I left the President said, 'I hope to sign a peace treaty with Israel. We will do it on the summit of Mount Sinai and I shall invite you to be present.' Alas, shortly afterwards he was assassinated. I recalled this impressive man who seemed to have an inner quietness of spirit, and was filled with sadness. Some who seek to make peace pay a heavy price for their commitment.

Abel Hendricks of South Africa

During the tour of South Africa to which I referred earlier I stayed for several days with the Rev. Abel Hendricks and his wife Freda. He is a Methodist minister, twice honoured by being elected President of the South African Methodist Conference. He left a comfortable appointment to go and live among the black and coloured people in Capetown not far from the infamous Crossroads. He is a gentle soul but was a formidable opponent of the apartheid system. Once when there was a protest march he went to see the police to ask them to keep a low profile, assuring them that there would be no trouble. As he crossed the road to return he was arrested and taken to prison. There he was tortured. Lighted cigarettes were applied to his genitals. The experience severely affected his health. He told me not to worry if there was a noise in the night: it would be the police searching the house for weapons. Abel never owned or handled a gun in his life.

We went together to visit Crossroads. At one shabby little home I was greeted with open hostility until Abel, himself coloured, explained that I was from London and 'he is on our side'. Suddenly frowns and growls of suspicion changed to smiles of welcome. In all his work Abel Hendricks has been marvellously supported by his wife. Their home is a haven of peace and tranquillity and she herself does marvellous educational work among the poor children of the area. I regard them both as among God's saints. Through all the dark years of apartheid they never allowed the flame of hope to be extinguished.

Lord Soper of London

Few occasions have given me greater personal pleasure than when we presented the 1981 Peace Award to Donald Soper. He is without doubt the outstanding Methodist minister of this century. His open-air ministry on Tower Hill and Hyde Park is known all over the world and, amazingly, is maintained in his nineties. He has been a consistent and fearless advocate of the pacifist position and has been tireless in his work for peace and reconciliation. Inevitably he has found himself at the centre of much controversy but I have never seen him lose the equanimity which enables him to treat opponents with respect. For many years he has been a greatly respected member of the House of Lords. He is President of the Fellowship of Reconciliation and of the Methodist Peace Fellowship. The major part of his ministry has been taken up with the superintendency of the West London Mission with its network of social work agencies. His political views spring directly from his understanding of the Christian gospel and at the heart of his life and work is a deep love of the sacramental side of religion. He presides every week at the service of Holy Communion on Sunday morning at Hinde Street Church in London.

Kenneth Mew of Zimbabwe

Kenneth Mew is the Principal of Ranche House College, Harare, established to promote racial unity and responsible citizenship after the pattern of the folk schools in Denmark. In the years following Rhodesia's declaration of independence the College became a centre for many types of inter-racial activity and a powerful opponent of apartheid policies. Members of both government and opposition used the facilities of Ranche House and Kenneth Mew won deep respect as an accomplished mediator. Since independence the College has been used by the government for the training of diplomats and civil servants. Mr Mew was a man made for the moment and his work has greatly influenced the development of an independent Zimbabwe. He received the award in 1982

Dr Tai-Young Lee of Korea

The following year we moved from Africa to Asia and honoured the work of Tai-Young Lee, a Methodist attorney who for thirty years had campaigned for the restoration of democracy in Korea and the establishment of human rights. She has used her skills as a lawyer to defend many of the victims of injustice. She said, 'The work I have done was brought about by Jesus Christ dragging me and pushing me along. It is he who should be receiving the award.' Dr Lee has been one of the leading figures in Korea in the struggle to establish the rights of women.

President Jimmy Carter of the USA

In 1985 the World Methodist Council made its Peace Award to President Carter at a ceremony in Emory University presided over by Bishop William Cannon, at that time the Chairman of the WMC and a friend of the President. Jimmy Carter, who is a devout Baptist, made a speech in which he revealed some of the ambiguities inevitable in one who has to handle great power on behalf of a nation. He asked the question, 'How does one measure the greatness of a nation?' He made clear his own conviction that service is the measuring-rod of greatness. He said, 'Peace cannot be assured nor human rights enhanced through political timidity or abandonment of principle. But neither can we expect to succeed through arrogance, vituperation, jingoism or the disparagement of others. The resolution of conflict, once begun, should be sought through diplomacy and negotiation, not by encouraging further hatred and bloodshed.' He went on to speak of the difficulties he had encountered in trying to apply these fine principles in the world of practical affairs.

The Rev Sir Alan and Lady Winifred Walker of Australia

Alan Walker and his wife have shared a remarkable global ministry and have been responsible for organising impressive evangelistic campaigns all over the world. Their presentation of the Christian gospel has never divorced the personal and the social. They have emphasised in particular the Christian call to be reconcilers and makers of peace. Alan has not shrunk from taking unpopular stands. He has consistently condemned war. When the atom bombs were dropped on Japan he said, 'The verdict of history on the dropping of bombs on Japanese cities could be: "They won a war and lost a civilisation."'

For many years as Superintendent of the great Methodist Mission in Sydney Sir Alan presided over a network of social agencies and founded an organisation called 'Lifeline International' which has helped countless people in distress. He has been honoured for his work by the heads of many countries. The WMC Peace Award was presented jointly to him and his wife at the 1986 meeting of the Council in Nairobi.

Bert Bissell of England and the Hon Woodrow Seals of America

Unusually the 1987 Award was made jointly to two men from different countries. Bert Bissell has spent his life building bridges of friendship with people of differing faiths and of no faith. In his home town of Dudley he has helped establish projects to assist immigrants from the West Indies, Kenya, India and Pakistan. He has been very successful in gaining the support of official bodies and civic leaders. He was still, in his eighties, climbing to the summit of Ben Nevis where he built a peace cairn – the focal point of the Ben Nevis Peace Fellowship, established to inspire peacemaking all over the world. The familiar image of Bert is of a figure clad in a long raincoat and wearing a battered hat bending before the wind that sweeps the mountainside. Many young men have entered the Christian ministry from his weekly Bible class. I was privileged to make the presentation to this grand old warrior at one of the sessions of the Methodist Conference.

Judge Woodrow Seals is well-known in the USA for his championship of human rights. He founded the Society of St Stephen which has over one hundred branches throughout the USA caring for the poor. His courageous rulings in court have often attracted virulent criticism from opponents. His decision that children of undocumented Hispanic workers should be given the opportunity of education in Texas public schools was a landmark which has improved the lot of thousands of young people. He has worked tirelessly for peace and has been especially involved with the attempts to bring an end to hostilities in the Middle East.

Gordon Wilson of Northern Ireland

In one terrible moment the name of Gordon Wilson became known throughout the world. On November 8 1987 Mr Wilson and his daughter Marie, a nurse in training, were buried under tons of rubble caused by the IRA bomb which killed eleven people in Enniskillen and injured sixty-one. Marie died of her injuries while holding her father's hand. Interviewed on television following this great tragedy, Gordon Wilson said that he felt no bitterness towards those who had perpetrated the crime. The Queen referred to him in her Christmas broadcast and to his witness to a love that is stronger than hate. The experience deepened his resolve to redouble his work for reconciliation and peace in his troubled land. Methodist people everywhere rejoice to know that this brave man was of their number.

President Mikhail S. Gorbachev of Russia

The citation read when the 1990 Award was presented to Mr Gorbachev referred to the part that he had played in changing for the better the relations between East and West and to his policy of granting greater freedom to churches and religious bodies. It went on, 'You have lifted your voice for restraint and a peaceful solution to the crisis in the Persian Gulf. While you have condemned the aggression committed, you have reinforced persuasively the idea that dialogue is always preferable to war, and face-to-face communication to bloodshed.'

Barbel Bohley of Germany

Barbel Bohley was born in Berlin and brought up in a city devastated by war. She devoted her life to the cause of justice and peace. She sold many of her own works of art to assist prisoners of conscience. She was several times arrested for her opposition to arms production and the laws on conscription. At one point she had to flee the country. Because of her public witness she was forced to resign from the Executive Committee of the Federation of Fine Arts in Berlin. She has made an outstanding contribution to the building of democratic institutions in post-war Germany. The Award was made to her in Leipzig in 1991.

Pastor Zdravko Beslov of Bulgaria

In 1992 I was in Bulgaria and saw something of the work of the small but lively Methodist community there. I attended the breaking of the sods on the central site in Varna presented to the Methodists for the building of a new church and community centre. Their old church had been confiscated by

the government and turned into a puppet theatre. When a
new government offered to restore their building to them the
Methodists said, 'No, the children of the city love the puppets
and we do not want to rob them of that facility.' The city
fathers were so impressed by this magnanimity that they gave
them the new site. The leader of the Bulgarian Methodists was
a frail old man, Pastor Beslov. He had been in prison for many
years because of his championship of human rights. It was
moving to observe the reverence with which he was treated by
his people. The presentation ceremony was held in a large
public hall and attended by a huge crowd including civic
representatives. The years of confinement and torture had
taken their toll and he died shortly after I saw him.

Dr Elias Chacour of Israel
The 1994 Award took us to the Middle East. As a boy Elias
Chacour saw his Palestinian village of Biram destroyed by
explosives and bulldozers and the land belonging to his family
for centuries confiscated. But his parents brought him up to
believe that forgiveness alone brings healing and peace. He has
never deviated from this belief and has spent his life seeking to
break the cycle of violence, vengeance and death which has
distorted the relationships between Israelis and Palestinians.
Much of his work has been done through the Prophet Elias
Community College which he created. He is a frequent
participant in television programmes and is widely respected as
a spiritual guide and teacher. The presentation ceremony at
Ibillin in Galilee was attended by many friends from his
College, from the West Bank, from Lebanon and from other
nations. It made a great impression on all who were present.

Bishop Stanley Mogoba of South Africa
I have known and admired Stanley Mogoba for many years.
Short in stature and quiet in speech, he has been one of the
leaders of the large Southern Africa Methodist Church and a

stalwart in the fight against apartheid. He is a close friend of President Mandela and was, like him, imprisoned for many years in the infamous gaol on Robben Island. It was while he was in prison that Stanley heard the call to the Christian ministry. He stood courageously for peace through negotiation when few people believed this possible. History has vindicated him. He is playing a notable part in helping to tackle the very great problems confronting the new South Africa. He was an ardent supporter of the World Council of Churches' Programme to combat Racism and it was as a result of a plea from him that the Council launched its more recent Programme to Overcome Violence. It was fitting that he should preach the sermon at the inauguration of Nelson Mandela as State President. The 1996 Award was made to him in East London, South Africa.

The Community of St Edigio

The 1997 award was given to the Community of St Edigio, a volunteer service group organised along the lines of Catholic lay movements in Renaissance Italy. This is the first time the award has been granted to a community. The community was founded in 1968 by students and young professionals who made a commitment to serve society. Andrea Riccardi, a professor of Christian History at Rome University, was one of the founder members. The community takes up the issues of the Day of Prayer for Peace in Assisi which was convened by Pope John Paul II.

The community has been constantly courageous and creative and communities have been formed in other countries, including Latin America, Europe, Central America, Africa and Asia. Many peace initiatives have been made. Some of the work of bringing hostile groups together is described in the chapter on Mozambique in this book. The community has regularly brought together government and religious leaders, to talk and to share in prayers for peace. In Rome alone the community members minister to six thousand children, five thousand elderly people, two thousand five hundred disabled people and six hundred AIDS patients. Hospitality is given to immigrants and a soup kitchen has been set up to feed homeless people. Hot meals are taken to people on the streets.

Andrea Riccardi has said, 'Hatred is the basis of all wars because it inflames and devours the hearts of some people and of entire groups. Religions do not desire wars. They do not intend to become instruments of war. There is no such thing as a sacred war. Religion insists: only peace is sacred!'

Reconciliation: What Price

Some Biblical and Practical Reflections from Africa

Cyril C. Okorocha

Introduction

I would like to present this brief reflection on the vast and fascinating theme of reconciliation in the form of some biblical insights and practical stories from the African experience. These stories are true life experiences but personal and place names have been altered to protect the identity of the people concerned. But the lessons from the stories remain unaffected. A critique on current events in some parts of Africa will be followed by a brief resume to the command to forgive *vis-à-vis* the appeal to reconcile.

The Gospel of reconciliation

The theme of reconciliation is woven like a golden thread through the pages of the Bible from Genesis to Revelation.

For example, Adam offended God and naturally decided to avoid God. But God in his love, took the initiative to find Adam and to arrange a new relationship. The Gospel certainly begins here: the scenario of sin and shame, of grace and generosity is at the heart of the biblical story of reconciliation. But it is also the story of God's initiative. The Christ event is the classic example of that redemptive initiative and the normative instance of God's reconciling movement towards humankind. In Paul's words: 'In Christ God was reconciling the world to himself' (2 Cor 5:19). Therefore argues Paul, the message of reconciliation is at the heart of the gospel.

So to be a missionary is to be an agent of reconciliation: reconciliation, between God and humankind and between people. The proclamation of the love of God revealed in Christ and of God's reconciling movements towards humankind is the logical basis for a proclamation of reconciliation between people. For example, when we ask people to forgive one another, it is because Paul argues, 'God in Christ has forgiven you' (Eph 4:32).

When we ask the World Bank and the Western nations to consider remitting burdensome debts of the poorer nations of the world by the year 2000, it is because the Bible speaks of the year of Jubilee and Jesus spoke of a year of God's favour, a remission of debts of which Jesus' own vicarious self giving was the climax: 'When we were still sinners, powerless and without hope, Christ died for us' (Rom 5:6-8; Luke 4:18; Lev 25:1; Pet 3:18).

Therefore it is appropriate to describe Christian mission with Paul as a ministry of reconciliation (2 Cor 5:16). Paul thus argues that the primary work of the Christian evangelist is to call people to be reconciled to God – as a basis for inter-personal reconciliation (2 Cor 5:14-21).

Reconciliation with people:
essential to reconciliation with God
Sin
In the Decalogue, which some scholars argue is a Mosaic adaptation of a typical Ancient Near Eastern Suzerainty Treaty, Moses links inter-personal relationships closely with a redemptive relationship with Yahweh. To claim to love God or to claim to honour God's name, but fail to honour one's aged and responsible parents, is as immoral as to commit adultery. To lie against one another or to fall foul of perjury is as evil as murder and both sins result from impiety which can be expressed in the form of blasphemy or idolatry. In short, from the Mosaic perspective, crime against humanity is indistinguishable from sin against God (see Ex 20).

The prophets take it further as Micah argues that God's understanding of true piety goes far beyond a 'beautiful liturgy' or an exhilarating 'personal experience of God' – dancing or laughing in the Spirit. It is often more than giving generously, as this also can be selfishly motivated. True piety, he insists, has to do with loving and fair relationships with one's fellow human beings! 'What does Yahweh require,' asks Micah. 'But to do justice, to love mercy, and to walk humbly with God'.

These ingredients are essential to good relationships. Most wars and conflicts in the world, in homes and in the work place, begin with arrogance on the part of one party and intolerance on the part of the other (see Micah 6:8).

Murder is in the heart
Jesus' words were even more potent. He argues that to snub, or look down on, or marginalise someone for whatever reason amounts to murder. Thus the attitude of inner snobbery or spite is as evil before God as open racism. To stereotype people – 'you Africans!' 'you white people!' 'you black people!' 'you . . .' is worse, than open murder. It is to castigate them. Such prejudice, our Lord insists, makes it impossible for us to see anything good in such people. We are afraid of showing them appreciation lest we suddenly discover that they are not as evil or as incompetent as we have always held them to be on account of their ethnic, national or racial origin. The result is that we find it easier to say 'Can anything good come out of Nazareth?' than to say a whole hearted (and indeed exhilarating) 'well done!' We put them down, say 'Raca!' rather than affirm them. So we marginalise rather than included them. Deep down inside, we rejoice whenever misfortune comes their way and are happier if they are out of the way. All that, says the Lord, is unpardonable murder (Matt 5:21-23).

A liberating encounter
A positive attitude towards people helps us to appreciate the good qualities that people have which, if we should focus,

would make working or living with them easier for both parties. But we often take a negative position which euphemistically we describe as class consciousness or at worst personal or cultural prejudice. 'It is the culture we live in', or 'It is the way I was raised, so don't blame me blame my parents'! But Jesus calls prejudice murder. If it persists, he warns, it becomes 'a sin against the Holy Spirit' for which there is no forgiveness from God. This is frightening. Can God condemn anyone for being a product of their time and of the cultural prejudices into which they are born? But are we right to stereotype people and fail to appreciate them? Are we right to put them down and fail to value them? We fail to acknowledge what they do well.

Jesus performed a miracle, but those who felt threatened by his integrity and 'success' chose to put him down. They insisted that he worked through the power of the devil. Jesus warns those who claim to belong to him that to escape the condemnation due to this most fearful of all sins (see Matt 12:24-32; Luke 12:10) so as to experience God's true peace now and ultimate salvation, we need a complete mental, spiritual and moral reorientation which can only be described in terms of a rebirth. 'You must be born again!'

This rebirth is a powerful and liberating encounter which like a recreating force turns us around and we become new people 'born of the Spirit' (John 3:3-5). For then the old value system must be discarded and the new one must replace it. In short, we need to be freed from fear of others' prejudice and other trappings of our unconverted background, Paul argues, in order to belong to God's family (2 Cor 5:17; Rom 12:1-3).

Prejudice is the root of murder, argues James, as greed is the source of a contentious and quarrelsome spirit. Arrogance makes us marginalise people, and pride keeps us from repentance and then results in the sin against the Holy Spirit (James 4:1-6). Prejudice results in favouritism in the workplace and in social relationships both in the church and in the wider community and means that people are often denied their basic right and justice (James 2:1-10). Our Lord's invective against the Pharisees was expressed in the strongest of terms. They were guilty of hypocrisy and prejudice. They would strain out a gnat but swallow a camel! They would make a meticulous observance of their religious rituals with a view to controlling and manipulating people, but neglect the more important matters of the law – justice, mercy and faithfulness' (Mat 23:23-24). The gospel of our Lord is a gospel of forgiveness, of reconciliation. A gospel that says to the sinner, 'Go and sin no more' and provides for the weak the power to 'sin no more'.

More than material gifts

To forgive, insists our Lord, is more important than to pay tithes and bring gifts to the altar – or to give to the poor or for mission. Before presenting a gift to God, we need to search our hearts and take practical steps to rid ourselves of pride, prejudices and social or economic sins against our neighbour. 'First be reconciled to your brother or sister, and then come and offer your gift' (Matt 5:24).

Forgiveness brings healing

Isaiah links physical healing with spiritual wellbeing and argues that true piety is evidenced in acts of social justice. This is the fast 'spiritually' that God has chosen: 'to loose the bonds of injustice, to undo the thongs of the yoke, to let the oppressed go free, and to break every yoke . . . to share your bread with the hungry, and bring the homeless poor into your house; when you see the naked, to cover them, and not to hide yourself from your own . . . Then your light shall break forth like the dawn, and your healing shall spring up quickly; your vindicator shall go before you, the glory of the Lord shall be your rear guard. Then you shall call, and the Lord will answer; you shall cry for help, and he will say, "Here I am"' (Isaiah 58:6-9).

Spiritual, physical and material blessing, argues Isaiah,

can be a direct fruit of the practical and social expression of the Gospel. It is not enough, he maintains, to speak for the poor. We must learn to act in their defence. It is not enough to speak and sue for peace. We must work to remove the things that cause war. It is not enough to apologise for past wars and ancestral sins or to indulge in a rhetoric of repentance; it is important to act to see that justice is being done and that we do not repeat the sins of our forbears or perpetuate the oppression or marginalisation of those whom they had oppressed and marginalised. In short, if we condemn the racism or tribalism of our forebears we must stop to ask ourselves what our attitudes are to people of other races and cultures living close to or working with us. But don't be fooled, some of them can be quite difficult to work with!

As the Saviour of the world stretched his hands wide to embrace the universe he breathed those final words, 'Father forgive them . . .' This is what he has called us to do and to be in the world. This is the most powerful point in the gospel narratives. Jesus argues on: 'I have glorified your name. . . I have kept your word . . . I have done the work you have sent me to do. . .' It is finished. . .' The final sacrifice has been made 'once and for all', therefore forgive them.' This I believe is the call to the church and to all humankind. To bring healing to the nations, healing to families, healing to ourselves and to others through *forgiveness*.

That man must be God
Some years ago a student came to me. He was very ill. Available medical services could not help him. After several visits and times of prayer with him I gave him a book to read. He later told me that as he read the story of the life and death of Jesus he was captivated by the story of the crucifixion. And as he read those final words of Jesus, 'Father forgive them . . .' a powerful sense of awe gripped him. How could a man forgive his enemies? The student, Ibrahim, jumped off his bed with a scream, 'This man must be God!' He fell back

on his bed and a deep peace descended on him. He fell asleep. Ten hours later his worried flat mates woke him up. (He had not been known to sleep for more than two hours at a stretch for over three years, even with the help of medication.) When Ibrahim woke up, he was a different person. He was healed, physically, emotionally and spiritually.

He came to me full of excitement: 'Sir, I am healed and I am now a follower of Jesus Christ.' I asked him to explain further: 'That man must be God' was all he kept shouting. Forgiveness brings healing and opens the door for a new hope and a new relationship. But to insist on my 'pound of flesh' perpetuates hatred and tension.

Reconciliation: undergirded by trust
Oriko

The Igbo of South East Nigeria have a special traditional ritual to signify that reconciliation is rooted in trust. After a serious feud, reconciling parties, whether a kindred group or family or – and especially – husband and wife, are brought together by the elders of the community to test the depth of their forgiveness of and therefore trust for each other. They are asked to eat together. Commensality is regarded as vital to interpersonal relationships among the Igbo. It is a symbol of trust, of hospitality and of willingness to sustain each other's life by replenishing it – through food. To refuse to share one's food with anyone is an indication not only of stinginess but of a deep down hatred which points to a wish for the expiration of the other person's life through starvation.

But it is not enough to throw food to someone – as to a dangerous animal or to the evil spirits to ward them off. Commensality that connotes life affirmation and trust involves eating *together*, preferably from the same bowl. Each party brings a meal to the ceremony. The food is mixed together and all those entering a new covenant of reconciliation and mutual *trust* eat each others' meals out of the same bowl. Then they feed each other, taking a piece of food with

191

the fingers and putting it directly into the other person's mouth. This is reciprocated repeatedly until the food is finished. There is a sense of rejoicing and celebration. This is called *oriko,* 'reciprocal eating together'.

Igba ndu

If a serious venture lies ahead then animal sacrifices are introduced. This is called igba ndu: 'bonding lives' or 'at-one-ment'. Literally, it means: 'I hand my life to you: I trust you unreservedly and I know you will never intentionally harm me. In my absence you will defend my cause and the honour of my name.'

Igbo politicians, soldiers especially in war time, and business associates are known to enter into 'igba ndu' covenants with each other as they form serious alliances. Those who breach this covenant are known to meet with sudden and often mysterious death! But no one would dare break it. To reconcile means to work to enhance life. And to the Igbo, ndu bu isi, life is supreme.

Examples from the Polynesians of Tonga and Fiji Islands show that similar rituals abound. The Kava drinking ceremony used to welcome visitors, like the Igbo 'kola hospitality', is indicative of good will, expressed through commensality.

In short, at the heart of the concept of reconciliation is a willingness to enter into a bond of mutual trust.

Reconciliation is not free

If we go back for a moment to the Gospel origins in Genesis 3 with which we began, we notice that reconciliation not only involves a sense of initiative on the part of one of the parties, but also a sacrifice. The amazing factor is that here the offended party who should have been insisting on 'justice for the injured' paid the price for peace! God took the initiative to find Adam. God provided the means of concealing Adam's shame so as to 'empower' him with a freedom that will make dialogue and meaningful relationships possible.

What a generous Saviour. Captured by this sacrificial love, John writes, 'In this is love, not that we loved God but that he loved us and sent his Son to be the atoning sacrifice for our sins'. (I John 4:10)

In short, there is always a price to be paid for peace. The Bible seems to assert that in a situation of conflict, whoever pays the price for peace is the nobler character. To sue for peace is to be willing to pay this price. It could involve losing face. It could mean a painful refusal to retaliate or to avenge oneself or to fight for one's right. It could mean being willing in a world of self assertiveness, to turn the other cheek and be called a wimp and a fool, and to appear to be the loser. Peter enjoins Christians of his time to endure suffering with patience and a forgiving attitude towards their persecutors because 'For Christ also suffered for sins once for all, the righteous for the unrighteous, in order to bring you to God (1 Peter 3:18).

In other words, some one has to let go and take initiative to end the vicious circle of aggression and retaliation.

Reconciliation and national healing: a Nigerian experience
We are all guilty

During the pogrom that precipitated the Biafran tragedy, Obi Okafor had fled Kano to return to his native home, Alandu in Eastern Nigeria, (Biafra).

There was a widely held fear that behind the war machinery was an agenda for Igbo genocide. That fear was justified by the pogrom that presaged the war and the ruthless conduct of the war by the Federal Nigerian Government, including indiscriminate air raids: bombing of open markets, schools, churches and hospitals. Most Biafrans believed that to lose the war was as suicidal as to fight on. Therefore, for an Igbo Christian to return to Kano, Hausa-Fulini and Muslim heartland so soon after the war, was either madness or utter foolishness.

That was what Obi did. He had no choice. The end of the war left him as hopeless as its beginning. So returning to

Kano was a desperate gamble by a desperate man. But he was surprised by joy.

His friend Alhaji Sule Gambo received him with open arms and deep apologies. Obi argued that Sule owed no apologies. 'I should be thanking you, I owe you my life: you helped me to escape,' Obi argued.

'No,' replied Sule falling on his knees before Obi, tears rolling down his cheeks, 'No, my friend,' he insisted, 'you owe me nothing. I owe you many apologies. May God forgive me. And please I beg you to forgive me. We are all guilty. I and my people. We are all guilty. We killed you. What I cannot understand is why we did it. You were such a friend – loved by all. We ate together, played and did business together. What drove us into such barbaric behaviour? How did we turn to fear and hate so bitterly the people who had been so close to us? Please forgive me!'

Obi also fell down and both men began to weep together. 'What causes so much hatred? Why should one set of people decide to wipe out another set of people or to dominate them for ever?' they asked in unison. Sule went on, 'I hear there will be a Commission of Enquiry; they will invite the United Nations and the International Committee of Justice. I will confess and I will report all the people I know who killed and who looted.'

'Don't be silly,' Obi cut in as he sat up. 'If you start that kind of enquiry, where will you begin and where will it end? Do you know how many hundreds of thousands of people were killed? And how are you sure people will not use the inquiry to falsely incriminate their enemies? You know our country and our people. It will never end. The war will start all over again and there will be more inter-tribal killings and perpetual hatred and bitterness!'

'What shall we do then – just leave it like that?' Sule asked as he too got up, his voice quivering and his face bowed in pain.

'Yes, Sule,' Obi insisted. 'You do not overcome hatred with hatred.'

'How about justice?' asked Sule.

'Yes, we need justice, but we need to accept God's justice which is revealed in Jesus Christ. Forgive me sounding preachy!' Both men laughed.

'You see,' Obi went on, 'justice must be tempered with mercy. If we insist on tit-for-tat, there will be no room for healing. Revenge breeds further revenge and hatred breeds more hatred. Forgiveness is stronger than retaliation and love is stronger than hatred. I have lost everything but I still have my life. There are some people who lost their lives in addition to their property. If we kill their killers in the pursuit of austere justice, we plunge the nation into another deluge of killings, bitterness and hatred and we will not be able to forget.'

'What shall we do then?' asked Sule in a very sober voice.

'The answer,' replied Obi, 'is repentance and a firm determination never to do it again, directly or indirectly. There should be a day of national repentance and reconciliation, when we get together and apologise to each other for our various prides and arrogance that brought us to this horrid situation. As you rightly said, we are all guilty, both the killers and the killed. There is too much hatred, too much selfishness, too much tribalism and xenophobia among us!'

Call to corporate repentance: no intention to retaliate
'But how can you get all my people to repent?'

'You can repent for them, Sule,' Obi replied. 'You told me just now that you identified with the guilt of your people. In the same way, begin to repent for them. That is how it begins one by one. We must let bygones be bygones. Otherwise we will never settle down to enjoy this peace that God has given us. I think the best policy is to say, "No victor, no vanquished". As for myself, forgiveness is greater than hatred. It brings healing both for me and for you and indeed for the whole community and nation. So, my friend, it is all over! Each of us must search our hearts and learn how we may make restitutions to show that we have indeed repented. National change and rapprochement will take time to achieve but it must begin with us as individuals. I speak for my people. We have no plans or intent to retaliate. We have forgiven you and we want to settle down to rebuild our lives. Tell your people to also go back to their businesses in the East. There is nothing to fear.'

The joy of reconciliation

'Obi, when did you become a preacher?' Sule asked with an excitement in his eyes. Obi laughed with his usual roar. Sule reconciled his old friend. Both men hugged each other, tears of joy mingled with the exhilaration of forgiveness, reconciliation and reunion. For them life was beginning all over again. It was a new life, not only for Obi, who claimed to have been 'born again' while in Biafra, but also for Sule, who had just received a new revelation of true love. From then on Sule set his mind to find the source of that light that gave his friend Obi's face this fresh new shine.

Restitution and national healing

Later that evening, Sule invited his kinsfolk and neighbours to welcome Obi home. He had Obi repeat what he had said to him about healing – personal and national – through forgiveness. Then he surprised everyone as he handed Obi a cardboard box full of the New Nigerian ten pound notes. 'I sold your chickens and the goods in your shop but kept the money, because, somewhere inside me, I believed that you would be back. I couldn't imagine life without you Obi. Here it is: thousand, one hundred and fifty-seven pounds, fifteen shillings and ten pence. It is your money. This is your home. Go again to Alandu and bring back your wife and children. We need you. Yes, you have so much to teach us.' Most people began to weep. Obi could not believe he was not in a dream. Not the money but the thought, he mused. The news of what Alhaji Sule did spread like wild fire

throughout Kano and others followed his example spontaneously. Through these two men, the healing of the nation
had begun!

A great contradiction
A foreign faith

Many people have described the recent genocide in Rwanda
as the greatest blot on the history of modern African
Christianity. How could Rwanda which was the cradle of the
East Africa revival become the scene of the most heinous
pogrom in recent human history? The brutal slaughter of
fellow human beings and fellow country folk and in some
cases one's fellow Christians simply boggles the mind.

The answer may be traced to a revival movement which
presented salvation as an 'otherworldist' experience which
was indifferent to social questions, and to a Christianity
which was clothed in too much foreign garb and therefore
seen as a 'foreign religion'.

Two faiths in the one mind

Such a colonialist view of Christianity and Christian mission,
produced Christians with a schizoid attitude to life. The
Church was seen as foreign – the 'New' or European way of
doing things. It was irrelevant to or at least did not understand the intricate issues of everyday life in the local African
culture. The result was that issues that related to Church life
and polity were viewed obsequiously from the perspective of
its foreign purveyors. But for traditional questions, because
they were rooted in their cultural ethos, the people resorted
to traditional practice for solutions.

This would include settling old scores the old ways. Tribal
wars were a regular cycle of life in primal African societies.
This schizoid mentality, 'two faiths in one mind' is the bane
of African Christianity and of modern revival and church
growth movements in Africa. The question remains: has the
Christian faith, judging by what we see of African Christian

behaviour, been able to penetrate beyond the surface of African life? Is it more than skin deep? In short, how converted are African converts?

Questions of depth of transformation
How could primal values persist so powerfully within and shape the behaviour of people who claim to have been converted to a new faith? Christianity is supposed to be a transforming religion. Why then were Rwandan Christians not transformed? John argues that any one who harbours hatred does not know God, for 'God is love' (1 John 4:10). So what effect did the revival have on them?

The Rwandan problem seems to present modern African Christian leadership with some specific questions:

- The question of hastiness in evangelism and the depth of conversion. Statistics could be simply triumphalist.
- The question of 'earthing' the gospel and expressing it in the idiom of a people's life and culture.
- The question of training high quality and relevant leadership for the church. Leaders who embody and model the gospel they proclaim. African social life does not major in theories and passive philosophies. It is practical and dynamic. Leadership both in the church and state needs to reflect this modelling motif.
- The question of the transformation of the people's culture and values and therefore the question of identity and loyalty. Which comes first, one's Christian identity in and loyalty to Christ or one's ethnic identity and loyalty?
- The question of foreign control and the 'Peter Pan' Syndrome that results from it, *vis-à-vis* the need for maturity, self-reliance and self-determination for the church.
- The question of continuous conversion and renewal. Many of the people engaging in some of the most harrowing ethnic squabbles in Africa today claim to have been 'born again' or received 'new life' during the revival years. That they seem to behave in ways that do not reflect that claim

suggests that we cannot live in the glory of the past. The power that set the spirit of revival and renewal in motion needs constant renewal so that conversion may at all times touch every aspect of a people's personal and collective life. This requires bold discipleship on the part of leadership and of all who would describe themselves as Christian in that context.

• The question of theological education and discipleship. If Christianity in Africa is to convert society, then for Christian leadership, relevant and high quality theological education is no longer a luxury but a must. My concern here is not merely with a parrot-fashion reproduction of Western Christian Theology by African 'scholars'. We have plenty of that already. We refer to a theological reflection that is biblical and Christo-centric and which is a result of honest struggle with the realities of a cultural situation, as the word of God revealed in Christ seeks to become redemptively incarnate in that local milieu. Perhaps this is the greatest challenge for African Christian leadership today. Stated differently: how do we make Christianity relevantly and redemptively African, and African Christians universally and authentically Christian?

• To find healing and lasting peace in Rwanda and Burundi, we need to 'earth' the Gospel of forgiveness and reconciliation in the soil of that context. The leadership of the Church there needs to know that there is a difference between following a foreign faith and therefore relying on foreign aid, and becoming self-reliantly and relevantly Christian. They must come to own the Gospel and take responsibility before God for their own actions. They need to find a Christian hermeneutic that is life affirming and culturally relevant so as to overcome hatred with love and death with life.

Reconciliation and forgiveness

The question people often ask is what is the difference between forgiveness and reconciliation? The Bible commands us to forgive unconditionally – 'just as God in Christ forgave us' (Eph 4:32; Matt 5:24*ff*). We are also warned that to forgive is not optional (Matt 6:14-15). We are advised to forgive others 'from the heart' to expect complete forgiveness from God (Matt 18:21-35).

We are advised to live at peace with everyone while it is in our power to do it, and commanded never to take our own vengeance or retaliation (Rom 12:17-21). But we are also commanded to repent so as to enjoy the fruit of God's forgiveness. To fail to do so is to live in fear and 'torment' (1 John 4:17-19). Whereas 'perfect love casts out all fear'. But it is those who repent that enjoy a reconciled relationship with God (Mark 1:14-15). This is closely linked with being reconciled to people (2 Cor 5:15-19).

However, the case of Abraham and Lot suggests that separation could pave the way to reconciliation and a better relationship. The proof of having forgiven is not always physical closeness, but the absence of bitterness. When there is no ill-will, no intention to revenge, then I know that forgiveness has taken place and reconciliation has been replaced by an attitude of good-will. Abraham loved Lot, the arrogant, ungrateful and greedy nephew whom he had raised and helped. They separated to make peace, but Abraham still loved – kept an attitude of good will for – Lot, the worldly incorrigible backslider. He risked his life for his rescue (Gen 14) and finally interceded for him and worked for his salvation – his physical as well as spiritual well being (Gen 18).

What a challenge!

Reconciliation and the World Faiths

Barbara Butler

A Maasai story tells of three bulls, red, white and black, a lion and a hare. The lion wanted to kill the bulls but could not do so because they were friendly towards each other. The lion persuaded the hare to divide the bulls and the hare succeeded. He first of all persuaded the black and white bulls that the red bull was a dangerous colour. The red bull was driven away, and then caught and killed by the lion. The hare then persuaded the black bull that the white bull was dangerous because he could be seen by enemies. The black and white bulls separated and both were killed by the lion.

There are many who are only too eager, sometimes unwittingly, to play the part of the hare between people of faith, telling the worst possible stories of other people's faiths and cultures and causing suspicion and even hatred, leading to separations, quarrels and sometimes wars. The Christian denominations have, throughout their history, also been divided in a similar way. The twentieth century ecumenical movement has made a lot of progress, but divisions, misunderstandings and wars continue. It is salutary to reflect on how recent most of the attempts at understanding and reconciliation between the world faiths have actually been.

It was as late as the Second Vatican Council in 1965 before the Catholic Church said officially that the suffering and crucifixion of Christ 'cannot be charged against all the Jews'. The Jews faced centuries of persecution by Christians. The fourth century archbishop St John Chrysostom said that Jews were no better than hogs and goats. Martin Luther recommended the burning down of synagogues and the houses and schools of Jewish people.[32] There were pogroms

201

in medieval England and the most horrendous cartoons against Jews were published. Christianity surely played a part in building up, over a long period, a misunderstanding of Jewish people, including the condemnation that they failed to recognise the Messiah, which many feel contributed to the horrors of the holocaust.[33] Even when the Second World War ended Jewish suffering did not. In one area of Czechoslovakia the people were told, as they were released, that there were no Jews in Poland and they were aware that 'the hope of finding alive any member of any family that had been separated years back and sent to Belzec, Treblinka, Auschwitz, and other accursed camps was dashed . . . it transpired that the survivors had nowhere to go, because Jews were not liked anywhere.'[34] Marginalisation and cruelty to Jewish people is not unknown in the 1990s. In Britain alone there are daily examples of prejudice and rejection.[35] It is only very recently that some theologians have struggled to change people's attitudes to Jews, to encourage listening to the Jewish people and appreciating that God's relationship to Jesus was a relationship of love and trust to a Jew living in a Jewish culture.[36, 37] Jews have also made efforts to portray Christianity in a positive light, some seeing it as God's gift to the Gentile world and encouraging understanding and friendship.

As friendship and understanding have developed between Jews and Christians the difficult question of the state of Israel has arisen. It is undoubtedly vitally important to Jews that Christians should relate to Israel and should understand their attachment to the land as part of their identity. For many Christians, saddened by the legacy of the holocaust, especially the unbelievable mass extermination of over one million Jews at Auschwitz, and struggling to make amends, it has been straightforward to accept Israel as the promised land of the Jewish people uncritically and without looking at the context in which Israel was formed and now exists. Unconditional support to Israel by many people, especially in Britain and

America, has led to the deprivation and marginalisation of the Palestinian people, Muslim and Christian, many of whom have suffered the loss of their lands and homes and are still struggling for a secure and peaceful future.

In May 1993 a conference was held in England entitled 'Christians in the Holy Land.' Palestinian Christians gathered from all over the world to share a few days together and it was immediately obvious that no matter how well educated and comfortable some of them were they were endlessly insecure, most of them living in exile and longing for their homeland. They sang songs of longing for home, 'Oh Jerusalem on our behalf, with certainty and dignity, let all people understand, that all we seek is life.' Rafiq and Najwa Farah were two members of the conference. They are a Palestinian Christian couple who have lived with struggle and suffering for most of their adult lives and are now living in retirement in Britain and Canada. Najwa wrote of her trauma in 1947 when, 'We were cut off from the world of the living and imprisoned in caves and camps, our condition deteriorating from one crisis to another . . . bewildered, shocked, broken-hearted, humiliated . . . I saw one city after another attacked and occupied, one village after another wiped out . . . my . . . people . . . becoming in one night refugees"[38] Rafiq and Najwa worked for human rights in the Middle East for many years, first in Israel and later in the West Bank, where they experienced the 1967 war and subsequent occupation, which Najwa later described as like seeing a horror film twice. In 1977 they moved to live in Beirut where they stayed in constant insecurity for nine years, living through the war and the 1982 siege, ministering to the injured and bereaved. Najwa and Rafiq are typical of Christian Palestinians who live in exile, and their numbers are increasing as their situation becomes more precarious. Forty per cent of them have left to go overseas since 1947. At the 1993 conference the Palestinian Christians who remain in their homelands spoke of daily problems and disruptions, including the lack of work opportunities and the take-over of church property and the lack of easy access to the holy places of Jerusalem for those living outside. The problems continue and so do the movements of the people into exile.

The Palestinians at the conference were at pains to understand their Jewish neighbours and to work with them where possible. They also expressed solidarity with their Muslim sisters and brothers, also Palestinians, sharing the same challenge and hope for a future. Jeanne Kattan, an academic from Bethlehem University, said passionately, 'I am not a minority. I am a Palestinian, an Arab and a Christian. I speak Arabic and have something in common with all Muslims . . . I have shared life with Muslims, I was brought up with them, at home and in school. When a colleague died the Christians and Muslims listened to each other's scriptures.' Jeanne conducted a survey of the students at Bethlehem University which indicated that their identity as Palestinians is stronger than their identity as Christians or Muslims.[39] Many people who live outside the Middle East are only aware of Muslim Palestinians and, unfortunately, their awareness is sometimes limited to the negative image of Muslims and of the Muslim world which has been conveyed to them by newspapers and on radio and television. The hare from the Maasai story seems to have good friends in spreading bad stories.

The Western media is particularly hard on Islam and many Muslims feel that it is almost impossible for them to have a fair hearing. This may be because there has been a history of competition between Christians and Muslims over many years, including the Crusader wars and centuries of strife, all leading to the gradual development of a climate of opinion which is very difficult to dislodge, which sees Muslims as alien, fanatical and 'wrong' in faith and culture. Muslims who live in the West sometimes say that they get the impression that the more secular they become, or appear to become, the more acceptable they are to many people. There is a general lack of willingness on the part of white British people to meet Muslims and to learn about their religion. There are of course many opportunities to do so and many organisations willing to give help.[40] If the barrier and ignorance could be overcome then much fear could also be overcome, for the Qu'ran so obviously teaches that Muslims are to strive for peace with those who are not Muslims.[41] The Qu'ran also states that, ' . . . there can be no compulsion in religion'.[42] The Western bias against Muslim religion and culture could be seen very clearly in much of the reporting of the Iranian revolution, when the religious fervour of the people was labelled very quickly as 'fanatical', 'fundamentalist', even 'barbarian', without any attempt to see developments from the point of view of the people who supported the revolution. Muslims find this unjust, especially since Western reports of the tragedies of Rwanda, Burundi and Zaire rarely include the fact that most of the people involved, as oppressors and oppressed, are Christians. John Simpson was one Western journalist who did spend a lot of time in Iran in the 1980s and he made an honest effort to convey his experiences truthfully. He communicated the harshness and sometimes cruelty of the revolution but he also shared something of the friendships he made with real and dignified people who had a different, but none the less authentic, view of life from his own and his insights into a rich and ancient culture. He wrote, 'To the outside world, Iran seems a dangerous and uncontrollable place, and there is a positive desire for horror stories about it. But the prosaic truth is that it is neither Cambodia in Year Zero nor Uganda under Idi Amin; it is in the grip of an ideology, but in most respects it is run like other countries, and more logically and efficiently than many.'[43] When Jeanne Coker, an Englishwoman, went to Iran in 1992 to teach athletics to women she was happy to discover that, though women live separate and, to Westerners, restricted lives, they often have great responsibilities. She worked with provincial leaders, scientists and teachers. She was given wonderful hospitality.

The report by the Runnymede Trust, *Islamophobia, a challenge for us all*, was brought out in 1997:[44] 'The word Islamophobia has been coined because there is a new reality which needs naming: Anti-Muslim prejudice in Britain has grown so considerably and so rapidly in recent years that a new item in the vocabulary is needed.'[45] The report makes it clear that Islamophobia does not include disagreement with Muslim beliefs or practices, nor does it include criticism of Muslim states where internationally recognised human rights are not allowed. Islamophobia includes unfounded and ignorant prejudice and hostility, the pigeonholing of all Muslims in the same box: identical, inferior and very different. It does not recognise the richness and diversity to be found in the Muslim world, or the possibility of mutually enriching relationships between Muslims and other people. The report tackles the consequences of Islamophobia, and its effects on young people and on employment. It is important not only because it faces unpleasant truths directly, but also because it paints a clear picture of the development of the various Muslim communities in Britain, including people of all traditions and ethnicities. It gives useful summaries of where bridges have been built, in national life and in community projects and dialogue. The check-list of recommendations given at the end of the report is a very useful tool for every aspect of life. The hope of the team who produced the report is that whenever prejudice against Muslims is voiced in public it will be challenged. Muslims will not be left to defend themselves.

Muslim women generally feel that they are badly and incorrectly represented as being down-trodden and marginalised by Muslim men. When meetings between women of different faiths take place Muslim women in particular are normally at pains to let everyone else know that they are full members of the faith, there because they have chosen to be there and that they are recognised as having equal status and dignity with men. One Muslim woman who works as a teacher in London and gives talks on Muslim women, carries a list around with her entitled, 'Islam and Women', which includes misconceptions and the reality of women's rights in Islam, including education, property, business and careers. We read that the reality is that 'Islam acknowledges the status of women and gives them rights equal to men', and 'Islam states that the mother is respected more than the father'. This Muslim teacher is a hard worker towards understanding and reconciliation between people of faith in an environment where many people somehow tend to remember the worst stories of other faiths and are inspired by the best stories of their own faith.

Muslim and Christian women worked together to bring peace in Bradford, during and after the riots of June 1995. They were able to do this because they met together regularly, in each other's homes, to share news and concerns about local and wider issues. One of the main discussions of the group had always been the nature of Islam in Bradford, where the first mosque was opened in 1959. Today there are more than thirty-four mosques. Two of the mosques are of the Shia tradition and the majority are Sunni. There are about fifty thousand Muslims in Bradford, so they are one in nine of the population, mostly living in the inner-city, and with a high proportion of young people. Unemployment is high, and this was later seen to be the main cause of the disturbances, together with the struggle young Muslims often have to work out who they are, often torn between the traditional demands of their faith and the expectations of secular youth culture. On June 9th 1995 four young men were arrested, followed by rumours and the gathering of crowds. There were more arrests and the attempts at mediation by the community leaders broke down. Then fires were lit in the streets and some shops were damaged. On Saturday, June 10th the situation had escalated and between two and three hundred people were involved in disturbances which many who experienced them felt were wildly exaggerated by the media. Molly Kenyon is a United Reformed Church

Minister who lives and works in Bradford and has written:

I went over on Sunday afternoon and walked around the upper part of Oak Lane, near the police station. There were a few broken windows, but many shops were open as usual with no sign of the devastation reported on the radio. I didn't realise until the next day that other areas had received much worse damage . . . A Muslim friend rang up on Sunday night with the idea of an action for peace, to stop the riots continuing for a third night. Eight of us had gathered by 11.30 pm. and we set out with candles and a makeshift banner saying 'Peace' in English, Urdu and Arabic. Four Asian and four white women walking together drew attention: women had kept away from the riots. There were groups of young men along Oak Lane, and quite a crowd at the police station – television lights blinded us as we approached it. The media surrounded us on the station steps for about half an hour, and by then the crowd had dispersed. We wondered if trouble would break out elsewhere, but in fact the night ended quietly. I was home by 1 am feeling very grateful to have been part of a positive action in the midst of so much distress, anger and fear. Women from different backgrounds had grown to trust each other. We were able to act together in a crisis as well as in day to day matters.[46]

Understanding and reconciliation with others is a challenge to all the main world faiths. The Incarnation of God as a human being, which is central to the faith of Christians, is a model of bridge-building between God and the earth and its people, who are challenged to be 'Peacemakers'. The Bible teaches that God created all that is, including all of life. Christians are challenged, especially in St John's Gospel, to see the light of God in every person. Christians in Britain have a special responsibility to build bridges towards people of other faiths because we have the space and the freedom to do so. We may be pioneers in a world where freedom is rare, where many people live in difficult and even dangerous situations. People of faith living in precarious situations do however often work bravely for reconciliation with those who are of a different faith. The Coptic Orthodox Church in Egypt has faced many attacks in recent years and hundreds of members have been killed by extremist groups. Early in 1997 thirteen people were massacred in Abu Qurquas. Copts feel marginalised in their own country and many feel that they do not have equal opportunities in education or employment, but they go on developing a strong and powerful spirituality and offering service to all around them, regardless of their religion. Christians in Pakistan are often very poor and people with little freedom. Mano Rumalshah, Bishop of Peshawar, estimates that seventy to eighty per cent of Christians work as sweepers or toilet cleaners. The church responds to this not by working with Christians, but by offering health care and education for whole communities. In this way Christians and Muslims meet each other at school and at the health clinic. The church is now working to offer opportunities for people to set up small businesses and in the long run there will be a spinning and weaving factory.[47]

Christians in Japan have always been a small minority and are less than one per cent of the population even today. Missionary activity was forbidden in the sixteenth century and Christianity was forbidden altogether in 1637, so that torture and death followed a confession of faith. In the middle of the nineteenth century Japan became more open and Christian missionaries began to return. It was then discovered that Christians had continued to live their faith secretly throughout all the centuries of persecution. There is a Christian museum at Oiso where there are many reminders of the time of secrecy and suffering, including crosses hidden in carvings and crucifixes hidden in the backs of buddhas. There are blocks of wood with relief carvings of Mary and Jesus. The reliefs were used for block painting prints, which were then used to detect hidden Christians; they were asked to step onto the prints, and were killed if they refused. The early paper prints were later replaced by bronze images.

There are also wooden blocks with the figures of mother and child, but without faces. The blocks had been produced by Buddhist woodcarvers to help the Christians in their time of trial, because they need not avoid treading on the images without faces and so could save their lives. Buddhist help to Christians in Japan is a challenge to all people of faith who live in privileged positions, perhaps where they are the majority or have a special place. Japanese Christians today are a small but strong community, at ease with people of other faiths and in their largely secular surroundings. They work hard as normal members of their own country and to join forces with the rest of Asia and with Europe. The significance of their contribution is a separate chapter in this book.

The Sanskrit word 'Yoga' means 'to join' or 'that which unites'. Yoga arose within the Hindu tradition and is a challenge to people of the faith to unite within the self, with others, with the environment, with the universal, with God.

Yohan Devananda is an Anglican priest in Sri Lanka, who has written and spoken about the dance of the Hindu god Shiva as one of the world's most powerful symbols of faith in action. Shiva, wearing a belt of austerity, and surrounded by a ring of fire, is poised with his knee raised in a dance of creation and of destruction. His foot is placed on a creature representing the evil forces of the world and his hand is pointing downwards in commitment to the world and its people, in commitment to work for justice and harmony.

One Hindu who built a bridge of understanding between Hinduism and the other faiths, especially those in the West, was Vivekananda, who attended and spoke at the first World Parliament of Religions in Chicago in 1893 which was celebrated by the 1993 inter-faith gatherings in India and around the world. Vivikananda set up the Ramakrishna Mission and the Vedanta societies in Europe and America. He appealed for people to work for understanding and to build up whole and wholesome lives by linking meditation with service. His appeal for contemplation and action, for work and worship, or work as worship, has been taken up by other world-famous Indian religious leaders and philosophers, including the poet, artist and musician Rabindranath Tagore, and Mahatma Gandhi.

Gandhi was inspired by the Hindu scriptures, especially the *Bagavhad Gita*, to strive towards loving devotion, understanding and selfless service of others. He was deeply influenced by the Quakers and by the Sermon on the Mount. He found common ground between the lives and teachings of Jesus Christ and the Lord Buddha. Gandhi's main challenge to all people of faith remains invaluable, especially in the late twentieth century. It is a challenge to ordinary living and working together, especially in serving others, so that spiritual experience arises naturally out of the service freely and lovingly given. His understanding has much in common with Celtic Christianity, which pointed to God in the ordinary work and everyday lives of the people. He founded ashram communities which were very practical, where people of different faiths and abilities worked at cleaning, cooking, farming and spinning. He spoke of being given energy for his campaigns from ashram life and work, and of seeing the face of God in the faces of the poor.

In India today approximately forty-seven per cent of the people live below the poverty line. Ill health and hunger are normal for such people. Those who are carrying on where Gandhi left off are not necessarily in ashrams, though they would include Mother Theresa's Sisters of Charity. Most are ordinary people, living and working in the rural and growing urban communities, like members of the 'Silence' community who '. . . can neither hear nor speak except visually and who cannot go places except in their imaginations'. The community of the disabled numbers seventy-two people who earn their own living by craft-work, and who encourage others to do the same. The Calcutta Young Men's Welfare Society is made up of ordinary people, Hindus, Muslims and Christians, all working together to share skills with the poor, so that they may develop in their own way. Priority is given to education at all levels and one of the most inspiring sights in the world is that of slum children studying in YMWS schools. Twelve hundred children attend these schools, and study as they would in a normal primary school, except that they go to school at night when they are free from their daytime labours and when the classrooms are free from the fee-paying children. There are also pavement schools and schools for Muslim girls. YMWS also works at community development and primary health care, including the mobile medical clinics. The organisation OFFER works with street children in Calcutta, those whose parents have abandoned them or are dead and who therefore live on the streets and on railway platforms. Members of OFFER give a home and education, but above all they give love and hope to children who were without either. Another group of people for whom work is worship makes up the Society of Developmental Action in Orissa where many projects have been started with the tribal people, for their future, including legal training and health education, a family counselling programme and an orphanage. There are many faith-filled, loving and dedicated people and communities in India; people for whom there is no dichotomy between the sacred and the secular. They offer a glimpse of the possibility of a whole, wholesome and holy India, even in the face of Hindu nationalism, and of a world where a whole cross-section of people of all faiths, classes and tribes are enabled to make their contribution to their people and country.

Buddhism began in North India in the sixth century BCE. Siddhartha Gautama was an Indian prince who, realising the inequalities and divisions of life, left his family and palace to go on a journey of faith towards reconciliation with himself and with others. The chapter on 'Buddhist Insights into Peace-making' gives us a clear awareness of the Four Noble Truths of Buddhism. The challenge of Buddhism is to see conflict as an opportunity for peace-making. To embark upon peace-making it is necessary to go to the roots of conflict. It is also necessary to live peacefully, through the eight-fold path and to develop detachment, wisdom and compassion.

Sogyal Rinpoche has written to enlighten Western readers on Tibetan Buddhism. He has given invaluable advice on how to awaken love and compassion which may eventually become boundless, encompassing the whole universe, but also people we dislike and even hate. He has pointed to a way forward by going back, in our thoughts, until we can re-create an experience of love. We should then dwell upon the person who loved us and the happiness this gave us. We should remember a specially vivid experience of love and feel grateful and loving towards the person who loved us. Gradually we will then become aware of being worthy of love. We may then give love, beginning with those closest to us and extending slowly outwards, to friends and neighbours, and then to strangers and the people we may call our enemies, until finally we are able to embrace the whole universe.[48]

No people are in greater need of this teaching than the Tibetan people themselves, because they have faced so many cruelties since their country was invaded by China in 1950, including war, death, torture and exile. Buddhism has been the religion of Tibet from the time when the Buddhist masters were invited there in the seventh century CE. In the seventeenth century CE Buddhist monks became the rulers of Tibet and the present Dalai Lama is the fourteenth 'monk ruler'. After the 1950 invasion the Tibetan culture and heritage were systematically destroyed, especially the monasteries and temples. Well over a million of the Tibetan people have died and those who have survived have vivid stories to tell, mostly of suffering. It is surprising that many Tibetan people living in India and Britain are patient, peaceful and seemingly without bitterness, building up their faith and culture as best they can and caring for the young people and children who are orphaned. There are eighteen Tibetan children's villages in India and all reach a high standard in care of the children and in education, especially in art and handicraft work. Three of the monasteries which were rased to the ground in Lhasa have been lovingly rebuilt in India, exactly as they were. India, a largely Hindu country, gave a generous welcome to the Tibetan refugees. From the moment when they arrived at the Indian border they were accommodated in transit camps and then sent off to settlements, some arranged personally by the Prime Minister, Jawahalal Nehru.

Losang Yeshi is one of many hundreds of Tibetan refugees who left Tibet in 1959 when he was five years old and went first to India where he was in a children's village and then came to Britain when he was eleven years old to be brought up in the Pestalozzi Village. He has worked in Pakistan and in Britain for the Ockenden Venture. He has spoken about being a refugee: 'I never quite have a sense of belonging. I feel that my experience of being a refugee is of benefit in the work I do with refugees.'[49]

The Dalai Lama himself is a well known religious leader who works for justice and peace for all. He stands in the fine tradition of Tibetan Buddhism which embraces the ideal of the Bodhisattva, the one who has gained enlightenment but who renounces the final entry into Nirvana in order to relieve the sufferings of the world.

> If I do not exchange my happiness
> For the suffering of others,
> I shall not attain the state of buddhahood,
> And even in samsara
> I shall have no real joy.[50]

Since his exile from Tibet in 1959 the Dalai Lama has supported his people in exile whilst at the same time striving to persuade China to give the Tibetan people and culture a future. His attempts to have Tibet turned into a peace zone where his people could live in dignity and with respect for the natural environment have so far failed, as have his attempts to build understanding between the Tibetan and Chinese people. He has faced his failures honestly, even sharing his frustrations and inability to understand what has happened to his people. He has even confessed that it is natural for anyone to feel hostile towards those who do harm to them. At the same time he has not given up in his attempts to bring reconciliation between his people and the Chinese people and he has further shown his care for the Chinese people. When the Tiannenmann Square demonstrations were crushed by the Chinese authorities he spoke out: '. . . the brave students and their supporters showed the Chinese leadership and the world the human face of that great race.'[51] He has continued in the face of very obvious and public failure. In 1994 he gave the John Main Seminar in London, when he commented on the gospels. When he spoke on Chapter 5 of St Matthew's Gospel, 'Love your enemies and pray for your persecutors', he referred to a Mahayana Buddhist text, *The Compendium of Practices*, in which Shantideva asks, 'If you do not practise compassion towards your enemy then towards whom can you practise it?' He also introduced *A Guide to the Bodhisattva's Way of Life*, in which Shantideva stresses that it is vital to develop the right attitude towards an enemy and goes on to say that an enemy may be the best spiritual teacher, providing an opportunity for the development of tolerance, patience and understanding, all of which may lead to the development of compassion and even altruism, equanimity and calmness.[52]

No one has practised compassion, altruism, equanimity and calmness more in the late twentieth century than Aung San Suu Kyi who was placed under house arrest in Burma in 1989 for challenging the long-standing military dictatorship. Elections took place in 1990 and Aung San Suu Kyi's National League for Democracy won eighty-two per cent of the seats, but the military refused to stand down. She was awarded the Nobel Prize for Peace in 1991 and officially released from house arrest in 1995. However, the reality of her restricted life remains the same, whilst military control continues. On November 3rd 1997 Aung San Suu Kyi's husband, Dr. Michael Aris, delivered the Pope Paul V1 Memorial Lecture, *Heavenly Abodes and Human Development*, which she had written.[53] In her paper she examines the Buddhist values which, as a Buddhist herself, she considers crucial for peace and human development. As she explains Buddhist values she often links them to Christian values, and at one point quotes from St Paul's First Epistle to the Corinthians. She does not consider development to be material but rather spiritual and enabled by the four 'heavenly abodes' of Buddhism: loving kindness, compassion, sympathetic joy and equanimity. It follows that any development must put people and their human rights first and that any work for development and justice must be motivated by love and compassion, always balanced by wisdom.

The Nipponzan Myohoji Buddhist Order is a branch of Japanese Nichiren Buddhism which was founded by Nichidatsu Fuji, a disciple of Gandhi who devoted his life to work for peace whilst living through World War Two, the Holocaust and the bombing of Hiroshima and Nagasaki. He worked for peace by making a world-wide pilgrimage during which he established peace pagodas. Members of the order continue to build peace pagodas and to walk for peace. He said, 'Civilisation is not to have electricity, nor aeroplanes, nor to produce nuclear bombs . . . Civilisation is to hold one another in mutual affection and respect.'[54] In 1994 the order organised a pilgrimage of ten thousand miles, from Auschwitz to Hiroshima, of which three thousand miles were on foot. The Reverend Gyoshu Sasamori has said, 'We started our journey at one of the most tragic places of the war, where there was a massive killing industry; we ended it at the place where the first atomic bomb was dropped on human beings, ushering in the possibility that all humankind and the earth herself could be destroyed . . . We offered prayers for the victims of all wars. We heard the voices of the victims in our hearts, voices of survivors, voices from the war zones, voices from areas of conflict. All those voices, overcome with sorrow, seeking hope. I believe that if we face the painful facts of history unflinchingly and convey the lessons drawn from them to future generations, we will be able to bring peace to the souls of those who died in anguish in time of war ... we can establish new values today and for the future.'[55]

One of the main homes of Theravada Buddhism is Sri Lanka where seventy per cent of the people, the Sinhala people, follow an orthodox Buddhist path, keeping as close as possible to the teachings of the Buddha. Very sadly many people of faith have not listened to each other in Sri Lanka, and the long civil war has not been curtailed. Many people feel that they do not have a future. Sinhala extremists have tended to bring out their idea of Sri Lanka as a Buddhist holy land, which has not helped to build a bridge with the Tamil people, who are mainly Hindu. When Prince Charles visited the country, for the fiftieth anniversary of independence celebrations on February 4th 1998, he was heavily guarded and no members of the public were admitted to the ceremony. President Chandrika Kumaratunga said, 'We must, with humility, examine our failures. We have failed in the essential task of nation-building. We must proceed with fortitude to face the daunting challenges of terrorism and the political and social violence it has engendered within the entire social fabric of our country.'[56] I refer to Sri Lanka in my introduction, giving examples of destruction in a country where more than fifty thousand lives have been lost but also of those who are working for human rights and for reconciliation, without whom the situation would be darker and the future more hopeless than it is. Like the Dalai Lama some of the people of all the faiths in Sri Lanka have been able to go on working for peace in the face of failure and humiliation and there is great hope in those who do this and in the link between the public work and the ordinary day to day living in faith of many like Ainsley and Evelyn Samarajiwa. They are members of the

Methodist Church who brought up their own family and then adopted two Buddhist girls. Their home is open to people of all faiths. Much of the grassroots community work in Sri Lanka shows clearly that most ordinary people are not religious extremists, but want an end to war. Yohan Devananda is the co-ordinator of the World Solidarity Forum, which includes people of all faiths and was founded in Thailand, with representatives from nineteen countries. The forum has published *A noble eight-fold path. Eight musts for peace.* This publication came from many months of work and discussion with grassroots community groups and with people of all religions and races in Sri Lanka. The eight points are an excellent basis for working towards permanent peace, including a challenge to the political parties, the ethnic groups and people of all faiths to seek to understand each other and to work together towards justice for all.

There is a lot of work to do because most Sri Lankan families have lost a member, many are poor and destitute. Perhaps the worst situation to face is of having lost a family member and of not knowing what has happened to them. Sunila Abeyesekera is the head of the Women and Media Collective in Colombo who works with refugees in Colombo, mostly women and children, many of whom have seen their husbands and sons killed. She has said, 'The level to which the whole cycle of killing has sunk is all so incredible; no-one is safe, from an infant of three or four months old to an old grandfather who is lying in bed partially paralysed.' Sunila says that those who suffer the most are those who do not know what has happened to their relatives. 'There is the need to get a body into your own hands to really know that a person is dead, not just to rely on word of mouth . . . people just want to see and reclaim that body so that at least they may bury it with some dignity, the dignity that they did not get in life.'[57] People of all faiths in Sri Lanka are bringing relief to those who suffer, in the refugee camps, in their homes, and by travelling, sometimes at great personal risk, to the stricken northern area, simply to be with the people who are suffering. The Colombo Cathedral organises relief and justice work, including rehabilitation projects for people who have returned to the villages. Seeds and plants are provided and people of faith are encouraged to work together. Counselling is organised for trauma victims.

No one has encouraged people of different faiths to work together in community in Sri Lanka more than Aloysius Pieris, a Jesuit who runs the Christian-Buddhist Dialogue Centre of Tulana. He challenges Christians not to try to fit Jesus into society as they find it, but rather to change the society which Jesus is already in, so that it is fit for him and for all his people. Change is most likely to be successful if people work together across the faiths, by joining basic human communities. Christians in such communities may discover more about themselves, and about Jesus, through working with non-Christians in the context of a common concern for liberation.[58]

The Sikh people have always worked for people of all faiths to understand and respect each other and to join forces in work for justice and peace. Sikhism developed in the Punjab, in North Western India, and is in itself the result of the interaction of Hinduism and Islam. It emerged as a separate faith with the teachings of Guru Nanak who was born in 1469, and its beliefs may be summed up in the phrase, 'One God and One Humanity'. Guru Nanak's teaching on the equality of all people has been well expressed in the development of the community kitchen or 'langar' where all people eat together, sitting in rows. A popular story is of the Emperor Akbar visiting Guru Amar Das. Before the emperor was allowed into the guru's presence he had to sit on the ground and share food with the people who happened to be there at the time. Sikhs also worship together, and during worship they share in *karah parshad*, which is a food made of ghee, flour and sugar which is offered to everyone present from the same bowl. Guru

Gobind Singh introduced a new ceremony at the festival of Vaisakhi in 1699 when he founded the *Khalsa* or community of the initiated. As part of the ceremony all the initiates drank amrit or nectar from the same bowl.[59] Sikh beliefs are not divorced from everyday life and Sikhs are taught to fight for what is right on every level, including the social and political, and their history includes persecution and struggle. Sikhs have travelled to live all over the world, including Canada, East Africa, Australia, America and the United Kingdom and they have established 'gurdwaras' or temples, for worship and social outreach, everywhere they have settled. In the UK Sikhs have quickly become local councillors and mayors. They have fought for recognition and acceptance everywhere. In 1984 more than fifty thousand Sikhs demonstrated in London against a headteacher who had refused to admit a Sikh boy with a turban. The Sikh battle has largely been won in Britain, and second generation Sikhs are completely at home whilst remaining Sikh.

In the modern world global communications, trade and politics have brought the world faiths together as never before although there have been good and bad examples of interaction throughout history. John Hick has argued that the faiths have developed from 'self-centredness to reality centredness', which he describes as a turning away from destructive egotism and a movement towards a compassionate, loving and caring attitude to all. 'The function of religion is to bring us to a right relationship with the ultimate divine reality, to awareness of our true nature and our place in the Whole, into the presence of God.'[60] Many people of faith are learning to respect each other and even to work together, whilst recognising that their faiths are different and that it is not possible fully to appreciate another faith without the 'eye of faith'. It is important that people of faith also recognise that it is reasonable for them to find someone else's faith unattractive and yet to respect it and to recognise the holy spirit of God within it, and to love and trust its followers.

When the Dalai Lama gave his speech in acceptance of the Nobel Peace Prize he focused on what people of faith have in common, as people, and he went on to challenge all people to take up their responsibilities for the world. 'We need to cultivate a universal responsibility for one another and the planet we share.'[61] He said that he believes that religion and spirituality have a greater role to play than ever before in the late twentieth century, complicated and troubled as it is. He believes that people of faith must strive to build a better world together, by recognising that we pursue the same goals and by strengthening each other.

The Dalai Lama's appeal to the religions to unite and to strive together for reconciliation and justice was in part reinforced by the *Declaration Towards a Global Ethic* launched by the 1993 gathering of the world's religions. This statement is the first to be supported by religious leaders from all over the world. Its creation is inspiring in itself, but the harder task of bringing the communities of faith from all over the world to support it remains.

The declaration states that:

> The world is in agony . . .
>
> Peace eludes us . . . the planet is being destroyed . . . neighbours live in fear . . . women and men are estranged from each other . . . children die.
>
> This is abhorrent.
>
> We condemn the poverty that stifles life's potential, the hunger that weakens the human body, the economic disparities that threaten so many families with ruin.
>
> We condemn the social disarray of the nations; the disregard for justice which pushes citizens to the margin, and the insane death of children from violence and hatred in the name of religion.
>
> But this agony need not be.
>
> It need not be because the basis for an ethic already exists . . .
>
> We are women and men who have embraced the

precepts and practices of the world's religions.

We affirm that a common set of core values is found in the teachings of the religions, and that these form the basis of a global ethic.

We affirm that the truth is already known, but yet to be lived in heart and action . . .

WE DECLARE:

We are interdependent. Each of us depends on the wellbeing of the whole, and so we have respect for the community of living beings, for people, animals, and plants . . .

We take individual responsibility for all we do . . . We must treat others as we wish others to treat us . . . We must have patience and acceptance. We must be able to forgive, learning from the past but never allowing ourselves to be enslaved by memories of hate . . .

We consider humankind our family . . . We must not live for ourselves alone, but should also serve others, never forgetting the children, the aged, the poor, the suffering, the disabled, the refugees, and the lonely . . . There should be equal partnership between women and men . . .

We commit ourselves to a culture of non-violence, respect, justice and peace . . .

We must strive for a just social and economic order . . .

We must speak and act truthfully and with compassion . . .

We must move beyond the dominance of greed . . .

Earth cannot be changed for the better unless the consciousness of individuals is changed first. We pledge to increase our awareness by disciplining our minds, by meditation, by prayer or by positive thinking. Without risk and a readiness to sacrifice there can be no fundamental change in our situation. Therefore we commit ourselves to this global ethic, to understanding one another, and to socially beneficial, peace-fostering, and nature friendlier ways of life.

We invite all people, whether religious or not, to do the same.[62]

The declaration is encouraging and uplifting in expressing the commitment of people of faith to reconciliation, peace and justice for the future of the world, whilst at the same time it is depressing because it also sets out the state of the world as it is and is a stark reminder of how much needs to be done, how difficult it all is and how few examples there seem to be of faith commitment being put into practice. There are more examples perhaps of the use of religion for political power and the oppression of others and some of these are touched on elsewhere in this book. The largest part of the hope is that many people of faith will not give up the struggle for wholeness and harmony simply because it is a long way off. There are also smaller crumbs of hope in people of faith throughout the ages, and also in the twentieth century, who have given their lives for the good of others; and they have not died in vain. The twentieth century has produced politicians of vision, including Jawarhalal Nehru of India and Julius Nyerere of Tanzania. Some great and inspiring changes have been made towards a more inclusive and wholesome world, the civil rights legislation in America and the downfall of the apartheid regime in South Africa being but two, in which people of faith played a great part. Late twentieth century conferences on the environment and on issues of population and war and peace have seen people from all over the world working together for change and sustainability. Many grass-roots groups around the world, of people of many faiths, are turning back to the challenge of Mahatma Gandhi, to recall the face of the poorest and most helpless person they have seen and to ask if the action they take will be of any use to him, 'Will it restore him to a control over his own life and destiny?'[63] Many people of faith who are working for the cancellation of the debts of the poorest countries in the world are doing so in the hope that dignity and equality may be restored. In 1987 the Interfaith Network was established in the United Kingdom, and now fulfils a vital role in linking up local interfaith groups all over the country. It encourages dialogue at every level, and provides resources and information. Its belief is, '. . . that in our plural society there needs to be mutual respect for one another's integrity and convictions, and this should characterise all our relationships with people of other faiths and beliefs.'[64]

The development of mutual respect, trust and working together between people of different faiths is essential for the future of the world. There must be no place for the hare who carried the bad news of differences in the Maasai story, but rather the spreading of the good news of all the world faiths, leading to an appreciation of the strength and richness of differences where those who are different work together for a whole and holy world.

Buddhist Insights into Peacemaking

John A. McConnell

'Keep in the wisdom of God that spreads over all the earth, the wisdom of the creation that is pure. Live in it ... // ... then you will come to walk cheerfully over the world, answering that of God in everyone.' Thus George Fox, founder of the Religious Society of Friends, urged Friends in 1656 in a letter from Launceston prison, Cornwall. The notion that our own spiritual searchings can encourage and discover like potential in others, and thus lay a foundation for reconciliation, lies at the root of the Quaker adventurousness in peacemaking. It results in an attitude that searches beyond the division and bitterness of conflict for a potential for goodness that has been obscured, and upon which a constructive way forward might be based.

Answering that of God in others also has implications for the way in which we relate to other faiths. If there is that of God in others, is it not likely that spiritual leadings towards peace are manifested in other religious systems as well as our own? My own research on resources of peacemaking in the Buddha's teaching confirms both that this is so and that there is much we can learn by such inter-religious study.

The four noble truths – a challenge for peacemakers
The basic insight of Buddhism is that conflict is the result of psycho-spiritual causal processes, and that if we can engage with and undermine those causal processes then the conflict too will be transformed. Like good doctors, peacemakers need to be able to diagnose and respond to underlying conditions rather than just treat symptoms. We need to understand the roots and inner workings of conflict with

enough precision to see points where the process of peace-making may engage.

In his first sermon at the Deer Park near Benares the Buddha gave what is at once the simplest and most comprehensive formulation of his teaching — the proclamation of a middle way of spiritual living (*majjhima patipada*) and the enunciation of the four noble truths (*ariya-sacca*). Even after two thousand years these lines have a tangible sense of spiritual discovery about them. The sermon, delivered to the five ascetics with whom the Buddha had earlier associated, is recorded in the *Samyutta Nikaya* as follows:

Monks, these two extremes should be avoided by one who has gone forth as a wanderer. What two? Devotion to pleasures of the senses, a low practice of villagers . . . unworthy, unprofitable, the way of the world; and devotion to self-mortification which is painful, unworthy and unprofitable.

By avoiding those two extremes the Buddha has gained knowledge of that middle path which gives wisdom, which gives knowledge, which causes calm . . . enlightenment, *Nibbana* . . .

Now this, monks is the Aryan truth about ill: birth is ill, decay is ill, sickness is ill, death is ill: likewise sorrow and grief, woe, lamentation and despair. To be connected with things we dislike: to be separated from things which we like – that also is ill. Not to get what one wants. In a word, this body, this fivefold mass which is based on grasping – that is ill.

Now this, monks, is the Aryan truth about the arising of ill: it is that craving that leads to birth, along with the lure and lust that lingers longingly . . . namely craving for sensual pleasure, craving for being, craving for non-being. Such, monks, is the Aryan truth about the arising of ill.

And this, monks, is the Aryan truth about the ceasing of ill: verily it is utter passionless cessation of, the giving up, the forsaking, the release from, the absence of longing for this craving.

> Now this, monks, is the Aryan truth about the practice
> that leads to the ceasing of ill: verily, it is this Aryan way:
> right view, right aim, right speech, right action, right living,
> right effort, right mindfulness, right concentration.'[65]

What the Buddha taught was basically that once we turn
our attention to our unhappiness and observe just how it
arises we gain the power to change the psycho-spiritual
processes that are its continuing cause. The fourth truth, the
eight-fold path, suggests a way by which self-awareness can
be made more profound, and other aspects of life brought
into harmony with spiritual progress.

The *Dhamma* (the Buddha's teaching) challenges us to let
go of habitual ways of coping with conflict, get closer to
experience and experiment with peace. Thus we can apply
the four truths to conflict as follows:

The truth of suffering – conflict is part of the human condition
The first step in responding to conflict is to be aware of the
patterns of conflict that have become built into our relationships with others at home, at work, and elsewhere – patterns
so familiar that we hardly notice them until things go badly
wrong. The challenge of the first truth is thus to ask ourselves:
'What is our experience of conflict? What are its qualities
and dimensions?' and simply to be aware, without avoiding
the reality in any way.

*The truth of the arising of suffering – what are the roots of
conflict?*
When the Buddha spoke of conflict it was often as the result
of the three unwholesome roots of action (the *akusala-mula*)
– greed (*lobha*), hate (*dosa*) and delusion (*moha*). All three
have in common that they are self-centred, rooted in spiritual
ignorance and unskilled. In conflict, greed, hate and delusion
interact within and between the minds of conflictants, leading
conflictants to extremes of emotion and behaviour that are, in

a very real sense, out of control. The *akusala-mula* can be used to analyse conflict – to trace, stage by stage, the psychological interactions that have caused and still sustain it.

A somewhat finer tool is to be found in the Buddha's teaching of Dependent Origination, the *Paticcasamuppada* which, in its psychological interpretation, charts out processes of attachment which distort our understanding and exaggerate our wants. Use of the *paticcasamuppada* as a 'tool of mindfulness' – to quote a recent Thai thinker, Buddhadasa Bikkhu – lets us identify successions of mental changes from the initial stimulus of a physical event or mental image, through various stages of attachment, to a change in the way we perceive ourselves and others. The challenge of the second noble truth is, using mindfulness, to seek out these psycho-spiritual roots of conflict and analyse the dynamic that has resulted in escalation.

The truth of cessation – that peace can emerge from conflict
Even though the causes of a particular conflict may lie in the injustices of the past, the conflict cannot be sustained over a protracted period without development and repetition of patterns of thought, awareness and feeling in the present. It is in the minds of conflictants here and now that transformation can begin. The third truth then, is that suffering peters out once the clinging which causes it comes to an end. Similarly with conflict, as the self-centred psychological processes that sustain the conflict are undermined through mindfulness and compassion, so the conflict starts to be transformed.

Peace and conflict are closely inter-related processes rather than distinct and different states. The three self-centred *akusala-mula* (greed, hate and delusion) are paralleled by three non-self-centred *kusala-mula* (wholesome roots of action) detachment (*alobha*), hatelessness (*adosa*), and clarity of mind (*amoha*). The Buddha taught that the psychological processes which produce suffering can be transformed, without remainder, into wholesome processes that yield health and enlightenment. The challenge of the third noble truth then is to see conflict, with all its messiness and pain, as an opportunity for peacemaking. It challenges us to develop a peace process that engages with the roots of the conflict.

The truth of the cessation of suffering – that peace is a way of life
The fourth truth is that we do not have to wait for release from suffering. We are free to begin, here and now, to live in a way that is conducive to the reduction and extinction of suffering. The eight-fold path (*atthangika-magga*)[66] consists of the following steps:
- Right understanding – understanding the four noble truths.
- Right thought – having thoughts free from desire, ill-will and cruelty.
  Together, right understanding and right thought are classed as wisdom (*panna*).
- Right speech – not lying, using harsh language or gossiping.
- Right bodily action – not killing, stealing or indulging in irresponsible sex.
- Right livelihood – not engaging in work or activity that brings harm to others (fishing, contributing to military activities, deceit, trading in arms, etc.)
  Right speech, bodily action and livelihood are said all to be part of morality (*sila*).
- Right effort – the effort to overcome unwholesome tendencies and promote wholesome ones.
- Right mindfulness – self-awareness of both mental and physical dimensions of our experience. When we walk we are mindful of the experience of walking. When we feel unhappy we are mindful of the feeling and the images associated with it.
- Right concentration – the concentration used in meditation and associated with wholesome (*kusala*) states of consciousness (i.e. cultivation of goodwill, renunciation of desires and obtaining a clear understanding)

Right effort, mindfulness and concentration are all brought together as meditation (*samadhi*).[67]

Practice of the eight-fold path has to be tailored to each individual's situation. Right speech is one thing for the teacher, another for the shop-keeper, another for the soldier – and different too for the peacemaker. Likewise, techniques of meditation adequate to practice in a quiet and solitary environment may not be so easily applicable to the situation of the peacemaker trying to stay mindful as he or she mediates a conflict awash with feelings of hurt and anger. The challenge of the fourth noble truth is to devise the most appropriate way of putting the eight-fold path into practice as a peacemaker. Peacemaking relates directly with the self-awareness with which we live each day.

Implications for peacemakers
• One of the deepest and most intractable roots of conflict lies in the basic attitudes, self-concepts and values of con-flictants. Peacemakers have a role, not just in juggling with a range of external options, but in engaging with the psycho-spiritual roots of the conflict too.
• The spirituality of mediators – their detachment, wisdom, compassion and quality of awareness – is a real and very practical resource in dealing with deep-rooted conflict. In the midst of anger, bitterness and confused accusations the mediator comes as a friend, with goodwill and a steady determination to make peace.

However intractable or overwhelming a conflict may seem, we should bear in mind that it needs causal processes of self-centred attachment to sustain it and that these processes are susceptible to change. Ven. Maha Ghosananda of Cambodia has said: 'There is little we can do for peace in the world without peace in our minds. And so, when we begin to make peace we begin with silence – meditation and prayer. . . . // . . . Peacemaking requires selflessness. It is selflessness taking root'[68]

The Buddha's mediation between Koliyan and Sakyan states

Introduction:

This section examines an incident in which the Buddha intervened between two neighbouring states – the Koliyas and the Sakyas – who had reached the brink of war. We will try to detect elements of the Buddha's approach which are relevant to mediators today. There are two different but overlapping versions of the incident in the *Kunala Jataka* and the *Dhammapada Commentary*. The accounts complement each other rather than conflict.

The situation

The Sakyas and Koliyas lived on opposite sides of the river Rohini. Fields lay on each side, next the river, and behind them, the capitals of the two small states. Kapilavatthu was the Sakyan capital, Ramagama the capital of the Koliyas. The royal families of the two states had intermarried and both were related to Gautama Sakyamuni – the Buddha. We know that, until the time of the conflict, there had been considerable co-operation between them because a common dam had been constructed and used by both to irrigate their fields. No dispute over the ownership of the river is mentioned.

The cause of strain in this amicable relationship was a drought in the weeks preceding harvest. The waters of the Rohini were low and people were uncertain whether or not there would be further rain. No fears of starvation are mentioned but there clearly was concern about what proportion of the corn could be brought to harvest if the drought continued.

A suggestion is made

One of the workers or foremen in the fields – a Koliyan – suggested that, since the water was insufficient to bring the crops of both sets of fields to maturity, all the water should be diverted onto Koliyan land. The text does not mention promise of a fair return for the Sakyas – say, half the crop – but we can assume there was something like that. The Sakyan workers, however, already worried by the prospect of a poor harvest, were suspicious of possible Koliyan moves to monopolise the water. They expressed their fear clearly: 'When you have filled your garners with corn, we shall hardly have the courage to come with ruddy gold, emeralds and copper coins and with baskets and sacks in our hands to hang about your doors. Our crops will thrive with a single watering. Give us the water.'[69]

The plan would cause dependence on the Koliyas and the Sakyas faced having to trade their treasures for rice and having to become hired labourers. The reference to 'hanging about your doors' indicates the loss of self-respect that this would entail.

The conflict escalates
At this juncture the problem was not especially difficult, and had they approached it jointly a mutually acceptable solution could surely have been found. Possible elements of an agreement might have been to give priority to the highest-yielding fields with the condition that the harvest would be divided equally. However, rather than discussing a range of alternatives, the parties argued for and against the Koliyan demand. Each was worried that the other would gain control. There was an impasse:

'We will not give it . . . neither will we.'[70]
Emotions ran high and fist-fights broke out.
As words ran high, one of them rose up and struck another a blow, and he in turn struck a third, and thus it was that with interchanging blows and in spitefully touching on their princely families they increased the tumult.[71]

Since the quarrel was between communities rather than individuals, it was the self-pictures of the communities – that is, their royal households – that were attacked: 'Be off with your people of Kapilavatthu, men who like dogs jackals and such like beasts, cohabited with their own sisters. What will their elephants and horses, shields and spears avail against us?'

The Sakyan labourers replied, 'Nay, do you wretched lepers, be off with your children, destitute and ill-conditioned fellows, who like brute beasts had their dwelling in the hollow of a jujube tree (*koli*). What shall their elephants and horses, their spears and shields, avail against us?'[72]

The royal families become involved

Reports were received by the princes and their advisors whose prime concern was, of course, the insult to their good names. Neither could deny the insults because they were drawn from legends of their shared history. That the water problem did not feature in their deliberations is confirmed by the complete absence of its mention in the challenges issued on the following morning.

Reading the challenges it is clear that the two sides are intent on making each other respect them by use of force. Since words could not put the other side in its place and restore the illusion of self at the centre of reality, they would regain their 'face' with military force.

Then the Sakyas said, 'We will show them how strong and mighty are the men who cohabited with their sisters,' and they sallied forth for the fray.

And the Koliyas replied, 'We will show how strong and mighty are they who dwelt in the hollow of a jujube tree,' and they sallied forth ready for the fight.[73]

The leadership of each state prepared for war, not to enforce or resist a policy on the water issue, but over the insults to their royal houses.

The Buddha's decision to intervene

The Buddha's decision to become involved is portrayed differently in the two texts. In the *Jataka* consideration focuses on the efficacy of his intervention: 'He wondered if he were

233

to go there the problem would cease, and he made up his mind and thought, "I will go there and quell this feud" . . ."[74]

Among the factors the Buddha may have considered in reaching the conclusion that he could indeed be of some help were his good relations with the two peoples – Gautama's mother was of Koliyan stock and his father had been an earlier Raja of the Sakyan republic – as well as Gautama's own friendship with King Pasenadi of Kosala to whom the leaders of both states were subject.

The account in the *Dhammapada Commentary* stresses the suffering likely to take place should he not intervene: 'If I refrain from going to them, these men will destroy each other. It is clearly my duty to go to them.'[75]

Out of compassion the Buddha decides to intervene.

Immediate effects of the Buddha's presence
With the appearance of the Buddha, the Sakyans evinced first dismay and shame: 'The master, our noble kinsman has come. Can he have seen the obligation laid upon us to fight?'[76]

As happens when children are caught in the act of some particularly naughty activity, his presence paralysed action and brought about some degree of change of heart:

> 'Now that the master has come it is impossible for us to discharge a weapon against the person of the enemy' and they threw down their arms saying, 'Let the Koliyas slay us or roast us alive.' The Koliyas acted in exactly the same way.[77]

The spiritual integrity of the Buddha threw the pettiness of the leaders into stark relief. The Koliyas were no longer referred to as beasts but became persons once again.

The Buddha sought the causes
The *Jataka* version has the king of the Sakyas tell the Buddha that the fight is about water – a reply intended to save face and, as we know, not quite true. In the *Dhammapada*

Commentary the Buddha questions the Sakyan king about the cause. The underlying humour in this dialogue is unmistakable:

> Said the Teacher to his kinsmen, 'What is all this quarrel about, great King?'
> 'We do not know Reverend Sir.'
> 'Who then would be likely to know?'
> 'The Commander-in-Chief of the army would be likely to know.'
> The Commander-in-Chief of the army said, 'The Viceroy would be likely to know.'
> Thus the Teacher put the question first to one and then to another, asking the slave labourers last of all. The slave labourers replied, 'The quarrel is about water sir.'[78]

The planned war could not be construed as in any way justified and the Sakyan king was profoundly embarrassed. His civil servants did not attempt to explain the situation in terms of the drought: they knew that the real motivation was wounded pride. It is left to the slave labourers to mention the water: that was how the conflict started, after all, and they would not wish to embarrass their masters by exposing the insults. Faces were saved but the actual cause of the preparations for war concealed.

A challenge to values
The Buddha then confronted the kings with the implications their actions would have had and challenged them to be clear about their values:

> Then the Teacher asked the king, 'How much is water worth great king?'
> 'Very little Reverend Sir.'
> 'How much are Khattiyas (warriors) worth great king?'
> 'Khattiyas are beyond price Reverend Sir.'
> 'It is not fitting that because of a little water you should destroy Khattiyas who are beyond price.'

They were silent. Then the Teacher addressed them and said, 'Great kings, why do you act in this manner? Were I not present today you would set flowing a river of blood. You have acted in a most unbecoming manner. You live in enmity, indulging in the five kinds of hatred. I live free from hatred . . .'[79]

The commentator links the incident with verses 197, 198 and 199, the first of which reads, 'Oh happily let us live free from hatred among those who hate; Among those who hate let us live free from hatred . . .'[80]

The root of the conflict
Throughout their dialogue with the Buddha neither of the kings mentioned their wounded pride as a motivating factor. In terms of the Buddha's teaching, delusion would be the condition for such feelings to arise. Thus, at the end of the dialogue between the Buddha and the king there is an indirect allusion to it: 'Verily, there is no satisfaction in this quarrel, but owing to a feud, sire, between a certain tree sprite and a black lion which has reached down to the present aeon.', and with these words he told them about the Phandana birth.[81]

The story referred to is of a black lion and a tree spirit who, through repeated intrigue against each other, furnish a wheelwright with the ideas and information needed to destroy them both – to make a wheel with a lion-skin tyre.[82] The sense is that this quarrel can only bring suffering to the people involved. The only beneficiaries are the two illusory ego-identities of the royal households – which were objects of insult. They have no existence except in our deluded minds, having been passed down from generation to generation.

It is interesting that, although delusion is central to the Buddha's own interpretation of the situation, he does not raise it till the end. He works with the moral and pragmatic concerns that would be of most immediate concern to the conflictants, first, but this last remark is actually the most profound. The theme of there being no satisfaction in conflict is picked up later in two stories. In one it is said that if animals seek out the weak points in each other they can do harm irrespective of weakness or strength. The second echoes the advice concerning the Vajjians in the *Mahaparinibbana Sutta* – that unity is the true foundation of strength:

'In the case of such that dwell together in unity, no one finds any opening for attack – but when they have quarrelled one with another a certain hunter brought about their destruction and went off with them. Verily there is no satisfaction in a quarrel.'[83]

The 'certain hunter' is Mara (the Devil): disunity brings disaster.

Another teaching, stressed in several ways, is about the importance of mindfulness: 'There ought not to be this blind following of one another.'[84]

Here, the Buddha is referring, particularly, to the way anger spread among the workers and to the royal households of each side. The rather amusing scene in which the Buddha questions king, commander in chief, generals and advisor in turn is linked with another *Jataka* tale in which a hare, frightened by the sound of a falling vilva fruit, causes panic among the other animals with the story that the earth is collapsing.[85] If we are unmindful, things get completely out of hand.

Lessons to be learned

There are certain aspects of the Buddha's intervention which are relevant to the practice of mediators today. Firstly, the Buddha became aware of the conflict at a critical juncture, just as serious violence was about to develop. His timely response probably averted an incident which would have blighted Sakya-Koliya relations for years to come. Conflicts have a way of escalating out of control very quickly and it is important to become involved – if only to make contact with the parties – as early as possible. The Buddha's decision to mediate took into consideration the urgency of the case.

Secondly, the established spiritual integrity of the Buddha had considerable effect on the conflictants. Although the kings had considerable military power the Buddha was clearly the more powerful – but in a different way. Beside him the two kings realise the unworthiness of what they are about to do. The cycle of escalation is interrupted as conflictants suddenly interpret their own behaviour as they know the Buddha would see it. Monks have retold similar experiences of people desisting from argument in their presence. This provides an opportunity to begin a process of dialogue. Thirdly, even though he is Sakyan, there is no question about the Buddha's neutrality in the dispute. This is probably because he is recognised as being 'above' the petty concerns that feed the quarrel. Detached compassion has a very practical application for mediators. The motivation for his involvement is recognised to be compassion for all who suffer and not just for a particular community.

The qualities requisite of a mediator
In another Sutta (appended to an account of a mediation between two groups of the Buddha's own monks) we find a description of the kind of monk suitable to handle conflicts within the Sangha. In parts the qualities outlined clearly relate to the role of mediator. The words are attributed to Upali. 'In the Order's affairs and deliberations and in matters arising for investigation, what kind of man is here most needed? How is a monk fit for leadership here? 'Above all, one blameless in moral habit, of careful conduct, his faculties well controlled.' The first qualification of the mediator then, is to live mindfully, with his personal affairs in good order.

'Opponents do not censure him in respect of a rule, for there could be nothing to say against him.' Mediators should live in such a way that they are beyond the reproach of any conflictant and so cannot easily be blackmailed or discredited.

'Opponents come under his control, and the many-folk come under his tuition . . .' Mediators need to be able to speak clearly and with moral authority when the need arises.

'And he does not neglect his own creed, (skilful) at question and answer, unhurting.' That the mediator should be 'unhurting' suggests that skill at questioning and the control he exerts are of a deliberately non-coercive kind. In the Kosambi situation we have seen that, despite his frustration at the pettiness of the monks, the Buddha relied on the skilful application of Dhamma and the unfolding of events.

'Able in doing a messenger's duty . . .' The mediator needs to be able to carry responses accurately from one conflictant to another.

'And well-informed in what they tell him of the Order's affairs.' Mediators need background knowledge about the affairs of the organisations within (or between) which they are mediating.

'Sent by a group of monks he is obedient, but he does not therefore think, "I am doing this".' Since mediation has obvious importance to people and events there is a temptation to think of oneself as a 'great mediator' – to enhance one's own self-picture. Ego-illusions like this can interfere with the patient and careful work of carrying messages in disastrous ways.

'Into whatever matters one falls, whatever is an offence and how to remove it – both these analyses are well handed down to him, he is skilled in the features of offences and removal, being sent away and good habits – he goes by these: he is sent away and what are the grounds, restoration of a person who has completed this – he knows this too, skilled as he is in analysis.' Mediation in matters which relate to the law require that the mediator have a working knowledge of the law. The reference to being 'sent away and what are the grounds' might imply a good knowledge of the requirements for legal actions (as in this case with regard to the suspension of the *Dhamma* teacher) or it may suggest that the mediator himself should wield some sanctions – probably the former.

'With esteem for senior monks, for newly ordained, for

elders and those of middle standing, a helper of the multitude, clever herein, monk such as this is fit for leadership
here.'[86] The mediator should relate to conflictants of
different rank equally – with respect and compassion. This is
especially important since conflictants tend to exploit, or be
disadvantaged by, differences in status more in conflict than
in ordinary life.

Summary

The Buddha taught that the way to extinguish suffering is to
remove the roots that sustain it. In order to achieve true
peace, peacemaking must undermine the roots of conflict.
The challenge to the peacemaker is thus to identify and
engage with greed, hate and delusion as they are manifested
in the conflict faced. The spirituality of the peacemaker is an
important practical resource.

The Buddha's own intervention to avert war between
Sakyan and Koliyan states demonstrates an engaged
approach to peacemaking and shows how personal qualities
associated with spiritual practice contribute to the ability of
the peacemaker to function effectively.

The list of qualifications of the mediator from the *Vinaya*
is, startlingly enough, as relevant today as it was in the Buddha's
day.

This chapter is adapted from chapters 1,19 & 18 of *The
Mindful Mediation: a Handbook for Buddhist Peacemakers* by
the author of this chapter. It is available in the UK from
Wisdom Books, Hoe Street, London and also from the
Friends' Book Centre, Euston Road, London. NW1 2BJ.

Reconciliation, Justice and Peace in India

B. J. Prashantam

I would like to deal with this subject in terms of four issues or four aspects of Reconciliation, Justice and Peace in India. The four aspects are: Communal Harmony, Children, Youth and Women.

Communal harmony

Communal harmony has been a hall mark of our civilisation for several thousands of years wherein the people of India welcomed, were hospitable to absorb, synthesised and integrated the various cultures, be they of the traders, or the invaders, or the colonial powers or other visitors to our country. It is because of this that today we have in India people of many backgrounds in terms of religions, in terms of languages, in terms of customs, of food habits, in terms of patterns of dress, in terms of ideologies and so on. A customary glance at the Indian Philosophy will indicate that there is a whole range of thoughts, starting all the way from *Charvaka*, which means atheism to *advaita vedanta*, which is belief in one God. This kind of heterogeneity is rarely found elsewhere in the world. Now, in terms of heterogeneity on an eight point scale, India is rated as six. This kind of pluralistic reality of an Indian society necessarily calls for high degree of tolerance, great maturity in accommodation. There are also periodical problems of conflict whenever, intentionally or inadvertently, the aspects of life that are important and precious to one community are in any way treated with disrespect or damaged by any other individual or community. Hence one has heard from time to time of Hindu-Muslim tensions or tensions among Christians and Hindus such as in Nagercoil and different communities in other places. What I would like to stress is that, whilst these problems existed, where both common people and leaders have tried to encourage reconciliation many of the efforts have been successful.

The Constitution of India itself seeks to do a lot of justice to the importance of communal harmony by granting freedom with reference to personal laws for people belonging to different groups. Needless to say that, every now and then, for the sake of political expediency, there are elements in our society who use or misuse, abuse or incite feelings of communal disharmony to their advantage. By and large, the common person has given a rebuff to such efforts, though at times with severe costs. Some aspects of such communal tension are promoted by forces outside the country which are inimical to the success of communal harmony in the Indian society. The Bombay blasts, the Madras blasts and other events are examples of that kind. Some of the events in Kashmir for example are supposed to be those kinds of issues.

Consequently, the question of reconciliation also involves dealing with the appropriate root causes of communal harmony. Gandhi very much wished to start what is called *Shanthi Sena* or peace army. Vinobha Bhave, who was a close aid and follower of Mahatma Gandhi, started one in 1958 with a small group of people in Kerala. This group, utilising young people and others, has been from time to time trying to serve as catalyst for peace in different conflicts and tensions around the country.

Madurai Gandhigramam, a University devoted to the pursuit of Gandhian ideals, has been very active in promoting the *Shanthi Sena*. Prof. Radhakrishnan, of course, describes some of the activities and issues connected with this Gandhigramam as well as activities of the *Shanthi Sena* in working for communal peace and communal harmony.

Looking into the future, politically and otherwise, communal harmony is going to be a very important focus.

The judgements of the Supreme Court, the verdict of the electorate, the interviews by common people of India, firmly and strongly stand by communal harmony and reconciliation. Aberrations from this idea are not totally absent but their minimum presence is sometimes very disturbing and also effective steps are being taken. Ultimately, it is the vigilant and aware citizens who can prevent such situations from escalating, who can nip in the bud any problems that may begin to rise. As the preamble of Unesco states: 'Wars start in the minds of [people] and it is the minds of [people] that defences of peace should be constructed.'

Children

Justice related to children emerges out of a commitment to the beliefs that children have rights to a decent living, healthy food, secure home and opportunity to develop themselves. Since children cannot fend everything for themselves, the family, the community, the society and the state have a major responsibility in ensuring that this vulnerable group of people are not exploited. Now, if you look at the society in India it is stated that one out of three labourers are children. That there are considerable number of child labourers in various cottage industries like Beedi, carpet making and others. Their nimble limbs and nature are taken advantage of and they are used. They are also used in quarries and in factories that make fire crackers. There is a problem of bonded labour for children where poor parents are forced to sell their children for labour in return for money. This has been exploited to the hilt. There is a socio-economic problem here that needs careful handling. Then, when it comes to female children, in certain parts of the country, there is a discrimination against female babies leading, in some extreme cases in certain places, to female infanticide and foetacide. This intolerable condition has to be condemned and treated as a matter of justice. Many voluntary agencies and the government at the state and the central levels have become very alive to the issues involved here and are taking steps to eliminate this ghastly practice from the daily life of the people where this is in vogue. Now and then, one hears about child marriages. Now this is again not very common. However, it is not non-existent. Somehow illiteracy among people seems to be connected with lower aged marriage, higher rate of fertility, bigger size family, higher infant mortality and malnutrition.

Added to all this is the phenomenon of street children who according to varying estimates number several millions and they need special attention to help them to cope with their difficult circumstances. It is gratifying to note that a large number of countries have signed the convention on the rights of children and are attempting to practise them. But they are nowhere near the complete elimination of the abuse of children.

Even in the tourist industry, one hears about the sexual abuse of children and this is again a highly condemnable practice that debases the dignity and humanity of children. The criminal justice practice in certain parts till recently has been inadequate in dealing separately and appropriately with children as the Children Act was not uniformly present in all states. Now several steps are being taken and a large number of voluntary agencies is coming forward to provide guidance and support, including shelters and education, medical aid and advocacy for the rights, privileges, welfare and wellbeing of children. A uniform law for the country called the Juvenile Justice Act has been passed in 1986 and came into operation in 1987, from the time of the birth of Mahatma Gandhi on October 2nd.

These are encouraging signs but there is a lot that needs to be done between the cup and lip. More priority has necessarily to be given to children and their welfare. Consequently, in the eighth five-year plan, the Government of India has made a commitment to reduce illiteracy to absolute bare minimum and also the allocation for education has grown from three to six per cent of the budget. In addition to all this, I would also like to state that there is hope and need for meaningful education, joyful education, practical education being imparted to children.

The values in which today's children are growing is another area of concern, arising out of the globalisation of communications with vast exposure to television. It is found that traditional values are rapidly eroding. There is definitely a need to retain some of them and to give to the children the benefits of moral values that may guide their lives towards being useful citizens, constructive in their functioning towards themselves as well as towards others.

Youth

Youth constitutes a sizeable chunk of our population. India is one of the predominantly young nations with an estimated forty per cent or more of the people in this age group. Access to education and access to employment constitute a major challenge here. In the suicide rates among the various age groups, youth constitutes seventy-four per cent of suicides in our country. This is a very large number indeed, that needs to be specially attended to. In a recent article on what is called the 'Gulf Syndrome', a psychiatrist in the Southern part of India stated that where parents go away in search of jobs that pay better, some children have developed problems of emotional adjustment. There is also the problem of terrorism in certain parts of the country, attracting some of our unemployed youth to join destructive and destabilising activities through which their life is spoiled. We have the problem also of drug-addiction and drug abuse in the tackling of which a frontal attack has been launched by government and non-governmental organisations together.

Youth deserves a better chance. The youth of India are highly talented. Many of them are highly frustrated as well. Social justice therefore needs to be accelerated and this is the direction in which the policies of the Government and the NGOs are aimed, though one must admit, when it comes to actual implementation, there is always hope for improvement. There are many loose ends that need to be tied. There are many loopholes that need to be plugged. I am confident however that this will be done.

Women

Women constitute half our population. Women have been the back bone of employment, very much so in the informal sector, where much injustice is done. Equal wages for equal work, equal opportunities for all kinds of employment for which they are suited is slowly opening up. Literacy as well as education are being emphasised. Wherever women's literacy is high, it is found that the fertility rate is low, the size of the family is low, the health of the family is high, the aspirations of the family and the success achieved by the family are also much better. Some regions of our country have achieved this, other regions are seen to be far behind. Therefore, we need a policy; we need a programme that will further strengthen the emphasis on women. Injustices against women in terms of dowry harassment or in terms of domestic violence, in terms of discrimination, in terms of crimes against women, in terms of job opportunities for women and girls are very great and great attention needs to be given. One of the few good things that people talk about through the involvement of the World Bank is that the developmental activities of our country are increasingly, during the past decade focused on women's development. There has been an insistence on a higher allocation of the money that is given from the World Bank for the education of women and children. This has enormous benefits far beyond the direct purpose for which that money is granted. There are many women's organisations which are trying to encourage women to organise themselves towards empowerment and towards realising their destiny along with the men as children of God.

South Africa on a Road to Transformation

Livingstone Ngwewu

Introduction

It is now a long time since South Africans of all races queued either in sweltering heat or in soaking rain to cast their votes in an election which was designed to transform South Africa into a democratic country. The elections of April and the inauguration of the first State President of the new South Africa in May 1994 meant, *inter alia*, that South Africa will never be the same again. Before April 1994 the races of South Africa were slowly but surely moving towards a precipice and they were not far from the brink when they either took or were made to take a U-turn.

The intention of this chapter is to spell out briefly some of the changes that have been brought about by the events of 1994 and also to highlight the extent to which each of the constituent races in South Africa has benefited from the negotiated settlement. When the people of South Africa patiently stood in long queues between the 26th and 29th of April 1994 what were their expectations of a democratic South Africa? Have these expectations been fulfilled? Because of the internecine conflict between blacks and whites in the apartheid era it would not be altogether incorrect to suggest that the expectations of a fair number of whites in South Africa were and might still be the polar opposite of those of the blacks. This conflictual situation could be attributed to the fact that both blacks and whites were, in various and in varying degrees, victims of apartheid. It would be quite misleading to imagine that in South Africa the tussle was just between blacks and whites. There is a race in South Africa about which very little is said which also found itself in a political quandary in the apartheid era, and that is the coloured race.

It is very misleading to imagine that apartheid was designed solely for the blacks. A close analysis of the South African socio-political scenario reflects that not only blacks but also whites and coloured people became victims of apartheid. The rationale behind apartheid was not just to keep blacks away from white people and whites away from black people but to isolate each racial group from the others. This constitutes what could be referred to as the method behind the madness of apartheid. Apartheid, however, meant one thing to the blacks and quite another to the whites as it did to the coloured people and the overriding concern of its protagonists was to create, promote and sustain the 'jangling discords of our nation'.[87]

Apartheid and blacks

As far back as the 1950s the architect of apartheid, Dr Hendrick Verwoerd, summed up how he perceived the role of the blacks would be in South Africa when he said that there was no place for black people 'in the European community above the level of certain forms of labour.[88] The crime committed against the blacks in South Africa was two-pronged. It consisted of psychological as well as physical attacks on them. This two-pronged attack on blacks was designed to remove the very penetralia of their being so that they cease to be human beings in their own right but become *iizinto*, i.e. objects or nonentities.

The psychological attack on blacks manifested itself in the distortion of their history as well as the denial of their humanity. It has been pointed out that white historians 'with few notable exceptions, have worked to bring about an amnesia. The true past has been distorted or obliterated. There are omissions of absolutely basic facts'.[89] Black school children who studied history books in South Africa were subjected to unmitigated distortions with the intention of calling into question the integrity of the black race. Historians seem to have been on a special mission of beguiling their readers with fudged ideas which intended to obscure rather than clarify the issues.

Black potential historians would not venture beyond the dominant historical paradigm. History books were published by companies which were under white control and every care was taken to ensure that the consumers received a well-spiced ideological *plat du jour*. No publisher would risk publishing what could be seen to have the capacity of rabble-rousing. The few black writers who quaffed in the white literature pool did so on the backs of their white masters who designed and determined the editorial policy. White researchers prowled about black communities looking for and finding great raconteurs whose stories they would tone down to suit the mass consumption. In 1994 the blacks went to the polling stations with no history to be proud of except the authorised distorted version which they were obliged to imbibe and guzzle from white writers.

The other manifestation of this psychological molestation on blacks has been the denial of their human rights and their basic needs. It was somewhat instilled in the minds of the blacks that they did not and could not share a common humanity with their white compatriots. The denial of their humanity was so degrading that it resulted in an inevitable self-doubt leading to self-demeaning and self-disparage-ment. This effectively meant that the South African blacks were pushed into an unenviable position of losing respect for and confidence in themselves.[90] These blacks found themselves pushed into an abiding sense of guilt and complete self-rejection. It must have been out of this profound sense of self-rejection that at some stage some blacks took it upon themselves to try and 'improve' what they both assumed and were made to understand to be the murky colour of their skin by applying on it all sorts of ointments and creams so as to 'whiten' it. For some blacks in South Africa one of the greatest dreams was to be white and the hope remained nothing more than a mirage. Even with this conscious attempt to be like their oppressors blacks were still discriminated against. The irony of this whole misplaced harlequinade was that a fair number of white people in South Africa were basking in the sun trying to be brown or suntanned and thereby become like the very people they detested intensely.

Not only were black South Africans victims of the pernicious psychological attack but also victims of physical abuse. In a vast country which could have provided enough land for all her inhabitants blacks were denied a fair share of the land. Homelands or Bantustans were set up as areas where blacks could be dumped. There were some blacks who were inveigled into accepting the partitioning of South Africa and these black mavericks enjoyed great financial benefits from the South African government – yet this was all a ruse. With the setting up of the Bantustans the South African government continued its policy of uprooting the blacks from areas that were designated white areas. People saw their houses demolished so as to make room for the erection of houses for whites.

Those who resisted the government inroads into the penetralia of their being either disappeared or died under very mysterious circumstances. It is no exaggeration to point out that '[Physical] assault by police and prison officials has long been a fact of life for Africans'.[91] All this happened because the Nationalist government was engaged in a systematic pogrom against blacks. Blacks were made to suffer the *ne plus ultra* of shame just by being black. The protest against this objectification of blacks is encapsulated in the freedom song – sung effusively by blacks – which puts the indictment at the doorstep of the heavenly kingdom. The song said:

Senzeni na, senzeni na?
Tyala lethu, tyala lethu
bubumnyama.
Tyala lethu, tyala lethu
bubumnyama.
What have we done, what have we done?
Our crime, our crime
is blackness.
Our crime, our crime
is blackness.

For the majority of blacks the events of 1994 could not have meant anything less than the transformation of 'the jangling discords of our nation into a beautiful symphony of brotherhood [and sisterhood]'[92] In April 1994 blacks held their heads high in quietude, completely content that after a long period of molestation and mortification they were going to be responsible for the destiny of their lives. As Dr Kevin Shillington has observed, what took place in South Africa in 1994 was to a very large extent the restoration of the human dignity of the blacks; it is this profound realisation that led one black man to say immediately after casting his vote, 'Today I became a human being.'[93] It is perhaps very important to note that as far back as 1960 it was stated quite categorically that what black South Africans basically wanted was 'to be free to make their own mistakes and to order their lives as they desire them to ordered. In short, they want to live as human beings'.[94]

Whilst the restoration of the black humanity is vital, this certainly was not the be-all and end-all of the quest for liberation. Surely, blacks wanted more than simply the affirmation of their humanity, important though this is. There remains the question whether or not the present South African government has fulfilled the expectations of the black people. There is no doubt that so much has changed in South Africa since the events of 1994, but paradoxically nothing has changed. There are two spheres which highlight the fact that blacks remain completely riveted in the positions they held before the elections of 1994 and those areas are the issues of land redistribution and education.

Land redistribution
One of the salient features of South Africa has not been an unprecedented rise in conurbations but a remarkable increase in shanty towns. Just outside the city of Port Elizabeth and at Crossroads in Cape Town there are thousands and thousands of black families who live in shacks which have very inadequate sanitation. Some of these are people who at some stage or another had very decent homes before they were evicted by a sheer government order. It was aptly remarked that 'Since the Afrikaner Christian Nationalist government came to power in 1948 removal and "resettlement" of blacks . . . has taken place on an ever increasing scale . . . '[95] These people who have been dispossessed of their land have been patiently expecting broad land reform policies that would lead to the restoration of land to all those who were dispossessed under racial laws.[96] If in other issues the government may be excused for muddling along, it will not be excused forever in this area.

White South African farmers have vast tracts of land that they use either for rearing live stock or for agricultural purposes. The question that is vexing many minds in South Africa is this huge discrepancy between the amount of land that whites own and the amount of land that is assigned to blacks. White governors in South Africa seem to have been on an escapade to grab as much land as they could from the natives. Sir George Cathcart who was appointed Governor of Cape Colony and High Commissioner between 1852 and 1854 'set out to reduce the (African) tribes to impotence by systematic invasion and confiscation of their lands'. To a very large extent the Governor and the missionary worked very closely in grabbing as much land as they could. There were exceptions like the Scottish missionary who fruitlessly urged that 'the Government should show that it does not conquer in order to dispossess'.[97]

The Methodist and Anglican missionaries grabbed as much land as they could in the area which was called the British Kaffraria. This is illustrated by a letter written by a missionary who was posted at Holy Cross in the Western Pondoland at the turn of the twentieth century. This missionary wrote to his father on 30th September 1912 informing him that on a previous Thursday a 'very nice and friendly magistrate from Lusikisiki' came out to spend the night at Holy Cross and whilst at Holy Cross this magistrate excised some land for the Anglicans. This missionary gleefully reported that the visiting magistrate 'marked out our boundaries and was most generous in his measurements'.[98] It is clear from this correspondence that the distribution of the land was in the hands of people who had the interests of a particular class of people at heart. To some extent this explains the vast tracts of land that are owned by few whites in the country.

The rightful owners of the land are squatters on white people's farms who sell their labour for a pittance. The bulk of the work on such farms is done by the black farm labourers who constitute the most exploited group of people in South Africa. What farm labourers get from their white masters can still be described as paltry wages, if any. There are farm labourers whose wages do not come in cash but in kind, and in lieu of cash these are usually given mealie-meal, samp and beans, some sugar and other consumables. The whole philosophy governing the mentality of most of the South African farmers is that a labourer's concern is to eat and that is all that there is to him or her.

Farm labourers were, to a very large extent, properties of the farmer. A man and his family may still reside in shacks on a white man's farm and all members of the family will be obliged to offer their services unreservedly to the farmer. Moreover, if for some reason the farmer is no longer satisfied with the usefulness of any of the labourers he is 'at liberty' to dispense with such a labourer at no cost at all. Most farmers have a mental grip on the vast majority of their labourers – who themselves would regard it as somewhat oafish to sever the links with the white farmer.

There seems to be some kind of fantasy to which both the farmers and the labourers are privy. For some white farmers the 'philosophy of oppression' has become 'perfected and refined throughout civilisation as a true culture of injustice'. This 'philosophy of oppression' does not, of course, achieve its greatest triumph when its propagandists knowingly inculcate it; rather the triumph is achieved when this philosophy has become so deeply rooted in the spirits of the oppressors themselves and their ideologues that they are not even aware of their guilt".[99] White farmers oppress black farm labourers not because they want to but because they sincerely think that they have to. They cannot imagine any other way of treating a black person besides the one they have adopted.

Black farm labourers accept the insults and outrageous treatment meted against them by white farmers as a divine order of things. Some labourers must sincerely believe that their white masters are the representatives of God on earth. The most disturbing factor about such farm labourers is their profound sense of almost servile quiescence when one would have expected them to be in a state of vibrant inquietude. The explanation for this kind of supine state is that they are victims of 'the most perfect type of slavery . . . that of not only not knowing that one is a slave, but holding as an ideal of life a situation which objectively is slavery'.[100] Farm labourers constitute a class of people who live on the land to which they have absolutely no claim. It would be no exaggeration to say that such people expect the government to rescue them.

It would be very unrealistic to imagine that the white farmers would ever willingly relinquish their hold on the land and break away from the principle of primogeniture.

Time will tell whether the present government or the future governments will continue to protect the selfish interests of the few who have feathered and still continue to feather their own nests at the expense of others. High political dissatisfaction with the government's land restitution policy could cetainly be a powder keg. The landless and the dispossessed people are patiently waiting for a just and equitable distribution of the country's resources, particularly the land.

Education
Education was used by the Nationalist government of South Africa as a useful ploy to enslave the blacks. Dr Verwoerd expressed his determination to reform Native education 'so that natives will be taught from childhood to realise that equality with Europeans is not for them.'[101] This educational system was therefore designed in such a way that blacks would not just be incapable of thinking for themselves but it also aimed at making social, political and academic imbeciles out of them. For forty years from 1954 to 1994 an African child was subjected to a poisonous form of education. The child was expected to imbibe without question whatever the teacher told him/her and at some stage the child would be expected to regurgitate what s/he had learnt by rote. Those who were in the teaching profession in 1954 when Bantu Education was introduced knew that there was something fundamentally wrong with this education but unfortunately they could not raise a finger in protest because the government had adopted a policy that whoever pays the piper calls the tune. The Bantu education system was profligate.

It was out of a deep sense of frustration that black students let loose their pent up anger in 1976 in what has come down to be mistakenly known as the 1976 Soweto riots, as if the riots were confined only to Soweto. This was not just a rejection of Afrikaans, and those who thought it was were misinformed and misadvised, but an outright rejection of the entire system and culture of Bantu Education. The slogan of the black school children soon became 'Freedom now and education tomorrow!' There is absolutely no doubt as to the wisdom of what appeared to be an importunate and impetuous demand at the time, especially in a country where education had become intricately interwoven with and become a vehicle of government propaganda. These children sincerely believed that only a new and democratically elected government could promote the interest of its people, of which education was one.

South Africa is in an educational crisis and perhaps the crisis even pre-dates the implementation of the Bantu education and might have been intensified when the Nationalist Party won the general elections in 1948. The Revd Arnold Stofile has pointed out that no less than 100,000 teachers have been left under-qualified by apartheid and yet in a miraculous fashion it is hoped that these teachers must and will be instruments of educational transformation. Stofile's concern has been reiterated by a member of Rhodes University's Eastern Cape curriculum unit, Mr Bruwer, when he said that no less than eighty-seven per cent of Eastern Cape's teachers were not properly qualified. In the sphere of education schools have had an interim curriculum which has been expurgated. But to what extent education will be an instrument of transformation in South Africa still remains to be seen.

Apartheid and whites
Apartheid permeated all spheres of life in South Africa. It would be naive to imagine that whites in South Africa were unscathed by this contagious malady. In 1963 Verwoerd as Prime Minister of the Republic of South Africa made it absolutely clear in his Parliamentary speech what the role of the Nationalist Party was when he said: 'We want to keep South Africa white . . . "keeping it white" can only mean one thing, namely white domination, not "leadership" not "guidance" but "control", "supremacy" if we are agreed that

it is the desire of the people that the white man should be able to protect himself by retaining white development'[102] When the Nationalist Party came into power in South Africa it effectively meant that it was bliss to be born white in the country. Each white person in South Africa had to decide how she/he was going to fit in within the system.

Whites in South Africa could be divided into three groups in the way they responded to the policy of apartheid. The first group comprised those whites who not only hated but detested intensely and resisted the policy of apartheid with all their might. These whites were not particularly liked by the rest of the white community and more often than not they became objects of scorn. A retired Bishop of Pretoria, Knapp-Fisher, believes sincerely – or seems to believe sincerely – that such characters were engaged in what he chooses to call 'raucous campaigning' which, needless to say, led some members of the white community to feel rancour against them.[103] These are men and women who as a result of their resolute commitment and unwavering zeal for justice were either deported, if they were not South African citizens, or were consigned to languish in the profound misery of stuffy and fusty South African dungeons.

This was a very small group of whites in South Africa. When Dr Nelson Mandela gave his first presidential speech in parliament in 1994 he paid a special tribute to one of these, a certain Ingrid Jonker, an Afrikaner woman who consciously chose to dissociate herself from the Afrikaner narcissism. It was out of a deep sense of frustration over, and a profound hatred of, what the Afrikaners were doing that some time in the 1960s Ingrid Jonker 'died by her own hand'[104] Whites who remained implacable enemies of segregation were inveighed against as recalcitrant radicals.

The second group consists of those white who in terms of Knapp-Fisher's classification did not have any sense of conviction that open 'confrontation with the civil authorities about the racial injustices' would achieve much but sincerely 'believed that more would be achieved by behind the scene pressure'.[105] There has always been some kind of dissonance between what these whites said and what they actually did. Most of them were victims of the cognitive dissonance syndrome which manifested itself in the peaceful coexistence in the same human being of two contrary strands: that of vociferously opposing injustice in public, on the one hand, and that of overtly practising injustice in private, on the other. A typical example of this syndrome was that of church leaders who denounced in the strongest possible terms 'various forms of oppression, while maintaining a high degree of inequality within their own organisation'.[106]

These whites were usually known as liberals and they tended to pick and choose what suited their fancy in the multifarious manifestations of apartheid and only appeared to be opposed to this policy. Most liberals were English speakers whose salient feature has been aptly described as the ability to 'speak with a Progressive tongue, vote with the United Party and thank God for the Nationalists'.[107]

These were whites who spoke patronisingly about doing things for blacks. They understood their role to be nothing less than subsuming the blacks. The liberals liked to believe that they were on the side of the blacks and became agitated when they were fobbed off by the very blacks they sought to impress. The basic problem with the liberals is that in the final analysis they were people who were not on the side of real and radical change but they would have been quite happy with some few ameliorations. They were particularly impressed with the Nationalist Party reforms of the 1980s because on the whole such reforms seldom involved genuine reform but were basically attempts 'to deceive and co-opt, while effectively simply revising the terms under which white supremacy (was) retained'. An Afrikaner academic referred to these reforms as 'little more than a public relations exercise to improve the image of apartheid and not endanger the Afrikaners'.[108] After all is said and done these liberals occupied a position which would 'allow them to maintain a position of privilege without having a bad conscience about it'.[109]

The third and final group consists of whites who have been uninhibitedly opposed to any form of integration with blacks. The apparent reforms of the Nationalist Party in the 1980s led to an unprecedented rise of the ultra-right wing 'hate movements' like the Afrikaner *Weerstandsbeweging* (AWB) under the leadership of Eugene Terreblanche. It was this hatred that in 1988 drove Barend Strydom to shoot 'twenty-two black bystanders in central Pretoria, killing seven'.[110] The hatred of this third group of whites constitutes a matrix out of which the policy of apartheid was born. Their intense hatred for blacks could be described as xenophobia and probably bears very close resemblance to that of the Ku Klux Klan in Georgia. These are people who introduced laws of discrimination in the country and if they had the means they would have seen to it that blacks inhaled a different kind of air, caustic air perhaps, and received a different kind of rain, acid rain perhaps. In South Africa they are not part of the transformation that is taking place there and somehow they think it might be possible to have a *Boerestan* where they would promote solipsism.

Before the general election of 1994 South African whites, almost without exception, were very anxious. Some of them must have wondered whether blacks would not hoist them with their own petard. To a fair number of white people in South Africa, particularly those who belong to the last two groups mentioned above, the events of April and May 1994 must have subjected them to an unprecedented kind of phantasmagoria which is that confused dreamlike changing scene of different things, real and imagined. These must have found it hard to believe themselves to be in South Africa which has a black State President.

In so far as whites are concerned it is true to say that since April 1994 little has changed in South Africa. Whites are still trapped and prisoners in their sumptuous houses in white suburbs whilst the majority of blacks are in cramped houses in the townships. The location of the whites is a clear demonstration of where the power is. The power still remains in white hands – particularly in the offices of the white senior civil servants. The present government is lumbered with thousands of white civil servants which it inherited from the previous government. There is also 'the problem' of thousands of civil servants from the Quondam 'independent states' which probably means that the present civil service must be almost bloated. The process of amalgamating these services and redeploying people is slow and some people are anxious that they might lose their positions in the process. White Christians in South Africa belonged to either of the three groups mentioned above. There were very few white Christians who not only opposed but also resisted apartheid in South Africa. Few whites like Trevor Huddleston, Ambrose Reeves, Joost de Blank, took an unwavering and courageous stand against apartheid, The bulk of the English speaking white Christians were liberals in the bad sense of the word and were quite happy to run with the hare and hunt with the hounds.

Apartheid and coloureds
In South Africa people are classified according to the skin colour they wear. This means that the racial divide is basically between black and white. It so happened that in the country there were and still are those who could not be classified as either black or white. Since the juxtaposed colours were black on the one hand, and white on the other, those who were neither were referred to as coloured. Insensitive and unscrupulous writers like Sarah Millin define coloured people as half-caste and half-breed, 'the fruit of vice, the folly, the thoughtlessness of the white man'.[111] There is no doubt as to the popularity of Millin's highly offensive book because it was reprinted eight times between the date of its first publication in 1926 and 1931. Nicholas Mansergh

points out that he once heard a Ceylonese diplomat describe the coloured all too romantically 'as the product of European gallantry and native indiscretion . . . '[112] There is no doubt that ideas like Millin's played a very significant role in the wording and shaping of what eventually emerged as the Population Registration Act No 30 of 1950 which defined the coloured people by exclusion, presented them as 'a distinct racial group defined negatively in relation to other racial groups . . . ' They are defined as 'those who do not look like or are not accepted as being white or African, they are those who are generally lighter skinned than Africans, but darker than Whites'.[113]

The racist South African legislation put the coloured people in a very precarious and unenviable ethnic ambiguity. It was instilled in the minds of the coloured people, as it was in the minds of all South Africans, that whiteness was the colour which signified all the good things of life, a colour that represented 'the epitome of achievement' whereas black was an outrageous colour. The difference between being black, on the one hand, and being white, on the other hand, was that some coloured people 'moved into the white community where skin colour made that possible. The advantage of "passing for white" made many sections of this community deeply conscious of colour . . .'[114]

The effect of the South African racist laws on the white people was to make them victims of inflated delusions of grandeur and self-glorification. The same laws made blacks feel that they had forfeited their self-respect whereas the effect was most damaging to the coloured people as it mauled their being. The process of making some coloured people 'pass for white' was responsible for many break-ups in families as some coloured *parvenus* started mounting up the social ladder and severing links with their friends and sometimes with their kith and kin. The coloured people were those who were not good enough to be white and who were not bad enough to be black.

261

The damaging effect of racism on the coloured community can be illustrated by the manner in which the coloured
people of Western Cape voted in the general elections of
1994. For the substantial majority of the coloured contin-
gency in the Western Cape to have voted for the Nationalist
Party, an action which shocked all self-respecting South
Africans, simply highlights the gravity of the coloured
identity crisis. These are people who were defined by the
Nationalists in most degrading terms as "dit se wat die
Kleurling nie is nie . . . As hy iewers anders tuishoort nie, dan
is hy n Kleurling."[115] (This describes what the Coloured is not
. . . If she/he doesn't belong anywhere else, then she/he is a
Coloured.)

For so long most South African whites, particularly the
Afrikaners, regarded the coloured people as objects of
ridicule and yet these coloured people were so befuddled as
to imagine that if they returned the Nationalist Party into
power the Nationalists would suddenly find the coloured
people somewhat pulchritudinous. The whole political
atmosphere in the Western Cape illustrates, rather glaringly,
two things:

(i)   The coloured people did not quite understand what the
      1994 elections were all about. After years of oppression
      the oppressors were saying they no longer were eager to
      continue paltering with the oppressed, but the
      oppressed coloured effectively said they were happy
      with oppression. The general elections of 1994 were
      about the affirmation of the dispossessed, the alienated,
      the coloured people.

(ii) The events of 1994 also highlight the extent to which
      the coloured people have internalised the country's
      racism. As far back as 1958 a coloured gentleman put it
      so well when he said: 'Having learnt as much as we have
      from the white South Africans we have not been slow
      to acquire their vices too. One of the chief of these is
      colour prejudice . . . [and we seem to think that] being

white represents the epitome of achievement.'[116] The Western Cape coloureds could not see themselves identifying with the blacks.

What the coloured people did in the Western Cape illustrates that the country's problem does not simply revolve around the question of being either black or white. Unless South Africans address the reality of the coloured people in South Africa they are nowhere near solving the country's problems.

Transforming South Africa

There is a lot that South Africans need to do to transform the country and make it a haven where everybody could nestle. A sense of personal safety and freedom should pervade the whole of society. In so far as black and coloured people are concerned, something of a therapeutic nature has to be done so that the events of the past do not tarnish their attitudes towards the future. The black and coloured South Africans were subjected to such grave violence in the past that they now need to be healed. The government of National Unity has put in place the Truth Commission whose *raison d'être* is to unravel some of the unsolved mysterious murders and assassinations of the past. It would be somewhat unrealistic to imagine that the Truth Commission is or could ever be an organ of reconciliation for most people in the country. The Truth Commission is gradually demystifying the issues and for some the clear knowledge of what happened has proved healing and has enabled reconciliation, whilst for others it has not.

At the beginning of May 1995 there was a television documentary in Britain about a South African white man who had been a member of the hit squad under the Nationalist Government. One of the victims of this hit squad was a Civil Rights lawyer, Griffiths Mxenge, who was brutally murdered by the members of the squad. The mastermind behind the squad, Mr Dirk Coetze, decided that he wanted to be reconciled with the family of the deceased lawyer. He plucked up courage and visited the family but unfortunately his visit was not welcomed. Some people might not wonder why.

The whole episode looked like some kind of a histrionic display. In African culture it would not be morally acceptable, and in fact it could be regarded as *contra bonos mores* for an offender, a murderer or an assassin in this case, to visit those whom he deprived of their member and expect to be accorded any measure of respectability. If the offender had any regard for the feelings of the bereaved he would have asked someone else to visit that family on his behalf and start preparing the family for his eventual visit. As things are at the moment it is doubtful whether the bereaved family will ever want to have any contact with the offender, except by making sure that proper nemesis is administered.

Sometimes South African whites make the mistake of assuming that the rambunctious and effervescent nature of black and coloured people means that they are so magnanimous that they are likely to forget about the past. Sometimes people could make the mistake of assuming that all people who are other than white share a common temperament, either that of Archbishop Tutu or that of President Nelson Mandela. It would be a fatal mistake to imagine that all these people are as ready to forgive and let bygones be bygones as Dr Mandela is, or are as magnanimous and benevolent as Archbishop Tutu. Indeed the events of 1994 were a great success but the wild enthusiasm must be rooted in reality for a long time into the future.

It was not so long ago that South Africans detested and hated one another like poison. They gashed gaping wounds on one another and where wounds have healed they have left bad scars. They have been so alienated from one another that they need to discover one another. There is need to talk about the traumatic experiences of the past and they need to come to terms with that past otherwise it will haunt them like an albatross around their neck. It is very tempting to say, 'Let us simply forget about the past', but to do so would be a very dangerous enterprise tantamount to papering over the cracks. South Africans have to deal with the past not in a manner that hurts but in a manner that heals and gives rise to reconciliation.

Reconciliation is a painful process to both the offender and the offended. It is also very important to remember that reconciliation is very costly. For the murderer, one of his/her overriding concerns should be the realisation that no amount of rhetoric will ever revive the dead. The South African government has put into place the Reconstruction and Development Programme which aims at making life reasonably comfortable for the marginalised members of the South African society. The RDP is seen and understood to be concerned with the mundane aspects of life which basically mean providing communities with electricity, good roads, and water. Without proper reconciliation it is only possible that people might use those roads as the easiest way of getting to their opponents, use the electricity as a means of ferreting out and incinerating their enemies, and use water as a means of navigating towards and drowning their foes. The greatest contribution of the Reconstruction and Development Programme should be seen as nothing less than the rebuilding of the broken humanity. This cannot just be the task of the government but that of each and every citizen of the country.

Reconciliation to be proper should be able to weld the South African people into one community. There is still enough polarisation to suggest that the South Africans have not taken any significant strides to move away from the apartheid era.

Some blacks still believe that South Africa is a white person's country and as blacks the best that they can do is to play second fiddle to white people. Not all whites have made the effort to be completely enmeshed in the joy of living in a democratic South Africa. There is a profound realisation with which white South Africans must come to terms, and it is that it is no longer *démodé* to be white. With the exception of the United States of America there is no other country in the world which has laid such a heavy stress on the pigmentation of its people. It has to be remembered that the argument that came as a facade to hoodwink the gullible was that the *sine qua non* of apartheid was separated development. The basic intention of apartheid was to keep a white race in its pristine purity, if Afrikaners ever had such. Whites have had such an obsession for whiteness and this was counterpoised by the black obsession for blackness.

The South Africans need to strive towards living as human beings not simply as whites, blacks or coloureds. The greatest discovery that South Africans still need to make is that humanity rather than colour constitutes the essence of their being. The status to which all should aspire is 'the status of being, not just "the Coloured people" [or white or black people] but full South Africans'.[117] There is no doubt that the racist nomenclature which we have internalised for so long will take a long time to jettison. South Africans are still living as whites, blacks and coloureds and have not started to relate to one another as human beings in the true sense of the word. It might take some time before the entire world, and not just South Africa, begins to move towards an ideal society as envisaged by Julius Nyerere where the individual would matter 'and not the colour of his [or her] skin or the shape of his [or her] nose.[118] Each South African citizen is expected to contribute in the onerous task of nation building and this can only happen when every effort is made painstakingly to remove all the impediments to sound and genuine relationships. The South Africans will not earn that genuine relationship by simply offering one another a deprecatory smile.

When black people voted they understood themselves to be voting for jobs, and yet years later most of those blacks who were unemployed at the time of the general elections are still unemployed and may be unemployable. In South Africa unemployment is horrendously high, particularly among the blacks. In a situation like that it is easy for people to become somewhat despondent and be resigned into some kind of lethargy. This malaise is borne out by voter registration in South Africa which was described by one newspaper as having 'gone . . . appallingly badly in many sections of our province . . . '[119] This lack of enthusiasm probably suggests that some people are gradually losing patience or are slowly becoming disillusioned with the government and are quite happy to distance themselves from it.

There is no doubt that some of the expectations that people have had are quite unrealistic. Some people have expected instantaneous solutions to the country's problems. It might help to remember that those who are at the helm are still in the process of knowing the ropes. Whilst there might be a lot to grumble about, quite justifiably so, it might help to remember, as Desmond Tutu does, that the present government has 'inherited a mess: an educational crisis, inadequate health care and a huge housing backlog'.[120]

There is need for some psychological transformation insofar as blacks and coloured people are concerned. These need to 'own' the present government as their own creation. In the past blacks and coloured people were always suspicious of whoever was in power but this situation should no longer apply. In the past the government was seen and understood to be doing things for the people but today people can no longer be passive recipients of the government largesse.

Violence, strikes and protests

One of the most disconcerting aspects about living in South Africa is the question of violence. It is estimated that 'South Africa has an armed robbery every seven minutes'.[121] After the release of Dr Mandela from prison there was an unprecedented escalation of violence in the country. He attributed this to the presence of the 'third force' and some people found the suggestion of a third force rather far-fetched, but today there is no doubt that the third force was and still is a reality in South Africa. Members of the third force were employed to wreak havoc in the country and it looks as if these members have allowed themselves to get into a rut. The State President 'vowed to clamp down on lawlessness and against people using protest action to conduct criminal activities'.[122]

The solution to the problem of violence is far more complex and complicated than the State President seemed to suggest. Beating people to submission could be one of the solutions but certainly not one of the best solutions. It is important to remember that people who perpetrate violence are those who could be said to have been conceived in violence and brought to birth in turmoil. People who have been nurtured in the culture of intolerance and confrontation need to be transformed rather than beaten up to become agents of negotiation and reconciliation. The desire of any human being who has lost his/her humane bearings is the restoration to him/her of the joy of being human. It is no exaggeration to say that it is usually victims of violence who perpetrate violence and it was not long ago when in South Africa the only language that was common to both the oppressor and the oppressed was violence.

One of the problems which does beset the present government as it did the previous one is the number of strikes. It was not so long ago that people used strikes and protests as effective means of non-verbal communication. The strikes and protests were absolutely essential in the past because the authorities had chosen to be impervious to reason and common sense. Is it not possible that those who embark on strike action are still cast in the old mould and need to be transformed rather than to be castigated? In the past the strikes could be said to have been morally justifiable because of the huge discrepancy between what the previous government was paying to white workers on the one hand, and what it was paying to black workers on the other.

Conclusion

There is need for all South Africans to be very patriotic without being nationalistic. That spirit of patriotism can only come about when South Africans begin to own, not only the country but one another as well. What will hold South Africa together is when each South African does not feel devalued but feels wanted and appreciated because of his/her unique being. For South Africa to become a truly democratic and peaceful country each of her citizens must be prepared to give and to lose in order to gain.

A New Start for Mozambique: Peace at Last

Clive Larkin

The purpose of this chapter is to provide a simple background to the sixteen year civil war which ended following peace negotiations in Rome on 4th October 1992; then to focus upon the churches' role in those negotiations.

Mozambique shares common borders with five Commonwealth members in Southern Africa and has a coastline of approximately two thousand kilometres. It lies to the North of the Transvaal, East of Zimbabwe and South of Tanzania. Mozambique contains the 'great grey greasy green Limpopo' and the Zambezi rivers. The capital is Maputo (Laurenco Marques) and the population is generally accepted as being approximately fifteen million. One final informative point, Mozambique is assessed as being one of the world's poorest countries, with in excess of ninety per cent of its GNP being measured in terms of foreign aid; per capita income is $54 per annum.

The Frelimo[123] party, led by President Samora Machel came to power on 25 June 1975 following a ten-year liberation struggle against the colonial Portuguese. The liberation struggle came to an end once the Portuguese army faction was successful in mounting its coup against Prime Minister Caetano in Lisbon in April 1974. The coup leaders were determined to prevent continuing loss of life in Mozambique and Angola, and determined to reach agreement with the rebel forces. A period of joint Frelimo/Portuguese administration held the ring from September 1974 to June 1975 after which Portugal formally handed Mozambique over to the Frelimo Party as the only viable way forward.

This direct handover of power without election rankled with many Mozambicans including some of the leadership. This disaffection was increased following the 1977 Party Conference which spelt out the new Marxist alignment of the party. At this time Ian Smith's Rhodesia was being attacked by Mugabe's ZANLA[124] guerrillas from bases in Mozambique, often with Mozambican support. To operate better against such forces Ken Flower, head of the Rhodesian Central Intelligence Force, recruited disaffected Mozambicans to make use of the language and local knowledge in planning and later carrying out raids initially against ZANLA bases but also against economic targets such as bridges and communications facilities in order to destabilise Mozambique. In response to these needs Renamo[125] under its first leader Andre Matangaidze was founded. By 1978 Matangaidze had been killed in action near Gorongosa, the present Renamo field headquarters, and Dhlakama, a deserter of both the colonial army and Frelimo, had taken his place. By 1979 it was clear to Ian Smith's planners that their battle was lost against the forces of Mugabe and Nkomo. As a result they handed Renamo over to the South African Defence Forces who during the next three years developed it into an effective offensive force to support South Africa's own destabilising campaign against Mozambique. The Frelimo government by 1983 was finding it difficult to counter Renamo; the Soviet supplied weaponry it received was designed for conventional European operations, not guerrilla actions in the African bush. During 1983 preliminary discussions were held at ministerial level hosted by the South African government; they failed due to Renamo's escalating and continuing demands for greater participation in government at cabinet level. As Renamo actions increased in effectiveness, Machel was forced to come to terms with Pretoria. During late 1983 and early 1984 a series of ANC[126] launched car bomb attacks had caused panic in Johannesburg. The two presidents signed the Nkomati Accord on 16 March 1984. The prime purpose was for each country to refrain from allowing its territory to be used against the other or any third party. Following the Nkomati Accord, Machel forced the ANC operatives to leave Mozambique. Unfortunately, South Africa continued to provide succour to Renamo daily and the infrastructure of Mozambique in terms of roads, railways, schools and hospitals was greatly diminished. Such cumulative destruction continued until the peace agreement of October 1992.

In 1986 Samora Machel died with many of his senior advisers and Cabinet ministers in an aircrash whilst returning to Maputo. Foreign Minister, Joachim Chissano took over the Presidency and began to search for a means to end the fighting – but on his terms. He was fully alert to the failure of the Nkomati Accord.

Chissano, who had been Frelimo's chief negotiator with the Portuguese in 1974/5 and head of the interim government, was also aware of the shortcomings of the Soviet bloc alignment. He sought, through a visit by Margaret Thatcher to Mozambique, a way of moving slowly closer to the West without disturbing the Soviet link which had the benefit of providing cheap oil. The Chissano/Thatcher relationship was both immediate and one of mutual respect. The UK agreed to fund the rebuilding of the Limpopo railway, allowing Zimbabwe an important outlet to the sea. To guard the investment against the Renamo attacks, Britain agreed to train Mozambican soldiers at its base in Nyanga in Zimbabwe. Thatcher was then able effectively to support the Front Line States in their struggle against South Africa without entering into sanctions considered harmful to Black South Africans, thus gaining considerable kudos.

By 1986 Zimbabwe, Tanzania and Malawi had all come to Chissano's aid and deployed sizeable contingents of soldiers within Mozambique. The immediate effect was at least temporarily to remove Renamo from its Gorongossa base. By 1987 it was clear to both Chissano and Dhlakama that stalemate had been achieved and that total victory was unattainable unless new factors were introduced into the equation and this was unlikely. What neither could have forecast was the power of the people when harnessed by the church in their desire for peace and the effects of the 1991/2 drought, particularly its savage effects upon Renamo operations. In 1988 a series of events took place which were to enable the church to bring about the train of actions which led to the final peace. Both Chissano and his advisers and Dhlakama and his advisers visited the US and began their process of enlightenment. Chissano also visited the Holy See and the Pope visited Maputo and Beira. The necessary close liaison, developed between the church and Chissano's staff during the Holy Father's visit, strengthened the position of the church in Mozambique and was instrumental in Chissano apologising for the previous anti church legislation and for his agreement to gradually returning stolen church property including churches, schools and seminaries. The 1977 legislation forbade christenings and the teaching of religion to young people. Many members of the church, including Bishop Sengulane, the British trained Anglican Bishop of Maputo, today claim that the church gained credibility and a sense of mission during this harsh period: it learnt how to survive; it relearnt the duties and responsibilities of priesthood and became a much more resilient and dedicated force, a force much closer to the people, and thus a force with temporal as well as spiritual authority. Although Dhlakama turned down an invitation to an audience with the Pope on the basis that the visit was a Frelimo spectacular in which he, Dhlakama would be seen as a puppet, yet Dhlakama had begun to renew his faith. He had spent some time in a Roman Catholic Seminary and maintains that he has always been a practising Christian. Before the Pope's visit Dhlakama's forces had killed some Catholic priests and captured another. This caused the Bishop of Beira, Don Jaime Gonclaves to try to act as mediator and after much thought the Bishop took it upon himself to seek out Dhlakama in his jungle lair in Gorongosa (Meringue). Both Don Jaime and Dhlakama are Ndau speakers and share the same birth place, Chibabava in Sofala Province, and they had briefly met during the course of Dhlakama's brief seminary training. The meeting to secure the release of the hostages was a success in terms of personal relationships and also in achieving its objective.

The Church continued to build on its new found liaison with the state, in particular Bishop Sengulane was determined that the church should seize the opportunity to contribute towards bringing the people to peace. To this end Sengulane established the movement entitled 'Preparing the People for Peace'. This built upon his church's earlier initiative in co-operation with the national disaster commission (DPCCN)[127], established to bring succour following a disastrous cyclone in 1983. Sengulane's determined efforts in this field of helping the people enabled the church to reach the people despite government restrictions. This ground preparation placed the Anglican Church in a strong position to prepare the people for peace. Sengulane could visualise the needs of a population torn apart by civil war and his crusade was targeted towards the people at all levels in all provinces to enable them to believe in their inherent ability to secure peace on their terms, given the support of the church. Sengulane devoted renewed efforts to re-vitalise the Mozambican Council of Churches (nineteen associate Protestant Churches) to support his work in all provinces. In tandem with this approach was a policy of convincing Chissano of the benefits of using the church to act as a politically neutral force for peace. Sengulane also addressed the problems of the war orphans, setting up campaigns, often with 'Save the Children' and other international charities, to help provide basic skills training, local education and other schemes to keep them from Renamo recruiters. A well publicised scheme was devised to prohibit the use of warlike toys.

This programme, 'Swords into Ploughshares', gained the public support of the government.

Finally, Sengulane used the Anglican Church, predominant in the surrounding Commonwealth countries, and his mentor Archbishop Tutu, President of the AACC[128] in South Africa since 1987, to establish the necessary links to bring pressure upon both Renamo and Frelimo to come to the peace table. The support of Presidents Mugabe (Zimbabwe), Moi (Kenya) and Banda (Malawi) was enlisted and they through senior civil servants such as Machingaidze, Kiplagat and Tembo set up the initial talks in Blantyre and Nairobi. Chissano was kept informed throughout and although the talks were declared deadlocked by Mugabe on 8 December 1989 they had provided the essential spark – peace was now on the agenda.

It was agreed that new mediating strength was required in order to convince Dhlakama in particular of the need for peace and the opportunity for the church to achieve a balanced solution. It was agreed that this need could be met by a two pronged approach enlisting the full support of the Roman Catholic Curia. Bishop Don Jaime was the ideal person to bring this to reality. His links with both Dhlakama and the Curia were a vital asset. As Chairman of the AACC he was also in a pivotal position in Africa enjoying a sound working relationship with Bishop Sengulane, the previous chairman.

During the 1980s Don Jaime had frequently visited Rome and had been introduced to the Sant Egidio Community. This lay community, founded in 1968 by Christian students in Rome, has under the guidance of Don Mateus Zuppi developed a world wide membership of ten thousand, each of whom agreed to provide their skills and expertise to support requirements of the community when so requested. The community, although not a formal element of the Catholic Church, enjoys the honour of a Papal audience each year.

The Community had been kept in touch with developments

in Mozambique by Don Jaime during his visits and they had earlier put him in touch with the Italian Communist Party and Trade Union leaders including the veteran Sr. Berlenguer with a view to engaging the Italian Communists in discussions with Frelimo in order to allow the church in Mozambique greater freedom. Don Jaime was therefore an important link between Rome and Mozambique and was able to alert the Sant Egidio Community to the need for their help in trying to progress the failed talks held in Blantyre and Nairobi in 1989. It was fortunate that the Community counted amongst its members Professor Andrea Riccardi, a brilliant historian, and Sr Raffaelli, a Socialist Deputy Foreign Minister in the Andreotti government. The formation of a team to continue this mediating work was then agreed between Zuppi, Don Jaime, Raffaelli and Riccardi. These four were to continue to be mediators and were largely responsible for supervising the detailed negotiations between Frelimo and Renamo in Rome until peace was finally signed on 4 October 1992. The grouping of the Catholic Church, the intellect of Riccardi, the political acumen and access of Raffaelli was to prove a very successful strategy. They operated in the formal political field, being accepted by both parties and being responsible for the parties' signing of the partial ceasefire in Rome on 1 December 1990. Bishop Sengulane and his Anglican Church meanwhile were instrumental in galvanising the people of Mozambique for peace, producing finally an unstoppable pressure for the peace talks to succeed.

The partial cease-fire involved the withdrawal of all eight thousand Zimbabwean forces stationed in Mozambique in the narrow six kilometre wide corridors astride the Limpopo and Beira railways, which provide Zimbabwe with its vital strategic links to the coast. The arrangement meant that Renamo had effectively removed their most efficient enemy from the battlefield; Zimbabwe gained the guarantee that its essential economic links would remain open. The partial agreement was witnessed by a group of nations who established a committee at ambassadorial level in Maputo to oversee the peace arrangements and to bring pressure to bear and give guidance to both Renamo and Frelimo with a view to reaching a comprehensive and lasting peace.

The Ambassadors were supported by military attaches or experts whose task was to verify on the ground any infringements of the agreement and to provide advice as to how disengagement could take place. Both the Ambassadors' committee, titled the Joint Verification Committee (JVC)[129], of eleven members, and the Military Committee (MIVECO)[130], were chaired by the resident Italian Ambassador to Maputo, His Excellency Incisa da Cammerana, who provided the essential political link between Rome and Maputo.

The year 1991 started with great expectations of achieving a full peace but such hopes were quickly dashed by the intransigence and mistrust shown by both sides. Renamo claimed that in fifty-two locations they had evidence to show that Zimbabwean forces had failed to withdraw inside the corridors. MIVECO asked for details and investigated 12 such locations but found no such evidence. Renamo, embarrassed by such findings, prevented MIVECO from visiting other alleged sites by refusing to guarantee MIVECO's safety. The withdrawal of Zimbabwean troops from the Tete road corridor, (part of the partial agreement) linking Malawi with the coast via Northern Mozambique, caused this route to close to traffic until August 1991 when Frelimo forces redeployed and drove out Renamo forces. Renamo, on the basis of their contention that the Zimbabwean forces had not withdrawn as agreed, initiated a series of attacks against the Limpopo Corridor and some areas within the Beira Corridor which resulted in the loss of railway staff, soldiers and locomotives. Each locomotive cost almost one million dollars to replace. Very quickly the capacity and value of the Limpopo Line was dramatically reduced. Such attacks were in addition to Renamo operations continuing throughout the country. By March 1991 negotiating teams had reached deadlock as to progressing the peace process and there seemed little that the international mediators could do.

The summer of 1991 also saw the rise of the *Naparamas* (Baramas) a 'Spirit' group founded by Manuel Antonio in the pattern of Alice Lekenya some thirty yeas before in Uganda. The Naparamas were provided 'protection' against bullets through taking part in various rituals and by imbibing certain potions. Armed only with spears and knives they banded together with great heroism and put to flight many isolated Renamo forces, particularly in Zambezia Province. Being a strategic central province and the most populous, Dhlakama determined to leave the peace talks dormant and to direct operations against the Naparamas himself. By October Renamo had regained much of its hold on the Province but a new factor was emerging; the November rains had not arrived, those of the previous year had been less than usual and the effect particularly in the remote Renamo areas soon became apparent, forcing by early 1992 the release of Renamo held children and the sick who were becoming a drain on Renamo's decreasing resources.

Late 1991 had seen the return to the negotiating table by both sides and Dhlakama on 18 October decided to finally comply with the partial cease-fire agreement by ceasing attacks against the Limpopo and Beira Corridors. This was also the day he signed Protocol I which laid down the basic principles guiding the process leading to a general cease-fire. It also required Frelimo to be a consonance with future protocols arising from the talks. Both parties became convinced of the urgent need for agreement; even the respective military commanders were broadly agreed that a military victory was not possible. Throughout this period the involved international community continued to exert pressure on both Renamo and Frelimo to allow MIVECO free access to the country in order to stimulate stability and confidence and thereby to extend the partial cease-fire. This requirement was accentuated by the increasing severity resulting from the drought. International Agencies such as *Medicin Sans Frontiers* and The Red Cross continued to develop imaginative plans to bring food and medicine to all drought affected areas but this required both the agreement and protection of Renamo and Frelimo forces. Whilst the government was usually content to guarantee such freedom of movement Renamo were not. They reasonably viewed such international action as being at the behest of government, using government escorts and vehicles which might quickly allow hard won Renamo areas to be re-absorbed into government control. Renamo placed the emphasis upon air supply as opposed to vehicles, yet it was clear that it was not possible to mount sufficient air lifts to address the situation country-wide. Undoubtedly those denied sustenance in Renamo areas suffered needlessly and it became clear to Dhlakama that compromises would have to be struck.

In early 1992 Dhlakama launched a so called 'battle for the cities' in a last attempt to gain at least one provincial capital and to put pressure on Maputo and to impress upon the international community there as well as to convince the Frelimo government that Renamo remained a force to be reckoned with. Due in part to a lack of popular support, for which credit should go to Bishop Sengulane's programme to prepare the people for peace, and due to the Renamo soldiers' fear of entering and fighting in the confines of dark and unfamiliar cities, the strategy totally failed causing further desertion within Renamo and further convincing Dhlakama and most of his advisers of the need to arrive at an acceptable peace.

Away from the battlefield other players were beginning to take part in bringing peace to Mozambique. President Chissano had attended the fringes of the Harare CHOGM[131] in October 1992 as a guest of President Mugabe. Later Mugabe met with Dhlakama and began to reduce the levels of Zimbabwean troops deployed to Mozambique. The situation in South Africa was changing quickly; by late 1991 it was clear that elections would soon take place and would herald the election of Nelson Mandela, a supporter of regional peace, as President. In the interim, President de Klerk continued to do all possible to rid the security forces of mavericks and to sever links with Renamo. Dhlakama could see the drying up of South African support. When the Renamo negotiating teams arrived in Maputo in January 1991 they had been shaken by what they saw; having spent years in the bush they had to adjust to traffic, to international standards of behaviour and to adopt the trappings and language of diplomacy and discussion. Much of the credit for providing such education is due to the mediators and the San Egidio Community who worked hard in the process of preparing Renamo for the final negotiations in Rome during the summer of 1992.

The international community involved in the peace process also played their part in moderating the sometimes intransigent stance of Frelimo and in providing the necessary confidence to enable Chissano to be more statesmanlike and generous. A continuing difficulty throughout the negotiations was the reluctance of the principal players, Chissano and Dhlakama, to meet face to face to decide key issues. Allied to this difficulty was the lack of negotiating flexibility allowed the Renamo delegates under Raoul Domingos who constantly had to be looking over his shoulder and delaying discussion in order to gain more instructions from Dhlakama.

By 1992 the focus of discussions had firmly shifted to the San Egidio Community in Rome where the four mediators, often joined by Ambassador Camerana, took a firm hold of the agenda and the discussion format. The various pressures previously discussed had forced the two parties to talk seriously and to compromise. It was clear to both delegations that post war Mozambique would require massive and continuing international aid to reconstruct and renew its infrastructure, Donor nations would be required; these would likely be the same countries who had assisted in the peace process. If money and expertise were to be provided then it would be sensible for the parties to take note of the donor countries' wishes; intransigence was unlikely to bring funding. This leverage was carefully employed by the donor countries but not without some difficulty in retaining cohesion between the countries in terms of applying the carrot and stick approach. With equal fervour Portugal, the previous colonial administrator of Mozambique, was more than willing to assume the reins of responsibility from Italy during particularly difficult discussions in mid 1992 and had to be restrained from this competitive, potentially harmful approach.

A central theme maintained throughout by the mediators was the need for Renamo publicly to recognise the Frelimo government and President Chissano as the *de facto* if not *de jure* authority of the Mozambican state at least until elections were held. For Dhlakama this was always a difficult concept to come to terms with, preferring to adopt the previous Portuguese stance prior to independence whereby a form of joint coalition was achieved. Associated with the concept of Frelimo as the *de facto* authority was the proposed constitution first put forward by Chissano in draft form for comment by Renamo in January 1991. The draft with few changes (Dhlakama preferring to produce his own alternative a short while later) was accepted into law by the Frelimo Assembly in January 1992. The document proclaimed a multi party Western style democratic system, a total reverse of the Marxist regime exercised since the Party's Third Conference held in 1977. Most Western countries supported the constitution with few changes.

Following the elections of October 1994 and the continuance of Chissano as President, (this time elected) winning fifty-seven per cent of the presidential votes, the constitution is likely to remain in place. Much of the credit for encouraging and leading Chissano to adopt such a relatively radical constitution must be laid at the door of Bishop Sengulane and the churchmen who gained the President's confidence and were able to convince him to take such a stance.

During May to July 1992 the negotiators, mediators and advisers worked hard in Rome to ensure a lasting peace agreement. A series of protocols were drawn up and it was agreed that the UN should be invited to provide supervision during the transition to peace. To this end a Brazilian Colonel (UN) was attached to the talks to ensure that the UN planners were kept abreast of developments. In effect Sr. Aldo Ajello (the Italian Special Representative to the Secretary General) arrived in Maputo with a small staff within twenty-four hours of the peace agreement coming into effect on 16 October 1992. The First Protocol (Basic Principles) signed in Rome by both parties in 1991 related to the partial cease-fire, the Second and Third Protocols laid down the provision of the electoral and party laws. These essential protocols, largely drafted by the mediators, in particular Sr. Raffaelli, were used to good effect as the basis for the 1994 elections and were shown to be extremely sound in their construction.

The Fourth Protocol dealt with the vital matter of demo-bilisation of the Renamo and Frelimo military forces and the recruitment and training of a new joint force. The military experts from France, Italy, Portugal, the US and the UK devised an establishment including a rank structure, deployment plan and an equipment scale which was broadly accepted by both parties following detailed talks. Renamo with a declared force of about twenty thousand, but not including any naval or airforce personnel, wished for a small force (fifteen thousand) of only soldiers whilst initially Frelimo, with a declared force of approximately sixty thousand plus reserves and including naval and airforce units, proposed a force of about forty thousand. They considered this as a minimum force necessary to defend the frontiers. However once it was agreed that it would not be reasonable to attempt to wage war against either South Africa or Zimbabwe both parties agreed that each should provide fifty per cent towards a force of twenty-four thousand soldiers, and in addition two thousand five hundred sailors, and three thousand five hundred airmen. Renamo finally had agreed the argument that to disband and lose the valuable technical skills of the Airforce and Navy would be a negative and harmful course for Mozambique. Renamo negotiators under General Morais agreed that their monitoring of these forces could be achieved through the placement of Renamo officers in deputy appointments.

By 3rd October all were ready to sign an overall peace agreement in Rome but once more Dhlakama proved to be reluctant to come to the talks to sign. He may have been uncertain of the support of some of his military commanders. The mediators once more played a critical role explaining the arrangements and highlighting the benefits whilst making clear that a failure to sign after more than two years of negotiations with the assurance of UN supervision would be unthinkable in terms of prolonging the agony of the Mozambican people. Dhlakama requested the mediators, with President Mugabe present, to make this clear in a presentation to his delegation, both military and civilian. He followed up the arguments deployed with his decision to accept the mediators' arguments and assurances. He felt that the power of the mediators' arguments was better expressed by them rather than him. In this fashion he was able to show any doubters that it was not just himself but the international community which required the agreement to be signed and that the rationale was sound. Renamo had achieved as much as could be expected.

Following the October Agreement both parties took up the arguments as to how to interpret and translate the Agreement into practical terms. Such matters as the holding of elections, planned for October 1993, demobilising of military forces and national rehabilitation were a long way from agreement. The HVC and MIVECO were wound up following the Agreement and the UN military force and civilian experts, including election staff, specialist agencies such as UNHCR, arrived to help bring the agreement into effect. Quickly it was realised that the elections would have to be delayed by one year until October 1994. Renamo refused to allow free access to their 'sanctuaries' and Dhlakama refused to come to Maputo, initially on security grounds and later due to the lack of 'suitable' accommodation. These matters, together with the disclosures that Renamo had spent $600,000 on the purchase of a non flyable airfreighter worth only $150,000, precipitated Renamo's withdrawal from the talks in March 1993.

Dhlakama resisted accepting the UK Government's offer to train the new armed forces until February 1993 when he grudgingly agreed in principle. What annoyed him was the fact that the training would take place at the British Army Training Centre at Nyanga in Zimbabwe. When finally he authorised General Ngonhomo to visit and inspect Nyanga the General was undiplomatic enough to describe the camp to his Zimbabwean hosts as 'the camp where you train Mozambicans to kill Renamo'. It was not until October 1993 that joint Renamo/Frelimo training took place. This prolonged delay (a year) put considerable pressure upon the UK if they were to complete the training of the Army forces prior to the elections. Both France and Portugal agreed to assist in training specialists but Dhlakama did not take up their offer until late 1933. This was particularly so as the monies voted by the UK Parliament to fund the training in 1993 were not to be available in 1994. In the event due to lack of recruits the new combined army at the time of the election totalled only ten thousand, less than fifty per cent of the planned figure due to lack of pay and adequate terms of service.

In conclusion, Bishop Sengulane was awarded the AACC Peace Prize in October 1992 in recognition of his patient dedication to the cause of peace in Mozambique. The monies received have been dedicated by the bishop to establish a Peace Centre in Maputo. One of the final key sticking points thrown up by the peace process was the control of the Security Police, the clear enemies of Renamo. As part of the General Peace Agreement in answer to Renamo's fears, a supervisory organisation, Commission for Information (COMINFO) was established independently to scrutinise the operation of the Security Police. Bishop Sengulane was the nomination acceptable to both parties to be its first co-chairman with Abd Al Aziz a senior Islamic Cultural Organisation (ICO) representative.

The Peace Process in Bishop Sengulane's words was successful due to 'Prayers, Bible study in the hope of peace, talking to governments about the urgent need for dialogue with Renamo, educating the children against conflict in all its forms, setting up skill options for youth, particularly the wounded of both sides, and developing self support projects to rebuild confidences'.

The Sant Egidio Community provided patience, an overall synergy and focus to the process and a permanent supportive and listening access to the outside world, particularly for Renamo. The Sant Egidio Community would add that the security offered by them was vital as was the non-political, non-partisan approach which by its very nature prevented or at least reduced the chances of either party being made to look foolish. The religious, patient, hopeful environment allowed contemplation and for parties to change their minds without undue embarrassment. A lack of publicity was judged essential. A further key to success was the decision to make both Dhlakama and Chissano feel that the world was watching and requiring them to act as responsible statesmen and bringers of peace. Both responded well to this concept, which they saw as enhancing their status.

The General Peace Accord is based upon the transformation of Renamo into a political entity and self limitation by

Frelimo, accepting democracy yet retaining authority, and both parties temporarily surrendering some sovereignty to the UN until the elections. The standing of the churches of all denominations has risen dramatically as has its membership. Finally, all recognised the need for help. The church was always there to cajole, morally challenge, educate, counsel, guide and above all to channel and focus the power of the people's will to the extent that peace survived and this was due in large part to Bishop Sengulane's painstaking policy of preparing the people for peace. The timing of the Angolan election in September 1992 could have been critical to the peace process in Mozambique. It initially provided, on the one hand an example and hope as an environment for the signing in Rome, yet in its tragic failure it could have undone the putting into effect of that agreement on the 15 October 1992.

President Chissano had tried to limit the loss of sovereignty and the role of the intermediaries, including the UN. The mediators had tried desperately to involve Dhlakama at every stage, binding Renamo into organisations, committees, agreements and understandings, a policy supported by President Chissano. Renamo's ambitions to achieved democracy and a Western economy with a multi-party state and a Western constitution were achieved. The churches will continue to maintain the engagement of both parties to the commitment to peace. In Bishop Sengulane's words, 'The urgency is to build up a spirit of consensus.' Had the church not taken the initiative to develop and pursue an environment for peace and to offer its services it is unlikely that peace would have been achieved either within the schedule obtained or, if later, then it is equally unlikely that the peace would have been so well constructed in terms of political reunification.

Neither party had foreseen the necessary complexity involved in establishing a permanent peace after sixteen years of civil war. The details contained in the protocols were essential to remove misunderstanding and provide confidence through transparency. From a donor point of view such transparency was vital. The Protocols do offer a guide to establishing future agreements of this nature and stand as testimony to the negotiating and drafting skills of the church's mediators.

The Transformation of Power in Malawi 1992-95

The Role of the Christian Churches

Kenneth R. Ross

From the time of independence in 1964, the churches in Malawi appeared to be compliant supporters of 'Life President' Kamuzu Banda and his repressive one-party regime. Every Sunday in churches of all denominations leaders prayed for the long life and prosperity of the dictator who was ruthlessly exploiting and brutally oppressing the people. At every national occasion the church leaders were present to provide religious legitimation for the political status quo.

With the end of the cold war, the subsequent wave of democratisation sweeping across Africa and the increasingly apparent political bankruptcy of the Banda regime, hopes rose for positive change in Malawi in the early 1990s. Still, few expected that the church would be the source of such change. The system of political control was so complete that most people had difficulty even imagining anything different. When a delegation of British lawyers visited Malawi as late as September 1992 they reported that 'the emotion we encountered, among citizens at every level, from villages to government officials, was fear'.[132] In the land 'where silence ruled' (to use the title of a 1990 *Africa Watch* report on Malawi), who could break the spell of fear?

The bishops' letter
In March 1992 Malawi's Roman Catholic bishops issued

their pastoral letter 'Living Our Faith'[133]. Rarely in modern times has a church document had such an immediately explosive effect in the life of a nation. Within four days the ruling Malawi Congress Party (MCP) was convened in emergency session to pass an unreserved condemnation of the bishops. Possession of the letter was declared an act of sedition, punishable by severe penalties. There were unrestrained calls at the party convention for the bishops to be killed; and the publication of an editorial entitled 'No Mercy' in the government-controlled newspaper led experienced observers to fear that the bishops were being set up for assassination.

Yet even as the one-party system mustered its forces to stamp out the dissent, it became evident that there had been a dramatic shift in power. The bishops' polite but blunt statements about the shortcomings of the prevailing political order had such a ring of truth that the MCP regime was suddenly exposed. Things could never be the same again. Practically overnight the mode of discourse in everyday conversation began to change. The once all-powerful MCP was becoming a laughing-stock. The sense of liberation was palpable.[134]

The critically important function of the pastoral letter was to introduce, quite suddenly and dramatically, accountability to Malawian public life. First of all, it made the regime accountable to reality. Whereas government propaganda ceaselessly promoted the myth that all Malawians had prospered under the beneficent reign of Kamuzu Banda, the bishops bluntly observed that 'many people still live in circumstances which are hardly compatible with their dignity as sons and daughters of God. Their life is a struggle for survival. At the same time a minority enjoys the fruits of development and can afford to live in luxury and wealth (p. 2). Shortcomings in the national education system were noted: widespread illiteracy, falling standards, overcrowding, shortage of teachers and materials, unequal access to education and indiscipline. Concern was expressed about the shortage of health centres, overcrowding and lack of personnel, the poor quality of medical care and inequality in medical treatment (pp. 4-7). These were all matters of common knowledge – 'People will not be scandalised to hear these things; they know them,' the bishops wrote (p. 10) – but no one had dared to mention them publicly for fear that this would be regarded as tantamount to sedition. Now the myth of the prosperous Malawi was exploded and people began to address the serious problems of poverty faced by the country. Much of the power of the pastoral letter lay in the fact that it broke the culture of deceit which had been allowed to develop.

The bishops, however, went further to question the entire nature and structure of Malawian political life, stating that 'People are entitled to know how their representatives fulfil their duties. No disrespect is shown when citizens ask questions in matters which concern them' (p. 10). This call for accountability to the people marked the beginning of a process of democratisation which would transform Malawian political life during the coming two years.

Perhaps the most powerful part of the letter was its section on 'the participation of all in public life'. The bishops drew on both Biblical texts (Ephesians 4:7-16 and 1 Peter 4:10-11) and traditional African proverbs to argue that society can be strong only when it enjoys the participation of all its members:

> Human persons are honoured – and this honour is due to them – whenever they are allowed to search freely for truth, to voice their opinions and to be heard, to engage in creative service of the community in all liberty within associations of their own choice. Nobody should ever have to suffer reprisals for honestly expressing and living up to their convictions: intellectual, religious or political. We can only regret that this is not always the case in our country . . .

> Academic freedom is seriously restricted; exposing injustices
> can be considered a betrayal; revealing some evils of our
> society is seen as slandering the country; monopoly of the
> mass media and censorship prevent the expression of
> dissenting views; some people have paid dearly for their
> political opinions; access to public places like markets,
> hospitals, bus depots, etc., is frequently denied to those
> who cannot produce a party card; forced donations have
> become a way of life. (p. 9)

The effect of all this on national life and consciousness
was 'an atmosphere of resentment', 'a climate of mistrust
and fear', so that 'the talents of many lie unused and . . .
there is little room for initiative' (p. 9).

First steps towards the restoration of a climate of trust
and openness were proposed, and these became Malawi's
political agenda for the next two years: establishment of an
independent press, open forums of discussion, free association
of citizens for social and political purposes, government
accountability, establishment of independent, accessible and
impartial courts of justice. These were all measures designed
to recover the accountability of government to the people
and to increase popular participation in political life.

For these goals to be achieved, however, another level of
accountability played an important role. Johann-Baptist
Metz has written of the 'dangerous memory' or 'subversive
memory' of Jesus Christ which the church carries through
history. Time and again 'this definite memory breaks
through the magic circle of the prevailing consciousness'[135].
MCP propaganda had succeeded in creating in the country
such a culture of deceit that people began to lose their
bearings and even their thinking was 'colonised' by the system.
The pastoral letter broke through that false consciousness by
making the system accountable to the norms and values of
the kingdom of God. Thereafter the MCP government could
no longer be a law unto itself for the church was measuring

its policies and actions against the norm or criterion of the Biblical message of the kingdom of God. By weighing the existing order against the demands of God's impending kingdom, the church supplied a gauge which freed people to make their own assessment of the prevailing system and to take action accordingly.

In a predominantly Christian country like Malawi, where the Biblical message has tremendous resonance, making the exercise of power accountable to God in this way was a formidable political challenge. When the MCP government made the mistake of asking people to choose between their loyalty to the church and their loyalty to the regime, it soon became clear that its legitimacy was crumbling. The church's memory certainly proved to be 'dangerous' and 'subversive' so far as the one-party system in Malawi was concerned.

By establishing these three levels of accountability, the Catholic bishops ensured that Malawi would never be the same again. What remained was to see whether a peaceful process of political reform could be developed to put into effect the vision expressed in the pastoral letter.

The public affairs committee

Despite intense government intimidation, support for the pastoral letter was soon made apparent. Catholic students issued a letter of support, and the following Sunday students of the University of Malawi marched in support of the bishops, an action which resulted in the closure of the main university campus for the first time in its history.

When Chakufwa Chihana, the Malawian secretary-general of the Southern African Trade Union Co-ordinating Council, returned to Malawi to begin a campaign for democratic change, he appealed in his speech upon arrival (before being arrested) to the pastoral letter as an indication of the need for political reform[136]. Later in April an unprecedented wave of strikes swept both the public and private sectors, forcing the government to implement massive wage rises.

The strikes were accompanied by rioting and looting directed particularly at properties identified with the MCP.

Although the government obviously faced a serious crisis, it was unclear for some months how the initiative of the pastoral letter could be taken up in a positive and constructive way. The bishops themselves found it advisable to take a low profile for a time. It fell to the Presbyterians to begin to chart a way forward. It now proved to be significant that the Church of Central Africa Presbyterian (CCAP) belonged to an international fellowship of mutual accountability, the World Alliance of Reformed Churches. In early June WARC sent a delegation to meet with the leaders of the Presbyterian churches in Malawi, and together they presented an open letter to the Life President entitled 'The Nation of Malawi in Crisis: the Church's Concern'. They made direct reference to the Catholic pastoral letter, still technically a seditious document, and insisted that the government must address the issues which it raised.

But more was needed at this stage than a Presbyterian echo of the Catholic social critique. Practical proposals were required. The church leaders accordingly called for the appointment of a broadly based commission with the mandate to make specific proposals for structural reform towards a political system with sufficient checks and balances on the use of power, and guarantees of accountability at all levels of government; to review the judicial system, in line with the rule of law; to look into the distribution of income and wealth required by the demands of social justice.

At the same time, the government must take immediate steps to remove injustices: end the practice of detention without trial; release or bring to early and fair trial all political detainees; reform conditions of imprisonment, in accordance with human dignity; allow freedom of expression and association, so as to encourage open discussion of the nation's future.

These demands were powerfully reinforced by the decision

in May of the Western donor communities to suspend all development aid to Malawi until there was evidence of greater respect for human rights and 'good governance'. A process of reform was immediately undertaken by the government. Many political detainees were released. The International Committee of the Red Cross was invited to inspect the prisons. The practice of forced donations and the harassment of people who did not possess party cards was stopped. Slowly and painfully, with many obstructions along the way, the door began to be opened to freedom of expression and freedom of association.

However, it was apparent that the government was hoping to placate its critics with relatively superficial reforms while maintaining the underlying structures of repression. Though the President had given a favourable reply to the Presbyterian open letter and had invited church leaders to meet with his ministers, the government stalled and was clearly reluctant to accede to the formation of a forum where fundamental political issues would be addressed[137].

The delay proved to be a blessing in disguise to the forces of reform, for it provided the opportunity and the constraint to work towards a more broadly representative commission, including not only church leaders but also representatives of the Muslim Association, the Malawi Law Society and the Associated Chambers of Commerce and Industry. Significantly, the church leaders included not only clergy but also elders with a wealth of experience in national affairs. Throughout July and August the Presbyterian church leaders worked hard behind the scenes to bring together a truly national and representative commission. The open letter to the government issued by the Christian Council of Malawi on 26 August 1992, calling for a referendum on the system of government, was signed by representatives of the Anglican Church, all three Synods of the CCAP (one later withdrew), the African Methodist Episcopal Church, the Seventh Day Baptist Church, the Churches of Christ, the Zambezi

Evangelical Church, Providence Industrial Mission, the Baptist Church and a number of parachurch organisations. Two days later, when the church leaders wrote to the government again, their letter was signed by representatives not only of the Protestant churches but also the Roman Catholic Church, the Muslim community, the business community and the Malawi Law Society.[138]

This was the first time in Malawian history that Christian and Muslim leaders had publicly united to take a strategic socio-political initiative. Despite the fact that the Muslim participants were later disowned by the more conservative leadership within their own community, the formation of the Public Affairs Committee was a significant event in the history of Christian-Muslim relations in Malawi. The significance of this united front was not lost on the government, which immediately responded by insisting that the committee should be composed of church leaders only and must exclude the business community and the Law Society.[139] In a series of exchanges the government maintained this position but the church leaders were not to be moved:

> The initiative of the church should not be interpreted in a narrow sense, as if the issues for discussion are exclusively religious. The issues which moved the church to call for a national dialogue were and remain national issues affecting all aspects of the lives of the citizens of this country.[140]

When the Public Affairs Committee (PAC) finally sat down with the Presidential Committee on Dialogue (PCD) on 19 October 1992, it did so as the representative organ of a truly national constituency. It was the first time that a non-party organisation was recognised as having a role to play in national political life. The PAC planned to press at this meeting for a national referendum on the question of a one-party or multi-party system of government; but in order to seize the initiative, Banda himself announced a day earlier that the government intended to hold such a referendum.[141] This announcement prompted a second 'pressure group', the United Democratic Front (UDF), to join Chakufwa Chihana's Alliance for Democracy (Aford) in the public arena. Chihana himself was by this time on trial for sedition. His two-year sentence, was reduced on appeal to six months (keeping him in prison until just after the referendum campaign was completed). Chihana's 'mitigation statement' during the appeal began: 'I come from a family which has strong Christian traditions, i.e. the fear and adoration of God, respect for human beings and the readiness to assist others in need of help. Throughout my life these Christian values have had considerable influence and have become the rockbed of my present social and political behaviour.'

While focusing on the institutional role of the churches in the changes in Malawi, we should not neglect the witness of lay Christians in the political arena. At the same time, it must be observed that at this early stage the budding political parties worked to a considerable extent under the umbrella of the PAC, which remained the engine of political reform during the referendum period. For example, it was the PAC which forced the government to address the issue of violence and even to sign a joint statement indicating their resolve to 'prosecute all persons who engage in incitement to political violence and violence itself and . . . to protect the fundamental right of persons to hold political views' (13 November 1992).

This paper agreement did not prevent the MCP government from continuing to use its familiar tactics of intimidation and violence in a vain attempt to stop the tidal wave of support gathering behind the multi-party movement. In the aftermath of the pastoral letter it had been immensely important that there were individuals who were prepared to defy such intimidation and to suffer for their convictions. The bishops themselves had stood by their letter and had defied all attempts to force an apology and retraction. Their

firm stand encouraged others to speak out. In an interview
in November 1994. PAC Secretary Misanjo Kansilanga
described his experience two years earlier:

> MCP top brass went to our home areas and informed our
> relatives that we were not good people. We had become
> rebels. They were inciting people in our home areas to
> bash our cars, to burn our property and all sorts of things.
> I lost a whole granary in my home area and my two houses
> were burned down during the referendum campaign
> period . . . My car was stoned and I was followed on
> several occasions – a car following me wherever I went.
> So we knew that we were in danger.

When Kansilanga's relatives and friends advised him to
withdraw from his involvement with PAC he told them:

> I am not doing my own thing. I did not choose this. But I
> believe that this is God's work. If it is God's work then it is
> God himself who has life in his hands, so if I am killed
> praises will go to God and you shouldn't cry.

The presence of individuals moved by this level of faith
and commitment demonstrated that the long-established
system of control by means of violence was breaking down
and that accountability was being introduced to Malawian
political life.

As the national referendum of 16 June 1993 approached,
it became ever more apparent that the government was
fighting a losing battle. Huge crowds flocked to the multi-party
rallies while MCP campaign meetings in much of the country
were subject to a virtual boycott. Only in its heartlands in the
Central Region were traditional MCP tactics successful in
retaining substantial support.[142] It was no surprise when the
electorate voted for a multi-party system by a two-thirds
majority. Significant for the future was the fact that the
one-third which supported the maintenance of the one-party
system was largely concentrated in the Central Region.

The churches were prominent in the conscientisation process necessary to achieve this result. The PAC set up an organisation called PACREM – Public Affairs Committee Referendum Monitoring – which quickly drew attention to any abuses and gave people confidence that they could vote freely.[143] When interviewed in November/December 1994, many people indicated that it was at church that they learned of the possibility of political reform and began to give their support to the multi-party cause. Officially, the churches limited themselves to spelling out the principles which should guide people in voting, but the gap between Christian principles and MCP rule was so obvious that the church was clearly perceived to be on the side of political reform. With few exceptions the 'mainstream' churches had effectively taken sides with the multi-party movement.[144]

The church as power-broker

The victory of the multi-party advocates in the national referendum of June 1993 led to the legalising of opposition political parties and the promise of a general election which was finally held on 17 May 1994. In the struggle for legitimacy between government and opposition during this period the churches played an important role as power-brokers. Since they were not seeking political office for themselves church leaders came to exercise a distinctive influence on the unfolding political drama. Aware of the ideological power of religion in the political realm, the MCP had over the years systematically and successfully pressed the churches into supplying the government with religious legitimation.

Much was made in the party propaganda of the fact that Banda was an elder of the Church of Scotland. Indeed, the review of the year in the *Daily Times* of 30 December 1991 singled out as the highlight of 1991 (with a full-colour front-page photograph) the 'triumphant moment' when Banda was presented with a commemorative scroll to mark the fiftieth anniversary of his ordination to the eldership. It was a serious blow, in the aftermath of the pastoral letter, when the Church of Scotland made it clear it no longer regarded Banda as an active elder.[145] The serious over-reaction into which the government was stung is a measure of how much it depended on the unquestioning support of the church.

This was further underscored, after almost all churches had rallied behind the work of PAC, by the importance the government attached to the continuing support of the Nkhoma Synod – the Central Region section of the CCAP which had strong historical links with the MCP leadership.[146] Struggling to retain an air of legitimacy, it turned to ministers of the Nkhoma Synod to officiate at government functions and generally to show solidarity with the MCP. This they were willing to do during the early referendum period; only later did the synod seek to draw back from its unqualified support of the MCP government with a statement in April 1993 that 'genuine Christians can support either side of the referendum question without violating the genuine ideals and principles of Christianity.'[147] This attempt at 'neutrality' did not convince the other churches, which saw it simply as an evasion of the demands of the gospel, and left the government even more bereft of the church endorsement on which it had depended in the past. In desperation the MCP attempted to supply its own religious legitimation. In its own campaign newspaper, *Guardian Today*, a striking number of articles were devoted to portraying the MCP as having a divine mandate, epitomised by a cartoon series on the theme 'MCP points to God! Multi-party – homs of the Devil!'[148]

On the other hand, the emergent opposition was able constantly to appeal to the prophetic critique of the churches as justification for its political initiative. Indeed, the July 1993 manifesto of the United Democratic Front, the first to be issued by an opposition party after the referendum, began with a quotation from the pastoral letter and stated that the movement for political reform had been initiated in response to the call from the Catholic bishops. Occasions such as the requiem mass in May 1993 for four politicians widely believed to have been assassinated by government agents ten years earlier were highly charged politically and very damaging to the credibility of the government.[149] It was no surprise that UDF leader Bakili Muluzi went out of his way in his victory speech after the referendum to thank the churches: 'In particular, I would like to single out the seven Catholic bishops and the [Presbyterian] Blantyre Synod.'[150] At the popular level, a significant factor in the conflation of Christian belief with the call for political reform was that many church songs were adapted to give expression to the movement for political liberation, especially among young people. So *Ndiri ndi Bwenzi Langa Yesu* ('I have my beloved friend Jesus') became *Ndiri ndi Bwenzi Langa Muluzi* ('I have my beloved friend Muluzi'). Particularly influential were the songs of Paul Banda and the Alleluya Band, a well-known Malawian musical group. In the powerful song *Tiyamike Chiuta* ('Let us praise God'), they played on the symbols of the opposing sides in the referendum – the hurricane lamp of the multi-party side and the black cock of the one-party side – to suggest an identification of multi-party with the light of Jesus Christ and of one-party with the darkness of Satan.

A notable feature of the ideological struggle was that the opposition began to argue that Baptist pastor John Chilembwe – not Kamuzu Banda – was the father of Malawian politics.[151] There were good historical grounds for doing so: Chilembwe led an armed rising against British colonial rule in 1915.[152] A popular song during the campaign period, *Kuno Kwathu ku Malawi*, suggested that just as Chilembwe had fought against the oppression of the colonialists so he would have fought against the oppression of Banda and the MCP. When the new government announced the public holidays for the 1995 calendar, Kamuzu Day was missing and Chilembwe Day had been introduced.

For the churches, adaptation to the new role as power-

301

broker did not come without struggle. On the one hand, some church leaders became so involved in the political arena that they eventually left the ministry in order to devote themselves to politics. Peter Kaleso of the Blantyre Synod became Aford vice-president before later joining the UDF and becoming ambassador to South Africa; Aaron Longwe of the Livingstonia Synod embarked on full-time human rights work with the newly established Foundation for Justice, Peace and the Integrity of Creation; Emmanuel Chinkwita of the Baptist Church became first a shadow cabinet minister and parliamentary candidate, then ambassador to Mozambique. In each case it had to be made clear that they were acting as politicians in their own right and no longer as representatives of their churches.

On the other hand, there were those who believed that the churches became too detached from the political process in the post-referendum period. When parliament was debating legislation to establish the bodies which would oversee the transition to a multi-party political system, the PAC declined to be represented, thus leaving the process of reform entirely in the hands of the political parties and allowing the government later to claim that PAC was a body which had a role only in the pre-referendum period and which was now obsolete.[153] However, the Christian Council responded by affirming very clearly in a press release (12 November 1993) that 'PAC is a relevant body and there is need for its continuity now and after the general elections. The church being the conscience of society shall continue to play this noble and prophetic role . . . PAC is here to stay for ever in Malawi.' In the run-up to the general election PAC was particularly active in working to avoid the 'Kenyan scenario' – a divided opposition allowing the old regime to remain in power.[154] In civic education and election-monitoring the churches remained by far the most effective organisation and contributed significantly to the general election being a very peaceful and highly efficient exercise. PAC made the church a significant force as a power broker. Integral to this development was the unity of the various groupings, which allowed the PAC secretary to sign communications with government 'on behalf of the countries' regional communities'.

The spectre of regionalism

The unity which had been found ecclesiastically in the PAC and politically in the multi-party movement was soon put to the test by the threat of regionalism. From colonial times Malawi has been divided administratively into Northern, Central and Southern Regions, each with its own cultural, ethnic, linguistic, religious and political identity. These divisions had been transcended in the formation of the nationalist movement in the 1940s and 1950s which, organised as the Malawi Congress Party, finally succeeded in achieving independence in 1964. Almost immediately, however, this national unity was fragmented as Banda, with his own authority under threat, played the tribal-regional card and sought to maintain his authoritarian rule by mean of a hegemony of his own Chewa-speaking people of the Central Region.[155] While the substantial issue in the cabinet crisis was the nature of government, it could not be ignored that the ousted ministers came either from the north or the south, nor that 'the repression which followed the break-up of the cabinet was clearly directed by region. Chiefs from both the Northern and Southern Regions were dismissed but none from the Central Region. Likewise a majority of regional councils in both the Northern and Southern Regions were dissolved – but again none from the Central Region'.[156] This set the scene for a political dispensation in which the ruling party continued to employ the language and symbols of the nationalist movement while reinforcing the dominance of the Chewa-speaking people of the Central Region.[157]

In crude regionalistic terms the multi-party movement of 1992-94 can be interpreted as the North and the South striking back against the Centre. Moreover, while the two powerful opposition parties sought to be national movements it soon became apparent that Aford was predominantly a northern party while the UDF was predominantly southern. This was borne out in the results of the 1994 general election, when each of the three regions gave overwhelming support to the party with which it identified – Aford in the North, MCP in the Centre, UDF in the South.[158] It could be argued that UDF won the election simply because the Southern Region is the most populous. The problem of national unity now came into the open as an urgent political issue[159] – so much so that Aford and the MCP, sworn enemies hitherto, were able to justify their sudden and short-lived alliance on the grounds of the need to secure national unity.

There was a real danger that politicians would regard their accountability in regional terms. National political life in the post-election period often appeared to be no more than a contest between competing regional power blocs. It remains to be seen whether the exercise of power can be conditioned by a sense of national identity and national accountability.

Although the churches through PAC provided an early rallying point for a united national movement, they were themselves seriously compromised by regionalism. This was most apparent in the Presbyterian Church where the Nkhoma Synod of the Central Region took a line which suggested that its political loyalty came before its ecclesiastical unity with the other synods.[160] In 1992, when the other church leaders were making their risky and costly prophetic social witness, the Nkhoma Synod acted in solidarity with the MCP Government. The other churches felt betrayed by its apparent decision to line up against them in the struggle for justice and truth in Malawi, and in November 1992 the Nkhoma Synod was suspended from membership of the Christian Council of Malawi.[161] Even so, the Synod continued working, hand in hand with the MCP to resist the forces of political change. Pastors often admonished the people to vote against any sort of political change and pronounced the

Banda regime to be ordained of God. In Dowa anyone who was suspected of sympathising with the multi-party movement was excommunicated.

But even though the churches had not been immune from the regional fragmentation which was the legacy of the Banda years, they had also been able, however imperfectly, to act as the custodians of national unity. In the pastoral letter of 1992 the Catholic bishops appealed to the need to 'guarantee the progress of the *nation*'; likewise, PAC was concerned to explain to the Government that it was concerned with '*national* issues affecting all aspects of the lives of the citizens of this country'[162] The churches had the capacity to affirm a sense of national identity and establish a sense of national accountability. In the aftermath of the general election this was strongly expressed by Paul Banda in his song *Tiime Pamodzi* ('Let us stand together'), which presents fragmentation as the work of the devil and Christian faith as a resource for fostering national unity. A sense of accountability to God can serve to relativise regional loyalties and thus orient the exercise of power to national responsibility. The extent of the churches' ability to contribute to the resolution of this problem will be determined by the success or failure of their own struggle for unity among themselves in the gospel.

The exercise of power in the new Malawi

There has been a vast increase in the accountability of those in power in Malawi between 1992 and 1994. The life president has been replaced by a state president elected to serve for five years with a maximum of two terms. The executive authority of the presidency is balanced by a careful separation of powers, with a serious attempt to secure the integrity of the legislature and the judiciary. All officers must operate within the constraints of the constitution provisionally implemented after the 1994 general election and ratified by parliament, with minor amendments, in March 1995. A parliamentary opposition offers vociferous criticism of the government. The press is free; and while some newspapers remain highly partisan, others are achieving an impressive level of independence and impartiality. All political detainees have been released and all exiles are permitted to return. Academic freedom is assured for the university. There are active 'watchdog' organisations, such as the Civil Liberties Commission and the Foundation for Justice, Peace and the Integrity of Creation, which publicise alleged abuses of human rights and any failure to meet the requirements of the constitution. Citizens who believe that their rights have not been duly respected can appeal to an ombudsman.

The churches' activity in the public arena has sustained the sense of the accountability of political life to the standards of the kingdom of God introduced so dramatically by the 1992 pastoral letter. When Bakili Muluzi accepted the office of presidency he immediately invited the churches to offer correction to his government whenever it might stray from the path.[163] Just two years earlier, when one individual had absolute power, parliament was a rubber stamp, the law courts were politically manipulated, the press was a government-controlled organ for propaganda, any suspected dissident was detained or assassinated and the witness of the churches was silenced.

Why, then, are many ordinary people saying that nothing has really changed, or that the change has been in name only?[164] A major part of the explanation is that the radical political reforms which have taken place have scarcely disturbed the profound economic inequalities bequeathed to Malawi by the colonial system and entrenched under the Banda regime. The small educated élite which took over the apparatus of the colonial government in 1964 was able to use its position to enrich itself at the expense of the rural masses, essentially continuing the colonial system but with a new set of beneficiaries. Both the 1992 pastoral letter and the WARC/CCAP letter had called for addressing the disparity in living conditions between the rich and the poor. It was this part of their critique which was most neglected. Kamuzu Banda's Press Corporation continues to dominate the small Malawi economy; it has a near or complete monopoly in many sectors and is accountable only to its shareholders. This secures the economic dominance of the tiny wealthy élite associated with Banda but offers little hope to the impoverished majority.

The removal of the MCP from government has not brought much tangible change. Indeed, though the UDF government was elected on a ticket of poverty alleviation, it was not long before the popular joke was that it was actually 'PPA' – personal poverty alleviation – as government ministers manifestly used their new positions for personal economic advantage![165] The suspicion grew in the popular mind that the political change had amounted to little more than a game of 'musical chairs' among the small dominant élite. There had been a tremendous sense of empowerment among the rural people when they were able to exercise their vote to elect a president and member of parliament of their own choice. Now they wonder whether that sense of empowerment was an illusion as they see the benefits continuing to flow to the urban élite while they remain in deepening poverty. In the recent play *Tisaiwale*, by the popular Kwathu Drama Group, a bishop tells his people that if you divorced a husband who constantly beat you and remarried only to find that you could not eat or clothe yourself, you would wonder if the change had been worth it.[166] A sense of disillusionment compounds the hopelessness and lack of initiative inherited from the colonial and one-party periods. Until this situation is addressed and there is a genuine empowerment of the rural population, the exercise of power in Malawi is going to be skewed in favour of the small but dominant middle class. Civic education, particularly on the part of the churches, remains vital to the redressing of the imbalances in power which entrench poverty among the rural majority in Malawi.

A particular problem is the tradition of political messian-ism bequeathed by the Banda era. Ascribing messianic quali-ties to Banda, which began as a calculated tactic to unite and inspire the people in the struggle for national independence, ended up allowing the 'Life President' to develop the highly autocratic leadership style and the egotistical brand of oratory which was to be the hallmark of government in Malawi for thirty years. In religious terms Banda was understood to be the man sent by God to lead the nation; and even during the referendum campaign Nkhoma Synod pastors often applied to Banda the text in Mark 9:7: 'This is my Son, the Beloved; listen to him!' There is some reason to suggest that the reform movement has simply substituted one political messiah for another. Among the popular songs promoting political change in Ntaja were *Abale kodi mwamva*, which emphasises that it is God who has chosen Bakili Muluzi to rule Malawi and that all godly people are obliged to vote for him, *Kongeresi ife ayi*, which says that since God is punishing the MCP no God-fearing person will want to be associated with it, and a third song which uses the Christological text 'The stone that the builders rejected has become the very head of the corner' (1 Peter 2:7) to interpret Muluzi's political career.[167] In the north there is a different messiah but the same idiom. When Chakufwa Chihana was released from prison at the time of the national referendum he was addressed in these terms by the General Secretary of the Synod of Livingstonia:

> We believe that you, like Gideon of old, have been called to deliver us and lead us into a new and just way of living . . . We are delighted that you are out of prison, for your own sake and that of your family, but also for the sake of Aford which has been 'rudderless' in your absence. For many of us, our patience with Aford has been wearing thin, but we have stayed with it because of the trust and confidence we have in you as a leader.[168]

It has proved to be more difficult than first imagined to emerge from the decades of dictatorship and to move towards a more mature political life. This has been reflected even in the president's conduct of his office. While his style is much more realistic and down-to-earth than Banda's, Muluzi too displayed a tendency to rule by decree. Already on the day he assumed office he announced to a packed stadium that a number of prisons would be closed and that the new state house in Lilongwe would be converted into a parliament building.[169] The latter pronouncement, on which he had not consulted parliament, proved to be quite impractical. Serious concern was aroused by his appointment of Chakufwa Chihana as Second Vice-President at a time when there was no constitutional provision for such a position, apparently imagining that he had authority to act in this way. One small group of concerned citizens challenged this decision and took him to court for breach of the constitution; and in March 1995 the National Constitutional Conference voted against the introduction of the office of Second Vice-President.[170] Another issue arose when MCP leaders were arrested on murder charges after the release, the Mwanza Commission Report mentioned earlier. There were fears that independence of the judiciary was being compromised by government interference in the case, even to the extent of a ministerial team travelling to the UK to hire prosecution lawyers – something they should have known was not permitted under the new constitution.[171]

Questions are also being raised about whether the exercise of power within churches is not still conditioned by the authoritarianism of the one-party system. Younger Catholic priests have told interviewers that the very bishops who courageously championed democracy in the political arena were operating the dioceses on a basis of dictatorship. A similar concern moved women of Blantyre Synod early in 1995 to march to the administrators' conference with a petition 'Justice and Peace in the Church'.[172] The justification for this action was dramatically demonstrated by the administrators themselves: not only did they refuse to receive the petition but they also resolved to suspend all women workers of the synod.[173] A striking tone reverberates through a recent statement by the Blantyre Synod Office on the 'Born Again' (charismatic) issue. The Synod officers define a Presbyterian church as follows:

> This type has a moderator and senior clerk as leaders of the general synod, moderator and general secretary in a synod, moderator and presbytery clerk, moderator (minister) and clerk of the kirk session: Power in this type of church is exercised by ministers and members at a general synod, synod, presbytery and kirk session. People who are not pleased with the hierarchy and exercise of power secede to other churches.[174]

Clearly the church is not immune to the temptation of thinking of the exercise of power in authoritarian terms; and it would do well to turn the searchlight of its call for democracy and accountability in the public sphere onto its own life also. So long as the church understands itself in terms of a power structure, its effectiveness as an agent for the transformation of power will be limited. A key issue here may well be the church's position on the balance of power between men and women. The constitution conference made it clear that many women are finding little in the new political dispensation to redress the discrimination to which they have been subject in Malawi society and culture.[175] Many look to the church for a lead and there is clearly a struggle going on at this point. The general synod meeting in Chongoni in November 1994 decided that any synod may proceed with the ordination of women when it judges the time to be right. On the other hand, the confrontation which developed in the Synod of Blantyre described above demonstrates that sexism remains deeply entrenched in the church.

As in many other countries, a testing issue in the Malawi transition is how to deal with abuses of power that took place in the past. Following the referendum, Article 19, the International Centre Against Censorship, made a powerful plea for the establishment of a 'Truth Commission' to investigate alleged atrocities of the past and make a definitive record.[176] The commission established by the new UDF government in June 1994 had the remit to investigate only the Mwanza 'accident'. As noted earlier, when the report of the commission implicated Banda and John Tembo, they were arrested. But coming to terms with the numerous episodes of this type poses serious challenges to the transitional process, since so many people are implicated in one way or another in the atrocities committed during the one-party era.

Some have suggested that it is necessary to 'draw a line through the past'; and several church leaders have laid great stress on the need for reconciliation. Indeed, leaders of Livingstonia Synod visited Banda shortly before his arrest with this objective in view.[177] Others insist that there is no true reconciliation without repentance. Meanwhile, claims by MCP leaders that they have repented are treated with scepticism so long as that repentance does not find expression in public acknowledgment of specific offences and some measure of restitution in favour of those who suffered.[178] Without such a process there will be no convincing answer to the question of whether such things might happen again in Malawi. Yet the political life is unlikely to be productive without national reconciliation. To meet both of these requirements is one of the most testing demands of a truly accountable exercise of power.

The recent history of Malawi demonstrates that there are resources in the Christian faith which can effect positive transformation of power. It was a Christian prophetic critique which exposed the gross abuse of power in Malawi's one-party system and made the regime accountable to God. Moreover, it was a church-based initiative which took the

311

lead in dismantling the one-party state and replacing it with a democratic order. Yet the churches' witness has remained ambiguous, for their own structures of power have been found to be more often oppressive than liberating. They themselves stand in need of the transforming leaven of the gospel to which they have borne such eloquent witness in the political arena.

'Heiwa no utsuwa':
'Vessels of Peace'

The witness of the Japanese church to reconciliation

Michael Ipgrave

'Lord, make us vessels of your peace (*heiwa no utsuwa*).'

That was the prayer adopted by the *Nippon Seikokai*, the 'Holy Catholic Church of Japan' (Anglican-Episcopalian) for its centenary celebrations in 1987. The expression *heiwa no utsuwa* referred back, through the prayer attributed to St Francis, to St Paul's account of the apostolic ministry in 2 Corinthians 4-5. There he describes God as having entrusted to his people the 'ministry of reconciliation' which was revealed in his work in Christ.[179] Yet the context within which Paul sets this entrustment is the brokenness and affliction of the apostolic life; the treasure of God is carried in 'vessels of clay (*tsuchi no utsuwa*)' by those who 'bear in their body the death of Jesus'.[180]

When the bishops of the *Seikokai* described their church as being an *utsuwa* or vessel sharing in the mystery of brokenness which leads to reconciliation, they chose their language carefully. The witness of Japanese Christians in this century has been set in times often marked by the division, aggression, alienation, and misunderstanding which are the human predicament crying out for divine reconciliation. Moreover, as the *utsuwa* of which they are made is common clay, so the church itself has shared in that unreconciledness in the heart of its being. Yet the remarkable vocation of the

Seikokai has been, precisely because it is an *utsuwa* of clay, to serve as an *utsuwa* of peace also: by acknowledging their participation in a history of complicity, Christians have found themselves strengthened in the integrity of their witness to reconciliation.

I shall seek to develop this theme by outlining some of the key factors in the Japanese situation which have in this century generated barriers to reconciliation, and by considering the Christian involvement in and response to those factors. But of course authentic reconciliation involves the overcoming of barriers on every side; so it is instructive to begin with the following reminder of the formidable barriers to reconciliation with Japan which still exist on the part of many British people.

In 1995, city, town, and village communities across Britain staged events to mark the fiftieth anniversary of the end of the Second World War. These clustered around two weekends, 6th-8th May and 19th-20th August, which were referred to as VE ('Victory in Europe') Day and VJ ('Victory over Japan') Day respectively. Official government literature described the different characters of these two occasions as follows:

VE Day. The themes are:
- Thanksgiving for the beginning of the peace.
- International reconciliation and the coming together of Europe.
- Youth, and the advantages gained by succeeding generations from victory.
- The VE Day celebrations will involve the whole of our society. We also welcome the involvement of a wide international representation.

VJ Day. The Anniversary themes are:
- Celebration of the end of the war.
- Thanksgiving for and commemoration of the sacrifices of the wartime generation.[181]

The two nationally staged religious observances in London expressed the differences between the two weekends very clearly. On 7th May 1995, a 'Service of Thanksgiving, Reconciliation, and Hope' was held in St Paul's Cathedral, attended by a large number of heads of state, particularly from the European Community. On 19th August, an open-air 'Service of Remembrance and Commitment' was held outside Buckingham Palace; non-Commonwealth government representatives were not invited, though something of an international dimension was added by the presence of both veterans from across the former empire and also leaders of non-Christian faith communities.

In four significant ways, the very different characters of these two events highlight the particular challenges which have to be addressed in any British engagement of reconciliation with Japanese people.

Firstly, there is the mismatch of titles: 'Victory over Japan' (not 'in Asia') contrasts strikingly with 'Victory in Europe' (not 'over Germany'). Not only does the first single out, and thereby perpetuate, a particular national identity as former enemies; the differing prepositions, 'over' and 'in', emphatically reinforce this suggestion of continuing hostility.

Secondly, such verbal differences acquire greater significance when the backward-looking character of the VJ anniversary events is remembered. Nowhere in official publicity was there any emphasis on the fifty years of peace which have followed the ending of the Pacific War; it was only in the 'coming together of Europe' celebrated on VE Day that the 'advantages gained by succeeding generations' were seen to lie.

Thirdly, from such a perspective, it is not surprising that the idea of 'reconciliation' was conspicuously absent from the Government's publicity for the VJ celebration. At the churches' insistence, and after considerable debate, the form of service used at Buckingham Palace did in fact include the following words:

> Let us give thanks for the reconciliation that has been
> established between nations once opposed in war; and let
> us pray for the people of all nations and their leaders, that
> those divisions that remain may be healed.[182]

Yet the inclusion of the 'R-word' provoked a storm of protest led by sections of the tabloid press; the tone of the service was, it was claimed, an insult to veterans of the war with Japan.

Fourthly, it was this same argument from the experience of former Far Eastern PoWs which was used to justify the policy decision to exclude any Japanese participation, or even presence, at the Buckingham Palace VJ celebrations – though, ironically, the streets of London were at that time full of Japanese tourists taking advantage of the *o-bon* holiday season to travel overseas. The government had been told that several veterans' groups, notably the Burma Star Association, would not join in the commemorations if there was any question of Japanese involvement. Certainly this seemed to be the attitude of Air Vice-Marshal Sir Bernard Chacksfield, the Association's chairman, who was reported as saying:

> 'I am a Christian and I can forgive a lot. But the feeling
> among our veterans is that the Japanese in war were very
> different from the Germans . . . If a Japanese contingent
> was present, not a single man would turn out.[183]

There are, then, clearly major challenges which need addressing from a British perspective on reconciliation with Japan. Veterans' experience of inhumane treatment at the hands of the Japanese is certainly one issue which understandably features very prominently. The depth of bitterness, mistrust, and emotional damage built up among some former PoWs is possibly such that they are actually unable psychologically to come to terms with the idea of reconciliation.

And the memory of wartime atrocities has entered a much wider, and younger, generation of consciousness through such films as *Bridge on the River Kwai*. But still it must be stressed that some veterans do find it possible to come to terms with their experience, and even to forgive their former captors; given the character of the British press, it is perhaps not surprising that they do not attract the same high media profile as those who remain determinedly and vociferously unreconciled.

Yet veterans' memories, however vivid, are hardly sufficient of themselves to explain the remarkable persistence of anti-Japanese feeling among British people. Some of this may be fuelled by resentment of the extraordinary success of the former enemy's post-war economic revival: not only, like Germany, has Japan spectacularly outstripped Britain's performance, but also, unlike Germany, it is generally seen as a trading rival rather than a trading partner. It will be interesting to see if increased familiarity with Japanese industry through growing investment in Britain leads to a softening of such popular attitudes.

Much anti-Japanese sentiment can also be best described as simple racism on the part of some Britons. In a society where the caricaturing, stereotyping, or denigration of Jewish, black, or most other minority groups is no longer acceptable behaviour (at least in public), it is still possible to hear and see the most blatant examples of anti-Japanese feeling expressed with little hesitation. Such attitudes are no doubt reinforced by the unfamiliarity and apparent impenetrability of Japanese culture, characterised by such time-worn myths as those of Oriental 'inscrutability', or of exceptional cruelty.

However, barriers to reconciliation never operate on one side only, and so it is to Japanese attitudes that we must now turn. First it must be noticed that official statements have rarely been either entirely candid or totally constructive. In August 1995, Tomichi Murayama, the Japanese Prime

Minister, did finally issue a kind of apology for aggression and atrocities during the war years, but it was widely perceived as a half-hearted and even rather bungled affair, and did not appear to command the full support of his government. This in turn generated another in the long-running series of controversies – both overseas concerning the extent to which the nation had faced up to its behaviour, and also domestically in Japan concerning the extent to which it needed to apologise at all. In January 1998 however, coinciding with Tony Blair's visit to Tokyo, his Japanese counterpart, Ryutaro Hashimoto, this time speaking on behalf of his whole administration, expressed publicly his 'heartfelt apology' and 'deep remorse' over the suffering of British prisoners of war. He even took the unprecedented step of backing this up with a personal letter to – of all newspapers – *The Sun.*

Running through fifty years of debate on these twin questions have been a few recurrent themes. It is crucial to identify these themes if we are to understand the problems facing any attempted programme of reconciliation involving the Japanese past. If this is so in the context of Anglo-Japanese encounter, it is still more apparent in the relations of the Japanese people with their Asian neighbours, whose sufferings were far more appalling than those of the Allied personnel.

We can trace these themes in the very first post-war Japanese statement. At midday on 15th August 1945, following the dropping of nuclear devices on Hiroshima and Nagasaki, and with his country facing total devastation, Emperor Hirohito broadcast to his people to announce unconditional surrender. The imperial rescript announced his decision as follows:

> The war situation has developed in a direction not necessarily to Japan's advantage . . . The enemy has begun to employ a new and most cruel bomb, the power of which to do damage is indeed incalculable, taking the toll of

many innocent lives. Should we continue to fight, it would not only result in an ultimate collapse and obliteration of the Japanese nation, but also it would lead to the total extinction of human civilisation . . . We are keenly aware of the inmost feelings of you all, Our subjects. However, it is according to the dictates of time and fate that We have resolved to pave the way for a grand peace for all the generations to come by enduring the unendurable and suffering what is insufferable.[184]

Whatever questions may be raised about his overall responsibility for the war effort, it is clear that Hirohito at this point had taken a courageous personal initiative to accept unconditional surrender.[185] Still it is interesting to identify within the rescript four themes which both reflect the mentality which had led to Japan's disastrous militaristic programme, and also have continued to pose serious challenges to reconciliation in the post-war years. These four are: first, a proclivity to understatement which verges on the denial of reality; second, a perception of the Japanese people as primarily victims; third, an emphasis on the homogeneity of the Japanese people under the reign of the imperial family; and fourth, a sense of the unique destiny of the Japanese race on earth. We shall look at each in turn, before seeing how Japanese Christians have begun trying to address the challenges they pose to authentic reconciliation.

One of the most poignant, and most unsettling, images of Japan in the post-war years was provided by the gathering of vast crowds in Tokyo in 1974 to witness the visit of Lieutenant Onoda Hiro to the Yasukuni shrine. Fighting in the Philippines in 1945, Lieutenant Onoda had become isolated from his comrades, and to evade capture had made a hiding place deep in the jungle. Here he had survived for twenty-nine years; when eventually found, he had for long refused to believe that the war was over, finding it almost impossible to accept the psychological reality of defeat.

Returning to Tokyo, he was hailed as a hero embodying all that was admirable in the spirit of old Japan:

> Onoda has shown us that there is much more in life than just material affluence and a selfish pursuit. There is the spiritual aspect, something we may have forgotten.[186]

Though he himself had missed hearing it, it was to men such as Lieutenant Onoda that Hirohito's remarkably under-stated description of 'the war situation' had been addressed. Their mentality was deeply formed by the ideals of the *bushido*, the 'way of the warrior', which taught bravery in the face of insurmountable odds, extolled loyalty to lord and country above all other goods, and regarded capture and dishonour as the greatest of evils. In 1937, the Ministry of Education had issued *Fundamentals of Our National Polity*, an extremely influential booklet which explained that:

Bushido may be cited as showing an outstanding charac-teristic of our national morality.[187]

This was the spirit which in the last year of the Pacific War had inspired the kamikaze pilots who sang as they took off on their suicide missions:

> Never think of winning!
> Thoughts of victory will only bring defeat.
> When we lose, let us press forward, ever forward![188]

Much has been written in appreciation of *bushido*, which is closely linked to the spirit of Zen Buddhism; while recog-nising the terrible national disaster into which its reckless-ness led the Japanese people, it is certainly difficult at the same time not to feel stirred by its fearless heroism.

However, Onoda's visit to Tokyo also highlighted another, darker, aspect of 'the warrior's way'. The Yasukuni ('protection of the nation') shrine at which he paid his homage is the national memorial to those killed in war. The theology or ideology of 'enshrinement' at Yasukuni is that those who die fighting for Japan become appropriate objects of public worship.[189] Among those so enshrined are the wartime Prime Minister Tojo Hideki and at least a thousand other convicted war criminals.[190] And this is the shadow side of *bushido*: these 'national gods' were men guilty of gross crimes against humanity. According to the militaristic ethic, defeated civilians and military personnel, whether as prisoners or as conquered peoples, were deprived of any right to respect. So in some ways the reluctance of successive Japanese governments to acknowledge crimes committed during the years leading up to and including the Pacific War is the psychological complement of Onoda's heroism: both rest on a deep-seated disinclination to face the true dimensions of an unpalatable situation.

Perhaps another manifestation of the same mentality, though one rather in tension with the combative attitude of *bushido*, is a deeply ingrained perception of the Japanese people as being primarily cast in the role of victims. Much of the pre-war justification for military expansion had arisen from claims that Japan was being unfairly held back from economic development by the western powers:

It is just that since the Powers have suppressed the circulation of Japanese materials and merchandise abroad, we are looking for some place overseas where Japanese capital, Japanese skills and Japanese labour can have free play, free from the oppression of the white race.[191]

Viewed in this light, the war could be presented as an attempt to redress the wrongs of colonialism; unfortunately, in that tragic pattern of escalating victimisation which is repeated in so many settings, the Japanese in turn learnt to play the part of colonial oppressors, first in Korea, then in China, and finally throughout the whole of the so-called 'Greater East Asia Co-Prosperity Sphere'.

Since the time of the imperial rescript's reference to 'a new and most cruel bomb', this sense of victimisation has been centred on the Japanese people's unenviable distinction of being the only nation to have suffered military nuclear attacks. This has become an experience deeply etched in the consciousness of the post-war generation, not least through the educational visit which every Japanese schoolchild will make at some time to the memorial museums in either Hiroshima or Nagasaki. It is impossible to visit either site without being deeply moved by the scale of the horror portrayed there. There is a vastness of suffering which seems to be most immediately conveyed not in overall statistics but by the repeated and detailed experiences of lives suddenly ended: my own abiding memory of the Hiroshima A-bomb museum is of a 10-year old lad's lunchbox, instantaneously incinerated with him on his way to school.

Visiting these sights rightly creates a feeling of deep discomfort in the English or American visitor; yet it is noticeable that the Japanese reaction tends to be much more straightforward – a feeling of deep sadness, coupled with bewilderment as to why such terrible bombs should have suddenly fallen from the sky. This is because the presentation in both museums, as in most Japanese school history textbooks, emphasises the events of August 6th and 9th 1945 in isolation from the context which led to them – the aggressive military expansion pursued by the Japanese government during the decade from 1931 to the outbreak of the Pacific War in 1941. Without such contextualisation, it is inevitable that the primary perception should be that of collective victimisation.

The sense of sharing as a nation in the experience of atomic warfare naturally reinforces the shared sense of membership of a homogeneous society which is such a characteristic of the ideology of Japanese nationhood. Paradoxically, those bearing in their bodies the actual physical consequences of atomic radiation, the *hibakusha*, form a group who experience various disadvantages and a sense of exclusion in contemporary Japan – as this comment reveals:

Hibakusha are, by and large, reluctant to talk about their experiences. And surprisingly, many are critical of anti-nuclear movements.[192]

The *hibakusha* in fact share this experience of marginalisation with other minorities – for example, the *burakumin* or so-called 'untouchables', Koreans and other resident ethnic minorities, and the surviving remnants of the indigenous Ainu people of the northern island of Hokkaido. To some extent, this is also the experience of the small minority of Japanese people who profess Christian faith.

In official and mainstream Japanese self-understanding, however, the existence of such diverse groups has been ignored in favour of the myth of one united people, sharing a common origin and belonging to one national family of which the Emperor (*Tenno*) is the head. In the pre-1945 imperial ideology, this was reinforced by the teaching that the *Tenno* was the lineal descendant of the sun-goddess Amaterasu. This perhaps found most powerful expression in the Imperial Rescript on Education, issued in 1890 and ordered to be hung next to the portrait of *Tenno* in every school to be the subject of regular obeisance by pupils and staff. The Rescript enjoined:

Our Imperial Ancestors have founded Our Empire on a basis broad and everlasting, and have deeply and firmly implanted virtue; Our subjects ever united in loyalty and filial piety have from generation to generation illustrated the beauty thereof . . . Should emergency arise, offer yourselves courageously to the State; and thus guard and maintain the prosperity of Our Imperial Throne coeval with heaven and earth . . . The Way here set forth is indeed the teaching bequeathed by Our Imperial Ancestors, to be observed alike by Their Descendants and the subjects, infallible for all ages and true in all places.[193]

When Hirohito made his surrender broadcast to his people, many were so overcome with emotion to hear the voice of the *akitsu mikami*, the god manifested in human form, speaking to them, that they scarcely could take in his words;[194] their understanding was further impaired by the fact that he was speaking in a courtly form of the Japanese language far removed from the rhythms of everyday speech. At the following New Year, the *Tenno*, at American prompting, issued a further Rescript explicitly disavowing the 'false conception' of his divinity;[195] the 1947 Constitution, which still provides the framework of contemporary Japan, vested all authority in 'the people of Japan', defining the Emperor as 'a symbol of the state and of the unity of the people'.[196] It is remarkable, however, that the imperial role was retained, despite the misgivings of some who felt that it could serve as a focus for renewed militaristic and nationalistic sentiment. Despite the exemplary constitutional role which has been played by both post-war emperors, these fears have never been wholly allayed in some parts of Japanese society. Perhaps more significant than the survival of the imperial institution itself, however, has been the continuing promotion of the ideology of Japan as a united, homogeneous, egalitarian society.

This ideology is closely linked to another distinctive feature: the belief that the Japanese people have a unique destiny in the world. The Emperor's surrender broadcast reflected this in linking the threatened 'collapse and obliteration' of Japan to the 'total extinction of human civilisation'. Such a linkage can be seen as just the negative corollary of the pre-war ideology which maintained that Japan was entrusted with a solemn vocation to bring about a new world order. In particular, the nation was destined to be the champion of Asian enlightenment over against western barbarism:

> Heaven has decided on Japan as its choice for the champion of the East. Has not this been the purpose of our three

thousand long years of preparation? It must be said that this is a truly grand and magnificent mission.[197]

It is easy to see in such posturing a belated response to the equally inflated imperial ideologies of the western powers; yet the sense of a distinct national mission has roots deep within the Japanese tradition. Particularly influential in developing this awareness was the thirteenth century Buddhist teacher Nichiren, who taught that the world was to be renewed through the establishment of the 'Buddha-land' in Japan:

> The sun rises in the east and sets in the west; this is an omen that the Buddhist religion shall return from the Land of Sunrise to the country of the Moon-tribe.[198]

Many sects of Japanese Buddhism derive from Nichiren, and all of them in some way or another have kept alive his conception of a special mission assigned to Japan. Nichiren-inspired attitudes certainly fed the nationalism of the militaristic expansion of the pre-war years.[199]

Conversely, though, it is important to note that the Nichiren tradition has also produced groups particularly active in the work of reconciliation – for example, the Nihonzan order,[200] or the powerful lay organisation Rissho Koseikai.[201] For these post-war groups, Japan's unique mission is to be understood as being precisely the furtherance of world peace. A secular analogue to this latter position can be found among those Japanese who continue enthusiastically to endorse the unique stipulation of the 1947 Constitution that:

> Aspiring sincerely to an international peace based on justice and order, the Japanese people forever renounce war as a sovereign right of the nation and the threat or use of force as a means of settling international disputes.

In order to accomplish the aim of the preceding paragraph, land, sea, and air forces, as well as other war potential, will never be maintained. The right of belligerency of the state will not be recognised.[202]

One survivor of the Hiroshima bomb offered these thoughts on this clause:

The renunciation of arms was the first truly courageous attempt and challenge ever made and taken in thousands of years of history. Has mankind ever before come up with and adopted such a noble ideal? At the time, I believed wholeheartedly that no other country was more suited than Japan to abide by that spirit and develop into an ideal nation that kept its vow never to re-arm.[203]

However, the astonishing expansion in Japan's economic power, together with the strained international climate of the Cold War, soon brought pressure from the USA on Japanese governments to take responsibility for their own defence. This led in the 1960s and 1970s to a steady growth in the so-called 'Self-Defence Forces'[204] which caused great consternation among those who feared that this could signal a return to the militaristic expansionism of the 1930s. It is fascinating to hear the terms of this debate, and contrast with them domestic British arguments of the same period over defence policy. In both countries, appeal is made to the experience of the pre-war years; whereas in Britain, though, the danger highlighted has usually been that of 'appeasement', or at least the perils of inadequate preparedness, in Japan the spectre invoked is that of military aggression. With the end of the Cold War, though, defence seems in the last few years to have become a less contentious issue in both countries.

What now can we say about the response of the Christian church in Japan as it seeks to witness to the reconciliation of the gospel in a situation marked by this complex and continuing history? In what follows, I shall be considering principally the Anglican Church in Japan. Though small in numbers, the *Seikokai* has considerable influence, and has in many ways given a lead to other churches in the area of reconciliation. This is clearly demonstrated by the 'Statement on War Responsibility of Nippon Seikokai' adopted by the General Synod on 23rd May 1996. This is a remarkable document which begins:

> The *Nippon Seikokai*, after fifty years since the end of World War II, admits its responsibility and confesses its sin for having supported and allowed, before and during the war, the colonial rule and the war of aggression by the State of Japan.[205]

The statement goes on to detail the various ways in which the *Seikokai* recognises itself as having failed to fulfil its prophetic mission. It is important to note that this self-analysis applies to the post-war years as much as to the decades leading up to 1945; throughout both periods, the statement identifies within the life of the church itself the four themes which we have outlined above as challenges to reconciliation. Thus, there is a recognition of the need to face up to the historical reality of Japanese war guilt – the statement proposes 'as a sign of repentance':

- To share the confession of our war responsibility among all of the parishes.
- To convey an apology to the churches in the countries which Japan had invaded.
- To start and continue a programme in each diocese and parish, to review the historical facts and to deepen our understanding of the Gospel.

Again, the statement emphasises the need to refute the 'victim-perspective' of much Japanese thinking, pointing out that:

Despite its more recent internationalism, our church has not been able to see Japan as an aggressor in the war.

The importance of correcting such a viewpoint is underlined in a fiftieth anniversary Hiroshima-day message from the Bishop of Tokyo; speaking of Japanese attitudes to the A-bomb memorial museums, he writes:

> When we travel to neighbouring countries in Asia, we hear many voices for the victims of Japanese atrocities during military invasions and occupations of those countries. For us to become committed for world peace, we have to overcome the misleading conception that it was only Japanese who suffered in war, as represented by the bombing of Japanese soil and our defeat.[206]

A major part of the statement is then concerned with the *Seikokai*'s alleged complicity with the *Tenno* (imperial) system – it points out that, even after the war, the 1947 General Synod adopted the 1938 Book of Common Prayer, which prayed for the *Tenno* (literally, 'divine ruler') as reigning according to the will of God.

Finally, the statement claims that the church had subscribed to the myth of a special national vocation in seeking to 'justify Japan's rule over other ethnic groups'. Commenting on these points, Fr. Nathaniel Uematsu, the General Secretary of *Nippon Seikokai*, explains that:

> Many Asians do not trust the Japanese, and the NSKK is part of this problem. In the past the NSKK supported the militarist government, prayed for the Emperor Tenno who is the demigod and high priest of Shintoism. The NSKK even said that Shintoism is not a religion but an authentic way of life, even forcing this doctrine on Koreans in occupied Korea at a national shrine the Japanese constructed.[207]

How is the General Synod's Statement to be evaluated? It

was passed with little debate, apparently partly because of exhaustion following a lengthy discussion of the question of the ordination of women to the priesthood. However, it has generally been welcomed by other Japanese churches, most of whom have tried to formulate similar statements of intent. Two important points need to be made in qualification of the Statement's general acceptance, however.

Firstly, some feel that there is a danger of dwelling on the past in an unhealthy way; indeed, that this can be a way of evading the challenges of the present. So, for example, the Primate Bishop, writing after the Synod's vote, expressed his fear that:

> The Emperor System is more often than not used by the self-righteous Japanese Christians as an apology for their failure to evangelise the Japanese both before and after the Pacific War.[208]

In similar vein, some Japanese clergy whom I have met ask for how long the events of fifty years ago are to be the subject of agonised discussion. After all, they point out, the Church of England has not made any kind of apology for its centuries-long collusion with colonialism, imperialism, racism, and so on; more positively, there are also fifty years of peace which deserve celebration and require safeguarding. Nor is this attitude only found among Japanese:

> NSKK representatives accepted Papua New Guinea's invitation to attend the fiftieth celebration of the thirteen martyrs of Papua New Guinea killed by Japanese soldiers during the Pacific War . . . The NSKK representatives could scarcely believe that such a large measure of reconciliation had been achieved, despite the Bishop of Port Moresby exclaiming: 'No more talk about reconciliation. We are reconciled'.[209]

Secondly, the twentieth century history of the church in

Japan is far more complex than a superficial reading of the statement might suggest. The General Synod's resolution is indeed a brave and honest confession of a degree of complicity in militaristic ideology, yet the wartime record of the churches in Japan cannot at all be described as one of simple identification with the prevailing mood.

On the contrary, throughout Japanese history Christians have generally been regarded with great suspicion as adherents of a 'foreign' religion, and during the years of the Pacific War this xenophobic attitude led to constant harassment of pastors and congregations. In the case of the *Nippon Seikokai*, the difficulties were exacerbated by the resistance of some parts of the Church to the Government's religious policy. Designed to maximise state control and stifle dissent, this ordered that from 1st November 1941 all non-Roman Catholic denominations should come together in one pan-Protestant organisation, the *Nippon Kirisuto Kyodan*. Many Anglicans, seeing in these proposals an unacceptable compromise of their apostolic integrity, refused to participate, and the *Seikokai* split in two;[210] during the remainder of the war years, the 'unregistered' denominations were subjected to a serious persecution which led to the death of several clergy and the imprisonment and maltreatment of many others.

For Japanese Christians in general, and for the *Seikokai* in particular, the war years therefore have a double character: on one hand, a time of participation in a society set on a course of military aggression which ultimately led to its defeat; on the other hand and simultaneously, a time of alienation from that same society as the suspect embodiment of an alien ideology. Yet it is this double experience which also makes the longing for and commitment to reconciliation an attitude so deeply rooted within the corporate life of the church in Japan.

Given the course of Japanese history, it is inevitable and proper that such reconciliation should find its main focus in relationships with the country's Asian neighbours. Much has begun to happen here, particularly within the context of the oldest and most difficult of all Japan's shared histories, that with the Korean people. Close links between the two countries' churches have been developed; and the *Seikokai* has pioneered advocacy work with and alongside the large number of Koreans resident in Japan, who have long experienced disadvantage and prejudice.

Yet reconciliation with the west, and particularly with Britain, is also a theme of continuing importance. There is surely much that British Christians could learn from their Japanese co-religionists' costly commitment to reconciliation as expressed in the 1996 Synod Statement:

> The NSKK May 1995 resolution had such a powerful sense of humility about it. The Church of England has to show solidarity as well as responding honestly to its own C of E history, ethos, and culture – honest about the nature of its colonisation policies hand in hand with its world missionary impetus. One interpretation would see the C of E's history as one of domination and asset-stripping of poorer nations.[211]

Now this certainly represents only one interpretation: the history of English Christianity reveals a picture even more complex and ambiguous than that of the *Seikokai* in its combination of worldly complicity and authentic witness. Yet, however we read our own story, reconciliation must be an imperative for us too – genuine reconciliation, which acknowledges the past in humility and honesty at the same time as it looks to the future. Where may we find inspiration and guidance seeking this amid the messy complexities of our overlapping histories?

Amid the tangled and often conflicting evidence, sometimes there appear individual stories of great integrity which for those who come later present the challenge and the promise of reconciliation in terms of startling clarity.

These men, and those who opposed them
And those whom they opposed
Accept the constitution of silence
And are folded in a single party.
Whatever we inherit from the fortunate
We have taken from the defeated
What they had to leave us – a symbol:
A symbol perfected in death.[212]

Within the Anglican dioceses of Leicester and Yokohama, which have enjoyed a companionship link since 1989, we have found such a 'symbol perfected in death' in the figure of Vivian Redlich. Child of the vicarage at Little Bowden in Leicestershire, he was beheaded by Japanese soldiers on Buna Beach in northern Papua New Guinea in August 1942, aged thirty-seven. Contemporary records make it clear that it was his commitment to providing the sacraments for his people which led him to stay in a situation where he faced great danger of death; indeed, he is venerated as one of the 'Thirteen Martyrs of New Guinea'.[213] His final letter to his father expresses this commitment in language of a gawky sincerity:

Somewhere in the Papuan Bush.
July 27 1942.
My dear Dad,
   The war has busted up here. I got back from Dogura and ran right into it – and am now somewhere in my parish trying to carry on, though my people are horribly scared.
   No news of May[214] and I'm cut off from contacting her – my staff OK so far but in another spot.
   I'm trying to stick whatever happens. If I don't come out of it just rest content that I've tried to do my job faithfully. Rush chance of getting word out, so forgive brevity.
   God bless you all,
   Vivian.[215]

When Bishop Raphael Kajiwara of Yokohama visited Little Bowden in 1988, he was deeply moved by the story of this young English priest, in whose faithful death he saw a sign of the costliness of the peace for which British and Japanese people together had to strive. To mark the fiftieth anniversary of Vivian Redlich's death, in 1992 the Bishop composed in English and handwrote a scroll of apology which he then presented to the Diocese of Leicester. Its words express the humility which deeply marks Japanese Christians in their witness to reconciliation; in that humility there is a challenge to the church in Britain to show a like awareness of the past and a like hope for the future. Bishop Raphael wrote:

> Because I am one of Japanese Christians, I would like to express our regretful sorry for your sad memories of the past history of fifty years ago in Papua New Guinea and other southern Pacific areas, where Fr. Vivian Redlich and his fiancée and other people were killed by the violence of the Japanese soldiers.
>
> It was so sad, and shameful deeds committed by the Japanese.
>
> As a Japanese, I confess our deep sorry and regret to you all against it, and I am asking for your friendly benevolence to forgive our past.
>
> Remembering love and life and death of Vivian Redlich.
>
> Asking your forgiveness of our past.
>
> Seeking for Vision and Peace of God in this difficult world.
>
> Hoping to deepen our future mutual understanding and friendship.

Reconciliation and Bosnia

Adrian Hastings

Is reconciliation possible in Bosnia? The straight answer at present is, sadly, no. An examination of why that is so can greatly help clarify the meaning and parameters of reconciliation, and the way that it cannot function validly in a sort of moral vacuum of its own.

Why is this so? Let us briefly recall the essentials of the Bosnian situation. The war began in late March 1992 as an unprovoked attack by the Yugoslav army controlled from Belgrade on the Muslim and Catholic (Croat) populations of Bosnia. It was backed by many, though by no means all, the Bosnian Serb minority, already organised in armed militias on instructions from Belgrade. It followed the Serb attacks on Slovenia and Croatia, each consequent upon a declaration of independence by these states previously within Yugoslavia, prompted by determination to escape the Serb domination of Yugoslavia which President Milosevic of Serbia had been masterminding. Bosnia had been far less interested in independence than Slovenia and Croatia, indeed its leaders had steadily sought some sort of Yugoslav compromise. Nevertheless, once the departure of Croatia and Slovenia from Yugoslavia had been finalised, leaving it more than ever a Serbian state, it was inevitable that the large majority of the Bosnian population would want to separate as well. They voted by referendum to do so at the end of February 1991, and international recognition had been guaranteed.

The new Bosnian state, however, was virtually weaponless. It also had no access either to the sea or to a neutral country. Milosevic had encircled Sarajevo, the Bosnian capital, with his troops and artillery long before independence was declared, just as he had armed the Bosnian Serb militias organised by his (at the time) henchman, Radovan Karadzic. Both Serbia and the international community expected the war to be over very quickly. In fact the greater part of the country was overrun within a few weeks. Only a number of major towns – Sarajevo, Tuzla, Zenica, Mostar and Travnik being the most important – managed to organise their own defence, backed by some of the more inaccessible mountainous areas of the countryside. The EC and UN recognised the independence of Bosnia but refused for four years to intervene to protect it, taking refuge in the pretence that this was a 'civil war', resulting from age-old 'tribal conflicts', rather than a carefully organised invasion of one country, Bosnia, by another, Serbia, in which the so-called Bosnian Serb government, headed by Karadzic, and its army commanded by General Mladic, were paid throughout the war by Milosevic. At the same time a significant minority of Bosnian Serbs, led by many of their most notable academic, literary and business leaders, such as academician Professor Berberovic, loyally supported the legitimate government of Bosnia, led by President Izetbegovic.

When it appeared, late in 1992, that there was no hope of repelling the Serb invasion, given the refusal of the international community to help effectively, the Muslim-Catholic alliance fell apart, though again some Catholics continued to support the Sarajevo government. The majority of 'Croats', however, inhabiting the western part of the country on the Croatian border, were encouraged by President Tudjman of Croatia to seize control, expel the Muslim population and prepare to be incorporated into a 'Greater Croatia' while the rest of Bosnia would be incorporated into a 'Greater Serbia'. However, even after this disastrous development, the Bosnian government, backed by what was still a majority of the population, refused to give up and its position actually improved little by little in the following years. It was the July

1995 massacre at Srebrenica together with international recognition that the Serb plan to conquer Bosnia had failed, but that the Bosnian government was still not strong enough to recover the country as a whole, given the 'arms embargo' imposed on it by the United Nations as proposed by Douglas Hurd at the suggestion of no one else than Milosevic, which at last persuaded the American government and, more reluctantly, its allies to intervene militarily and bring the war to a halt. This was followed by the Dayton peace conference whose agreement was formally signed in Paris in December 1995. On one side, its terms accepted a largely divided country, on the other they required the return of refugees to their homes, general freedom of movement, and the punishment of war criminals. Two years later, none of these latter provisions has in any way been implemented. That is one of the reasons why reconciliation remains impossible.

The full reason, however, lies far deeper. The primary character of the war in human terms was not one relating simply to the political status of Bosnia and its inhabitants, but one relating to the very existence and character of its people. It was not merely a war of conquest but one of genocide. This was so from the very beginning. The Muslim population in areas controlled by the Serbs was immediately rounded up, murdered, thrust into concentration camps or deported. Within a very short time towns like Zvornik, Foca and Visegrad, all of which had had an absolute Muslim majority before the war, were left with no Muslim inhabitants at all, or a mere handful. Their religious and cultural monuments, including mosques and tombstones, were systematically destroyed in the determination to make subsequent ages believe that there had never been any Muslims there.

While the majority of the Muslim population escaped to become refugees in other parts of Bosnia or elsewhere in Europe, there were also large massacres carried out in many places including the numerous concentration camps, of which Omarska was the most notorious. Over two thousand prisoners were killed in the football stadium of Zvornik, over a thousand in the prison at Foca. All this happened very rapidly within a matter of weeks. It was quite clearly a case of genocide as defined by the International Convention on Genocide, though the British and American governments consistently refused to recognise its genocidal character, because that would have imposed an obligation upon them to intervene. But, of course, refusing to admit that genocide is taking place, when the evidence is overwhelming, is itself collusion in genocide and a crime for which one can be indicted at the International Court of Justice. When in July 1995 many thousands of men who had been living in the so-called UN 'Safe Area' of Srebrenica were massacred on the orders of General Mladic, this was probably the largest single atrocity of the war, but it was no different in kind from the many atrocities committed in 1992, to which the international community had turned a blind eye. This time, given that Srebrenica had been declared a 'Safe Area' and despite the continued British reluctance to do anything to stop further crimes, the UN, effectively the US, did intervene.

While Dayton brought an end, perhaps only temporarily, to the fighting, it has hitherto in no way dealt with the crimes committed or the inability of the refugees driven wholesale from their homes in Foca, Srebrenica and elsewhere to return to them. On the contrary, the very people who were responsible for the crimes committed remain in full control of the Serb-held part of the country. The survivors of Srebrenica have been prevented even from disinterring the bodies of their fathers, husbands and sons in order to identify them and give them proper burial. To suggest that 'reconciliation' can take place between those who escaped genocide and those who planned and carried out their eradication, seized their property and continue to prevent the Muslim people of Srebrenica (almost eighty per cent Muslim in 1990) and elsewhere from returning to the places where they had always lived, would be absurd. There is no comparability between the present situation in Bosnia and that, for instance, in South Africa. First, because the apartheid regime in South Africa never treated South African blacks in living memory in a way comparable to that in which the Bosnian Muslims were treated. Second, because there has been no removal from power of the criminals, no expression of remorse, no willingness to allow those most guilty to face trial.

Reconciliation is not something, either theologically or practically, which can take place within a moral and political void. 'Liberation', that is to say some manifest return to an order of justice involving the objective restoration of rights, must come first. It cannot be complete – wrongs can never be entirely put right – but it must be both significant in scale and public. In regard to such horrific crimes as happened in this decade in Bosnia, it must certainly involve the trial of some of those principally responsible. Without that, to argue for a strategy of reconciliation is to propose the abandonment of justice and the retrospective sanctioning of the most appalling atrocities which have happened in Europe since the second world war. This does not mean that there is no place for reconciliation now. There is, but only between those who accept that it is not a replacement for justice and that the objectivities of recent history require an enforcement of justice which is bound to be painful for the oppressors. Reconciliation can never be built on lies and a wholesale denial of moral responsibility. It depends above all on recognition of the truth of what has happened by those who remain identified with the criminals. Only thus can the Serb population and the Serb Orthodox Church themselves be liberated from the burden of the crimes committed either by them or in their name. Until that happens, the moral air remains irremediably polluted.

In 1985 in South Africa a large group of committed Christians produced the famous *Kairos* document which declared that 'Reconciliation, forgiveness and negotiations will become our Christian duty in South Africa, only when the apartheid regime shows signs of genuine repentance'. In 1989 I commented somewhat critically:

> Can we ever say that forgiveness is not our Christian duty now but only 'afterwards'? True Christian forgiveness is not soft forgiveness. It does not leave things unchanged. It does not imply any glossing over of injustice, structural or personal. It does not leave out issues of the repayment of ill-gotten gains, even tenfold. It is not an alternative to liberation, but rather is each internally part of the other. (*The Theology of a Protestant Catholic*, 1990, pp. 109-110.)

If that was true of South Africa, it is even more true of Bosnia. In 1989 it was just becoming possible in South Africa to contemplate moving forward from a strategy of liberation to one of reconciliation. That is still not the case in Bosnia. Without a serious beginning to justice, an appeal for reconciliation is neither Christianity nor humanism. It is merely opium.

Seeking a Common Future in the Midst of a Contested Society in Northern Ireland

Derick Wilson

What we are learning from meetings between adults in Northern Ireland

I was born into, and still live and work, in a place called Northern Ireland / The North of Ireland / Ulster / The Six Counties.

The very lack of an agreed name about the place conveys that it is a contested society, one where each major tradition within it has been and is involved in a contest, with one another and neighbouring parties, about the nature, name and character of this place and how it might be run.

We have no common sense

A contested society is one where there is no common sense of identity. Support for the institutions of the state are variable depending on the traditions people belong to and how they sense their position *vis-à-vis* the state at any time. Two very different experiences illustrate this.

> 'I was brought up in a very Nationalist, Catholic home. I am proud to be associated with that tradition, being very steeped in the Irish language tradition too.'

> 'To my family, the Royal Family was everything. We were brought up to value everything that was British, the Crown, Parliament and our laws. We could all say we were proud of being British.'

Fear pervades everyday relationships

The community mechanisms and institutions of the society do not resolve and dissolve the tensions and conflicts efficiently. These can:

- keep people from hearing about personal grief:
  'I feel so awkward, the troubles keep me in my own circles so much that I did not even know one of my workmates had someone close to him killed.'
- prevent normal good neighbourliness being counted on:
  'I was intimidated to leave my house. I live in an area where my neighbours were from the other tradition. I was feeling very hurt, not knowing if they were part of this threat, until some came to me and said they didn't want me to leave.'
- necessitate people taking avoiding and often stressful actions:
  'Is it right that we settle for working people being scared going off to do normal maintenance work on people's houses, streets and water supplies? Do you know in our place workers leave their driving licences behind them, they re-christen each other with appropriate names when they go out to hard line areas. Think of the stress that causes.'

Choices and actions are shaped by a force field

People like you and me easily become locked into what we call a 'force field', a field which continually shifts its ground as the issues and balances between the different parties change.

To seek a common future in such a place means that the nature of this force field itself needs to be acknowledged. In fact one educational starting point is to illuminate this dynamic influence on all of us, those from inside it and those coming in from outside too.

In the work we have developed over the last 15 years we have drawn heavily on the innovative political thinking about such contested areas by my late friend and former colleague Frank Wright. His political work about such contested areas identifies how peoples and groups in them deter each other either by threatening to use their favoured position with external groups or authorities or by hinting that the worst excesses of their own extremes will be unleashed.

This is represented by the force field model on the relative positions of the British and Irish governments *vis-à-vis* the different traditions in Northern Ireland. Working within our group work model these help people examine how their loyalties, traditionally associated with Britain and Ireland, evolve and change. People speak together about how their feelings change as they perceive the positions of the two governments change, relative to each other and to the traditions locally.

Within mixed groups, people from very different areas and traditions understand the changes they experience and, at the same time, listen to others identifying their experiences. The model helps to explain, rather than condemn, people's fears and shows how extreme views often became attractive to some who were, and are, very fearful.

The 'extremist' on the other side dominates 'me'

Internally people can explore how seeking to deter the other can readily drive people more towards those they believe they are like and away from those they are not like. As fears rise this allows people to become prey to those people who, at that time, offer safety for the group by promising extreme actions to defend people.

> Community workers spoke of how for weeks before a planned march people had been taking sides for, or against, the marchers and whether they had a right to march. We could see established community relations

links dissolving before our eyes. The contagion of fear spread almost at once, driving people into their respective camps, seeking safety and moving away from their new contacts.' (Cross Community Group, January, 1992)

In such moments I can begin to believe there are 'others', who are extreme, and that I am incapable of such actions.

In such moments I can only see the extremist on the other side, I am blind to the extreme position on my side and in me.

Fear only needs a vacuum to grow whereas trust needs relationships between people and eventually agreed structures which nurture these ways.

The task of people working for community understanding is to acknowledge these realities and, at times, be content to work in this fragile task of opening links, communication and trust between those who have been given to understand they come from different and threatening traditions, knowing it is so fragile in the face of fear and threat.

Some of the dynamics I outlined above can also apply to members of gender groups who feel diminished; minorities who are not given a secure place; children and young people who are bullied.

These dynamics, and others outlined later, are best understood for us out of a model of contested societies described by Frank Wright as 'Ethnic Frontiers'.

What if any political understandings do these meetings draw on as, people might rightly ask, 'Can bringing people together make any difference?' This is the put down which all community workers boil at!

Ethnic frontiers

On a typology of colonial history two major forms are colonies and settlements. There are also at least two more complicated structures associated with the remnants of colonial history.

These are a settlement colony where a very small settler group maintains their privilege by their own established legal structures or the threat of force. In such places the jobs of the settlers are protected from low wage competition by natives.

Another form with a different character is called the Ethnic Frontier.

Ethnic Frontiers are a product of forces where native and settler groups are relatively balanced with each other.

- The Ethnic Frontier is characterised by one or either group being unable to finally dominate the other.
- Peace such as exists within its boundaries equals an uneasy tranquillity, at best one group deters the other.
- Discrimination operates for a time rather than the legal protection of high wage employment for settlers and the economic separation of jobs which are found with the settlement colony.
- Over time the lines between settlers and natives become less distinct as both are now in long term residence in the one place.

In an Ethnic Frontier the competing traditions are close to those lands or nations with which the different groups identify, in our case Ireland and Great Britain.

Looking at some of the dynamics in such places
- The line of fear between the different traditions in the one place runs through all social and economic groups. At times of uncertainty fear drives identity. It is on either side of this line of fear that people locate in traditional groups, postured around points of identity which are 'unbargainables'. For us this means religious identity while in other ethnic frontiers it could be language, ethnic identity or culture.
- There comes a time when the economic and other differ-

entials, such as educational opportunities and skill levels, which may earlier have been unjustly kept at different levels for the different groups are no longer tolerated. This is the time of transition we have been going through.

- It is a place where people become partial about the law and ambivalent about violence, out of the differential relationships to the state mentioned above. The law and policing; equitable access to employment and education become central themes for justice and reconciliation work.

An example which highlights these themes

In practical work in support of 'Education for Mutual Understanding' between schools, Protestant teachers talked about: 'being fearful of unidentified parents challenging the mutual understanding programmes' whilst Catholic teachers indicated that they 'are more willing than their colleagues in Protestant schools to get involved in Education for Mutual Understanding initiatives'. (Stranmillis Seminar Groups on EMU, 1990)

Catholic/Nationalist fears revolve more around Britain than around Protestants, whereas Protestant/Unionist fears are of Catholicism and Irish Nationalism.

The Catholic school system is integral to the Catholic/ Nationalist community in Protestant eyes and thus, when 'Education for Mutual Understanding' asks Protestants to co-operate with Catholics it asks some Protestants to meet with their 'enemy'. When 'Education for Mutual Understanding' asks Catholics to meet Protestants it does not ask Catholics to take the same risk. Many Catholics do not readily understand this.

Protestant and Catholic 'being' is tied up in their relationship to the state, the law and the police

In circumstances where Protestant-Catholic meetings at school level are to be carried out under the auspices of the police community relations branch, some Catholic parents and teachers become fearful and object. In this situation many Protestants do not understand Catholic fears.

In group meetings, it is possible to visualise and analyse the reasons why two major traditional groups do not have symmetrical experiences of the state. Their relationships with each other are always affected by this structure.

The fears of Protestants have been dominated by views about the Irish Republican Army, and Catholic fears have been shaped through their experience of British law and order and their historical experiences of economic inequality.

In contested societies we learn how close to the surface the urges for retaliation and revenge are. In contested societies we learn how easily the cycles of vendetta and tit for tat can effect the whole of the society from top to bottom and bring all into instability.

Working for community understanding and trust means that we are seeking experiences where trust more than rivalry dominates relationships between people. Reasons to dislike the other side grow as people lose contact and trust with people from that side.

> ' . . . on the work buses, there was a deep fear of mentioning religion or politics. There was plenty of talk but most of it was gossip. I have seen this happening and noticed how silence descended when you went to join one of these groups. It looked as though they had been conspiring.' (Trade Union Group, 1991)

Insecurity and anxiety lie very close to the surface; people's secrets are much less secure.

> 'In our divided town people try to keep things down and yet something is said which sets off the feelings. People speak of being on the tip of an iceberg when they meet, they could see each other and were very aware of something grating under the surface.' (Trade Union Seminar Paper, p. 5)

In this example people do not trust each other, yet they act as if they do.

> 'Experienced teachers on a residential course spoke of how they had not met people from other traditions in depth before. Hearing about the life experiences of people brought up in the other tradition was completely new for them, a silence had been broken.' (Residential Course for Teachers)

People need atmospheres where disclosure is not 'exposure'. When people hear one another sharing these secrets, a new reality comes between them. People begin to marvel at the separated lives they often lead here.

> 'When I came to this group I only thought Catholics had cause to fear and be uncertain. How can it be that I only learn, when I am thirty plus, that Protestants feel vulnerable and carry hurts too. As a teacher I am sad that I only befriended my first Protestant when I was thirty years of age.' (Inter Church Group, 1994)

In the absence of meeting with each other in an atmosphere of trust people have no understanding of how they threaten the other, they only see how and where and when the other has threatened them. In such moments people settle to remain separate, avoid each other or be anxiously polite in one another's presence.

Settling for these ways we only try to make it through today. Such ways do not enliven and enrich us in going beyond the fears of the present.

In such fears we all can remain dominated by fear and shaped by the worst extremes of our traditions. People also need to know that those who, like them, wish community trust to grow meet opposition from their own groups too.

> 'There was a crowd surrounding my house . . . they lined themselves behind the hedge at the front. They had

burned the hedge of my sister who lived further down the
street.' (Female member of a Peace group)

'In our area the killings have been so many that even the
fragile links I have made with people in the different traditions have become more fragile or broken off altogether as
I became fearful of my own.' (Community Worker)

Building transcendent experiences step by step

As fears rise people seek to be with those they are like,
moving away from those they believe to be different and
threatening. A victim in this process can so often be the
space people have to meet together across the fault lines of
distrust; in the so-called middle ground, populated by so
many different and, often, surprising people.

Without these meetings there are few relationships in
which the experience of trust can grow. In such relationships
the memory of trust and the reality of change is carried.
Education for peace means that we value all community,
institutional and physical spaces in which people meet and
trust one another freely, without the anxious politeness
which so easily generates sectarian misunderstanding. Such
places enable people to understand how society is dominated
by fears which continue to mis-shape and influence the very
choices people have to make.

All issues can become hostage to sectarian, cultural or racist
loyalties. The issues, whether of gender, culture, disability,
poverty etc., can be used by one group for their own ends or,
with care, can evolve into spaces for meeting and common
action; meetings and action which transcend; meetings
and action in which different people experience inclusive
communities of difference; communities of contrast.

To grow up in the midst of the majority tradition in Northern
Ireland was to be immediately introduced not only to beliefs of
the group and tradition I belong to but also, in many subtle
ways, to be introduced to 'the others' in the midst of us.

'The other' – the Catholic – was a member of a group which was not talked about in ways which were complementary, there was always a degree of fear and anxiety surrounding them.

Members of the 'other' tradition who were friends of my family were always treated as 'exceptions', 'one offs' not like the rest of that tradition. Members of the other side who were exceptions to the rule were to be trusted and, in a strange way, this also reinforced that the rest were not to be trusted, they were a threat.

I was brought into the stories, rituals, traditions and views of a non-political and deeply faithful Presbyterian family. In this family and community atmosphere I was introduced to ways in which those who were different were kept at distance, except for our exceptional friends.

In such ways history was laid down in me – a history which introduced me to my group, those who would protect me and those whom I was to be careful of or keep my distance from.

In fact I was introduced to who the scapegoats of my tradition were.

Those who were numerous and different were treated a little intolerantly because they were seen as a threat. These were Catholics.

Those who were different and few in number were treated in a rather more tolerant way: these were members of the Jewish population and of minority ethnic traditions.

All, however, were made scapegoats in one sense or another. In both situations we were brought into communal ways which were about protecting our tradition and remaining one up, superior to the other.

Coming many years later to work in practical programmes linking schools and community relations work it was discouraging to note that the attitudes of my parents were not very different from many others thirty years on – on all sides. In practical programmes linking churches and community relations work I found many clergy to be amongst the most resistant to integrated education.

These patterns of communal living and the fears were and are a response to living in a contested society. In such places people in opposing groups seek to secure their future for their children in their cultural values and beliefs – so education is a form of battleground between the traditions.

In such places too, religious values and beliefs (which for me are different from faith) also become points people accumulate around for security. So clergy and religious leaders feel themselves drawn to become guardians of traditions at the cost of the inclusiveness and acceptance which, for me, characterise the Christian gospel.

Unless education for peace work is to be dragged into the scapegoating and blaming of others – seeking to be superior to them – we need to understand the nature of the forces which shape people and groups in places which are uncertain, and build relationships in which the fears people have can be heard and the relationships with those who are different can be built.

Central to our work is inviting each of us to seek to live in ways which are not at the cost of someone or some group being scapegoated – personally, economically, culturally, etc.

Peace education in the middle of a contest is a very emotional vocation! Many political commentators fail to record proper respect for this fact because they too easily focus on the importance of structures without realising that no structures will begin to work equitably in such places unless there is trust. Trust, as Fugiyama argues, is the irreducible core of democratic society.

It is possible to meet together in a stable society without the strong emotions and historical feelings which so easily infuse meetings between people from different traditions meeting together in a contested society.

Rituals and the contest
The very nature of a stable society means that much about it

doesn't need to be spoken of. The nature of its peace and stability is that difficulties and tensions in day to day life are carried and resolved within its rituals and institutions, more or less.

History and the contest

With the contest at the centre of a contested society every meeting is potentially under a cloud of fear and threat. In fact the unresolved difficulties and tensions of previous history can continually erode the present possibilities.

Education for peace in the midst of a contest means that people are always being invited to meet and acknowledge the scapegoats in their midst. This meeting therefore, for many, indeed for all of us, can be highly charged and full of uncertainty, risk and emotion. In this experience we come into the vicinity of the chaos and upheaval associated with previous scapegoating – here we approach the deep cultural fear that it could now be us who are scapegoated again or anew.

The cultural ways people are brought up in such contested areas means that we are more prepared to stay apart and remain apart than prepared for meeting and being at ease with those who are different from us.

Education for peace in such places needs to recognise the deep emotion and strong force fields associated with colliding and opposed identities. These forces influence the choices people make and feed fears prejudice and suspicion of the other.

The fears people have often drive us into the grip of those who offer us security and protection; moving into the vicinity of those who speak the more extreme views we hear from those around us, thus providing even more confirmation of our fears and the rightness of our position. In this process the fragile links between people across the line of fear become threatened even more and all can become hostage to those who peddle fear. Fear only needs a void to grow – trust needs people and relationships.

The extremes grow at the expense of the links between different people

In such contested places we learn that the most important reality in a conflict is to seek opportunities where possible, to met each other in a new way.

We learn that peace making is, at root, not about problems and skills, although these are important at certain times, it is about relationships and people meeting together, taking risks to trust each other.

Peace work is not a question of persuasion but a question of meeting each other in such a different way as to undermine all previous certainties.

When people speak together about changes in their own feelings towards Britain and Ireland it becomes clear that there are many different experiences and feelings around the actions of the state in Northern Ireland.

The practice of our work

The ideas that underlie the practical group work are concerned with relationships, structure and freedom.

Human experience is in relationships. Who a person is and will be emerges out of the relationships he/she has had, the relationship he/she is in, and the relationship which he/she will form.

The structures which grow out of relationships here will often be full of emotion, uncertainty and hurt. In rivalrous and scapegoating actions, much hurt and unhappiness is buried and can emerge at any time. In such contexts, relationships are often very fragile, unless they are supported by agreements and procedures which give them structure.

The need for structures, within which people feel free to act with others, using agreements and procedures they have negotiated, is a central theme in our work. It comes out of previous community relations work and experiences of developing new institutional arrangements, which transcend different traditions such as joint Catholic/Protestant projects, integrated schools, establishing an ecumenical centre; assisting trade union groups develop procedures and agreements on shop floors which transcend sectarianism.

'Meeting together' is about:

- the search for structures through which daily life and organisations can continue.
- ways in which people can deal with their problems together.
- ways which assist people take difficult decisions about ordering their relationships within a contested society.

The need for such practical structures also applies to work with people in community groups, professional organisations, inter-professional groups and training courses, since, in a contested society, all is fragile, as the following examples illustrate.

A member of the Corrymeela Community, who was Catholic, was upset and very angry at the time of the hunger strike. During this time, there was great polarisation in the community at large. She lived beside the home of one of the hunger strikers. Having known the members of that family well, she was very deeply involved in the emotions of that period. The woman came to a community meeting some time later, and described how her links with her Protestant friends in the community had diminished during that period, 'No one seemed to ring me again,' and she became totally thrown back on friends, who were Catholic.

'All of us on the estate did not all agree about everything surrounding the strike and yet by leaving me alone I had no one else to go to. Why didn't you call? Why didn't you ring me and speak to me?' she asked. 'Even now people remain silent about it rather than speak about it.'

One of those people she spoke about in the meeting, replied after a long silence; 'I didn't know what to say to you and so I didn't say anything. I didn't ring up. I too then got caught up in all the traditional views of my side at that time. I missed you to give me a balance.' (Wilson, 1989)

Here, even within the membership of a long-established reconciliation group the different cultural loyalties were too strong at a time of crisis. The mass of fears submerged the possibility of even a small phone call, to show someone they were remembered.

In such ways, unless the relationships and structures for remaining in contact are well established, the potential of cultural traditions to erode fragile agreements is always there. A contested society has few, if any, transcending institutions through which difficulties and differences are resolved and regulated. Cultural peace is only possible when people are recognised as being different, each having their own place, a place which is respected by everybody. In small ways this work supports such local experiences between people in the belief that these can then be experienced and modelled elsewhere.

The Nuclear Issue in the Pacific

On the Challenges Towards a peaceful and Healthy Future

Akuila D. Yabaki

'The Pacific is not just an ocean. It's a people – people who see themselves as the trustees of the environment.' (Bishop Leslie Boseto, Solomon Islands)

The Pacific is a world of small land masses dispersed over part of the world's largest ocean. Life depends to a large extent on the natural environment and is vulnerable to a wide range of natural disasters. There are thirty-three island states and territories (including Irian Jaya and Galapagos) with over eight million inhabitants rich in their diversity of cultures, languages, traditional practices and customs which are central to their close relationship to their environment.

Thanks to eighteenth century geographers modern maps still divide the Pacific Islands into three major groupings; Micronesia, Melanesia and Polynesia. Important systems of authority vary between these groupings. Melanesia tends to be the larger and higher islands where positions of authority are taken by the dominant members of the society. Polynesian islands are spread out covering a wider expanse of ocean area; their chiefs are determined by patrilineal descent, whereas Micronesia, in small and low islands generally to the North Pacific, has a system of chiefs which is commonly matrilineal.

World issues
The nuclear issue is an issue for the world, not just for the

Pacific. Missile testing in Tahiti is just one manifestation of a Pacific-wide militarisation dating back to the 1940s which has turned the Pacific into a 'Nuclear Lake.'

The overriding rationale for all weapons testing has been provided by the Cold War. The USA assumed for itself the right to develop a nuclear umbrella which would shield the 'free' world from Soviet aggression and expansion. So when the atom bomb was dropped on Hiroshima and Nagasaki the world entered a fundamentally new era in the conduct of international relations. The possession and threat of nuclear weapons became a constant factor in political relations, scientific research and development. Nation states who own nuclear arsenals belong to an élite club of nations regardless of the state of their economies and the grinding poverty of the population; India and Pakistan in fear and suspicion of each other resort to possession of nuclear weapons at heavy cost. This is because nuclear weapons have the potential of mass destruction; mere possession of them is a powerful argument which can be used in diplomacy.

Choice of the Pacific

Five nuclear powers have been involved in the testing of nuclear weapons; the United Kingdom, USA, France, and to a lesser extent China and the former Soviet Union.

USA was the first to enter the nuclear race. France and United Kingdom joined in the 1950s. Both ended up choosing the Pacific as their testing ground; France after losing the Sahara test sites following Algerian independence in 1962. The UK carried out testing in the Pacific and Australia between 1956 and 1963.

In 1980 China tested two intercontinental ballistic missiles over the Pacific. The USSR has also tested missiles with splashdowns in the Pacific Ocean.

The large expanse of low populations of the Pacific are perceived to make it ideal for two types of testing: long-range weapons delivery systems and arms too dangerous to use near populated areas. The Pacific has always had a counter logic to this Eurocentric perception. A poster competition held by the Pacific Conference of Churches in the 1980s was won by a young Solomon Islander who had the legend: 'If it is safe dump it in Tokyo, test it in Paris, store it in Washington, but keep my Pacific nuclear-free.'

The manner in which the nuclear powers have used the Pacific islands without the inhabitants' having a free choice as to whether they would agree to the use of their land and seas for nuclear testing is an act of grave injustice and casts doubt on whether these nuclear nations could be relied upon as credible partners in the international community.

Nuclear effects

Pacific islanders leading a life of simplicity in their island existence were often not told the frightening truths about what was happening to them and their land and sea. In fact they were assured of the contrary. When the military governor of the Marshall Islands first explained to chief Juda in 1946 that the removal of their population to another atoll would contribute to the ending of all wars on earth, the paramount chief said, 'If the US government and the scientists of the world want to use our island for furthering development, which with God's blessing will result in kindness and benefit to all mankind, my people will be pleased to go elsewhere.'

The 'Bravo' test 1954, carried out by the US in the Marshall Islands, showed the effects of radioactive fallout on human health. Medical problems of major proportions have surfaced since then. Women especially suffer as victims from radiation related illnesses; stillbirths and miscarriages among Rongelap women rose to more than twice the rate of unexposed Marshallese women. Long after the nuclear weapons test has dropped its fall-out or the nuclear waste has been dumped, radiation continues to affect people through the food they eat.

Scientists have tried to explain the dangers from nuclear wastes in the depth of the ocean. Radio activity from leaking nuclear waste dumped on the ocean floor will surely find its way into the ocean food chain. All plant and animal members of the ocean food chain can all be affected by poisons from the leakage. Also on land, radiation falls into the soil and enters the food chain through grass, to cows, to milk, to humans. The limited data already available indicates great migration of fish and sea mammals, in addition ocean currents are able to carry contaminants throughout the world thus making the Pacific nuclear threat a global concern.

Evacuation of island inhabitants
Whole populations have been evacuated for relocation from eight different islands in the Marshalls including Bikini, Enewetak, Rongelap and Wotho atolls, and Kwajalein. In 1946 with less than a month's notice all Bikini inhabitants were evacuated to Rongerik Atoll with 10 islets merely a quarter of the size of Bikini. Some of the islanders have been allowed to return to their island homes while still unsafe; some islands will be off limits for human habitation forever.

Secrecy
Military priorities and military secrecy continue to dominate the world's political and scientific agenda. Collusion and conspiracy suggested to be going on amongst nuclear powers leave small island states of the Pacific much more vulnerable. The causes of cancer death became unavailable in Tahiti since 1963 three years prior to the test. Hospitals were run by military doctors with lack of independent data thus making it difficult to prove the link between nuclear tests and health problems on the islands.

Following the end of the last series of French tests in 1996 the first comprehensive study of the possible effects on the health and wellbeing of the French Polynesians is being conducted by two experts from Holland with the co-operation of the Evangelical Church in Tahiti and the non-governmental organisation, *Hiti Tau*. During the thirty years of French nuclear testing no such independent survey has been allowed. The French government has always maintained there has been no harmful effect on health and environment.

If reliable data about the health effects of nuclear tests is hard to come by, even greater is the paucity of data on environmental effects. Clean-up efforts are extremely costly. The clean-up of Enewetak and Bikini in the Marshall Islands has cost millions of dollars yet has not resulted in the satisfactory resettlement of the atolls.

Nuclear-free constitution

Belau, an island with fifteen thousand people and five hundred square kilometres, is entirely dependent on US grants. The Belauans' struggle for a nuclear-free constitution is a remarkable show of democratic strength against an imposition of will by a major nuclear power. In July 1979, ninety-two per cent of the population voted in favour of provisions which would prohibit the use, testing and storage or disposal in Belauan territory of 'harmful substances such as nuclear, chemical, gas or biological weapons' without the express approval of seventy-five per cent of the votes in a referendum. The constitutional battle raged through the 1980s as the US tried in vain to establish military authority over Belau. In 1990 in yet another referendum only sixty per cent of the votes were cast in favour of the arrangement called Compact under negotiation. The democratic decision of the Belauans not to buckle under the weight of intense political and economic pressures by the US had been reaffirmed seven times over in a series of referendums. Despite severe social instability, sabotage, murders and even bombings the Belauans resistance did not diminish.

South Pacific Nuclear-Free Zone Treaty

This Treaty came into existence largely as a result of the impact of the Nuclear-Free and Independent Pacific

Movement which had its birth at a conference in Fiji in 1975. This first Nuclear-Free Pacific Conference, the first of its kind in the Pacific, was made up of representatives of peace movements, ecological movements, churches, academics, unions and individual politicians.

The Conference produced the draft of a 'People's Charter for a Nuclear-Free Pacific' which later influenced the then Prime Minister of New Zealand to call for the creation of a nuclear-free zone treaty at the South Pacific Forum meeting of the same year. At subsequent conferences held in Pohnpei in 1978 and Hawaii in 1980 the movement's name was changed to include the independence issue. Nuclearisation of the Pacific, it was argued, was merely an extension of colonialism. Independence also means nuclear independence. A revised People's Charter incorporating these ideas was adopted.

This gave support to the Kanak independence struggle in New Caledonia, opposition to the Indonesian policy of transmigration in Irian Jaya (West Papua), endorsed protest against the dumping of nuclear wastes in the Pacific, condemned the use of the Kwajalein Atoll for testing of the MX and other missiles, called for an end to uranium mining in Australia and supported Belau's antinuclear constitution. The Movement was now undergirded by grassroots support and actions across the Pacific.

The nuclear powers took note of this widespread raising of Pacific consciousness but their superficial notion of the priorities of the so-called 'free world' bore no relation to the deep attachment which Pacific islanders have towards their environment and which was at the heart of their struggle for a nuclear-free Pacific.

The 1980 meeting also established a secretariat for the movement, the Pacific Concerns Resource Centre in Hawaii. Later the Centre was moved to Auckland, New Zealand and then more recently to Suva, Fiji where PCRC still has its headquarters.

At the largest meeting of the Movement held in Vanuatu

in 1983 the drafters of the South Pacific Nuclear-Free Zone
Treaty came under intense pressures from the USA and
France to tone down the Treaty according to their interests.

Later in drafting the nuclear-free pacific treaty, the South
Pacific Forum – a body composed of the heads of government of independent and self-governing states in the South
Pacific – also came under pressure from nuclear powers to
make compromises.

Hence, the drafters decided to establish a nuclear-free
zone only south of the Equator, excluding US-controlled
Micronesia. Ballistic missile tests were not prohibited nor
were facilities which are part of nuclear war systems and
networks. Vanuatu, which had become the first country to
impose a port ban on nuclear ships, refused to sign the treaty
because it felt it didn't go far enough. Nevertheless, the
treaty was signed by all remaining South Pacific Forum
members and came into force on 11 December 1986.

The signing by Britain, France and USA of the South
Pacific Nuclear-Free Zone Treaty ten years after could be
seen as a welcome sign towards the ending of nuclear
experimentation in the Pacific. But this came only after
France had confounded thousands of people across the
world and Europe in particular by resuming a series of six
tests after a moratorium of almost three years.

To many people's bafflement was Britain's apparent
endorsement of the French actions. It seemed that this was a
return for French support during the Falkland war and the
need to preserve the balance of power in the Pacific region
as a whole.

This view is further endorsed in a statement by the
speaker of France's National Assembly, Philippe Seguin,
addressing a seminar of the South Pacific in May 1996:
'France's presence in the South Pacific is, in my opinion, an
indisputable asset for the region. When other powers tend to
gradually pull out from the region, France emerges as the
natural intermediary between Europe and the South Pacific.'

There is probably some truth in all these explanations but none of them goes any way to allay the Pacific people's concern that Britain does not seriously care about the future of the Pacific.

Human issues raised
The first issue I believe is the issue of powerlessness. The French President Chirac having once stated that he will resume testing said his decision was irrevocable. For Chirac as well as other leaders colluding with his nuclear test schemes the people out there in the Pacific, and who were vocal against the tests, simply do not exist. A clear instance of the arrogance of absolute power. These nuclear powers could again decide to resume testing tomorrow and nothing could be done to stop them. Pacific people are totally defenceless against what has been a relentless destruction and despoliation of their lands, seas and people.

To avert the imbalance calls for a new kind of international statesmanship; a world where the powerful nations who wield power through possession of nuclear weapons must now yield power and heed the voice of the powerless.

The second issue I believe is the fact of our interdependence. In a development-conscious world enlightened self-interest is usually given as a reason why people of the North should be in solidarity with others from the South. But the Pacific people's interdependence has an indigenous inbuilt sense of oneness with the environment; human beings may not have lost this sense of interdependence with all created life. The integrity of creation is a perception we would do well to recover. Pacific people can share this message with the world out of their own cultures and traditions – an experiential truth: the ocean, land and people are closely interconnected. Hurting the land and sea with bombs is also hurting human beings because people's origins are bound up with land and ocean.

The third issue is about liberation. In 1982 the Pacific

Conference of Churches published a book on the anti-nuclear theme called *A Call to a New Exodus*. It was full-colour and easy to read, therefore called a primer. The title drew a parallel between the struggle for a nuclear free Pacific and the 'going out' in freedom of the Israélites when they escaped from Egypt. Pacific islanders bear in themselves and with their environment the marks of being made victims of our global nuclear technology. Would you join and participate in their struggle for justice, peace and the integrity of creation? The book made the point that 'Human beings now had the clear possibility of making frightening changes to life on earth as we know it not only through the use of weapons, but through accidents or the careless disposal of wastes'.

The warning is also a challenge to work for a better world.

The safest policy for both the Pacific Region and the planet would be the complete cessation of the nuclear testings.

Select Bibliography
E. Weingarten, *The Pacific: Nuclear Testing and Minorities* (Minority Rights Group, London, 1991)

S. Swatibau and D. Williams, *A Call to a New Exodus: an anti-nuclear primer for Pacific People* (Pacific Conference of Churches, Suva, Fiji, 1982)

The Europe-Pacific Solidarity Bulletin Vol. 4; Number 3 May/June 1996, ECSIEP Zeist Netherlands

The Thorny Road to Reconciliation in El Salvador

Marigold Best and Pamela Hussey

A whole series of Latin American countries has emerged from periods of internal conflict over the last few years, through different processes and with varying degrees of success. It would be hard to say, however, that any of them has managed to achieve true reconciliation and thus a situation of harmony in which conflict and repression will never occur again.

A basic problem is how you define reconciliation. It can come as a shock to those of us accustomed to revere the concept of reconciliation to discover that, like many other noble concepts, it has sometimes been so distorted as to become a dirty word. In 1986, the member of the Nicaraguan Sandinista government in charge of relations with the churches, on hearing that Quakers have traditionally worked for peace and reconciliation, responded not with a smile but with the blackest possible frown: 'Reconciliation! That is what the Archbishop [who had supported the Contras] preaches to us. We are just to forget all the Contra atrocities, sweep everything under the carpet . . . ' That kind of 'reconciliation' seems to him, and to many other Latin Americans, not a positive step forward towards peace but just another triumph for the old system of impunity and corruption which has produced so much suffering and conflict. Father Francisco Estrada, the Rector of the Jesuit Central American University (UCA) in San Salvador, defined reconciliation differently when he wrote in 1994, 'With the signing of the Peace Accords in Chapultepec [on 16th January 1992], there began the long journey of national reconciliation; not that of "forgive-and-forget", which is an offence to the victims and a protection to the victimisers. In the face of offences against society only a social forgiveness, achieved through a sufficient process of truth and justice, will guarantee an authentic and permanent reconciliation.'

El Salvador is the country we shall mainly concentrate on in this chapter as we both have a long involvement with it and have visited it together. Our visits enabled us to meet a range of unforgettable people whose experiences we can draw on to illustrate more vividly the problems of working for peace and reconciliation in a country with such a history of conflict. El Salvador is also a very important example to examine because it is the scene of the first attempt by the United Nations at peace building, not just peace keeping, and a lot of international support has been provided for the reconstruction process. The difficult question is whether there is sufficient will inside the country itself to bring all the elements of the fragmented society together in order to solve the problems of injustice and marginalisation which caused the conflict in the first place.

Causes of the conflict

Salvadoran society in the 1970s was controlled by an élite, loosely known as 'the fourteen families', who over generations had accumulated more and more land, pushing poor peasants onto the least fertile ground or reducing them to dependence on the pittance paid for seasonal work on the large plantations. In the cities a minority prospered from industrialisation based on meagre wages and terrible working conditions. The figures for infant mortality, malnutrition, illiteracy and other indices were shockingly high. In 1968 the second Conference of Latin American Bishops met in Medellin, Colombia, and, following the spirit of the Second Vatican Council, adopted the 'preferential option for the poor'. Although most of the Roman Catholic hierarchy in El Salvador was very conservative, Monsenor Luis Chavez, Archbishop of San Salvador from 1939-1977, was an enlightened church leader who encouraged priests and religious sisters to work with the rural poor, supported co-operatives and women's groups, and backed the priests like the Jesuit Father Rutilio Grande who in the 1970s were helping to organise Christian Base Communities, peasant organisations, the promotion of literacy and health care and other such activities. This was labelled Communism by the élite and intense persecution of the church began. In 1977 a death squad distributed leaflets in the capital saying 'Be a Patriot! Kill a Priest!' and many priests, sisters and lay workers were murdered during the 70s and 80s. One of them was Rutilio Grande, whose death was the final eye-opener for his friend Oscar Romero. Romero had been chosen to succeed the 'dangerously radical' Archbishop Chavez because he was thought to be safely conservative. But he was always close to the lives of his people and as he saw how they were suffering he developed the courageous prophetic stature which made him the 'voice of the voiceless', a role for which he too was murdered on 24th March 1980. He had just written to beg President Carter to stop sending military aid to the Salvadoran government. In his final Sunday homily on 23rd March he had appealed to the soldiers themselves to stop the repression against the peasants who were their own brothers and sisters.

By that time a civil war had been under way for several months. During the 60s and 70s every attempt to bring about reform by peaceful and democratic means had been violently repressed. Reformist politicians, trade unionists, peasant leaders, anyone who wanted to change the *status quo*, were liable to be assassinated. So a number of left-wing groups emerged, five of which eventually joined together to form the Farabundo Marti National Liberation Front (FMLN), and, deciding that armed resistance was the only alternative available, took to the hills where they were increasingly joined by peasants fleeing from persecution by the military. There is no time to tell the full story of the horrors of the war here but it left a toll of some seventy-five thousand dead, mostly civilians killed by the military (we met with a woman who was the only survivor when her whole village was massacred), and a terrible legacy of wounds and divisions throughout Salvadoran society.

The United Nations brokers peace accords

By the late 1980s even the United States government, which had given such enormous financial support to the Salvadoran Armed Forces throughout the conflict[216] was coming to realise that neither side was going to win a military victory. The shocking murder of six Jesuit Fathers, their housekeeper and her daughter, at the UCA on 16th November 1989 was a factor in increasing support for a new US policy favouring a negotiated settlement. Also the collapse of the Soviet Union greatly reduced the credibility of the Cold War rhetoric used to justify the US intervention. Talks between the Salvadoran government and the FMLN were held in September and October 1989 but failed to reach agreement on proceedings for a cease-fire. Both sides then requested United Nations mediation, and the dialogue resumed in Geneva on 4th April 1990 in the presence of the UN Secretary-General, Javier Perez de Cuellar. 'The two sides signed a "Declaration" setting out the aims of the process and stipulating that a cease-fire and the incorporation of the FMLN into civilian society should come after political agreements encompassing the armed forces, human rights, the electoral and judicial systems, and economic and social reforms.'[217] The talks culminated at last in the signing of a Peace Agreement at Chapultepec, Mexico, on 16th January 1992. The cease-fire itself came into effect on 1st February amid country-wide rejoicing.

'Post-conflict peace-building'

Among the important agreements which were reached even before the signing of the final Accords one was of particular significance. It was the first to be signed by both sides, in July 1990, and dealt with human rights and international verification, establishing a UN Verification Commission, part of a UN Observer Mission known as ONUSAL. 'The task of this Commission would be to monitor the human rights situation in El Salvador from the moment of its installation. This step is unprecedented in the history of the UN, and is the most powerful mechanism for the protection and promotion of human rights ever set up by that body.[218] The UN Security Council approved the setting up of ONUSAL in May 1991, after the Secretary-General had managed to persuade the US and Britain not to oppose the Mission starting work before the cease-fire, and ONUSAL actually began its task on 26th July that year. Before the cease-fire, its task was to include 'active surveillance of the human rights situation; investigation of specific charges of human rights violations; promotion of human rights, formulation of recommendations for eliminating violations and promoting respect for those rights'.[219] This sounds a big enough task by itself, but after the cease-fire, under the very wide mandate given to it by the Security Council 'to monitor all agreements concluded between the two parties', ONUSAL was given a task never undertaken by the UN before, that of 'post-conflict peace-building'. UN Secretary-General Boutros Boutros-Ghali, in his report *An Agenda for Peace: Preventive Diplomacy, Peacemaking and Peace-keeping* (UN, New York, 1992), describes peace-building as including 'disarming the previously warring parties and the restoration of order, the custody and possible destruction of weapons, repatriating refugees, advisory and training support for security personnel, monitoring elections, advancing efforts to protect human rights, reforming or strengthening governmental institutions and promoting formal and informal processes of political participation'.[220] It is interesting to compare this list of activities with the list of changes needed 'in order to guarantee real democracy' presented in a little 'popular'[221] booklet distributed in January 1991 by the Salvadoran Community Movement (MCS) in an effort to arouse enthusiasm and pressure for the peace process among ordinary Salvadorans. They call for 'strict respect for human rights . . . the demilitarisation of society . . . reform of the judicial system . . . complete functioning of a pluralistic political system [i.e. clean elections] . . . protection, support and use of the right to organise . . . a public and national system of democratic, scientific education . . . raising the standard of living of the majority [housing, health, infrastructure] . . . respect for the rights of women and children . . . equal access to the means of communication . . . defence of the purchasing power of workers' wages [by price controls etc.] . . . massive job creation with fair wages . . . deepening the socio-economic reforms . . . programmes to rescue the environment [there is real danger of desertification] . . . a new economic order to aid development and social harmony . . . the recovery of national sovereignty and non-alignment . . . working towards uniting the five Central American countries'.

Some of the MCS demands go well beyond even ONUSAL's broad remit but a good many of them are in fact present in the terms of the Peace Accords whose implementation ONUSAL was asked to verify. So it is clear that peace-building goes a good deal further than peace-keeping or even than reconstruction, necessary though both of those aspects are in El Salvador. Reconstruction implies restoring structures which were there before but have been destroyed by conflict but many of the agreements in the Salvadoran Peace Accords relate to conditions which did not exist at all before the conflict but which are seen as essential if peace and eventual reconciliation are to be achieved, things like an independent judiciary, a civil police not linked to the military, a military subject to civilian control, a real agrarian reform – in fact, the Peace Accords call for a thorough transformation of society.

It is not surprising then that those who have always

benefited from the *status quo* should not want to rush to implement changes which seem mainly to benefit those who have always been excluded, although there are those even among the élite who appreciate that addressing the causes of the civil war is essential for the development of the country as a whole. Alfredo Cristiani, then President of El Salvador, in his speech at the signing of the Peace Agreement, acknowledged the 'profound social and political roots' of the war. 'Now democracy belongs to everyone without exclusion or privileges. The agreement is an act of freedom for an entire people whose suffering and stoicism have given it the supreme right to hope for a more humane life.' Extending his hand towards President Cristiani, FMLN Comandante Schafik Handal said, 'We are not coming to this moment like stray sheep returning to the corral, but as mature and energetic promoters of the changes longed for by an immense majority of Salvadorans . . . From now on the entire nation will be the protagonist of its own transformation.'[222] Magnanimous words on the two sides sounded a note of hope but the completely separate celebrations they held showed how great was the divide that needed to be bridged.

The Accords and their implementation

The Act of New York, embodying the peace agreements, was signed at the United Nations just a few minutes before Javier Perez de Cuellar's term of office as General Secretary expired at midnight on 31st December 1991. The main agreements concerned the creation of a National Civil Police Force; the reduction and purging of the armed forces; socio-economic issues, including the transfer of land to ex-combatants and inhabitants of conflictive zones; and the political participation of the FMLN following a cease-fire. The first two weeks of January 1992 were devoted to working out an agenda for the implementation of the agreement and also a calendar of implementation to try and make sure that the procedures agreed were carried out as rapidly as possible. For example, the FMLN were to be demobilised and integrated into civilian life within nine months of the cease-fire and the five US-trained élite battalions of the army were to be disbanded within ten months. The calendar was carefully worked out in order to maintain the confidence of both sides in the process as each step was taken. In practice, not surprisingly, endless problems arose in keeping to the calendar, which had to be renegotiated several times. ONUSAL's original one year remit was extended first until the 1994 Presidential Elections, then further and further, as the implementation of the Accords delayed yet again. ONUSAL (after a year as a greatly reduced MINUSAL – UN Mission in El Salvador) finally left on 30th April 1996, with the peace process still by no means complete. This fact was recognised by their leaving behind a small United Nations Verification Office (ONUV) with a mandate until December 1996.

Achievements and problems

The UN has declared its operation in El Salvador one of the most satisfactory it has undertaken and the Salvadoran government claims that ninety-five percent of the Accords have been implemented. There have certainly been considerable achievements yet most observers feel there is still a long way to go to achieve the aim of reconciliation which is stated or implied in every aspect of the Peace Process. The Washington based SHARE Foundation, for example, has expressed concern that some components of the Peace Accords will never be completed. 'The diminishing UN verification role will make compliance more difficult. Further, the fact that it is diminishing is partly an indication of the determination of the Salvadoran government to declare an end to the Peace Accord process, rather than comply fully with its promises.'[223] We can only give a brief summary here of how the most important aspects of the Peace Accords have fared and direct readers to the Bibliography for further reading.

Human rights

Even before the cease-fire the presence of the ONUSAL observers did result in a considerable decrease in major human rights abuses. After the cease-fire the white ONUSAL vehicles were everywhere and we remember the excitement in a returned refugee community when a couple of ONUSAL helicopters were seen to be landing not far away. The mission received a flood of denunciations in its early days, far more than it could possibly investigate, so some people's unrealistic expectations led to disappointment. Those who did not want the truth to come out tried to denigrate ONUSAL, who were attacked in the press and even received death threats. Not all those who could have reported everyday human rights violations did so. A young man we know was stopped by the police in San Salvador and because he could not produce one insignificant document on the spot was taken to the police station, kept overnight without being allowed to contact his family (who spent the night searching the hospitals), and released the next morning minus his watch and his glasses. When it was suggested to him that this was just the kind of thing that should be reported to ONUSAL he said, 'I can't do that – those policemen would come back and beat me up.'

A major problem that ONUSAL, like many other UN bodies elsewhere, had to face was that its strongest instrument for ensuring compliance with the accords was simply public censure. The body to which the Accords gave strong legal powers to verify the implementation of all aspects of the agreements was the National Commission for the Consolidation of Peace (COPAZ). It was made up of two Salvadoran government representatives, two from the FMLN and one from each of the political parties in the Legislative Assembly. It was felt to be a very important mechanism for bringing all sides into the process and encouraging consensus decision-making, but unfortunately support for the government and support for the FMLN has usually been equal, resulting in stalemate.

There have been occasions when COPAZ has tried to perform a mediating function and has been undermined. It is supposed to have an important role in overseeing the most contentious changes of all, those relating to land distribution. In the early days after the cease-fire the question of land take-overs by peasants and evictions by landlords was making progress almost impossible. COPAZ members made a strong call for peasants to cease land take-overs, and landlords to end eviction attempts, to allow breathing room for the [newly installed land] commission. Yet the following day paid ads from the Ministry of Agriculture were run in various newspapers calling landowners together to begin legal proceedings to reclaim their lands. A media campaign denouncing take-overs as the tactic of 'bad Salvadorans . . . who don't respect private property' was launched with saturation exposure on commercial radio stations.[224]

The virtual ineffectiveness of COPAZ, therefore, meant that most of the responsibility for verification fell to ONUSAL which has not always been willing to use its public censure option to full effect. In September 1992 the US-based human rights monitoring group Americas Watch issued a report[225] in which it praised ONUSAL for dramatically improving the observance of human rights. It concluded, however, 'that some senior ONUSAL officials had mistakenly viewed its promotion of human rights and its overseeing of the implementation of the peace accords as contradictory. As a consequence, ONUSAL has been timid in openly criticising the government on human rights matters, even when its own investigations have pointed to state involvement in abuses . . . ONUSAL has yet to use fully the ultimate recourse of public censure, something which detracts from its effectiveness and allows perpetrators of abuse to escape broader detection.' Many people have felt that, in particular, ONUSAL's apparent reluctance to insist on full investigation of the death squads was unfortunate. Nevertheless, whatever its shortcomings, the UN mission has given the Salvadoran people an unprecedented glimpse of what a system of respect for human rights might be like. It remains to be seen whether the people can eventually insist that their national authorities provide such a system. A sign of hope is the appointment of a human rights ombudsperson under the Accords. She has proved an effective advocate and has gained considerable public confidence but has problems with lack of resources and of co-operation from those in authority.

National Civil Police (PNC)

There seemed some hope of a growing reconciliation between the police and the public with the establishment of the PNC which was to be made up of twenty per-cent ex-FMLN combatants, twenty per-cent ex-National Police and sixty per-cent civilians who had not taken part in the armed conflict. They were to receive training in the new style of professional policing at a new Police Academy. In spite of delays and serious under-resourcing, the first PNC groups deployed in selected regions made a good impression. The priest who one day in 1994 was driving us along the bandit-infested dirt road between a series of returned refugee com-munities and the nearest town stopped when we came to a PNC patrol and told them that a busload of boys and girls from the communities would be travelling to the secondary school in the town early the following morning and would they please be specially vigilant. That is something he never would have done with the old police but he said ruefully, 'Of course they will be corrupted.' And in fact the PNC has not only been given insufficient resources and training but, contrary to the Accords, former Army, Treasury Police and National Guard officers have been allowed to join and the habit of repressive violence has reappeared. Of the one thousand two hundred and seventeen human rights violations recorded by the ombudsperson's office in the first three months of 1996, seven hundred and ninety-one were attributed to the PNC. A MINUSAL study of the PNC in 1995 pressed for urgent reforms. Many elements in Salvadoran society are making the same demands and the fact that people are now more willing to report violations to the ombudsperson gives some hope of eventual improvement in this vital component of a new civil society.

Changes to the Armed Forces

Although the removal of a good number of officers with bad human rights records, as recommended by the ad-hoc Commission of three highly respected Salvadoran politicians, was continually put off after the military criticised the report as a 'leftist plot', there have indeed been big changes in the Armed Forces. About half the troops have been demobilised and all the wartime leaders have retired. However, the military are still being used, against the terms of the Accords, for internal security functions supposed to be carried out by the PNC, thus undermining the latter's authority. MINUSAL's final report, and many human rights organisations, including the Ombudsperson's office, express the fear that increased use of the military under a controversial new 'Transitional Emergency Law to Combat Delinquency and Organised Crime' might endanger the reform of the judicial system and other elements of the Peace Accords. Some people even told us they feared that some military officers were encouraging the crime wave in order to regain some of their lost power. The Law has not in fact helped to reduce the enormous amount of crime and violence – there is a daily average of twenty-one violent deaths now compared with seventeen a day during the years of conflict. Youth gangs cause mayhem in streets and schools, robbery is rife and shadowy death squads still exist. The UCA maintains that 'tougher laws will not resolve the problem, because it is not fundamentally a question of legal order, but one of a lack of investigation and administration of justice'.[226] The poverty and hopelessness in which many young people live plays its part in turning them to gang life. The Ministry of Education tried to help solve the problem by lengthening the school day until 3 pm but we were told that the main result in the capital was that many children either skived off at lunchtime to rob in order to eat or else fainted from hunger during afternoon classes.

Overhaul of the Criminal Justice system
ONUSAL found the judicial system so inadequate that it devoted the whole of its fourth Human Rights report to recommending changes. Some constitutional reforms have been made but essential legislation has still not been passed. In August 1994 a new Supreme Court of Justice was elected, the first to be elected unanimously by the Legislative Assembly and therefore with representation of different shades of opinion. But people have not seen it begin to take energetic action in the way they had hoped and so still have very little faith in obtaining justice through it.[227] However, the large number of judges condemned as corrupt or incompetent are gradually being removed and there are hopeful signs of the emergence of a more independent and reliable judiciary.

The Truth Commission
This was set up under the Accords with a remit that included 'the need to create confidence in the positive changes which the peace process is promoting and to assist the transition to national reconciliation'. Headed by Belisario Betancur, former President of Colombia, Reinaldo Figueredo, former Foreign Minister of Venezuela and Prof. Thomas Buergenthal, Hon. President of the Inter-American Institute for Human Rights in Costa Rica, the team was only given six months from 14th July 1992 to prepare a report on human rights violations on both sides during the 12 years of conflict so it could not examine every case. But it analysed the most serious incidents on the basis of evidence given by thousands of individuals and a wide variety of governmental

and non-governmental bodies. Responsibility for eighty-five per cent of the atrocities was attributed to State security forces, paramilitaries allied with them and death squads. The FMLN was held responsible for five per cent. The report recommended the removal from the armed forces and the public administration of all those named as responsible for violations and the replacement of all the judges on the Supreme Court, as well as reforms to bring the armed forces properly under civilian control, also the creation of a special fund for compensating victims and/or their families.

The Truth Commission's report, entitled *From Madness to Hope*, was published in March 1993 in a full version and also in a 'popular' version with cartoons, more accessible to the general public. It was received with opprobrium by the authorities. (The President of the Supreme Court of Justice denounced the setting up of the Commission as not only an error but an act of stupidity.)[228] Back in January 1992 the Legislative Assembly had passed an amnesty law (calling it the Law of National Reconciliation), 'but exempted those cases that might be taken up by the Truth Commission as well as cases tried by a jury (such as the Jesuit case)'.[229] Now headlines appeared in the press saying 'An Amnesty is Essential for Reconciliation', and the assembly readily acceded to the President's request that they should pass a law which gave amnesty to everyone except the FMLN members who carried out two murders of North Americans. (The FMLN accepted the Truth Commission's report.)

Although the reaction to the report may have been disappointing, the document itself is there for all to see and no one has been able to say that the facts it contains are not true so it has gone some way towards satisfying the demands of the families of the dead and disappeared to know what happened to their loved ones.

Reaction in the church
During the conflict there were many priests and religious

sisters who risked their lives remaining with their people in the conflictive zones and helping the many thousands displaced by the military scorched earth policy. Other parts of the Catholic Church supported the government in its fight to stamp out so-called Communist subversion. One bishop was even also a military Colonel. Archbishop Rivera Damas was, like his predecessor Oscar Romero, a source of strength and support for those working to defend human rights. From the early 1980s he also pressed constantly for dialogue to end the conflict and later, when talks did begin he frequently acted as mediator. In 1988 he brought together representatives from all aspects of society, including from the Protestant churches, in an ongoing National Debate for Peace. Both sides in the conflict saw him having an active role in furthering the Peace Process as a member of COPAZ. Father Ignacio Ellacuria, the Rector of the UCA murdered there with his fellow Jesuits in 1989, was also active in seeking to bring about negotiations which his colleagues feel was the reason for his killing. At grassroots level pastoral teams in resettled areas are working to bring together communities with different histories and allegiances.

So the progressive parts of the church were strongly committed to the peace process as a whole and especially saw implementation of the Truth Commission's report as essential to progress towards reconciliation. They were indignant and deeply saddened by the official attempts to denigrate the commission and to draw the veil of amnesty over terrible truths which needed to be faced. (One bishop of a different persuasion congratulated the judicial authorities for their rejection of the Truth Commission's conclusions.) Father Jose Maria Tojeira, the Jesuit Provincial, writing to deplore the amnesty in early April 1993, stressed that the authorities had no need to fear any spirit of vengefulness in the country. 'All of us in El Salvador are talking about the need to find rational mechanisms for legal pardon . . . (based on) a process of truth, justice and forgiveness . . . It is necessary to delve deeply into the truth in order that we can change structures and attitudes which are harmful to all Salvadorans. It is supremely important that there should be justice so that society can, through its institutions, sanction, formally and officially, the crimes committed, thus avoiding the risk of their repetition (and our suggestion in this regard was that the crime committed should be confessed before a judge, after which there should be some kind of pardon.'[230]

An editorial in the same number of *Carta a las Iglesias* expresses the hope that international pressure will bring about some degree of compliance with the recommendations of the report but it ends regretfully, 'When all is said and done, it has to be noted that the internal pressure in favour of this process is insufficient. There has been little mobilisation in support of the Truth Commission Report and against the approval of the amnesty. This facilitates manoeuvres against peace inside the country and makes international action difficult. 'Peace is the task of us all, and it therefore behoves all the forces in El Salvador which want peace, truth and justice to speak out more clearly and to demand the implementation of the Accords and of the recommendations of the Truth Commission Report.' (Our translation.)

The role of 'internationals'
It is perhaps not surprising that large numbers of ordinary Salvadorans who suffered great hardship before and during the conflict, and many of whom are suffering even greater economic hardship now, may, at least temporarily, have lost some of their energy or confidence to keep on and on struggling and campaigning for their rights. During the conflict many thousands of those suffering repression, the displaced and the refugees learned to rely for support on international solidarity from organisations and individuals. We ourselves first encountered Salvadorans through the international programmes to help refugees in camps in Honduras who came to feel, with some justification, that their very lives depended

on the presence among them of as many 'internationals' as possible. An effective level of international monitoring and support will be necessary for some time, even if the process of implementing the Peace Accords continues, but it is obvious in many parts of the world today that unless there is political will and public pressure inside a country or region to change the *status quo* the success of international efforts can only be limited.

Sometimes too much international involvement can inhibit the development of local initiatives. Holiday and Stanley suggest that the high degree of confidence placed in ONUSAL's human rights work meant that it 'effectively displaced, albeit unintentionally, the human rights work previously carried by non-governmental organisations and the church, without working with them to redefine their new role in the post-war period' (p. 28). At the grass-roots level some communities have relied so much on donations from abroad that their long-term economic viability is threatened. Some people feel that the exclusively non-Salvadoran make-up of the Truth Commission team reduced its credibility (in comparison, for instance, with the Rettig Commission in Chile which was totally Chilean) but that may have been the only way of getting a Truth Commission at all.

In fact the Peace Accords as agreed could not have come into being or been implemented to the extent they have without the dedicated mediation and lengthy accompaniment of the United Nations teams under Secretary General Perez de Cuellar and Boutros-Ghali. The Salvadoran military would not have reluctantly accepted the setting up of the Ad-Hoc Commission and the Truth Commission without strong pressure from their erstwhile supporters in the United States. The mechanisms for the implementation of the Accords could not have been set up without support and funding from the international community.

At an individual level an example of how helpful a non-national actor (or, in this case, actress) can be is shown in the role played by the American Friends Service Committee's representative in El Salvador, Sandra Dunsmore Pentland. In the period leading up to the signing of the Peace Accords she worked to bring together people of different views within the business community as well as labour leaders to talk about their common interest in addressing the socio-economic causes of the conflict. After one seminar she was delighted that the evaluation concluded, 'We're all Salvadorans. Despite our political or ideological differences, we're all Salvadorans, and we can talk to each other.' It was a very valuable step forward and Sandra had not expected her contribution to be more than that, but when the Forum for Economic and Social Co-ordination was set up under the Accords she was invited to become its executive secretary as being the only person that all sides could agree upon. She performed that function for a year, using many of the skills she had learned in facilitating the small seminars. The Forum 'did not result in major policy changes, but was very important at a key stage in the peace process. In a war-weary country, it built hope that former enemies could talk and act, even in small ways, in the interest of El Salvador as a whole'.[231]

The growing move towards regional integration of the Central American countries may have a positive role to play in strengthening civil society and therefore furthering the cause of peace and reconciliation in each nation. On 30th March 1995 the governments of Costa Rica, El Salvador, Guatemala, Honduras, Nicaragua and Panama signed a Treaty of Social Integration making an all-embracing commitment to every possible right and form of development for all their peoples. It may be that they can all encourage each other increasingly to live up to that commitment.

Reconciliation through reconstruction?
The crucial and sensitive economic and social aspects of peace-building, including the vital and tricky question of land distribution, were left till the last minute in the peace

negotiations and clear and detailed agreements about mechanisms for carrying out the process were not reached. The question of land distribution, with attempts at agrarian reform only minimally implemented over many decades, is still the biggest stumbling-block on the road to peace and reconciliation. At the moment not much more than half of the land identified for redistribution has been allocated and poor peasants fear that even if they get a parcel of land they may never be able to earn enough from it to pay off the cost. The huge problem of the land is much too big a question for us to go into further here but it is seen as a potential time-bomb by many people.

The FMLN and the Government have very different ideas about what reconstruction means. The FMLN wanted the National Reconstruction Plan (PRN) to promote economic development in the ex-conflictive zones through grassroots projects based on 'integral human development' – not just land or grants but the education, training, access to credit and other facilities to enable poor people to emerge from minimal subsistence level. The government on the other hand, anxious that reconstruction should not disrupt its structural adjustment programme, wanted the PRN merely to rebuild the infrastructure and install some short-term poverty alleviation programmes, leaving development 'to evolve through market-driven accumulation which would eventually create employment opportunities for the population, thus opening the path out of poverty'.[232]

The peace accords do 'call on the PRN to promote the "integrated development" of the ex-conflictive zones, and to contribute to national reconciliation among all Salvadorans'.[233] The international donors of funds for reconstruction, especially the Europeans, certainly saw the reconstruction process as a means of encouraging reconciliation, indeed they said they would not support any plans which were not agreed by both sides. The United States Agency for International Development (USAID), on the other hand, insisted on donating its reconstruction money to the government's National Secretariat for Reconstruction (SRN). The United Nations Development Programme (UNDP) did not have the resources to act as an independent administrator of the plan so the end result is that the government has been left with almost complete control of the process with a minimum of input from the FMLN or from the beneficiaries of reconstruction projects. The non-governmental organisations (NGOs) linked to opposition parties, with valuable experience of working in the conflictive zones, have also been largely cold-shouldered by the SRN, though they have been included in UNDP projects and those of foreign agencies.

The greatest potential opportunity for reconciliation as a part of reconstruction lay in the Municipalities in Action (MIA) programme. MIA was started by USAID in the last years of the war to finance infrastructure projects through local government. To the FMLN it was simply part of the counter-insurgency programme and where possible they blocked it by preventing mayors from serving. The local government system is now re-established throughout the country and MIA has received the largest share of the SRN reconstruction funds for projects such as building schools and rebuilding roads. 'At the core of the MIA programme is the *"cabildo abierto"*, or municipal assembly, in which residents can propose projects based on community needs. The mayor, perhaps with the municipal council, then establishes priorities and presents a project list to the MIA programme for approval . . . Negotiations between USAID, SRN and the FMLN resulted in two mechanisms to ensure the participation of the local opposition: expanded municipal assemblies which include local NGOs; and municipal reconstruction committees meant to enable opposition input on priorities.'[234]

What happened in Suchitoto is an example of how well the scheme can work and also of how easily it can be undermined. (This case and three others are fully documented in *Rescuing Reconstruction*.) The Mayor, from the government

ARENA party, (one of a number of well-intentioned ARENA mayors in various parts of the country) formed a very broad-based Municipal Reconstruction Committee, including the FMLN, to involve as many people as possible in the task of prioritising the reconstruction needs of Suchitoto. The Committee worked so well that it attracted attention and support from a number of international aid agencies and also, initially from the SRN and USAID. 'However, as the Committee consolidated, Mayor Figueroa began to receive pressure from ARENA and the SRN to withdraw from the Committee. He and others believe ARENA feared a "co-governing" situation was developing with groups linked to the FMLN.'[235] Funding for five PRN projects was frozen and Mayor Figueroa was first dismissed as ARENA Secretary General in Suchitoto and then charged with misspending project funds, arrested and imprisoned. 'After Mayor Figueroa was jailed, the Municipal Reconstruction Committee disintegrated, and the budding consensus and participatory process withered. The energetic priest who had been a strong advocate of the committee was transferred. Former Committee members now carry out activities separately. The Mayor appointed to replace Figueroa, his first cousin, Julio C'sar Figueroa, has had little contact with surrounding communities or the NGOs.'[236]

At least this example shows that people from different parties and organisations can, and often want, to work together constructively if they are allowed to do so. Local people from all sides lament the loss of the wide participation achieved through the Committee and one can only hope that they will find ways of recovering it. Their effort could have been an example of 'real democracy' as well as of 'real reconciliation'. Unfortunately there is still some way to go before the welcome increase in formal democracy translates into democracy as a means for people to achieve change. MINUSAL's final report stressed the urgent need for implementing electoral reforms in time for the 1977 legislative and municipal elections so that 1994's chaos over voter registration is not repeated. 'It is a crucial moment. If the Accords are not fully implemented in 1996, they may never be. The fragile process of democratisation must be consolidated, or it could quickly deteriorate.'[237]

Ex-combatants

The reinsertion of ex-combatants from both sides into civil society is a large part of the reconstruction programme (described fully in *Rescuing Reconstruction*). As with so many aspects of the peace process, this part of the programme has been implemented to some extent but not fully. With regard to the land there have been many delays in transferring it and providing title deeds. 'Those who did succeed in obtaining land have had trouble getting credit, technical assistance and training. The reduced size of the plots is a further obstacle to the development of productive and sustainable farming. This situation feeds the frustration of the ex-combatants on both sides. Many have abandoned their plots and have swelled the ranks of migrants to the United States.'[238]

One might think that reconciliation between those who have been physically fighting each other for so long would be the most difficult kind to achieve, but in reality it is probably easier than most. As Archbishop Romero said, both the soldiers and the guerrillas were mainly poor peasants with identical backgrounds. Many soldiers were forcibly recruited and all were brutalised into carrying out dreadful deeds against those they were taught to call 'subversives'.[239] Ought there not to be an international human right of soldiers not to be brutalised? The accounts of what they can be subjected to are horrifying.[240] Now communities of ex-guerrillas and their supporters and communities of ex-military are having to learn to live side by side again and realising that they all need health clinics, schools, loans to buy seeds, training for the disabled etc. There have been several joint demonstrations by ex-combatants of both sides demanding the help they were promised under the Peace Accords and have not yet received.

As well as reconciliation between ex-combatants of the two sides there is a need for reconciliation between ex-combatants and post-war civil society which can see them as a threat. A very imaginative project for tackling this problem is being developed by the Centre for International Studies (CEI) in Managua, Nicaragua, which is bringing together ex-combatants from Nicaragua, El Salvador and Mozambique to share their experiences and to explore ways of actively promoting reconciliation and reconstruction in their communities. CEI Director, Alejandro Bendana, writes, 'In and of themselves, cease-fires, elections and political power-sharing will not produce democracy and development. Institutional arrangements in each country remain fragile, as negotiated agreements at the top can rapidly unravel or indeed fail to hold much consequence for those at the bottom. Herein lies the importance of promoting peace-building and reconciliation from below, and specifically with the active participation of organised former combatants.'[241]

Divisions in the FMLN

It is not only between traditional opponents from right and left that reconciliation is needed. There are often serious divisions between those who are theoretically on the same side. The March 1994 elections gave Suchitoto an FMLN Mayor (succeeding the ARENA mayor mentioned above). It happens that four of the five FMLN parties are present in that area and members of the factions other than that of the new Mayor expressed concern that he might give preference to 'his own people', even though all the factions are represented on the Municipal Council.

During the conflict the five FMLN armies, as they then were, all strongly territorially based, subordinated their differences to the needs of the war but after the peace agreement it was understandably much harder for them to unite in a single political party with an agreed programme and a single presidential candidate. Two of the factions withdrew from the FMLN to form another party, now called the Democratic Party. The remainder are managing to become more united, with the old factions as 'tendencies' within a single party. Having to spend so much time on getting established as political parties in the capital, and to take part in so many negotiations, not to mention power struggles, meant that the opposition factions gave insufficient attention to their grassroots base in the countryside and we found much disillusionment among communities who felt they had been abandoned, even betrayed, by the leaders from whom they had expected so much in the post-war situation. So reconciliation between leaders and base is needed too.

The territoriality of the FMLN factions means that almost all the resettled communities in the ex-conflictive zones are also linked to one or other of the groups. We heard of one community which, unusually, included supporters of three different factions so they set up three separate management committees. Each faction also has NGOs linked to it, working with the communities, and they do not always co-operate fully with each other. With any luck this may just be a temporary post-conflict phase and there are people working at grassroots level to overcome it. The two North American religious sisters who were working with the women we met in Suchitoto said that the women's organisations there were managing to attract members from all parties and that women were better than men at surmounting such divisions and building friendships as individuals.

The women's movement
We met with a wide range of women in early 1994 to learn about their experiences and the part played by their faith in helping them to survive. We were very impressed and moved by their strength and their determination to improve not

only the lives of women but the community as a whole. They told us that they see their most important role as keeping little flames of hope alive in this time of transition and uncertainty. The key concept in their programmes is that of dignity. One of the most effective organisations is called *Women for Dignity and Life*. These are basic needs of all women, indeed all people. Yet it is not always easy for the various women's groups to work together harmoniously. Some groups are linked to political parties, others work within the church, but many women feel both these contexts are too male-dominated and undemocratic to allow women to develop fully within them and want their groups to remain autonomous. There is a co-ordination of many women's groups but some way to go before all are willing to work closely together. Nevertheless we felt that the women's movement, which is growing rapidly, is one of the most fruitful ways forward towards reconciliation. Mercedes Canas of the Centre for Feminist Studies told us, 'What unites us is the desire that our lives may contribute to transforming the lives of women, because we know that transforming the lives of women is to transform the world and to make a truly democratic El Salvador.' As well as meeting a wide variety of individual women we also attended a pre-election women's rally in the capital at which women candidates from the entire spectrum of political parties shared the same platform and responded to the same set of questions – the first time such a thing has ever been possible in El Salvador.

Reconciling perceptions
One of the things which repeatedly moved us deeply in our conversations with women was how little feeling of vengefulness or hatred one finds among people who suffered so dreadfully from the military repression, some losing ten or twelve family members in the most barbaric circumstances. Most of them seem to accept that the soldiers were forced to do what they did and would have been killed themselves if

they had refused. A very telling incident happened during our visit to a group of women in Suchitoto in 1994. Their tragic experiences had by no means crushed their spirit and they were all organising women's activities in their different areas. They pointed out to us a woman sitting outside on the pavement begging and told us she had been an informer and many local people had been killed because of her denunciations. But they explained that they did not feel bitter towards her as they knew she had only done it because she was desperate for money to feed her family and they now tried to help her when they could. Later, a lorryful of election campaigners for the governing ARENA party (founded by Major Roberto D'Aubuisson who is widely believed to have ordered the murder of Archbishop Romero) trundled along the road with loudspeakers blaring. Those same women rushed out into the street shouting 'Murderers! Murderers!' They can forgive the individuals who actually did the deeds but not those interests which were ultimately responsible for them.

It is harder for people in the capital who did not see so much of the repression and the conflict at first hand, but suffered from the FMLN blowing up electricity pylons, and who are influenced by the strongly right-wing media and ARENA propaganda blaming all the violence on the guerrillas. There is a great deal of 'perception management' at work even over such a famous case as the murder of Archbishop Romero. A delightful teenage girl we know, from a middle-class city family whose knowledge of current affairs comes mainly from the vituperative ARENA-supporting daily *El Diario de Hoy*, told us of taking part at school in a reconstruction of Romero's death and referred to a friend taking the part of 'the guerrilla who shot him'. That is what she is taught at school. Her older cousin kept a scrapbook of all the laudatory obituaries and reminiscences published on the occasion of Roberto D'Aubuisson's death. He is held up as a saintly figure by ARENA and we recently heard that on the fourth anniversary of his death masses were held for him in seventeen churches in San Salvador, praising him as a role model for the youth of the country. The majority of Salvadorans already regard Oscar Romero (to ARENA a 'communist sympathiser') as a saint. It will take a long time to bring reconciliation between those opposing perceptions.

Hope for the future
During the conflict, in the FMLN-controlled zones of El Salvador and in refugee camps and communities outside the country, people began to develop a society based on close co-operation and participation. That helped them to survive in their perilous situation and gave them confidence in their ability to organise their own lives and a vision for a better future. Many of them had also been strengthened in their faith by experiencing religion as a community activity in Base Ecclesial Communities in which everyone contributed. Now they find themselves living under a predominant ideology where individualism and market forces reign even more supreme than they do here. Without our social security safety net, cuts in already insufficient public spending, to meet structural adjustment conditions imposed by the International Monetary Fund and the World Bank, are increasing the already high level of poverty and making it harder for people to care about anything but their own survival.

Many of the communities of repatriated refugees and ex-combatants, who were held so closely together in wartime conditions, are finding it difficult to work co-operatively in the new context. However, we are hearing that in the cities and in parts of the country which were not so conflictive (it is extraordinary what big differences there are between regions of this tiny country the size of Wales) many successful new co-operative ventures are springing up to start small businesses, credit schemes, projects in appropriate technology, growing non-traditional crops, in fact a whole range of activities. Many of these, and of course the resettled communities too, are supported by aid agencies, including British ones. A good reconciliatory project would be to encourage links for mutual inspiration between these newer community ventures and the resettled communities which have developed their own health clinics and schools staffed largely by health workers and teachers from the communities themselves, facilities which the newer communities often lack. Young people who have been through this system of 'popular education' are now doing well in high schools and going on to university in the capital. Some of them, not surprisingly, are lured by city life, but others remain involved in their communities and will help them to progress.

People in the churches, as well as the women's movement, have told us that their hope lies in small initiatives slowly bringing about change, based on concepts such as human dignity for all people as children of God rather than on political theories. Sometimes during the conflict the needs of individuals were sacrificed for the survival of the community. Now the ethos urges individual advancement and the devil take the community. Somehow finding a way of life which reconciles the real needs of individuals with the needs of a healthy community and a healthy environment is a goal as important for us as for El Salvador. We have great faith that the richness of experience, both good and bad, of the Salvadoran people, and their spiritual strength will produce solutions from which we can all learn.

Select Bibliography

Kevin Murray with Tom Barry, *Inside El Salvador* (Latin America Bureau, 1995)

Phillip Berryman, *The Religious Roots of Rebellion: Christians in the Central American Revolutions* (SCM Press, 1984)

Jenny Pearce, *Promised Land: Peasant Rebellion in Chalatenango, El Salvador* (Latin America Bureau, 1986)

Pamela Hussey, *Free from Fear: Women in El Salvador's Church* (CIIR, 1989)

Pablo Galdamez, *Faith of a People: The Life of a Basic Christian Community in El Salvador* (CIIR, 1986)

Mandy Macdonald and Mike Gatehouse, *In the Mountains of Morazan: Portrait of a Returned Refugee Community in El Salvador* (Latin America Bureau, 1995)

Reconciliation in the Struggle

Theological reflections from the Rebellious
Women of Latin America

Marcella Althaus-Reid

A group of indigenous women from the north of Argentina is covering two tables with the clothes which used to belong to their neighbour. A well-used peasant hat goes at the head of the table, a poncho (traditional cloak) is put in the middle, while at the end someone arranges with care a pair of rubber sandals. Nearby, on another small table, the arrangement made is for a baby: an open tin of milk powder and a knitted shawl. Once the arrangements on the tables have been made, the whole community gathers together for the night to sing, pray and drink to the memory of the desaparecidos[242] (the disappeared), of the village. Finally, with songs and tears, they proceed to bury the clothes and belongings. The point is that for the indigenous people of Argentina, there cannot be funeral rituals without bodies, and without those rituals the souls of the departed cannot rest in peace. Neither can the souls of the survivors.

The cruel *Guerra Sucia* (Dirty War)[243] killed approximately thirty thousand people but never returned their bodies: they became known as *desaparecidos*. In response, the indigenous people of Argentina devised a new funerary ritual without the bodies, but with some clothes and belongings of the dear ones as a replacement. The women created the ritual, and gave it to their community as a gesture of reconciling them-selves with crime, injustice and the silence of God. It came from their spirituality of resistance and struggle, which at some deep level was not ready to accept the religious implications of *desaparecidos* bodies. They re-created the presence of their beloved ones through the ritual of clothes and belongings. They affirmed what the political repression wanted to deny, that is, that those people existed, belonged to a community and are remembered.

In Latin America, we cannot speak about peace and reconciliation without speaking first about concrete everyday things such as food, health and education and, more specifically, without speaking of the fate of the thousands of citizens who died under dictatorial regimes this century. A Peruvian theologian, Gustavo Gutiérrez, has spoken about the historical subject in Latin America as 'the cactus person' (*la persona cactus*),[244] as a metaphor for a person who is not only poor, but who has lost the basic elements of human dignity in her/his life; such an individual could be personified in the figure of the *desaparecido* because, in that case, a person's whole identity and existence has been obliterated from history. The *desaparecido* was a person whose belongings were also taken, his/her house sold, and even their clothes and decoration were distributed as 'war trophies' amongst the military forces. As the family and friends of the *desaparecido* were forced to remain silent, without talking about the abduction of that person, and since the media also ignored these abductions, the *desaparecidos* became the ultimate symbol of being a non-person in Latin America. Precisely for that reason, the *desaparecido* is the subject of our theological reflections, but from a different perspective from a traditional theology which tried first to think about God, and second about humanity. In this case, following the methodology of Liberation Theology, the order is reversed. What we want to know is what the women who struggle for human rights during the time of the *desaparecidos* can tell us about God, and God in our historical circumstances.

Under the present democratic systems in Argentina, as elsewhere in Latin America, the voices for peace and reconciliation have risen from different fields, identifying a need to heal the wounds of the past and start anew. However, the women who were active in the struggle for human rights in Argentina, such as the *Madres de Plaza* de *Mayo*,[245] have some lessons for a better understanding of how this process of reconciliation may be defined. Basically, what is needed for the woman and man *cactus* of the continent is a reconciliation process which can actually transform things and circumstances, and help to articulate a new social order. Latin American Theology of Liberation reappropriates the collective, transforming power of reconciliation processes, and tries to learn from them the genuine spirituality of the people in situations of oppression and rebellion. The issue of food, for instance, is a theological issue, because it confronts us with the violence of the structures of hunger and death, which take away not only lives, but also human hope and the dignity of people. However, Latin American Christians are in search of an efficacious spirituality; one that can actually challenge and eventually change the structures of death underlined in situations of poverty. For that reason, the concept of reconciliation has become alien to Latin Americans when understood as a synonym of a call to 'historical amnesia', and to forgive and forget a basic unjust order which tends to repeat its crimes with punctual regularity.

Reconciliation is then a concept which has been re-defined by Latin American people and has acquired other names: justice is one of them. Another name for reconciliation is as synonymous with women, especially with *Madres* and with their *Espiritualidad Guerrera* (Fighting Spirituality). This *Espiritualidad* has taken different forms through peculiar historical circumstances and the characteristics of different Latin American countries. From the Mexican women who fought with bows and arrows against the invasion of their country by Europeans in the fifteenth century, to the Widows of Guatemala and the *Madres de Plaza de Mayo* in Argentina, in all of them we find that the theme of reconciliation carries three main distinctive elements: first, they do not accept the unjust situation and denounce it in some form of confrontation; second, they keep the memory of what has happened, and oppose any form of officially declared amnesia; and third, they work to find ways to avoid the repetition of acts of injustice in their society. In this paper we would analyse the Latin American women's *Espiritualidad Guerrera* as a key to understanding the type of reconciliation processes we have highlighted. We will consider in particular the case of the Madres and from their experience in the struggle we will consider the emergent feminist popular theology which has opposed the forces of dictatorship in Argentina.

Reconciliation in struggle
First of all we need to understand the genesis of this reconciliation in struggle, which does not begin after a tragedy such as the gross violation of human rights which happened in Argentina during the 1970s. In fact, there have been always women in the 'hidden history' of Latin America who struggled for freedom in their countries, from the brave indigenous women who fought against the European invaders to women such as Domitila Chungara or Rigoberta Menchú.[246] For that purpose, we need first of all to define what we mean by reconciliation. Reconciliation is a word which literally means 'to bring together'. It applies to people but also to structures which are considered to be dissimilar in methods although not necessarily in purpose, but by any means reconciliation is a concept generally homologised with peace. However, Latin American women, through their action and reflection, have added to reconciliation the further dimension of 'reconciliation in struggle', when their process of reconciliation is started by bringing together the people who stood against the dictatorship and reconciling them in an ecumenical, broadly based political alliance for the lives of the *desaparecidos*. The women whose children were taken away by force to be incarcerated and killed

started their struggle with a process that involved bringing together anonymous people, whether or not direct victims of the political repression. Reconciliation in struggle, then, is precisely the process of bringing together, beyond personal circumstances (for instance, actually having been a victim of the repression or not) or even political ideas, the people who believe in the sacrality of human life at all cost. Latin American women have done this in situations where hunger, disease, racial oppression and violence required them to reconcile life, that is, the people who were ready to defend life in various ways, from organising free meals for children to political demonstrations. One of the most common types of popular women's organisations, the *Comedores Populares* (People's Soup Kitchen), were created by an alliance of poor women as protest and resistance against economic oppression, and also as political denunciation of official policies. To do that, women need to confront *Machista*[247] structures who do not allow them to leave the space of domestic life and intervene in public issues.

The organisation of movements of reconciliation in struggle made by women in Latin America is primarily contextual. The movements reflect the challenges and difficulties of a specific historical period but they have certain characteristics in common, such as the following.

- The women organisers come from the *Barrios* (poor neighbourhoods) and, more specifically, from the marginalised *Barrios*. They are women geographically and politically located at the margins of the centres of power of the big cities, by a conjunction of factors such as age, social class, gender and race.
- They respond to a concrete situation of need or injustice in their lives or in the lives of their communities. Their knowledge of the situation which needs to be addressed is first hand, and their reflection based on suffering experienced in their lives.

401

- At least at the beginning, the women consider their organisation to be apolitical and without any religious affiliation. The political awareness in most of cases comes as the result of their own analysis of a particular situation and their struggle to change the circumstances of oppression. In the case of the *Madres*, they themselves confess that they were simple housekeepers, and many said that they did not understand politics, nor were they interested in issues of the government of the country. Some say that they did not even read the newspapers before being confronted with the disappearance of their family.[248] In relation to the religious dimension that the *Madres* or other women's movements in Latin America may have, it is interesting to notice that although most women come from a Christian background, they find the development of a spirituality of struggle incompatible with any formal link to a church.

Espiritualidad Guerrera

The 'fighting spirituality' of the *Madres*, as with many other Latin American women historically, has not been able to find a place in the church or in other institutions, even political ones, without taking the risk of distorting their identity as an organisation and even some of their principles. Some of the reasons for that are contextual. Latin America is a very heavily patriarchal continent, where even radical movements up till today have silenced women, but there are other things to be considered too. Basically, the *Madres* are confronted with the difficulties of trying to institutionalise prophecy. This fighting spirituality does not produce unifying theological concepts or reflections, because it is grounded in the historical process of a nation, and therefore it acquires a dynamism of thought and action. Such spirituality could not be incorporated in the church without producing at the same time deep structural changes. The theology which encourages forgiveness without change has been called by Latin Americans 'Ostrich

Theology'[249] because, like the ostrich (a popular animal in the continent), it puts its head under the ground instead of facing the situation. Such theology uses a cover up of cheap forgiveness instead of being part of a process in whose origins we have the denunciation of the oppressive structures. Women like the *Madres* have made a theology of their call to all who want to defend life to form an alliance to protect life beyond boundaries of political or religious beliefs. In that sense, it is a prophetic spirituality. It does not offer easy bargains of peace and understanding; neither has it a solution for the broken lives for whom reconciliation is only a very abstract concept. Its strength is its prophetism, that is, the dynamism and analysis of the situations as they are in the present, denouncing the mistakes of the past and looking for a transformation which lies at the roots of the conflict. For the same reason, the prophets of the Hebrew Scriptures did not organise people into institutions, but remained at the edge of religious institutions in order to preserve their freedom of action and thought. The materialist, down to earth approach of women's spirituality in Latin America, apart from that element of prophetism, has a liturgical and a sacramental dimension which is very relevant for the present moment in the lives of Argentinian people and Latin Americans in general. Let us consider how these dimensions have key elements to understand and live this reconciliation in the struggle which seems to be so needed not only in Latin America, but in the rest of the world.

'To whom does a Cathedral belong?'[250]

On the 8th of July 1996, a day before the celebration of the Argentinian Independence Day, a group of thirteen *Madres* wearing their distinctive white scarf, the youngest being sixty-one years old and the oldest eighty-four, went to the Roman Catholic Cathedral of Buenos Aires. They went to pray in silent solidarity for the conditions of poverty under which many fellow citizens are living. In their hands they carried only the *misales*, that is, the prayer books which used to belong to their *desaparecidos* children. Some women walked into the Cathedral with the help of their canes, one needed a tripod. While they were kneeling in prayer, a priest came and told them to leave the Cathedral immediately. They refused and explained that they were there as Christian women to pray, but finally, the local priest called the police and the *Madres* were taken out by force from the Cathedral. Some later needed medical treatment in the hospital due to the injuries inflicted by the armed forces. After the episode, one of the *Madres* asked, 'To whom does this Cathedral belong?' For the people who were witnesses of the police intervention in the Cathedral, the theological reflections were centred around that very issue. Some asked if the priest 'had bought the Cathedral' and if so, 'with whose money, since they do not work'.[251]

It is interesting to notice that people recognise the prophetic, fighting spirituality in their spontaneous reflections on situations such as the one described. The figure of the Cathedral was compared by witnesses of this episode with the Temple in the New Testament's narrative in Mark 13 and the cursing of the fig tree in Mark 11. Someone pointed out that the fruits of the Cathedral, as a symbol of the Roman Catholic Church in the country, should be fruits of justice, of sharing in solidarity amongst the dispossessed and a project towards a society with peace and equality. Therefore, if the Cathedral cannot bear such fruits, it should be cut down as a fig tree without fruits, and the words of Jesus about the destruction of the Temple must then be applied to Buenos Aires too. At a popular level, such as the group of people (mainly students) who gathered opposite the Cathedral that day, many are inspired by the *Madres'* fighting spirituality to biblical reflections in which the prophetic style of the Hebrew communities described in the Scriptures becomes alive.

The prayer day at the Cathedral is a typical example of the

liturgical gestures of the *Madres*, who are still struggling for a reconciliation at a national level after the Dirty War, but not through forgetfulness of the facts lying beneath the tragic decade of the *desaparecidos*, such as poverty and injustice. The importance of liturgical gestures such as going to pray at the Cathedral of Buenos Aires (which represents the presence of the Roman Catholic Church in Argentina, and is located opposite the May Square and the Government Palace) lies in the fact that history is remembered at popular levels basically through symbolic actions. The *Madres* with their scarves and their children's prayer books present a counter liturgy to the services for reconciliation usually offered in the country. Their liturgies oppose the easy peace which 'ostrich theologies' proclaim, and introduce a rebellious sense of peace characteristic of prophetic movements.

Rebellious peace

The *Kairos* document from the Central American Churches asks Christians 'to make an option for the poor, but for the rebellious poor'.[252] The Madres from Plaza de Mayo are the rebellious poor women who disturbed the false feeling of peace created by a strong policy of censorship in the mass media, and a system based on accusation of political disagreements which extended from eavesdropping on other people's conversations on the public transports, to reporting things said in confession to priest supporters of the dictatorship. What needed to be reconciled, that is, brought together was people's trust and solidarity and also the dispersed hope of change which felt impotent under the heavy structures of dictatorship. This is why peace needed to be rebellious. The *Madres* acted by unmasking that false peace, and showing that real peace required political confrontation, but the strength needed for that could only come from their own spirituality, which basically has been a spirituality of life. As one of the *Madres* has said, 'We were called "the crazy ones" from Plaza de Mayo (May Square), because they [the dictatorship] had no concept of the strength of a mother and a woman, so able to confront a criminal dictatorship.'[253] Their madness seems to be linked to the crossing of religious and social boundaries of Latin American women, whose lives are meant to be spent in the domestic areas of life, but not in the public ones. They are also called *transgresoras* (transgressors) because they go against the prevailing injustice of a established social order. After leaving the Cathedral, one *Madre* commented 'Once again, we pulled down some masks . . .'[254] Unmasking the powers is done through symbolic gestures and actions where reconciliation calls for justice in the past and in the present.

Re-conciling as a sacramental act of re-membering
The phenomenon of the *desaparecidos* is different from other situations of political crimes. The *desaparecidos* literally 'disappear' from society without leaving a trace; suddenly, someone does not go to work, or to a place of study. From one day to the other, family and friends do not see their beloved one again. A child does not sit at the table for meals any more; a baby does not have a mother near her and a grandfather will never again go to visit his married children and grandchildren simply because they are not to be found any more amongst them. There are no witnesses of what has happened and enquiries to the police or to hospitals only receive either negative answers or threatening statements. The point is that it is against the logic of the *desaparecidos* to know about their fate. Therefore, *Madres* were asked to forget about their children and grandchildren, accepting that they have never existed. Reconciliation started then with an act of remembering as affirming the knowledge of the existence of a human being, and also of remembering as telling the society that the *desaparecidos* are part of it, and that they belong to a community which needs to re-member them, that is, to stake a claim for the ones who are an important part of that

body. This act of re-membering is the reconciliation act *par excellence*, reaffirming life and reclaiming it by saying that in reality, people do not disappear: people die, and then, there are bodies left, and their relatives have the right to claim their dear ones alive or dead. They are still part of us, of our communities and of our nations. When the *Madres* put home-made posters around Buenos Aires depicting silhouettes with a name and a date of birth and disappearance, suddenly the city, by that symbolic gesture, re-membered into its society thirty thousand women, men and children who were part of our communities, who although deliberately ignored by the government, existed and who, either alive or dead, formed part and influenced the context of our lives. The act of ignoring people who are considered '*desaparecidos*' matches the attitude of ignoring politics of poverty and injustice. In a way, the posters with the silhouettes of the people killed during the seventies and the sitting in the Cathedral are part of the same liturgy of re-membering with obstinacy which is a sacrament of remembrance in itself. The act is to re-member the suffering community as the body of Christ, denouncing while announcing a social order more in tune with the reign of God announced in the gospel. Re-membering is the Christ-act of final reconciliation of God with the world, in the sense of making God's people one body and also keeping a permanent memory of the passion of Christ when he confronted the structures of power of his time.

The problem of suffering and reconciliation in the struggle

Reconciliation in struggle as shown by the *Madres* teaches us how the actual process of reconciling starts with a prophetic denunciation of the injustice amidst us and a courageous alliance with people who believe in the sanctity and dignity of human life. The *Madres* represent the voice of a majority which is in reality a minority, considering how little political and theological representation women in Latin America have in general. The character of their work for peace is very significant because it fully acknowledges the human dimension of suffering without denying emotions, and in this case, women's emotions related to losing a child, and that knowledge and being in the world is relational. According to the traditions of Latin American Original Nations, people do not exist on their own and therefore it is right to say that the feminist principle of subjectivity demonstrated in the action and reflection of the *Madres* is already part of the cultural heritage of the continent. However, the concept of mutuality which exists in many orders of life has not been able to generate a practical answer to the problem of suffering in Latin America. Moreover, the spiritual response to suffering through heavy structures of sin such as economic policies of hunger and repressive regimes has traditionally been, amongst the poor, a response either of resignation or of over-spiritualisation of material suffering.

As the poor masses have been historically disempowered, the acceptance of poverty and violence either as the will of God or as part of the powers of evil in this world has taken the place of serious analysis and strategy for change in the continent. The traditional theology has found it easier to disembody people's suffering to the point of talking about reconciliation as the act of assimilation of suffering to a doctrinal meaning, in the same way that something considered 'minor' needs to accept a major, sacred global conceptualisation of the meaning of life and human suffering. This concept of reconciliation is close to the idea of harmony as a supreme value of the Christian faith, whose unmeasured cost is usually a feeling of impotence when confronting injustices, resulting in a consequent chronic lack of hope and action. Harmony as the idea of reconciliation at all costs eliminates human emotions and the subjective knowledge of the suffering community, and encourages instead an idealistic future where suffering still exists but is always subjugated to a sacred self-explanatory order.

The prophetic strength of the *Madres* lies in another theological space. It is the historical and not the metaphysical future which grounds their reflection, and therefore, it is not a process of harmonisation but of rupture which is required from the community. Harmony would come, in any case, through an acknowledgement of the tensions and contradictions involved in reconciling as a peace process while the causes of suffering still remain in society and there has not been a judicial procedure for the killing of thirty thousand citizens, plus the theft of their properties and goods.[255]

The sacramental memory of reconciliation in struggle
Women in Latin America are the keepers of the memory of the continent. Excluded from history in a very male dominated culture, they have traditionally kept the memory of their race through traditional religious ceremonies, ritual and story telling. The language of the silenced people, gossip, murmurs, denigrated by patriarchal systems as the fabric of lies and misinformation, is sometimes the only source of knowledge and communication when other forms, either by tradition or by political censorship, are banned. Women in Argentina have traditionally gone to the markets to buy fresh food but also for an opportunity to socialise and to engage in the political reality of the country through discussing the prices, the newspaper stories; and in that non-threatening atmosphere, they became a political community of women involved in the aspects of their country from which they have been traditionally excluded. While the media ignored the reality of the *desaparecidos* at the same time justifying ideologically and theologically the need to expurgate from society, in a 'justified war', anti-Christian communist elements, the *Madres* started to gather together for information, support and planning what to do, in the typical way of women, that is, observing and chatting with other women.

One of the Madres explained how she started. She had lost a son, and went into the ordeal of asking for her son at police stations, hospitals and even the city morgue. In all the places she had to wait long hours for a reply that was always negative, and sometimes ironic and hurtful if not threatening for her own life and the life of her surviving family. She decided to go and sit in the hospitals, looking for other women who perhaps, like herself, could come with a photograph of a *desaparecido*, trying to find some details about his or her life. In that way, she would see another *Madre* doing the same pilgrimage that she had been doing, and ask her if she was like herself, searching for a beloved one taken away by the state. At the beginning, other *Madres* reacted to her approach with suspicion and fear, but later, they were able to gather together trust and hopes and the organised search for their family began. In silence they went to sit on benches in the May Square, opposite the Government Palace. Because of the sun, they covered their heads with their big, old fashioned cotton handkerchiefs, while waiting for some answers from the government. The obstinacy of their memory, as the memory of their lost families and the strategy of political persecution in their country, not only kept them alive, but kept the country alive as the prophets of the Hebrew Scriptures did when they interpreted the presence of God amongst the suffering people.

The point is that in the long suffering Latin America, with five hundred years of human rights violations and cultural and political oppression, reconciliation as a concept has always been imposed over people in the name of Christianity as a way of not considering seriously the crimes that have been committed, the ideology behind them and a transformation of the conditions which gave place to such violations. For the women who devised a funerary ritual with the clothes of the *desaparecidos*, the reconciliation liturgy was a necessary sacrament in order to bring peace to the dead according to their traditional beliefs. The vehicle of the sacrament as an outward sign was represented by the belongings of the abducted people upon which God's peace was understood to be conferred. However, the permanent struggle of the *Madres* of May Square, not only in relation to the *desaparecidos* but also in the transformation of the political-economical structures of the country, has also developed sacramental liturgical acts coming from their fighting spirituality. In a Christian continent such as Latin America, this seems to be the force of transformation and courage which comes from the poor, and especially from poor women. Their reconciliation in the struggle is an example of the kind of reconciliation process which is necessary in order to achieve a long lasting, transformative peace as the one proclaimed in the gospels, with the creativity that the Spirit gives to the ones who dare to speak truth to power. The sacrament of reconciliation is given here by the permanent offering of their lives in the struggle for justice, in which God and God's people (both victims and those responsible for the massacres) can finally come together for a new beginning.

Some years ago, during a popular Bible study done in a poor community of El Salvador, a woman pointed out that to forgive means to liberate someone from a situation of sin.[256] Jesus' forgiveness is always liberating, as the start of a new life in real freedom. Perhaps one of the most significant aspects of the work of the *Madres* is this unquenchable thirst for forgiveness, demonstrated through the years in the systematic unmasking of the differences between a cheap forgiveness leading to a false sense of reconciliation, and a true reconciliation process that makes of people active subjects and not mere passive objects of forgiveness. That is the essence of what I have called reconciliation in the struggle, as shown by poor Latin American women as a gift not only to our continent but to the world.

Churches and Ecumenical Movements in Latin America Struggling for Human Rights

Aldo M. Etchegoyen

This frank chapter aims at being a contribution towards an understanding of the predicament of the church and the movements for human rights when protecting life in Latin America. The theme is a broad one and can be looked at from various points of view. I will attempt to recount some central issues knowing that others may be omitted.

The urgency of the problem

One morning somebody knocks at the door of the pastor's office. When it is answered a man with his family appears who says, 'We have had to leave our country and we need asylum and support. Can you help us?'

Another day a mother recounts her personal drama: 'Last night my son disappeared. I'm desperate. What can I do? Where can I turn?'

These simple stories bring me to the first point which I wish to make. The defence of human rights in Latin America is an outcome of the urgent need to preserve human life in the face of the military power which, in 1973, began the wave of domination and repression.

Many times, without the necessary organisation, we have to confront serious violations of human rights which demand our attention. In this there is a great similarity to what happened, in the Bible story, to the Samaritan who went down from Jerusalem to Jericho and came upon the wounded man hurled to one side of the road. The wounded man needed immediate help and the Samaritan gave it to him. The same sort of thing can be transferred to many situations in all Latin America.

Later came time for thought and the setting up of programmes but this was always in the middle of activity for preserving human life. It was a process of practical help and thought in which theology and concrete action opened up a way forward together.

An ecumenical struggle for human life

There was no time to consider our different Christian traditions, on the contrary, ecumenical action was essential. The life of one of our neighbours was in danger and we had to be united when helping those concerned and their near families. In this way arose various ecumenical movements and church projects which confronted the situation and I must highlight the firm support that the World Council of Churches gave in pastoral and economic help in the face of such overwhelming violence. Whoever exposed their lives in defence of human rights in Latin America will never cease expressing their deep thanks to God for the company of churches and other organisations and communities in the world especially in Europe, Canada and the USA. In this context I wish to express our appreciation and gratitude to the Reverend Charles Harper of the Bureau for Human Rights in Latin America of the World Council of Churches. He was much more than an official and became a real friend in this mission to save lives.

Nevertheless I am only telling half the truth when we think of ecumenism as just being between churches. Practical help and thought where lay people, pastors, priests, bishops, rabbis, agnostics, politicians, guilds, teachers, men and women of many different kinds of training and religious, political and social categories put their hands and minds into this struggle. I cannot continue without underlining here and now the real worth of this ecumenical scenario as a place for Christian witness and at the same time a setting for learning and mutual training. In this scenario where we are united we can read together signs of the times and together we make vital decisions where an error of judgement could cost us our lives. So we Christians learn that the arm of God is broader than that of the church and that the leaven of the kingdom of God is able to leaven the dough so that we may be nourished and able to accompany victims in their suffering and raise together a prophetic voice and walk together arm in arm to denounce oppression and defend truth and justice.

Criteria of action

From the perspective of the Christian faith the criteria of our actions were very worthwhile and founded in the Bible. They were values born of the word of God, his prophets, his patriarchs and in Jesus Christ and in the teaching of the apostles was the light which lit up our way.

As an example of this I go back to the Document of the Second Meeting of Latin American and Caribbean Ecumenical Organisations for Human Rights which took place in Quito, Ecuador, from the 16th to the 21st October 1989. On that occasion we were accompanied by our brothers from Canada, World Council of Churches, the Latin American Council of Churches and the Conference of Churches of the Caribbean. In an atmosphere of prayer, thought and brotherly communion was reaffirmed our commitment for the lives and the rights of both individuals and peoples. Our affirmation was the following:

> WE AFFIRM that our support and driving force for the defence of human rights we find in the Word of God. From this basis we consider the reality of Latin America and the Caribbean. The Bible gives us light to see true reality and points out our way.
> WE AFFIRM that humankind has been created in the

image and likeness of God as the highest point of his creative work. Consequently the life of everybody is sacred and of worth no matter what his economic position, his social condition, his culture or his education, the colour of his skin or any other condition whatsoever.

WE AFFIRM that the historic moment our peoples are living through now is comparable to the exodus of the people of God in their journey towards fullness of life. Our people yearn for freedom from the various forms of oppression to which they are submitted.

WE AFFIRM that the aim and objective of this journey is fullness of life expressed in food, land, work, education, health, culture, freedom, brotherhood and solidarity. We believe that all this bears witness to the majesty of God, his kingdom and his justice which are true and eternal.

WE AFFIRM that on our way towards this objective we confront the forces of death through injustice, dependency, oppression, terrorism, violence, falsehood, people disappearing, torture, the drugs trade, marginalisation and other realities of humanity. The words of the prophets nevertheless continue to condemn all these manifestations of sin.

WE AFFIRM that the suffering of our people and our martyrs contain the force of the resurrection, as when the grain of wheat dies in order to be born to a new life which gives food and hope. It is suffering like that of a woman in travail which precedes the new creation, the work of God.

WE AFFIRM that we find freedom in truth, that justice is the basis for peace and that in our neighbour in need is our meeting place with God moved by his love which drives us on.

WE AFFIRM that the way to reconciliation is opened when there is true repentance and forgiveness.

WE AFFIRM that our hope lies in Jesus Christ, the Lord of Life. Through him has burst upon us the victory of the resurrection over the forces of sin and death.

WE AFFIRM that his kingdom will come and that his will will be accomplished over everything and everyone, as the waters cover the bed of the sea.

416

Steps forwards and backwards

The people of Latin America and the Caribbean love life and aspire to living it in full. This aspiration confronts a contrasting sense of purpose which is that of foreign power centres and of people who are acting within their own countries and who seek to maintain and reinforce the structures of domination and injustice which violate the lives and dignity of individuals and populations.

When we contemplate the reality of our countries in this last decade we are aware of moving forwards and backwards in the struggle for life and justice. On the one hand we note that, looking beyond the diversity and complexity of different situations, those who benefit from structures of dependency and injustice have perfected their structures so as to maintain patterns of oppression. This has meant that in this decade our region has continued to exist under the reality of a structure of violence which has not merely been maintained but strengthened.

Nevertheless, on the other hand, we also realise that:

- we have managed to consolidate projects based on national self-determination and on a better sense of justice between social groups
- we have been given procedures leading towards democracy after long years of suffering military dictatorships
- we have put up resistance when confronting situations being maintained which mean the negation of human rights for a large part of the populace and the impossibility, for some national communities, of exercising their right to sovereignty.
- the struggle continues among people who are still suffering from a continuation of colonialism.

Perverse structures

When we carefully look at the contradictory reality of our region we realise that a particularly perverse barrier to the maintenance of human rights among our people is that of

417

foreign debt. The indebtedness of our countries towards creditor institutions and governments has as a direct result that the rich have increased their wealth while the great majority have been dramatically submerged in unbearable poverty. Besides this it has led to an increasing impoverishment of the middle classes. The mortgaging of society that repaying the debt produces has forced these economies to allow in international capital which at the same time reduces the possibility of investing in social and development programmes. This in turn implies the loss of self-determination of our people. The way foreign debt works has reinforced the economic structures which encourage the concentration of national income among small, dominant social groups and the transference of our wealth to creditor countries and institutions. It is necessary to point out that in many cases loans to various states were not used for the development of our people. The situation is made worse because there is an unjust arrangement in international economic relationships with unfair rates of exchange between rich and poor countries.

Another reality is the advance of international power groups which has reversed the working of national economies and enslaved peoples' own life styles. These centres of power promulgate their own ideology and cultural models by making use, among other mechanisms, of the systems of mass communication.

Linked with international activity is also that of internal power groups which reinforce an unjust social and cultural economic model which leads to violent situations and the systematic violation of human rights. The phenomenon of marginalisation is aggravated with peasants dispossessed of their land, millions of people having to move from the country to the town or to other countries. Unemployment becomes chronic, the numbers of 'homeless' increase, health services become out of the reach of the majority. The situation of children who wander in their millions through the streets of our cities is particularly sad.

The reinforcement of this structure aggravates discrimination where racial culture and gender are concerned. Even in so-called democratic societies they do not manage to guarantee the rights of native and different ethnic peoples to their own land, culture, language, communal socio-political structure, etc.

The actions of certain sections of the established churches and of some sectarian groups collaborate in maintaining this situation and in serving the interests of the rulers.

Repressive systems

In order to consolidate this social structure, power groups within these countries have set up systems of repression, often under a banner of pseudo-legality.

An extension of the East-West conflict provides an opportunity for adopting the doctrine of national security to suit different countries. In some the armed forces who seized total political power and oppressed the populace with the so-called claim of combating subversion, have managed to preserve their political autonomy even after the return of a legal state by guaranteeing their exemption from punishment, which weakens new democracies.

On the other hand, in Central America, the so-called low level conflict, which has a catastrophic impact on the people who endure it, shows up the realisation of USA strategy in maintaining its own interests safe and sound in the region. In many Caribbean countries USA intervention is more direct, including inducing states in the area to involve themselves in the internal affairs of sister nations, in an obvious adoption of foreign interests.

As a consequence of repressive action the right to life, freedom and personal integrity has been brutally violated.

We cannot forget State terrorism with its executions, torture, kidnappings, political prisons, and the exile of thousands of citizens. The consequences of these violations of human rights will continue for a long time to affect thousands of people and families, with repercussions on the whole body of society. The absence of truth and justice where past crimes are concerned brings with it a new violation of human rights.

The fact that authoritarian social and political structures have been preserved within new democratic regimes constitutes a threat to freedom and allows a system of state violence to work. The desire for peace among our people is seen to be obstructed by the phenomenon of militarism which pervades the culture and the social structure of our people. This process of increasing militarisation is fed by the requirements of the arms industry in which some countries of the region have an interest.

The increase in the phenomenon of the drugs trade has created a new threat for human rights in our countries. By arming themselves the confrontation between governments and drug traffickers strengthens military and police repression where, under the pretext of combating the drugs trade, they harshly punish people caught in the conflict.

The interests of the drugs trade have an effect on key sectors of political, economic, legal and even legislative structures. Nor do normal international operations escape this phenomenon.

This theological testament followed by a description of the decade 1980-1990 with its light and shadows enables us to gain a general overview of the situation. In this description we meet external factors which combine and complement each other creating a massive violation of human rights.

Violation of human rights
Other important elements have been provided by a report by the Commission of the Churches on International Affairs of the World Council of Churches which now takes up the theme.

Underdevelopment and violation of human rights in predominantly Christian countries
These aspects merit commentary. First of all, it is relevant for the Roman Catholic Church that violations of human rights

occur in a continent which in a few years, will represent fifty per cent of the Roman Catholics in the world. This is not a mere quantitative fact: it is also a qualitative one. What does it mean for the Christian faith and its mission in the world that a continent which contains fifty per cent of the Roman Catholics of the world violates persistently and systematically human rights, and furthermore, claims a religious legitimisation of that violation?

The parallel between these two problems does not have a merely pedagogical function. In reality it is a matter of two dialectical points, development and human rights are linked together. There are certain development models which imply a violation of human rights, and the repression which violates human rights in turn hinders forms of promotion of those rights.

We believe that Latin America's underdevelopment as a continent is a call to faith. Various theologies of development have attempted to simulate Christian responsibility concerning the task of progress. But if progress is to benefit all without discrimination, then power structures and relationships must be changed. All of this implies a liberating struggle. Violations of human rights are the most recent response aimed at subduing those liberation efforts, suppressing popular organisations and silencing the needs of the poorest. If one says that this is necessary because atheistic movements and ideologies were filtering through the protests of the oppressed, the response accuses Christians even more: it shows their incapacity to hear the cry of the poor, to raise their voices and unite their efforts with the oppressed to obtain their liberation. It indicates leaving it to ideologies which the Christian does not share.

Religious legitimisation of repression
Religious legitimisation of certain regimes which violate human rights is evident. We could cite many well known cases, publicised by the governments themselves, of bishops

who support oppression considering it necessary to combat the Marxist threat. Every country has outstanding examples. But even more, some episcopates seem to offer arguments in defence of the very existence of repression even when inadmissible excesses are obviously noted.

Religious legitimisation of repression raises an extremely serious problem for the evangelisation of Latin America. Evangelisation is proclaiming the salvation which comes to us in Jesus Christ through the love of the Father. Eternal life also calls upon present life. Some Christians interpret that salvation in Jesus Christ and that call as a questioning of the status quo. Thus on the basis of their faith they denounce misery and oppression. Other Christians, although they categorically declare themselves to be followers of Christ, defend their gospel by silencing and also exterminating Christians who denounce misery and oppression. When believing in Jesus Christ and his salvation lead to such different and serious conclusions, it represents a pastoral problem of primary importance, of clarifying who Jesus Christ is and what his salvation means. The great challenge to the church in Latin America is hardly how to continue to proclaim God in an urban industrialised and secular society. It is instead how to proclaim God to the poor who are crushed by industrialisation, achieved through conditions of external dependency which benefit a few who wish to maintain the monopoly not only on the goods of this world but also in Christian faith and, therefore, do not tolerate their privileged position to be questioned in the name of their faith.

We have pointed out the problem. Evangelisation in Latin America is defined, at least partially, by the positions which the church takes on the defence of human rights. It either proclaims a Christ who can be adored in injustice and slavery and who goes along with passivity and conformism, or it proclaims a Christ who brings us the love of the Father, makes us brothers and sisters and for that very reason leads us to reject all forms of discrimination and oppression. Which Christ will we proclaim?

The position of the church when confronted with violations of human rights

As I said at the beginning, the defence of human rights in Latin America is a consequence of the urgent need to defend lives when confronted by the inhuman powers that they are subjected to. As was said in a report by the Central Committee of the World Council of Churches in 1977: The ecumenical preoccupation with human rights has resulted less from intellectual speculation among clergy than from the needs and experiences of churches and Christians who often find themselves caught up in the struggle for justice and human dignity in their own environment.

Confronted with this urgent problem the churches, from various traditions, reacted in very different ways.

Collaboration with the ruling power

There are plenty of examples of clergy and laity, chaplains and bishops who collaborated with military power and justified their action more from an ideological than an evangelical position. The important thing was to fight Communism and any doctrine or viewpoint which justified a left-wing view. From this way of looking at things they justified repression and violence. Recently in Argentina a naval officer confessed that he used to throw kidnapped prisoners from aeroplanes into the sea and when he returned from this military action there were priests who would justify his action by using Jesus' parable of the wheat and the tares. What these officers were doing was cutting down the tares. It has been verified that there were priests in the torture chambers under the military regime in Argentina. For their part, bishops, especially those of the higher ecclesiastical hierarchy, condoned violence. One must point out a particular feature of this relationship which is that there were clergy who took up a position which we might call 'humanitarian' in that they used their relationship with the military power to save some victims from

423

torture and death. Underneath the 'umbrella' of a good relationship with the military they obtained information, they were able to intercede on behalf of some kidnapped victims and also smuggle people in danger out of the country. This methodology enabled them to wrest some advantages from those in power.

Indifference
Unfortunately, for many churches, and this includes evangelical, Protestant and Orthodox groups, violation of human rights was taken to be an ideological/political question in which they had no reason to intervene: Christians should lead a spiritual life and becoming interested in such problems would be to participate in worldly affairs. There were churches that were silent about what was happening, and what was happening were completely anti-Christian acts such as torturing, robbing and making thousands of people vanish including children and pregnant women. This act of indifference was the result of a theological position erroneously bent on heavenly things and on a reading of the Bible which ignores the Incarnation, something which is totally opposed to liberation theology.

A commitment to preserving human life
Just as there were clergy who collaborated there were also those who risked their lives to defend human rights. There were ministers and priests, bishops and theologians along with millions of believers, men and women who understood very well that being faithful to the gospel meant defending human life. There were many prophetic documents throughout the continent produced by churches, episcopalian bodies, church councils (like the Latin American Council of Churches and the Council of Evangelical Methodist Churches of Latin America and the Caribbean) who, through their declarations, condemned oppression, torture, people's enforced disappearance and all forms of violence.

Because of this commitment they visited prisoners, consoled broken-hearted families, denounced oppression and many gave up their lives and died in this cause. All this activity through words and commitment formed a network which extended throughout the continent and linked their wishes and their physical hands with millions of people who, from another position, were fighting for the same sense of human dignity. This Christian testimony was based on a clear understanding that defending human rights was defending God's rights who identified himself and showed solidarity with anybody in need and suffering.

These three attitudes went across churches, the collaborating hierarchies and the clergy working from a compromised base, the official declarations of assemblies and indifferent Christian people, in short, it was a mosaic of attitudes. All this activity in defence of human rights was, at the same time, a help towards a resumption of democracy.

One last word

Today we are living under democratic governments but which are enormously dependent on world centres of economic power. It is impossible to pay the foreign debt of Latin American countries. The military governments helped to create this situation as they represented at one and the same time, an economic means of domination. In Argentina alone when the military government took power in 1976 external debt was five billion dollars approximately. When it collapsed in 1983 it had risen to thirty-five billion. This phenomenon took place throughout the continent. Military oppression was an instrument of economic oppression.

Today our countries suffer from economic dependency which is leading at the same time to a deterioration in the human condition: unemployment, infant malnutrition, hunger, illness, violence and death. For this reason the economic problem has become for us today an article of faith because when God speaks to us this theme is our neighbour's life. We can no longer now study theology without considering, at the same time, economics and sociology.

The mission of the church in Latin America today implies fighting for the consolidation of democratic countries founded on truth, justice and peace which is in the sense of *shalom*, in other words, fullness of life.

Translated by Margery Hyde

Select Bibliography

The following bibliography was compiled by Roger Williamson to accompany the paper *Reconciliation: Conflict & Reality* presented at the July 1995 Christians Aware Summer School, Harrogate. It was compiled from the author's personal library and makes no claims to being exhaustive or academic.

Theology

Brian Frost, *The Politics of Peace* (Darton, Longman & Todd, 1991)

Basil Hume, *Remaking Europe: The Gospel in a Divided Continent* (SPCK, London, 1994)

Robert J. Schreiter, *Reconciliation: Mission & Ministry in a Changing Social Order* (Orbis, Maryknoll & Boston Theological Institute, Cambridge, Mass., 1992)

Military dictatorships in Latin America

History and political analysis

Leonardo Boff & Vergil Elizondo (eds.), *1492-1992 The Voice of the Victims (Concilium 1990/6)* (SCM, London & Trinity Press International, Philadelphia, 1990)

Catholic Institute for International Relations, *Nicaragua: The Price of Peace* (CIIR, London, 1993)

Eduardo Galeano, *Open Veins of Latin America: Five Centuries of the Pillage of a Continent* (Monthly Review Press, New York and London, 1973)

Eduardo Galeano, *Memory of Fire (Trilogy consisting of Vol. 1, Genesis, Vol. II. Faces & Masks, Vol. III, Century of the Wind)* (Quartet Books, London and New York, 1985, 1987, 1989)

Saul Landau, *Guerrilla Wars of Central America: Nicaragua, El Salvador and Guatemala* (Weidenfeld & Nicolson, London, 1993)

James Painter, *Guatemala: False Hope, False Freedom* (CIIR

and Latin America Bureau, London, 1987) (Updated edition, 1st edn. 1987)

Jenny Pearce, *Under the Eagle: US Intervention in Central America and the Caribbean* (Latin America Bureau, London, 1981)

Pablo Richard, *Death of Christendoms, Birth of the Church: Historical Analysis and Theological Interpretation of the Church in Latin America* (Orbis, Maryknoll, 1987)

The churches and liberation theology

Carmelo Alvarez, *People of Hope: The Protestant Movement in Central America* (Friendship Press, New York, 1990)

Trevor Beeson & Jenny Pearce, *A Vision of Hope: The Churches and Change in Latin America* (Collins/Fount, London, 1984)

Philip Berryman, *Christians in Guatemala's Struggle* (Catholic Institute for International Relations, London, 1984)

Philip Berryman, *The Religious Roots of Rebellion: Christians in the Central American Revolutions* (SCM, London, 1984)

Leonardo Boff, *Way of the Cross – Way of Justice* (Orbis, Maryknoll, 1982)

Leonardo & Clodovis Boff, *Salvation and Liberation: In Search of a Balance between Faith and Politics* (Orbis, Maryknoll & Dove, Melbourne, 1985) (1st edn. 1984)

James R. Brockman, *The Word Remains: A Life of Oscar Romero* (Orbis, Maryknoll, 1983) (1st edn. 1982)

Jose de Broucker, *Dom Helder Camara: The Conversion of a Bishop* (Collins, London, 1979) (1st French edn. 1977)

Dermot Keogh, *Romero: El Salvador's Martyr* (Dominican Publications, Dublin, 1981)

Martin Lange & Reinhold Iblacker, *Witnesses of Hope: The Persecution of Christians in Latin America* (Orbis, Maryknoll, 1981) (1st German edn. 1980)

Penny Lernoux, *Cry of the People: The Struggle for Human Rights in Latin America – The Catholic Church in Conflict with US Policy* (Penguin, Harmondsworth, 1982) (1st edn. 1980)

Daniel H. Levine (ed.), *Religion and Political Conflict in Latin America* (University of North Carolina Press, Chapel Hill and London, 1986)

John Medcalf, *Letters from Nicaragua* (Catholic Institute for International Relations, London, 1988)

Richard Shaull, *Heralds of a New Reformation: The Poor of South and North America* (Orbis, Maryknoll, 1985) (1st edn. 1984)

Jon Sobrino (ed.), *Romero: Martyr for Liberation* (Catholic Institute for International Relations, London, 1982)

Jon Sobrino (ed.), *In Memoriam: The Jesuit Martyrs of El Salvador* (CAFOD, CIIR, SCIAF, Trocaire; London, Glasgow and Dublin, 1990)

Elsa Tamez, *Bible of the Oppressed* (Orbis, Maryknoll, 1982)

Human rights in Latin and Central America

Cynthia Brown (ed.), *With Friends Like These: The Americas Watch Report on Human Rights and US Policy in Latin America* (Pantheon, New York, 1985)

Sheila Cassidy, *Audacity to Believe: An Autobiography* (Collins, London, 1977)

Joan Dassin (ed.), *Torture in Brazil: A Report by the Archdiocese of Sao Paulo* (Vintage/Random House, New York, 1986)

Ariel Dorfman, *Widows* (Vintage/Random House, 1984) (1st Spanish edn. 1981)

Andrew Graham-Yooll, *A State of Fear: Memories of Argentina's Nightmare* (Eland, London, and Hippocrene, New York, 1986)

Thomas Hauser, *Missing* (Penguin, Harmondsworth, 1982) (1st edn. 1978)

Emilio F. Mignone, *Witness to the Truth: The Complicity of Church and Dictatorship in Argentina 1976-1983*, (Orbis, Maryknoll, 1988) (1st Spanish edn. 1986)

Nunca Mas (Never Again): A Report by Argentina's National Commission on Disappeared People (Faber & Faber, London and Boston, 1986) (Spanish original 1984)

Alicia Partnoy, *The Little School: Tales of Disappearance & Survival in Argentina* (Virago, London, 1988) (1st edn. 1986)

John Simpson & Jana Bennett, *The Disappeared: Voices from a Secret War* (Robson, London 1985)

Jacobo Timerman, *Prisoner without a Name, Cell without a Number* (Penguin, Harmondsworth, 1982) (1st edn. 1981)

Lawrence Wechsler, *A Miracle, A Universe: Settling Accounts with Torturers* (Pantheon, New York, 1990)

South Africa

History and general political analysis

William Beinart, *Twentieth Century South Africa* (Oxford University Press, Oxford and New York, 1994)

British Council of Churches, *Violence in South Africa: A Christian Assessment* (SCM, London, 1970)

Catholic Institute for International Relations, *South Africa in the 1980s* (CIIR, London, 1983) (1st edn. 1980)

Commonwealth Committee of Foreign Ministers, *South Africa: The Sanctions Report* (Penguin, London, 1989)

Basil Davidson, *Let Freedom Come: Africa in Modern History* (Little, Brown & Company, Boston, Toronto and London, 1978)

Basil Davidson, *Africa in History* (Phoenix/Weidenfeld & Nicolson, 1991) (Revised edn. 1st edn. 1966)

Hermann Giliomee and Jannie Gagiano (eds.), *The Elusive Search for Peace: South Africa/Israel/Northern Ireland* (Oxford University Press, Cape Town, (in association with IDASA), 1990)

Desiree Hansson & Dirk van Zyl Smit (eds.), *Towards Justice? Crime and State Control in South Africa* (Oxford University Press, Cape Town, 1990)

R. W. Johnson, *How Long Will South Africa Survive?* (Macmillan, London and Basingstoke, 1977)

John Kane-Berman, *South Africa: The Method in the Madness* (Pluto Press, London, 1979)

Brian McKendrick & Wilma Hoffmann (eds.), *People and Violence in South Africa*, (Oxford University Press, Cape Town, 1990)

Sebastian Mallaby, *After Apartheid* (Faber & Faber, London and Boston, 1992)

Walter Rodney, *How Europe Underdeveloped Africa* (Zimbabwe Publishing House, Harare, 1983) (1st edn. 1972)

Susanna Smith, *Front Line Africa: The Right to a Future* (Oxfam, Oxford, 1990)

Pauline Webb (ed.), *A Long Struggle: The Involvement of the World Council of Churches in South Africa* (WCC, Geneva, 1994)

Black resistance, human rights and the church opposition

Stephen Biko, *The Testimony of Steve Biko* (Panther/Granada, London, 1979)

Allan Boesak, *If This is Treason, I am Guilty* (Collins/Fount, Glasgow, 1988) (1st edn. 1987)

Andre Brink, *Mapmakers: Writing in a State of Siege* (Faber & Faber, London and Boston, 1983)

Catholic Institute for International Relations, *Out of Step: War Resistance in South Africa* (CIIR, London, 1989)

Christian Concern for Southern Africa, *Speaking Out: Secret Interviews with Black Workers in South Africa* (CCSA, London, 1982)

John W. de Gruchy, *The Church Struggle in South Africa* (SPCK, London, 1979)

Shirley du Boulay, *Tutu: Voice of the Voiceless* (Hodder & Stoughton, London, etc., 1988)

Don Foster, *Detention & Torture in South Africa* (James Curry, London, 1987)

International Commission of Jurists (eds.), *The Trial of Beyers Naude: Christian Witness and the Rule of Law* (Search Press, London, and Ravan Press, Johannesburg, 1975)

Kenneth David Kaunda, *Kaunda on Violence* (Collins, London, 1980)

Ken Luckhardt & Brenda Wall, *Organise . . . Or Starve! The History of the South African Congress of Trade Unions* (Lawrence & Wishart, London, 1980)

N. C. Manganyi, *Being-Black-in-the-World* (Spro-Cas/Ravan, Johannesburg, 1973)

Fatima Meer, *Higher than Hope: The Authorised Biography of Nelson Mandela* (Harper & Row, New York, 1988)

Basil Moore (ed.), *Black Theology: The South African Voice* (C. Hurst & Co., London, 1973)

Indres Naidoo & Albie Sachs, *Island in Chains: Ten Years on Robben Island by Prisoner 885/63* (Penguin, Harmondsworth, 1982)

N. Barney Pityana *et al.* (eds.), *Bounds of Possibility: The Legacy of Steve Biko & Black Consciousness* (David Philip, Cape Town, and Zed Books, London and New Jersey, 1991)

Peter Randall (ed.), *Not Without Honour: Tribute to Beyers Naude* (Ravan, Johannesburg, 1982)

Albie Sachs, *The Soft Vengeance of a Freedom Fighter* (Paladin/HarperCollins, London, 1991)

Piniel Viriri Shiva, *A People's Voice: Black South African Writing in the Twentieth Century* (Zed, London, and Ohio University Press, Athens, Ohio, 1989)

H. J. & R. E Simons, *Class and Colour in South Africa 1850-1950* (Penguin, Harmondsworth, 1969)

Aelred Stubbs (ed.), *Steve Biko – I Write What I Like* (Bowerdean Press, London, 1978)

Charles Villa-Vicencio, *Trapped in Apartheid* (Orbis, Maryknoll, and James Philip, Cape Town, 1988)

Charles Villa-Vicencio (ed.), *The Spirit of Hope: Conversations on Politics, Religion and Values* (Skotaville, Johannesburg, n.d.)

Jim Wallis & Joyce Hollyday (eds.), *Crucible of Fire: The Church Confronts Apartheid* (Orbis, Maryknoll, and Sojourners, Washington, 1989)

432

Peter Walshe, *Black Nationalism in South Africa: A Short History* (Spro-Cas/Ravan, Johannesburg, 1973)
Donald Woods, *Biko* (Paddington Press, New York and London, 1979)
Michael Worsnip, *Between Two Fires: The Anglican Church and Apartheid* (University of Natal Press, Pietermaritzburg, 1991)

Europe
Abel Aganbegyan, *Moving the Mountain: Inside the Perestroika Revolution* (Bantam, London, 1989)
Trevor Beeson, *Discretion and Valour: Religious Conditions in Russia and Eastern Europe* (Collins/Fontana, Glasgow, 1974) (2nd revised edn. 1982)
Hans Magnus Enzensberger, *Europe, Europe: Forays into a Continent* (Hutchinson/Radius, London, 1989)
David L. Edwards, *Christians in a New Europe* (Collins/Fount, London, 1990)
Janine di Giovanni, *The Quick and the Dead: Under Siege in Sarajevo* (Pheonix House, London, 1994)
Misha Glenny, *The Fall of Yugoslavia: The Third Balkan War* (Penguin, London, 1992)
Stephen Iwan Griffiths, *Nationalism and Ethnic Conflict: Threats to European Security* (Oxford University Press, Oxford and New York (for SIPRI), 1993)
Vaclav Havel, *Open Letters* (Faber & Faber, London and Boston, 1991)
John Hutchinson & Anthony D. Smith (eds.), *Nationalism* (Oxford University Press, Oxford and New York, 1994)
William Green Miller (ed.), *Toward a More Civil Society?: The USSR Under Mikhail Sergevich Gorbachev* (Harper & Row, New York, 1989)
Czeslaw Milosz, *The Captive Mind* (Penguin, Harmondsworth, 1980) (1st edn. 1953).
Czeslaw Milosz, *Native Realm: A Search for Self Definition* (Penguin, London, 1981) (1st edn. 1968).

Jurgen Nowak, *Europas Krisenherde* (Rororo, Reinbek, 1994)

Oxford Research Group, *New Conflicts in Europe: Prevention and Resolution, Current Decisions Report No. 10* (ORG, Oxford, July 1992)

Pax Christi (Germany), (eds.), *Der Krieg auf dem Balkan* (Komzi, Idstein, 1992)

Erich Rathfelder (ed.), *Krieg auf dem Balkan: Die europaische Verantwortung* (Rororo, Reinbek, 1992)

Jane M O Sharp, *Bankrupt in the Balkans: British Policy in Bosnia* (IPPR, London, 1993)

Laura Silber & Allan Little, *The Death of Yugoslavia* (Penguin and BBC, London, 1995)

John Simpson, *The Darkness Crumbles: Despatches from the Barricades Revised and Updated* (Hutchinson, London, 1992)

Martin Sixsmith, *Moscow Coup: The Death of the Soviet System* (Simon & Schuster, London, 1991)

Dan van der Vat, *Freedom Was Never Like This: A Winter's Germany in East Germany* (Hodder & Stoughton, London, 1991)

Ed Vulliamy, *Seasons in Hell: Understanding Bosnia's War* (Simon & Schuster, London, 1994)

Ole Waever *et al.* (eds.), *Identity, Migration and the New Security Agenda in Europe* (Pinter, London, 1993)

Boris Yeltsin, *Against the Grain: An Autobiography* (Jonathan Cape, London, 1990)

The Israeli-Palestinian conflict

History

Sydney D. Bailey, *Four Arab-Israeli Wars and the Peace Process* (Macmillan, Basingstoke and London, 1990)

Colin Chapman, *Whose Promised Land?* (Lion, Oxford, 1989) (revised edition)

Martin Gilbert, *The Arab-Israeli Conflict: Its History in Maps* (Steimatzky, Jerusalem, 1992) (5th edn)

Walid Khalidi, *Palestine Reborn* (I. B. Tauris, London and New York, 1992)

David McDowall, *Palestine and Israel: The Uprising and Beyond* (I. B. Tauris, London, 1990) (revised edn.)

Nur Masalha, *Expulsion of the Palestinians: The Concept of 'Transfer' in Zionist Political Thought, 1882-1948* (Institute for Palestine Studies, Washington, 1992)

Everett Mendelsohn, *A Compassionate Peace: A Future for Israel, Palestine, and the Middle East* (Farrer, Straus & Giroux, New York, 1989) (revised edn.)

Benny Morris, *The Birth of the Palestinian Refugee Problem, 1947-1949* (Cambridge University Press, Cambridge, 1987)

Edward W. Said, *The Question of Palestine* (Vintage, London, 1992)

The peace process

Jane Corbin, *Gaza First: The Secret Norway Channel to Peace Between Israel and the PLO* (Bloomsbury, London, 1994)

Mark A. Heller, *A Palestinian State: The Implications for Israel* (Harvard University Press, Cambridge, Mass, and London, 1983)

Sari Nusseibeh & Mark A. Heller, *No Trumpets, No Drums: A Two-State Settlement of the Israeli-Palestinian Conflict* (I. B. Tauris, London and New York, 1991)

Palestinian Christians in the Holy Land

Naim Stifan Ateek, *Justice, and Only Justice: A Palestinian Theology of Liberation* (Orbis, Maryknoll, 1989)

Canon Naim Ateek, *'The New Consciousness'* – *CMS Annual Sermon* (CMS, London 1990)

Naim Stifan Ateek, *'The Basic Principles of Dialogue in the Israeli-Palestine Conflict: Respect, Honesty, Sincerity, Humility'*, in: Haim Gordon & Rivca Gordon (eds.), *Israel/Palestine: The Question for Dialogue* (Orbis, Maryknoll, 1991) (Also contains contributions by Hanan Mikhail-Ashrawi,

Faisal Husseini and Haidar Abdel Shafi and Jewish authors on the dialogue)

Naim Stifan Ateek *et al.* (eds.), *Faith and the Intifada* (Orbis, Maryknoll, 1992)

British Council of Churches, *Impressions of Intifada* (BCC, London, 1989)

Elias Chacour with Mary Jensen, *We Belong to the Land: The Story of a Palestinian Israeli who Lives for Peace and Reconciliation* (Harper, San Francisco, 1992)

Church of England (Board for Social Responsibility), *The Intifada (GS Misc. 372)* (Church of England, London, 1991)

Al-Liqa, *Journal from Al-Liqa, the Centre for Religious and Heritage Studies in the Holy Land* (PO Box 11328, Jerusalem)

Michael Prior and William Taylor (eds.), *Christians in the Holy Land* (World of Islam Festival Trust, London, 1994) Vital collection of statements by Palestinian Christians on their situation

Audeh Rantisi with Ralph Beebe, *Blessed are the Peacemakers: The Story of a Palestinian Christian* (Eagle, Guildford, 1990)

Patrick White, *Children of Bethlehem: Witnessing the Intifada* (Gracewing, Leominster, 1989)

Notes

1 Roger Williamson was Assistant Secretary (International Affairs) in the Board of Social Responsibility of the Church of England when he wrote this chapter. He is now an officer with Christian Aid. This chapter was written in his personal capacity and the views expressed do not necessarily correspond with those of either the Board of Social Responsibility or Christian Aid.

2 Fanon, F: *The Wretched of the Earth* (Grove, New York, 1966) p. 31. See the analysis of this and the following passage in Said, E. W: 'The Text, the World and the Critic' in Harari J. V. (ed.): *Textual Strategies: Perspectives in Post-Structuralist Criticism* (Methuen, London 1980) pp. 161-188. Quote from p. 182.

3 Galeano, E: 'In defense of the Word', in *Days and Nights of love and War* (Pluto Press, London, 1983) p. 183. See also his books *Open Veins of Latin America: Five Centuries of the Pillage of a Continent* (Monthly Review Press, London and New York, 1973) and the trilogy *Genesis, Faces and Masks* and *Century of the Wind.*

4 An extensive bibliography is included earlier in the book. Where reference is made to books in the bibliography, the section number will be noted after the name of the author, e.g. (Hume:1).

5 Ariel Dorfman has also treated the subject of 'disappearances' in his poetry. See, above all, Dorfman A: *Last Waltz in Santiago* (Penguin, New York, 1988).

6 ibid. pp. 14-5.

7 This is one of the central issues of Jürgen Moltmann's theology. See this quote in: Moltmann, J: *The Crucified God* (SCM, London, 1974) (1st German edn. 1973) p. 223.

8 cf. Havel, V: 'The Power of the Powerless', in Havel, V: *Open Letters: Selected Prose* (Faber & Faber, London and Boston, 1991) pp. 125-214. The piece was written in 1978.

9 Compare the following testimony from Argentina: 'Matilde de Mellibosky's . . . daughter was also disappeared. "We know that almost every woman who was detained by the junta was raped. Even if we have lost our daughters, perhaps somewhere we have grandchildren. We want to know the truth about what happened to our children but we also want to know what happened to grandchildren we might have who might have been given to the families of the military," she says.' Valentine, S: 'No memorial to 30,000 "disappeared"', in: *Democracy in Action* (Journal of the Institute for Democracy in South Africa, June 1995) p. 7.

10   cf. Lernoux:, P: *Cry of the People: The Struggle for Human Rights in Latin America – The Catholic Church in Conflict with US Policy* (Penguin, Harmondsworth, 1982). See esp. pp. 463-470 for a partial list of martyrs.

11   Valentine, S: 'No memorial to 30,000 "disappeared"' in: *Democracy in Action* (Journal of the Institute for Democracy in South Africa, 1.6.1995) p. 7.

12   Wright, A: 'Children of the disappeared' in: *New Internationalist, No. 270* (August 1995) p. 35.

13   For a peace researcher's comments on the dangers of a 'chosen people' self-understanding, see Galtung, J: 'The Challenge of Religion: Transcendent or immanent, hard or soft?', in: Race, A and Williamson, R (eds.): *True to This Earth: Global Challenges and Transforming Faith* (One World, Oxford, 1995) pp. 63-74. In his other writings, Galtung develops the theme of the dangers of chosen people and promised land ideologies with reference to the Biblical story and its applications to Israel, the USA, and South Africa.

14   For the text of the *Kairos Document*, subsequent international responses and a theological analysis, see: McAfee Brown, R: *Kairos: Three Prophetic Challenges to the Church* (Eerdmans, Grand Rapids, 1990).

15   ibid. Section 3.1. p. 38.

16   One of the clearest statements of the issues is still that by a former Brazilian archbishop, Helder Camara. Camara, H: *Spiral of Violence* (Sheed & Ward, London, 1971).

17   Biko, S: 'White Racism and Black Consciousness' in: Stubbs, A (ed.): *Steve Biko – I Write What I Like* (Bowerdean Press, London, 1978) pp. 61-72. Quote from p. 66. The original paper was published in a collection in 1972, which explains the sexist language.

18   cf. Harries, R: *Should a Christian Support Guerrillas?* (Lutterworth, Guildford, 1982).

19   Strikwerda, P: 'A veteran campaigner's recipe for South African justice', in: ENI Bulletin No. 8, 25.4.1995, pp. 12-14. Quote from p. 12.

20   Oxford Research Group (Hugh Miall): *New Conflicts in Europe: Prevention and Resolution* (Current Decisions Report No. 10, July 1992) pp. 32-35.

21   Nowak, J: *Europas Krisenherde* (Rororo/Rowohlt, Reinbek bei Hamburg, 1994)

22   Hobsbawm, E: 'Lost Horizons' in: *New Statesman and Society*, 14 September 1990. Cited in: Storm, R: *In Search of Heaven on Earth: The Roots of the New Age Movement* (Aquarian/HarperCollins, London, 1992) (first published 1991) pp. 174-5.

23   Drakulic, S: 'Overcome by Nationhood' (January 1992) in: *Balkan Express: Fragments from the Other Side of War* (Hutchinson, London, 1993) pp. 49-52. Quote from pp. 49-50.

24 For further information concerning the 1996 Lent Course and the European Conference on Reconciliation, contact CCBI, Inter-Church House, 35-41 Lower Marsh, London SE17 7RL.

25 From: 'Sarajevo' in : Motion, A: *Few concessions from a master*, (Review) of Milosz, C: *Facing the River* in: The Guardian (II – Books), 21.7. 1995, p. 6.

26 Williams, R: *Resurrection* (Darton, Longman & Todd, London, 1982) pp. 17-8.

27 Nolan, A: *God in South Africa* (David Philip, Cape Town; Eerdmans, Grand Rapids; Mambo Press, Gweru; CIIR, London, 1988) p. 7.

28 ibid. p. 108.

29 ibid.

30 ibid. p. 109.

31 ibid. p. 110.

32 Dimbleby, J: *The Palestinians* (Quartet Books, 1980) p. 35. Richard L. Rubenstein, John K. Roth: *Approaches to Auschwitz* (SCM, 1987) pp. 48 & 59.

33 Rosemary Radford Ruether, *Faith & Fratricide. The Theological Roots of Anti-Semitism* (New York, Seabury) 1974.

34 Gilbert, M: *The Day the War Ended* (Harper Collins) 1995, p. 362

35 The Runnymede Trust.

36 Vermes, G: *Jesus the Jew* (SCM, 1983)

37 Bayfield, T & Braybrooke, M: *Dialogue with a Difference* (SCM, 1992)

38 Farah, N: *The Colour of Courage* (Christians Aware, 1991) p. 7.

39 Prior, M & Taylor, W (World of Islam Festival Trust, 1994) p. 96.

40 *Meeting Muslims* (Christians Aware, 1995)

41 *Surah* 60:7.

42 *Surah* 2.256.

43 Simpson, J: *Behind Iranian Lines* (Fontana/Collins, 1988) p. 379.

44 *Islamophobia. A challenge for us all* (Runneymede Trust, 1997) available from 133, Aldersgate, London EC1A 4JA.

45 *Islamophobia* p. 4.

46 Kenyon, M: *Healing the Wounds* August 1995.

47 Rumalshah, M: *A New Paradigm* (Diocesan Centre, 1, Sir Syed Road, Peshawar, NWFP, Pakistan 25000).

48 Rinpoche, S: *The Tibetan Book of Living and Dying*, editors, Gaffney, P and Harvey, A (Ryder, London, 1992).

49 *What Lies Ahead? Listening to Refugees* (Christians Aware, 1992).

50 Bachelor, S (trans.): *Shantideva* (Library of Tibetan Works and Archives, Dharamsala, 1979).

51 Address by His Holiness the Dalai Lama on the acceptance of the Nobel Prize for Peace, December 10th, 1989, Oslo, Norway.

52 His Holiness the Dalai Lama: *The Good Heart* (Rider, 1996).

53 Aung San Suu Kyi, *Heavenly Abodes and Human Development* (CAFOD, 1997).
54 'Ashes & Light,' Nipponzan Myohoji, 1996, p. (i).
55 'Ashes & Light,' p. (ii).
56 *The Daily Telegraph*, Thursday, February 5th, 1998.
57 *Out of the Depths. Struggle and Hope in Sri Lanka* (Christians Aware, 1992) p. 70
58 See Pieris, A. SJ: *Love Meets Wisdom* (Orbis Books, 1988).
59 See *Meeting Sikhs* (Christians Aware, 1998).
60 Hick, J: *God and the Universe of Faiths* (One World, Oxford, 1993) p. 147.
61 From the Dalai Lama's Nobel Acceptance Speech in *Ocean of Wisdom* (Harper Row, 1990).
62 This declaration is reproduced in *A Global Ethic*, Eds. Kung, A & Kuschel, K. J (SCM Press, London, 1993).
63 From the Gandhi Talisman.
64 *Mission, Dialogue and Inter Religious Encounter* (The Interfaith Network, 1993).
65 SN V 420/LVI,XII,II,i.
66 The following definitions are based on entries in Venerable Nyanatiloka Thero's Buddhist Dictionary.
67 The apparent comprehensiveness of the eight aspects of the path should not lead us to think that the Buddha taught a rigid code by which every minute of our lives is regulated. He did not. Rather, the eightfold path can be seen as a tool for enabling us to integrate all aspects of our lives with spiritual endeavour.
68 Ghosananda, M., Ven: *Step by Step* (Berkely: Parallax Press) p. 51.
69 *Jataka* No 536, Bk. XII, p. 412.
70 ibid.
71 ibid.
72 ibid.
73 ibid. p. 412-3.
74 ibid.
75 DhA Bk. XV, N 3, 255.
76 J Bk. XXI p413.
77 ibid.
78 DhA Bk. XV N3, 256.
79 ibid.
80 ibid.
81 J Bk. XXI p. 414.
82 *Jataka* tale No 475, J bk. p. 208.
83 J Bk. XII p. 414.
84 ibid.
85 *Jataka* tale No 322, J Bk. IV pp. 72-74.

86 Vin Mahavagga X.6.3.
87 Graig M: 'Martin Luther King Jr' in *Candles in the Dark: Seven Modern Martyrs* (Hodder & Stoughton, London, 1984) p. 64.
88 Harrison, D: *The White Tribe of Africa: South Africa in Perspective* (British Broadcasting Corporation, London, 1981) p. 191.
89 Buckland, M: *History Begins Its Own Great Trek* in *Daily Despatch*, April 8, 1995.
90 Mosothoane E K: *Department of Religious Studies: The Department and The Reconstruction & Development Programme* pp. 2 – 3. (unpublished)
91 Hain, P: *Don't Play with Apartheid : The Background to the Stop The Seventy Tour* (George Allen & Unwin, London, 1971) p. 32.
92 Craig M, op cit, p. 64.
93 A quotation from Dr Kevin Shillington's presentation in the Christians Aware and College of the Ascension conference on 6th May 1995 held at the College of the Ascension.
94 Reeves, A: *Report on South Africa* (Christian Action, London, 1960) p. 7.
95 Nash, M: *Black Uprooting from 'White' South Africa: The Fourth and Final Stage of Apartheid* (SACC, Braamfontein, 1980) p. 1.
96 *The Star*, 3 January 1995 Art: "Land of Hope and Restitution"' p 9.
97 Macmillan, W. M: *Bantu, Boer, and Briton: The Making of the South African Native Problem* (Oxford at the Clarendon, 1963) p. 337.
98 Callaway, R. F: *Letters from two Fronts: A Selection of His letters from South Africa, 1900-1914 and from France, 1914-1916* (The Southern Publishing Company, Brighton, 1917) p. 72.
99 Miranda, J: *Marx and the Bible: A Critique of the Philosophy of Oppression* (SCM, London, 1979) p. xi
100 ibid. p. 8.
101 Hain P, op cit, p. 27.
102 Hain P, op cit, p. 34.
103 Knapp-Fisher, E: *Archbishop Selby Taylor: Apartheid's Subtle Foe* (*The Guardian*, Wednesday 10 May 1995, p 15).
104 De Klerk, W. A: *The Puritans in Africa: A Story of the Afrikanerdom* (Rex Collings, London, 1975) p. 341.
105 Knapp-Fisher, E: op cit, p 15.
106 Isichei, E: *A History of Africa: From Antiquity to the Present* (SPCK, London, 1995) p. 308.
107 ibid. p. 309.
108 Tomlinson, R: *Urbanisation in Post-Apartheid South Africa* (Unwin Hyman, London, 1990) p. 65.
109 Kleinschmidt, H (ed.): *White Liberation* (Spro-cas, Johannesburg, 1972) p. 16.

110 Manganyi, N. C & Du Toit, A (eds): *Political Violence and the Struggle in South Africa* (MacMillan, London, 1990) p. 59.
111 Millin S. G: *The South Africans* (The Constable & Co Ltd., London, 1931) p. 195.
112 Mansergh N: *South Africa 1906-1961: The Price of Magnanimity* (George Unwin, London, 1962) p. 32.
113 Fine, R & Davis, D: *Beyond Apartheid: Labour and Liberation in South Africa* (Pluto Press, London, 1990) p. 107. cf. Hirson, B: *Year of Fire, Year of Ash. The Soweto Revolt: Roots of Revolution?* (Zed Press, London, 1979) p. 216.
114 Hirson, B: op cit, p. 216. cf. Van der Ross R. E: 'The Coloured People' in Smith, P (ed.): *Africa in Transition: Some BBC Talks on Changing Conditions in Southern Africa* (Max Reinhardt, London, 1958) pp. 170-172.
115 Coetzee J. H: 'Die Kulture Identiteit van die Kleurling en Kulturele Verskeidenhede binne die Kleurlingbevolking' in Van Tonder, A (ed.): *Die Kleurlinge in Suid-Afrika* (Afrikaanse Studentebond, Johannesburg) p. 31.
116 Van der Ross, R. E: op. cit, pp. 171-172.
117 ibid. p. 177.
118 *The Times*, March 13 1961.
119 *Daily Dispatch*, April 24 1995, *Editorial Opinion: 'Register Now'*.
120 *Sunday Times*, April 23 1995.
121 *Daily Dispatch*, April 26 1995.
122 *Daily Dispatch*, April 24 1995.
123 Front for the Liberation of Mozambique.
124 Zimbabwe African National Liberation Army.
125 Mozambique National Resistance.
126 African National Congress.
127 Department for Prevention and Control of Natural Calamities.
128 All Africa Council of Churches.
129 Joint Verification Committee: Congo, France, Italy, Kenya, Malawi (Mid 1992), Portugal, Soviet Union/Russia, UK, US, Zambia and Zimbabwe.
130 Military Verification Committee
131 Commonwealth Heads of Governments Meeting
132 *Human Rights in Malawi*: Report of a Joint Declaration of the Scottish Faculty of Advocates, the Law Society of England and Wales and the General Council of the Bar to Malawi, 17-27 Sept. 1992 p. 8.
133 Later published under the title *The Truth Will Set You Free* CIIR, London, 1992).
134 Research conducted at Ntaja, Mwanza and Nkhata Bay in November and December 1994 revealed virtually universal recognition at the popular level that the pastoral letter was the turning point in recent

442

NOTES

Malawian political life; indeed, even MCP leaders, including its vice-president Gwanda Chakuamba, later declared that it was 'a blessing in disguise for the MCP (*Daily Times*, 29th April 1994).

135 Metz, J. B: *Faith in History and Society: Towards a practical Fundamental Theology* (Burns & Oates, London, 1980) pp. 89f.

136 cf. *The Independent* 8th April 1992.

137 Minister without Portfolio, W. B. Deleza told the church leaders on 15th July 1992 that it was no longer necessary for them to meet with government ministers since the life president had touched on all the issues in his address to the nation on 5th July 1992. (See the letter of Silas Nyirenda and Misanjo E. Kansilanga to J. Z. U. Tembo, 28th August (Public Affairs Committee file, 1992).

138 ibid.

139 Letter of J. Z. U. Tembo to Silas Nyirenda and Misanjo E. Kansilanga. 7th September 1992 (Public Affairs Committee file, 1992).

140 Letter of M. E. Kasilanga to Bestir Bison, chairman of the Presidential Committee on Dialogue, 12th October, 1992 (Public Affairs Committee file, 1992).

141 *Daily Times,* 19th October 1992.

142 These tactics included the use of poison to eliminate opponents, intimidation by Nyau dancers and the threat that all multi-party supporters would be exterminated after the MCP had won the referendum; G. Chikonga, research notes on interviews conducted at Madisi, 29-30 November 1994.

143 See document: *PAC Referendum/Election Monitoring Unit* (Public Affairs Committee File, 1992).

144 For studies of the 1992/3 period see: *Kirche und Gesellschaft in Malawi: Die Krise von 1992 in Historischer Perspektive* (EMW Informationen no. 98, Hamburg, Feb. 1993); *Malawi, a Moment of Truth* (CIIR, London, July 1993); Cullen, T: *Malawi, a Turning Point* (Pentland Press, Edinburgh, 1994); Nzunda, M. S. & Ross, K R (eds): *Church Law & Political Transition in Malawi, 1992-4* (Gweru Mambo, 1995).

145 Chris Wigglesworth, General Secretary of the Church of Scotland Board of World Mission & Unity, confirmed this in a BBC broadcast, 13th May 1992.

146 See Pauw, C. M: *Mission & Church in Malawi; The History of the Nkhoma Synod of the Church of Central Africa Presbyterian, 1889 – 1962* (dissertation, University of Stellenbosch, 1980).

147 *Daily Times*, 30th April 1993.

148 See e.g. *Guardian Today*, vol. 1, no. 7 19-25 May 1993.

149 See *The Monitor*, vol. 1, no. 13, 18th May 1993. One of the first actions of the newly elected UDF government in June 1994 was to appoint a commission to investigate the 'Mwanza accident'. The

release of its report in January 1995, confirming suspicions of foul play, led to the immediate arrest of Banda and his right hand man, John Tembo.

150 *UDF News*, Vol. 1, no. 21, 17-24 June 1993.

151 See e.g. *The Monitor*, vol. 1, no. 9, 28 April-4 May 1993.

152 A full account of the uprising is found in Shepperson, G & Price, T: *Independent African* (Edinburgh UP, Edinburgh, 1958).

153 cf. *Daily Times*, 9 November 1993.

154 On PAC meetings with leaders of different political parties, 14 December 1993 & 6 January 1994, see Public Affairs Committee files, 1993, 1994.

155 See Ross, K. R: *Christian Faith and National Identity: the Malawi Experience* (Journal of Theology for Southern Africa.)

156 *Where Silence Rules. The Suppression of Dissent in Malawi* (Africa Watch, New York, 1990) p.57.

157 This has been convincingly documented & demonstrated in Vail, L & White, L: 'Tribalism in the Political History of Malawi,' in Vail, L (ed.): *The Creation of Tribalism in Southern Africa* (James Currey, London, & University of California Press, Los Angeles, 1989) pp. 151-92.

158 *Daily Times*, 20th May 1994.

159 ibid, 19th May, 1994. cf. *The Enquirer* 21-24 May 1994.

160 The Nkhoma Synod grew out of a mission established in 1889 by the South Africa Dutch Reformed Church. There have always been tensions between Nkhoma and the synods of Scottish Presbyterian origin – Blantyre and Livingstonia – but they have been ecclesiastically united in the Church of Central Africa Presbyterian since 1926.

161 *Daily Times,* 6th November 1992.

162 M. E. Kasilanga to B. Bisani, 12th Oct. 1992. Italics added.

163 *The Nation,* 23 May 1994.

164 See Chigona, G: research notes on interviews conducted at Ntaga, 23 November 1994.

165 See *The Weekly Chronicle,* 29 August-4 September 1994.

166 *The Nation*, 2 May 1995

167 Chigona, G: research notes on interviews conducted at Ntaga, 23-24 November 1994.

168 O. P. Mazunda to Chakufwa Chihana, 23 June, 1993

169 *The Nation,* 23 May 1994.

170 *Daily Times,* 29 September 1995; *The Nation* 14 November 1994, 23 February 1995.

171 *The Nation,* 24 January 1995.

172 See *The Independent,* 19-24 January 1995.

173 See *The Monitor,* 18 January 1995.

174 CCAP Blantyre Synod Office Statement, *To be Born Again/ Fellowship*, 11 January 1995; tr. from Chichewa by O. Maliya; italics added.

175 See *Daily Times*, 20th February 1995.

176 *Malawi's Past: The Right to Truth* Article 19, no. 29, 17 November 1993.

177 See *Malawi News,* 12-18 November 1994.

178 See, e.g. *The Nation,* 12 May, 1994.

179 2 Corinthians 5:18-19.

180 2 Corinthians 4:7-12.

181 *VE and VJ Day Commemorations: Official Events* (HMSO, London, 1995).

182 *A Service of Remembrance and Commitment to mark the 50th Anniversary of the end of the Second World War* (Council of Churches for Britain & Ireland, London, 1995).

183 Quoted in Buruma, I: 'Why we find it so hard to forgive Japan' (*The Guardian,* 17th August 1995).

184 Storry, R: *A History of Modern Japan* (Penguin, London, 1960)

185 cf. *Pacific War Research Society, Japan's Longest Day* (Kodansha, Tokyo, 1968).

186 Mainichi Shinbun, quoted in Morris, I: *The Nobility of Failure: Tragic Heroes in the History of Japan* (Tuttle, Tokyo, 1975) p. xiv.

187 Kokutai no hongi, in Tsunoda, R, de Bary, W. T and Donald Keene, D (ed.): *Sources of Japanese Tradition, II* (Columbia University Press, New York, 1958) p. 284.

188 Morris, p. 312.

189 Shoji, T: 'The Church's Struggle for Freedom to Belief – An Aspect of Christian Mission' in England, J. C (ed.): *Living Theology in Asia* (SCM, London, 1981) pp. 49*ff*.

190 Koyama, K: *Mount Fuji and Mount Sinai: A Pilgrimage in Theology* (SCM, London, 1984) p. 264.

191 Hashimoto Kingoro, *Addresses to Young Men*, in Tsunoda, de Bary, and Keene, p. 289.

192 Chujo, K: *The Nuclear Holocaust: A Personal Account* (Asahi Shinbun, Tokyo, 1983) p. 107.

193 Tsunoda, de Bary, and Keene, pp. 138*f*.

194 Koyama, p. 25.

195 Koyama, p. 49.

196 Koyama, p. 205.

197 Okawa Shumei, in Tsunoda, de Bary, and Keene, p. 289.

198 Kangyo Hachiman Sho (1280), in Nichiren, M. A: *The Buddhist Prophet* (Harvard, Boston, 1916)

199 Cf. Snelling, J: *The Buddhist Handbook* (Rider, London, 1987) p. 192.

200 Founded by Most Ven. Nichidatsu in 1924, the Nipponzan order has established peace pagodas and pillars at sites in many countries around the world, including Britain.
201 Founded by Rev Nikkyo Niwano in 1938, Rissho koseikai has funded many conferences, centres, and programmes for reconciliation, especially with an inter-faith dimension.
202 Koyama, p. 202.
203 Chujo, p. 105.
204 Weinstein, M. E: 'Is Japan Changing Its Defence Policy', in Livingston, J, Moore, J, and Oldfather, F (ed.): *The Japan Reader 2: Postwar Japan, 1945 to the Present* (Penguin, London, 1973) p. 294.
205 Resolution 34 of the 49th Regular General Synod of Nippon Seikokai.
206 John Makoto Takeda: *Message for Transfiguration Day 1995* (NSKK Newsletter, Vol. 9 No 3, September, 1995).
207 In a seminar on 'The Role of the Church in Japan in Reconciliation and Peace', organised by the Church of England's Partnership for World Mission on 1st November 1996.
208 James Takashi Yashiro, writing in NSKK Newsletter, Vol. 10 No 2 (June, 1996).
209 PWM Seminar, 1st November 1996.
210 In 1944, 75 Seikokai churches were listed as participating in the Government-sponsored Nippon Kirisuto Kyodan, and 157 as non-participating (Akashi no Oji Diocese of Yokohama centenary history, Yokohama, 1984) p. 85.
211 PWM Seminar, 1st November 1996.
212 Eliot, T. S: 'Little Gidding, III', from *Four Quartets*.
213 Rowland, E. C: *Faithful Unto Death: The Story of the New Guinea Martyrs* (Australian Board of Missions, Sydney, 1964).
214 'May': Vivian's fiancée May Hayman, also executed by Japanese soldiers in 1942.
215 Medley, C. G & Herbert, P. C.: *Vivian Redlich: A Modern Martyr* (Leicester, n.d.), p. 18.
216 We realise that, at least in the first few years of the conflict, the FMLN received help from the USSR via Cuba and Nicaragua but it cannot compare with the huge scale of the US aid to the Salvadoran military.
217 *Step by Step Towards Peace in El Salvador: A chronology of the negotiations* (CIIR Briefing Paper, 1992). This Briefing Paper gives a concise account of all the ups and downs through the different stages of the talks.
218 CIIR Briefing Paper.
219 UN Dept. of Public Information, Press Release, July 1991.

220 Quoted in Holiday, D and Stanley, W: 'Building the Peace: the Role of the United Nations in El Salvador' in *Journal of International Affairs*, Winter 1992-1993.
221 Using 'popular' in its Latin American sense to mean 'of, or for, the people'.
222 CIIR Briefing Paper.
223 *The Salvadoran Peace Accords Land Transfer Programme: A Report on Its Progress, Problems and Sustainability* (SHARE Foundation, May 1 1996).
224 *Voices on the Border: Update*, Spring 1992, p. 5.
225 *Americas Watch Press Release, El Salvador. Peace and Human Rights: Successes and Shortcomings of the United Nations Observer Mission in El Salvador (ONUSAL)*, 2 Sept. 1992.
226 Quoted in Peace Brigades International Special Report from El Salvador: *The Changing Face of Violence*, 22 May 1996.
227 *Sentir con la Iglesia*, 15 October 1995.
228 *Carta a las Iglesias* (UCA, 1-15 April 1993) p. 5.
229 Holiday and Stanley, p. 31.
230 *Carta a las Iglesias* (UCA, 1-15 April 1993) p. 10. (Our translation)
231 AFSC, Quaker Service Bulletin, Spring 1995.
232 *Rescuing Reconstruction: the Debate on Post-War Economic Recovery in El Salvador* (Hemisphere Initiatives, May 1994) p. 1. This report gives an excellent account of the successes and failures of the first two years of the reconstruction process.
233 ibid., p. 50.
234 ibid. p. 22.
235 ibid. p. 24.
236 ibid. p. 25
237 SHARE report.
238 NACLA Report on the Americas, May/June 1995, p. 8.
239 Women were 'factories for producing subversives', children 'the seeds of subversives' and therefore fair game. Clements, C: *Witness to War* (Fontana, London, 1985). He was a Quaker doctor in the most conflictive zone in the country for a year.
240 *Children: the invisible soldiers*, a new report by the Quaker United Nations Office in Geneva, provides a grim picture of the training, even under-age soldiers (and often guerrillas too) receive in many countries.
241 *Demobilized Soldiers Speak: Reintegration and reconciliation in Nicaragua, El Salvador and Mozambique* (Education and Action for Peace Programme, Centro de Estudios Internacionales, Managua, Nicaragua, 1995, pp. 2-3.)
242 *Desaparecidos* is the name given to the victims of abduction, torture and execution during the political repression organised in Argentina

during the years 1976-1983. In this chapter the term will remain untranslated.

243 The term 'Dirty War' was a euphemism given to explain a political persecution carried out in the name of a supposed Communist plot to take over Argentina, in which women, men and children were supposed to have been recruited to fulfil their mission. For this point see Graziano, Frank: *Divine Violence. Spectacle, Psychosexuality and Radical Christianity in the Argentine Dirty War* (Westview Press, Oxford, 1992) Chapter 1.

244 See Gutiérrez, G: *Teología de la Liberación. Perspectivas* (CEP, Lima, 1971). The cactus is a popular plant growing in the desert areas of Latin America.

245 The 'Mothers of May Square' were so called by the public, because they went every week to the May Square (located opposite to the Government Palace) to ask for explanations about their children who were *desaparecidos*.

246 For this point see for instance Dillon, Susana: *Mujeres que hicieron America. Biografías Transgresoras* (Catari, Buenos Aires, 1992).

247 *Machista* is the Latin American term to define the patriarchal structures of the continent, characterised by a mixture of racial, class and religious oppression towards women.

248 See Fernández, Arturo, 'El Testimonio de una Madre de Plaza de Mayo' in *Movimientos de Mujeres y Pobreza en America Latina. Reflexiones a partir de un estudio en Perú* (Homo Sapiens, Rosario, 1994) pp. 96*ff*.

249 See Alvez, Rubén *et al: Reconciliación y Mundo Nuevo* (Tierra Nueva, Buenos Aires, 1981) prologue.

250 cf. Bonafini, Hebe: 'Comunicado de la Asociación de Madres de Plaza de Mayo' in *Madres de Plaza de Mayo*, XIV, 133, 1996, p. 11.

251 Idem, p 12-3.

252 cf. *Kairos Central America. A Challenge to the Churches and to the World* (Circus, New York, c 1988) point 101.

253 cf. Fernandez, Arturo, op cit, p. 97.

254 cf. Bonafini, Hebe, op cit.

255 We refer here to the Argentinian laws no. 23.492 and 23.521, plus the decree 1002'89. The first law is related to the principle of 'Obedience in war situation' (thus making unimputable the crimes committed by the army) and the second is called the 'final point', that is, that after the inquiries legally made about the disappeared it is now considered that the issue should not be brought to legal attention any more. The decree establishes the amnesty for the people involved in the repression who are no longer subject to imprisonment or any form of detention.

256 cf. Alvez, Rubén, *et al.*, op. cit., p. 72.